COMMUNITY NATURAL RESOURCE MANAGEMENT AND POVERTY IN INDIA

COMMUNITY NATURAL RESOURCE MANAGEMENT AND POVERTY IN INDIA

Evidence from Gujarat and Madhya Pradesh

Shashidharan Enarth
Jharna Pathak
Amita Shah
Madhu Verma
John R. Wood

Los Angeles | London | New Delhi
Singapore | Washington DC | Melbourne

First published in 2016 by

SAGE Publications India Pvt Ltd
B1/I-1 Mohan Cooperative Industrial Area
Mathura Road, New Delhi 110 044, India
www.sagepub.in

SAGE Publications Inc
2455 Teller Road
Thousand Oaks, California 91320, USA

SAGE Publications Ltd
1 Oliver's Yard, 55 City Road
London EC1Y 1SP, United Kingdom

SAGE Publications Asia-Pacific Pte Ltd
3 Church Street
#10-04 Samsung Hub
Singapore 049483

Published by Vivek Mehra for SAGE Publications India Pvt Ltd, typeset in 11/13 pt Minion by Diligent Typesetter India Pvt Ltd, Delhi and printed at Chaman Enterprises, New Delhi.

Library of Congress Cataloging-in-Publication Data Available

ISBN: 978-93-515-0652-2 (HB)

The SAGE Team: Supriya Das, Saima Ghaffar and Ritu Chopra

Contents

List of Tables

List of Figures

List of Images

List of Abbreviations

ADB	Asian Development Bank
AGM	Annual General Meeting
AKRSP	Aga Khan Rural Support Programme (NGO, Ahmedabad)
APL	Above the Poverty Line
ASA	Action for Social Advancement (NGO, Bhopal)
BJP	Bharatiya Janata Party
BPL	Below the Poverty Line
CADA	Command Area Development Agency
CBO	Community-Based Organization
CDP	Community Development Programme
CEH	Consumption Expenditure of the Household
CIFOR	Center for International Forestry Research
CISED	Centre for Interdisciplinary Studies in Environment and Development (Bengaluru)
CNRM	Community Natural Resource Management
CPLR	Common Property Land Resource
CPR	Common Property Resource
DANIDA	Danish International Development Agency
DCF	Deputy Conservator of Forests
DDP	Desert Development Project
DFO	Divisional Forest Officer
DPAP	Drought Prone Area Programme
DPIP	District Poverty Initiative Programme
DRDA	District Rural Development Authority
DSC	Development Support Centre (NGO, Bopal, Ahmedabad)
EC	Executive Committee
EDC	Eco-development Committee

FAO	Food and Agricultural Organization
FC	Fishing Cooperative
FD	Forest Department or Fisheries Department
FDA	Forest Development Authority
FES	Foundation for Ecological Security (NGO, Anand)
FF	Fish Federation
FGD	Focus Group Discussion
FPC	Forest Protection Committee
FRA	Forest Rights Act
FRL	Full Reservoir Level
GCA	Gross Cropped Area
GIDR	Gujarat Institute of Development Research (Gota, Ahmedabad)
GoI	Government of India
GoG	Government of Gujarat
GoMP	Government of Madhya Pradesh
ha(s)	hectare(s)
HCI	Head Count Index
HHS	household survey
HHs	households
HYV	High Yielding Variety (seeds)
IC	Irrigation Committee
ICEF	Indo-Canadian Environmental Facility
ICRISAT	International Crop Research Institute for the Semi-arid Tropics (Patancheru, Hyderabad)
ID	Irrigation Department
IRDAS	Institute for Resource Development and Social Action (NGO, Hyderabad)
ISEC	Institute for Social and Economic Change (Bengaluru)
IWDP	Integrated Watershed Development Project
IWRM	Integrated Water Resource Management
JFM	Joint Forest Management
JFMC	Joint Forest Management Committee
MCE	Monthly consumption expenditure (referring to household expenditure)

MDG	Millennium Development Goals
MGNREGA	Mahatma Gandhi National Rural Employment Guarantee Act
MHRD	Ministry of Human Resource Development
MJSI	Major Source of Income
MoA	Ministry of Agriculture
MoEF	Ministry of Environment and Forests
MoRD	Ministry of Rural Development
MP	Madhya Pradesh
MPCE	Monthly Per Capita Expenditure
MPFDC	Madhya Pradesh Fish Development Corporation
MPFF	Madhya Pradesh Fish Federation
MPWRD	Madhya Pradesh Water Resources Department
NABARD	National Bank for Agriculture and Rural Development
NCA	National Commission on Agriculture or Net Cropped Area
NGO	Non-governmental Organization
NRM	Natural Resource Management
NSA	Net Sown Area
NSSO	National Sample Survey Organization
NTFP	Non-timber Forest Product
NRAA	National Rainfed Area Authority
OBC	Other Backward Caste
O&M	Operation and Maintenance
PIA	Project Implementation Agency
PIM	Participatory Irrigation Management
PRA	Participatory Rural Appraisal
PRADAN	Professional Assistance for Development Action (NGO, Delhi)
PRI	Panchayati Raj Institutions
RGMWM	Rajiv Gandhi Mission for Watershed Management
SC	Scheduled Caste
SDO	Sub-divisional Officer
SE	Sub-engineer
SHG	Self-help Group

SLA	Sustainable Livelihood Approach
SOPPECOM	Society for Promoting Participative Ecosystem Management (NGO, Pune)
SPWD	Society for the Promotion of Wasteland Development
SRIJAN	Self-reliant Initiatives through Joint Action (NGO, Delhi)
SSP	Sardar Sarovar Project
SSNNL	Sardar Sarovar Narmada Nigam Limited
ST	Scheduled Tribe
UG	Users' Group
UNDP	United Nations Development Programme
UNCSD	United Nations Commission on Sustainable Development
USD	United States Dollar
VFC	Village Forest Committee
VLO	Village Level Organization
VRDP	Village Resource Development Programme
WDC	Watershed Development Committee
WDF	Watershed Development Fund
WDP	Watershed Development Programme (or Project)
WDT	Watershed Development Team
WUA	Water Users Association

Preface

In the year 2000, the United Nations, after surveying all the economic, social, health and environmental problems of our planet, announced the Millennium Development Goals (MDGs). They agreed on eight goals, the first of which was declared to be the eradication of poverty.[1] This was of immediate significance to all those concerned about poverty in India, which, going by the World Bank poverty standard of a per capita income of less than US$ 1.25 per day, implied that India contained one-third of the world's poor (2010 figures). The poor thus formed 42 per cent of the Indian population and lived mostly in rural areas. Despite recent overall increases in India's growth rates and an official downward revision of poverty estimates, the absolute number of rural Indians living below the poverty line is estimated at about 400 million (2010 figures).[2]

During the two decades leading up to the millennium, a new approach to rural development was introduced in many of the larger Indian states and this in turn gained governmental recognition. Titled as Community Natural Resource Management (CNRM), it featured the decentralization by government departments of the local management of natural resources to the rural communities most involved in their use. Thus, under the new approach, farmers were to take responsibility for the management of water, forest dwellers for the protection and management of their forests and fishermen for the management of the fisheries on India's inland

---

[1] The other MDGs were to: (a) achieve universal primary education, (b) promote gender equality and empower women, (c) reduce child mortality, (d) improve maternal health, (e) combat HIV/AIDS, malaria and other diseases, (f) ensure environmental sustainability and (g) develop a global partnership for development.

[2] See http://www.worldbank.org/content/dam/Worldbank/document//State_of_the_poor_paper_April17.pdf

reservoirs. This book explores two main questions, namely whether the promise of community managerial success has been realized and whether the CNRM projects and institutions have made an impact on Indian rural poverty.

The research reported here has grown out of the multi-institutional and bi-national collaboration of five scholars under the MDGs grant programme of the Shastri Indo-Canadian Institute. Three Indian and one Canadian institution took part: the Development Support Centre (DSC) and the Gujarat Institute of Development Research (GIDR) in Ahmedabad, Gujarat, the Indian Institute of Forest Management (IIFM) in Bhopal, Madhya Pradesh and the University of British Columbia (UBC) in Vancouver, Canada. The MDG Project, as we called it, was headquartered in the Institute of Asian Research at UBC in Canada and at GIDR in India, with DSC taking care of the financial transactions and accounting in India. The Project began with an inception workshop at GIDR in October 2008 and wound up with a final workshop at DSC in December 2011.

Apart from the Project Leader, each of the members of the MDG Project Team specialized in one of the CNRM programmes in India. In the order of their chapter contributions they are as follows. Dr Shashidharan Enarth is the former Executive Director of DSC and earlier worked with the Aga Khan Rural Support Programme in Gujarat. He had wide ranging experience in implementing projects in the Participatory Irrigation Management programme. Dr Jharna Pathak is an Assistant Professor at GIDR whose doctoral thesis at Gujarat University was a study of Participatory Irrigation Management in Gujarat and who moved on gamely to undertake research on inland Fishing Cooperatives for the MDG Project. Professor Amita Shah, former Director of GIDR, is an internationally recognized specialist on Watershed Development in India and a consultant to the national government who has made many important contributions on poverty and gender issues. Dr Madhu Verma, Professor of Environment and Development Economics programme at IIFM in Bhopal, is a specialist not only on Joint Forest Management but also on forest evaluation and forest certification in India. Dr John R. Wood, Professor Emeritus,

Department of Political Science, UBC, is a long-time specialist on Indian politics with a recent interest in the politics of resource management. As Project Leader and as a generalist in CNRM studies, he has written the introductory and concluding chapters with generous assistance from the partners.

In that regard, despite the division of labour outlined above, we agreed that this book would be considered as jointly authored because we set ourselves a common research strategy and agenda of questions for our fieldwork, used common instruments for our data collection and, as much as possible, endeavoured to write our findings according to an agreed comparative format. During the course of the project, moreover, we, along with our research assistants, field workers and invited guest specialists, held five periodic workshops for the presentation and sharing of the ongoing research findings as well as our thinking about 'comparative CNRM' in India.

We have read and commented on each other's chapters. Apart from all of the collaboration, each of us had a free rein to interpret all the information and data collected according to our individual disciplinary perspectives and theoretical preferences. Although we may not all agree with everything written here, we all have enjoyed and profited from the mutual give and take that has characterized this project.

We wish to acknowledge with thanks the contributions of the institutions and staff members that made our research possible. First, the Shastri Indo-Canadian Institute not only provided the grant but also provided encouragement, especially from Earl Cholden, Michele Neider, Mahmuda Aldeen and Sarah Sidane at the Canada Office and Prachi Kaul, Anju Taneja and Naresh Roy at the India Office. At UBC, we owe a great debt of gratitude to Marietta Lao of the Institute of Asian Research and sincere thanks to Paul Evans and Karen Jew.

In India, we are grateful to many friends at the GIDR, including R. Parthasarathy, its Director during 2008–09, who helped design the MDG Project and get it started. GIDR CNRM experts Hasmukh Joshi, Dipak Nandani and Shiddalingaswami Hanagodimath provided valuable fieldwork and analytical support. Research Associate Kairav Trivedi and fieldwork assistants Ramnik Chavda,

Santosh Kumar Chauhan, Antim Kumar Makwana, Alpesh Patel, Chirag Patel, Mukesh Kumar Rekwan and Pushpendra Singh Solanki put in long hours of fieldwork, especially during the household survey and data analysis.

We wish to thank Sachin Oza, Director of the DSC for his support to the project and Rajesh Mehta for his dedicated efforts in managing our project accounts.

At the IIFM, we received excellent cooperation from Vice Chancellors B.P. Pethiya and R.B. Lal. Dr Manish Mishra participated in much of the fieldwork and taught us a great deal about the vast non-timber forest products of India's forests. Munish Sikka carried out the bulk of the household survey interviewing and analysis.

Finally, we wish to thank the two keynote speakers at our workshops who provided valuable perspectives on our research: Dr S. Mahendra Dev, Chairman of the Commission for Agricultural Costs and Prices and Dr Ruche Ghate of Nagpur University.

Shashidharan Enarth
Jharna Pathak
Amita Shah
Madhu Verma
John R. Wood

1

CNRM in India: The Problem and the Context

John R. Wood

The management by local communities of natural resources such as water, forests or fish is hardly a new idea in India. Historically, in order to survive the uncertainties of a monsoon climate and the oppressions inflicted by indigenous feudalism or foreign conquest, the people of rural villages devised institutions for the sharing of resources that were vital for all.[1] Where the imposition of rule from outside the village was powerful and extensive enough, new resource management practices might have forced changes that would benefit the outsider. On the whole, however, the allocation of natural resource benefits was based on village politics shaped by caste and landowning dominance. In the vast majority of villages the allocation was not equitable, and some groups were excluded from access altogether. But loyalty to the village and deference to its institutions, especially those managing natural resources like water, forests and fish, have remained strong in rural India to the present day.

Once independence from British rule was won in 1947, there was widespread hope that village institutions would be reformed, ushering in a new era of greater productivity and social justice. Beginning in 1957, local governments were established through a system of democratically elected councils based on the traditional

---

[1] Indian ingenuity in building systems for water harvesting and distribution has been documented in Agarwal and Narain (1997).

panchayat or council of five. As Panchayati Raj Institutions (PRIs) came under state jurisdiction, however, there was unevenness in the creation and performance of village councils and generally a reluctance to give them much decision-making power (Mathew, 2000; Mathur, 1999; Narayana, 2005). Alongside the panchayats, the Community Development Programme (CDP) was created as the primary instrument for rural development, but soon became a means for dispensing political patronage (Mukherji, 1961; Taylor, 1956).

The 'agrarian revolution' was slow to materialize, despite limited attempts at land reform in the 1940s and 1950s and the more successful but patchy spread of 'green revolution' agricultural technology in the 1960s and 1970s. What was *not* changing was the iron grip on natural resource management (NRM) exerted by government departments and officials at the state level in all rural development decision-making. Particularly where natural resources like water, forests and fish were concerned, the Ministries of Irrigation, Rural Development, Environment and Forests, and Fisheries, respectively, ruled over farmers, forest dwellers and reservoir fishermen through 'top-down' policies backed by rules and regulations, many of them hardly changed since the British Raj. As a result, resource management deteriorated and rent-seeking by officials flourished. Local 'bottom-up' initiatives for management change and increased productivity remained weak.

The 'development era' promoted by the Planning Commission in New Delhi began with the primary motive of increasing rural productivity. Meanwhile, in India's nascent democracy, where four-fifths of the voters had to be wooed at the village level, it soon became inevitable that rural development schemes be driven by political as well as economic and social motives. In virtually every case, development schemes at the village level were captured by and used to the advantage of the 'haves', leaving the 'have-nots' far behind. Meanwhile, the imperatives of winning elections forced the process of political restratification to continue with each successive general election. At the all-India and state levels this meant a gradual devolution of power to previously less-advantaged groups and greater assertiveness on the part of lower castes with large voting potential. At the village level, however, the restratification was delayed or checked altogether by the power wielded in land-tenure relationships, hierarchies rooted in religious, caste and gender traditions, as well as dependencies based on money-lending and indebtedness.

1. The Emergence of CNRM

The emergence of CNRM—Community Natural Resource Management—a new strategy for managing natural resources by the local communities first appeared in the 1980s and spread widely in the 1990s, and was touted as 'a new paradigm' for rural development in India (Joshi, 1997; Joshi and Hooja, 2000). CNRM was to feature in varying degrees the decentralization of resource management control from government departments and officials to 'end-users', that is, villagers whose work and livelihoods depended on resources such as water, forests and fish. While its primary objective was to increase productivity, the arrival of the 1990s and the beginnings of the larger strategy of economic liberalization in India found a new justification for adopting CNRM as a policy, namely that it was in harmony with privatization and 'getting government off the backs of the people'. With the heavy hand of officialdom removed and control over NRM in the hands of end-users, it was argued that new levels of rural productivity would be unleashed. Moreover, there would be significant cost-saving for governments if people whose livelihoods depended on water, forests or fish took more responsibility for the local management of these resources. Perhaps it seemed like a dream at the time, but CNRM promoters also argued that CNRM institutions at the village level could eventually be both self-governing and self-financing.

Our research has arisen out of the question of whether the introduction and working of CNRM institutions in rural India have made an impact on poverty. Although CNRM programmes were introduced at different times and in different ways over the last two decades, we felt it was time to assess their performance, and especially their successes and failures in the reduction of poverty.

The inspiration for our research was drawn from the first goal of the Millennial Development Goals established by the United Nations in 2000: the eradication of poverty (UN Millennium Project, 2005). The more realistic goal of studying poverty reduction became the focus of our research in four of India's CNRM programmes: Participatory Irrigation Management (PIM), Watershed Development, Joint Forest Management (JFM) and Inland Fishing Cooperatives. All four programmes ostensibly share the following features:

1. Each of them was introduced in an apparent attempt to decentralize, in varying degrees, control over the management of an important natural resource from government departments to end-users who have the greatest stake in improving the productivity and sustainability of the resource.
2. The rationale for decentralizing control lies in the belief that those whose livelihoods depend on the effective use of the resource will have the most incentive and determination to take up the responsibility of its management.
3. In all four programmes, the control over resource management was previously exercised exclusively by government departments and officials. With the transfer of management control to end-users only partial governmental control would continue in various ways, both de jure and de facto.
4. In each programme a new institution was created at the village level with the intention of representing end-users' interests and facilitating to some degree their participation in the management of the resource.
5. In each programme, greater equity was expected not only in sharing the work of resource management but also in sharing the benefits and some of the costs by the end-users.
6. Improvement was expected not only in the overall prosperity of CNRM villages, but also in the livelihoods of their 'weaker elements', namely women, the Scheduled Castes (SCs) and Scheduled Tribes (STs), minorities, tenants, the landless and the land-poor.
7. The introduction of the new CNRM programmes was undertaken by government officials or non-governmental

organization (NGO) activists. Whatever their implementation approaches at the village level, one of the challenges was in transferring the initiative to the end-user institution so that the latter would become self-reliant and self-governing.

In view of these ostensible commonalities, our research project aimed as far as possible to study the four programmes comparatively, not only to learn about India's overall CNRM experience but also to explore the similarities and differences that have arisen in the implementation of the programmes and their impacts on poverty. Our aim was to be analytical, to explain why similarities or differences in the programmes and their impacts had occurred. In Chapter 2 we provide greater detail on the challenges encountered in trying to carry out a comparative analysis of CNRM in India, especially with reference to the conceptual and methodological challenges faced by us and how we attempted to deal with them.

The comparative aspect of the project was furthered by studying CNRM in the contexts of two states, Gujarat and Madhya Pradesh (MP). Ultimately, one would hope that similar studies might be undertaken in all of the Indian states so that the unparalleled diversity of India's regions, states and localities, as well as their CNRM programmes, might be represented. Unfortunately, such a study would require far greater financial and scholarly resources than were available to us. Therefore, we proceeded on the assumption that ours would be a pilot study, exploring amongst other things the potential of a larger study. In any case, given what we have learned about how CNRM has been implemented in a variety of Indian states as well as abroad, we feel confident that Gujarat and MP have been worthy laboratories for our study. Because Gujarat is a relatively well-off state and MP one of India's poorest we were able to explore programmatic impacts on poverty in a comparative framework that allowed us to see how differing approaches to implementation and operation in these two states made a difference to programmatic outcomes. The governments of these two states have generally taken opposite approaches to CNRM: a more 'bottom-up', gradual approach with more grassroot initiatives and NGO inputs in Gujarat versus a more 'top-down', rapid and government-led approach in MP.

In the 1980s and 1990s when CNRM was first introduced, the approach often took the form of experiments or pilot projects of limited scope. During this early phase the emphasis was on getting the programmes up and running. A great deal of scepticism had to be overcome and end-users needed to be shown that CNRM could not only work, but also that the results obtained would be significantly better than those from the formerly government-controlled resource management system. Little was said about CNRM reducing poverty, although in some of the experiments undertaken by NGOs, resolute efforts were made to include the 'weaker elements' in CNRM general bodies and executive committees (ECs).

Today, with 'inclusive growth' as one of the slogans widely adopted for judging development policy in India, the issue of equitability in the design, operation and results of CNRM programmes is of considerable importance. When the government was solely in charge of NRM, only programme effectiveness mattered, and was frequently found wanting, especially at the village level. Now, not only effectiveness but equitability, and a new concern for sustainability have been added as criteria for judging whether a CNRM programme is successful or not.

'Inclusive growth' became the slogan of the Congress Party-led United Progressive Alliance during the election campaign of 2004. It has also been endorsed by the Bharatiya Janata Party (BJP) government of Prime Minister Narendra Modi in the first President's address to Parliament after it came to power in May 2014. But what does the term really mean and how is it to be achieved? According to S. Mahendra Dev, inclusive growth is synonymous with 'equitable development', but is to be measured in more than just economic terms. It points to all those who are excluded from the benefits of development and asks not only why they are excluded, but also what strategies should be pursued to create and implement pro-poor and people-centric policies. Dev is an advocate of decentralization strategies that involve the growth of self-reliant institutions run by end-users. He calls this 'democratic decentralization', which, he argues, along with gender equity can have significant poverty-reducing effects in rural India (Dev, 2007: 97). In his words, 'Decentralization and governance in terms of improving performance of institutions are becoming important in determining poverty levels in the country'. (Dev, 2007: 99)

Early in our focus group discussions (FGDs) with villagers we too formed the opinion that it was not just the extent of decentralization of resource management control to CNRM institutions that would determine their impact on poverty, but the way they were governing themselves and performing their new tasks. Assessing the 'governance' of the new institutions eventually led us to conclude that governance components such as participation, transparency, accountability and the rule of law are often instrumental in causing the success or failure (or somewhere in-between) of CNRM institutions in terms of their impact on poverty.

2. The Plan of the Book

Beyond introducing CNRM, this chapter will provide a brief background on the beginnings of each of the four CNRM programmes in India. Chapter 2 explores the conceptual and methodological issues we have addressed in our research. The main concepts are some of the thorniest in the development lexicon: community, decentralization, institution, equity, governance, impact, poverty. The main methodological challenges included the selection of study villages, FGDs, a household survey (HHS), pre- and post-intervention asset and production measurements, determining the impact of CNRM on poverty, including attributing change in poverty status to CNRM.

Chapters 3, 4, 5 and 6 present our research findings and analysis of the four CNRM programmes of PIM, Inland Fishing Cooperatives, Watershed Development and JFM, respectively. Because of the special features of each programme, each author conducted the research and analysed the results in his/her own way. However, as far as possible, a comparative perspective was maintained, noting similarities and dissimilarities in de jure and de facto programme initiation, performance and outcomes.

Chapter 7 begins the Conclusion by exploring the comparative findings presented in Chapters 3–6; specifically, it reviews the authors' answers to the central research questions from the perspective of each of the four CNRM programmes. Chapter 8 presents The Way Forward and undertakes two tasks: (a) it presents the main deficiencies of CNRM in the two states, both generally and with regard to each programme and (b) based on the evidence and the analysis, it suggests policy changes regarding CNRM and its role in the reduction of poverty in India. We offer these suggestions to central and state governments (administrators and politicians, policymakers and implementers), taxpayers, NGOs, the academic community studying CNRM, and most importantly, CNRM practitioners at the village level.

3. The Evolution of CNRM in India

Between the years 1990 and 1995, the Government of India (GoI) took much of the initiative in each of the four CNRM programmes studied here by promoting reform, setting up model legislations and providing financial support. Two of the programmes, namely Watershed Development and Joint Forest Development, are all-India programmes based on a centrally-devised policy for the whole country and in turn framed by the Ministries of Rural Development and Environment and Forests respectively. But, according to the Constitution of India, it is the state governments that are jurisdictionally responsible for the implementation of policies regarding water, forests and inland fishing in India. It has therefore been primarily in the states that both administrators and politicians have had to be convinced that CNRM could work.

At the outset, the CNRM idea was greeted with scepticism: how could farmers, without engineering or management training, take on the huge responsibility of water management? Similar doubts were expressed about the administrative abilities of forest dwellers, or fishermen, and their ability to overcome their dependence based on poverty, illiteracy and isolation. For centuries rural people had relied on *sarkar mabap* ('government, our mother and father') to solve all problems. Inside the government, meanwhile, there were more than a few officials who feared that if CNRM were to become a success, they might eventually be out of a job. Outside of the government, there was suspicion that CNRM would never be allowed to succeed, because government officials controlling NRM would never let go of the authority that allowed them to add rent-seeking to their incomes.

Nonetheless, given the stagnant condition of India's agricultural production and the inexorable rise in population, a way had to be found to increase the efficiency of canal irrigation and to maximize the gains from monsoon rain for agricultural land that was not able to receive water by canals. In the forest areas, where poverty levels were amongst the worst in India, the crisis, ostensibly, had less to do with the production and more with the protection of India's forest, which were rapidly dwindling due to illicit felling and encroachment by an expanding human and animal population. In the case of inland fisheries in the large reservoirs created by a surge in dam-building, there was the need to not only increase fish production, but also to give employment to the growing numbers of 'oustees' whose land had been submerged by reservoir construction.

In addition to the increased need for production and job creation, there was a larger purpose that CNRM needed to address. With India entering its fourth decade of political democracy, there was pressure to show that India could not only manage its resources productively but also equitably. Thus CNRM, if it were to succeed, required not only decentralization of power that would challenge the authority of government officials, but also an equitable distribution of benefits that would challenge the existing politico-economic structure in every CNRM village. In other words, the CNRM initiative would have to confront the issues of poverty along with the marginalization of women, the SCs and STs, tenant farmers, the landless and the land poor.

The four CNRM programmes to be examined here are the largest and most widely adopted in India. They began in different ways in the two states, and the way each began at the village level is still an important factor affecting their operations today. In what follows, some brief historical background is provided, while the details of how they developed in Gujarat and MP will be presented in Chapters 3–6.

4. Participatory Irrigation Management (PIM)

Dams have been built in India for thousands of years and at present there are roughly 4,050 large dams as well as thousands of smaller dams and tanks. The irrigation systems deriving from their reservoirs fell under centralized state control during the British Raj and continued under the Irrigation Department's control after independence. The transfer of local control to end-users under the PIM programme began in the 1980s after it became clear that government control had resulted in inefficiencies, corruption and the breakdown of canals and other structures due to poor maintenance and an unviable user-fee structure. Irrigation management had become so inequitable that in many villages only 'head-reach' farmers, that is, those near the canal outlets received adequate water while 'tail-enders' received little or none (Chambers, 1988: 21–24). By putting control of irrigation management in the hands of farmers who depended on irrigation water, it was hoped that not only greater efficiency, but also greater equity in water distribution would be achieved (Chambers et al., 1989: 229–41).

The PIM programme involves the establishment of Water Users Associations (WUAs) as self-governing institutions regulating the allocation of water below the outlet from a canal or distributory, collecting water rates and maintaining field channels. The WUA general body consists mainly of landowners (in some states tenants are also included). Irrigation management transfer has taken place in different ways in different states. In West Bengal, control was taken over by the panchayats. In Andhra Pradesh, a 'top-down' approach was imposed whereby government legislation in 1997 instantly created some 10,292 WUAs and gave them the control of irrigation management at the village level in all the major irrigation projects in the state (Government of Andhra Pradesh, 1997). In other states, such as Gujarat and Karnataka, a more gradual 'bottom-up' approach was used, based on pilot projects and a significant role for NGOs in mobilization and capacity-building (Parthasarathy, 1998: 1–5).

5. Inland Fishing Cooperatives (IFC)

The inland fishing industry in India registered an eight-fold increase in production between 1950 and 1990. The catch, mostly of carp and catfish, takes place in 1.6 million ha of lakes, rivers, reservoirs and ponds throughout the country. As of 2010, there were over 11,000 primary fishing cooperative (FC) societies, federated into 108 central societies at the regional level, 17 state level federations and, at the apex, the National Federation of Fishermen's Cooperatives. The original intent was that the government would provide the policy framework for fish management and also operate hatcheries to replenish the reservoir stock. Meanwhile, at the village level, the cooperatives were to look after minor administrative matters and resolve conflicts that might arise.

After independence, fishing was relegated to a small department in the much larger Ministry of Agriculture in New Delhi. It was the states, however, that held the more important jurisdiction, but there too fishing was of little consequence until the 1970s. Inland fishing began to get more attention when it was realized that the market for fish was growing. With the proliferation of large dams in India, the potential for large reservoir fisheries increased. In some states it was decided that rights for fishing should be given to 'oustees', that is, those evicted from their land to enable reservoir construction, as compensation for their lost income and as a new means of employment.

6. Watershed Development Programme (WDP)

Our third CNRM programme, the Watershed Development Programme (WDP), is of vital importance to India's rain-fed areas, which make up 60 per cent of the 142 million net sown hectares in the country (Dev, 2007: 52). They are dependent mostly on monsoon rain and to a lesser extent on winter rain. In general, these areas are less productive and some are frequently prone to drought. The WDP uses techniques to capture every drop of water that falls in a watershed, and is intended to mobilize villagers to participate in building and maintaining structures such as check dams, nullah plugs, contour bunding and so on. It also facilitates other self-help activities such as the planting of orchards and other afforestation activities, animal husbandry or skill training for self-employment.

The GoI began its support for watershed development with the National Watershed Development Programme for Rainfed Areas (NWDPRA) in 1990. At this point, two related programmes were already functioning: the Drought Prone Areas (DPAP) and Desert Development Programmes (DDP). By 1994, the Hanumantha Rao Committee made recommendations on merging the funds available under DPAP and DDP and creating a new approach based on participatory watershed management principles. What were known as the 'Common Guidelines' were applied, promoting a 'bottom up' approach that featured community participation and the assistance of NGOs. The guidelines have since been revised four times. A fiercely contested point in these revisions has been the designation of the Project Implementing Agency (PIA), the support agency that helps villagers in planning and implementing the programme as per the guidelines. At various points in time, PIAs have included NGOs, PRIs, government departments and even corporate bodies.

At the district level, the District Rural Development Agency (DRDA) holds the responsibility of implementing the WDP at the village level. Watershed projects generally last 3–4 years, although the period is being extended to 5–7 years. Construction work is mostly funded by the state government, although approximately 5–10 per cent of the cost is paid by villagers, often in construction labour. The work is supposed to start at the ridge (i.e., the periphery) of the watershed and proceed gradually towards the valley (the middle). The technical advantage of such an approach is that treatment of the ridge lines optimizes water harvesting and lessens monsoon runoffs and erosion. An added benefit is that in many watersheds it is the marginalized people who live at the ridge.

7. Joint Forest Management (JFM)

In December 1988, the GoI passed the National Forest Policy Resolution which committed the Ministry of Environment and Forests (MoEF) to work with forest communities to protect and enhance existing timber stocks while at the same time 'meeting the requirements of firewood, fodder, minor forest produce, and small timber of the rural and tribal populations' (Sethna, 2000: 14). There was frank recognition that India was losing its forests at an unsustainable rate, both due to the encroachment on forest land by expanding populations and the illegal cutting of trees for profit. It was realized that unless local people, living in or near the forests, were included in the effort to save forests, there would soon be little to save.

In June 1990, the MoEF wrote to all state governments, encouraging them to implement the recommendation of people's participation. The resulting JFM Programme has taken several forms, but the central idea remains as joint action by the state Forest Department (FD) and local forest dwellers to (a) preserve forests by restricting access to forest and forest products, (b) rehabilitate rootstock and plant new forest on degraded land and (c) enable those formerly dependent on the forest to gain other means for their livelihoods. Restricting access to forests could mean different things, depending on the context. Sometimes it could be total, as in the Ecological Development Programme designed for protected areas like national parks and the buffer zones that surround them. Under other JFM programmes, access is more closely monitored and controlled on forest land, with the entire management control coming under the FD, forests grown on land owned by the local government or revenue department.

A large part of India's forested areas is populated by adivasis (aboriginals, also known in India as tribals), many of whom are among the poorest and the most vulnerable people in India. Therefore, although the JFM was conceived from the beginning as a 'partnership', it was clear that the FD would have the upper hand in policymaking regarding JFM and that its implementation would be tightly controlled by the FD. Under such circumstances, 'community' management of the forest per se was unlikely to happen. However, the FD, despite its position of dominance, knew that it would have to provide concessions and benefits if it wanted to have the cooperation of local villagers, especially those accustomed to using the forest for grazing livestock or collecting firewood and non-timber forest products (NTFP) such as medicinal herbs, *tendu* leaves for making *bidis* (Indian cigarettes) or *mahuva* flowers (used to distil liquor).

8. Can CNRM Reduce Poverty in Rural India?

CNRM as a means for managing local resources like water, forests and fish in India should by no means be regarded as 'here to stay'. The foregoing preliminary examination of the institutionalization of the four kinds of CNRM in the village-level projects that we examine here reveals wide disparities in performance across the resource management programmes and between the two states under study. In some projects, the institutionalization of CNRM as a vehicle for end-user initiatives was remarkably smooth and solid. In others, the programmes under discussion were too recent and too uncertain to be regarded as robust and self-sustaining. In any case, apart from a few studies to be discussed in Chapters 3–6, CNRM's impact on poverty in rural India, however, is unknown and is an issue that has not previously been investigated or analysed in any depth.

Hence, throughout our research we have tried to look beyond the question of NRM through CNRM to identify the beneficiaries of the programmes, and whether they included the poor. Did CNRM, directly or indirectly, make an impact on rural poverty? The answers to this simple question are complex, as the evidence and analysis to be presented in the following chapters will attest.

But first, a few caveats. There were significant differences between the four resource management programmes, not to mention their poverty-reduction potentials, partly due to differences in the nature of the resources and partly due to contrasts in the institutions that managed them. It is therefore first necessary to assess to what extent the resources in question were common property resources (CPRs), or open access resources (OARs), or resources that could be accessed exclusively by the members of the CNRM institutions. The distinction determines first, the extent of benefits that were to be gained from CNRM and who got them; second, the potential for the CNRM institution's ability to control resource management by creating incentives and sanctions and third, the commitment of CNRM institution members to collective decision-making and goals.

A second caveat is that in order to gauge a CNRM institution's ability to manage the resource in question, one needs to determine the extent to which real decision-making authority had been decentralized by the government to the CNRM institution. In all four resource management regimes, the appetite of government officials for retaining or increasing their control, both in the state NRM departments and locally, seemed unabated. One therefore needed to examine closely the de jure rights of the communities as per the new legislation or regulatory rules, and de facto how much control had really been decentralized.

The third caveat relates to the question of whether the CNRM institutions could govern themselves, if indeed authority was properly decentralized. Was the CNRM institution able to take decisions and implement them effectively? And, in view of equity concerns, could it do so democratically? The answer seemed to depend on a variety of factors, such as the unity of the end-users as a community, the quality of local leadership, members' respect for agreed rules and procedures, and so on.

Finally, in order to explain why CNRM worked better in some village contexts compared to others, one needed to examine how a CNRM project was actually introduced and supported at the village level. In this regard, the role of the PIA to initiate participatory behaviour and provide capacity-building inputs became very important. This study seeks to evaluate the ability of NGOs versus other agencies, principally government departments and their officials, to not only build the capacity of CNRM institutions to manage resources, but also become self-governing entities addressing concerns of equity and inclusiveness.

2

Comparative CNRM:
From Concepts to Field Research

John R. Wood, Shashidharan Enarth
and Amita Shah

Our project's original title, 'Community Natural Resource Management Institutions and their Impact on Poverty in Gujarat and Madhya Pradesh' raised many conceptual questions. The burgeoning literature on CNRM soon led us to debate, from our different disciplinary and resource specialization viewpoints, what exactly we understood by CNRM and central concepts such as 'community', 'decentralization', 'institution', 'governance', 'equity' and, especially for this study, 'poverty.' Once the field research was underway, we realized that agreement on definitions and the operationalization of these concepts for research would be a challenge.

Two aspects of our approach to the research demanded conceptual clarity. First, as stated earlier, we wanted our study to be comparative, in terms of not only how CNRM projects varied from site to site, but also across the four resource management programmes and across two Indian states. The advantage of a comparative study would be that by examining both similarities and differences in CNRM practices we would be able to better understand the reasons for the success or failure of CNRM performance and outcomes. Second, we wanted our study to be as inductive as possible, rather than to start with the imposition of a theoretical framework based on CNRM experience in other contexts. Thus fieldwork, including getting to know selected CNRM sites, usually villages, through FGDs, a large HHS and discussions with government officials and NGO activists became our continuing priority over two years.

What follows is an attempt to sum up as briefly as possible the results of our debate on the major CNRM concepts, including some of the stumbling blocks involved in operationalizing the concepts for research.

1. The Major Concepts

As stated in the Preface, 'CNRM' essentially means decentralization by government departments of the local management of natural resources to the rural communities most involved in their use. In the CNRM literature as well as in NGO parlance, CNRM is sometimes referred to as Community-based Natural Resource Management (CBNRM). The two terms are usually regarded as synonymous. We have opted for the term 'CNRM' partly because it is less unwieldy. However, it should also be noted that while CBNRM refers to the body of end-users to which resource management responsibilities are transferred, it leaves open the question of who is actually doing the management. Even with the community specified as its base, it may not be the case that the community per se has control over resource management—for example, in the JFM or FC cases, government control continues to be retained through the presence of government officials on the CNRM institution's executive. We believe the term 'CNRM' sharpens the meaning specifically to imply that the community of end-users, through its elected representatives, is truly carrying out the resource management.

The term 'community' is obviously important because it is to the communities that the control over NRM is to be transferred. We started our research assuming that villages would be the location of the communities that would manage the resources in question. With images of de Tocqueville's town meeting or Gandhi's village republic in mind, we expected face-to-face communication and interdependence amongst members of the new CNRM institutions. That was frequently, but not always the case.

The reasons were structural and based on the nature of each resource. For example, in the case of PIM, determining who belonged to a WUA depended on hydraulic considerations, that is, where a farmer's plot was located on an irrigation network, so that the 'community' might involve people of more than one village or part of a village. There were also cases where a farmer owned two hydraulically separated plots and belonged to two WUAs. In addition to farmers who benefitted directly from the irrigation network, there were also farmers who owned land outside the network that was affected by irrigation operations. There were farming families who owned no land, but directly depended on agricultural labour in the irrigated land for their incomes. The inclusion of these families as stakeholders further widened the scope of the term 'community'.

Similarly in the case of the WDP, it was the size and terrain of watersheds that determined how many villages belonged to a WDC along with hydraulic considerations. In this case, the 'community' included every family living in these villages because their livelihoods were affected by one or more of the resources in the watershed–land, water, vegetation and livestock. Meanwhile, in the case of the Gujarat FCs studied by us in the Ukai reservoir, multiple villages belonged to each cooperative. In addition to that, we also discovered that the real locus of decision-making for cooperatives was in the Fish Federation (FF), which in the Ukai reservoir consisted of three cooperatives.

Eventually, we decided that it was more accurate to conceptualize the members of a CNRM institution as not just members of a village community but as members of a community of end-users. End-users were people who worked most closely with and depended on a resource for their livelihood. Nonetheless, where the members of one village dominated a particular CNRM institution numerically, for simplicity's sake and in line with state policy whereby the CNRM institution was named after that village–frequently, but not always, that was the village studied by us.

The second problem facing the 'community' concept was that while common interest in a resource may have united or induced a 'community feeling' amongst the end-users, there may have been other factors that divided them. The internal socio-economic heterogeneity of an Indian village based on religion, caste, tribe, faction, land tenure status or other differences may very well undo the cohesion ordinarily associated with the term 'community'. During the time of the survey it was also commonly found that when such divisions became politicized, the partisanship aroused during elections might have itself become an additional and enduring basis for division and conflict. During our research we made every effort to be aware of divisions like these and to focus on how they might or might not affect the ability of a community of end-users to work together. We also tried not to prejudge, or jump to any conclusions about the effect of such divisions on CNRM performance. In other words, we did not assume that social heterogeneity would be a determinant of CNRM failure.

Although we did find one instance of a woman President of a WUA in MP, women were generally under or completely unrepresented on the ECs of the CNRM institutions we studied. We heard a variety of excuses ranging from 'this is not women's work', to the fact that meetings were held usually at night, a time when women were often too busy to attend meetings because of their domestic duties. And, repeatedly we learned that even if women did attend meetings, they did not speak. Thus we often found that the female part of the community in a particular village had no voice in CNRM deliberations.

Several geographical and demographic factors may also have had an influence on the nature of a 'community'. In some JFM villages, for example, the 'community' did not live in the usual village where all households live in a single cluster, but in a number of small hamlets (*falia*) strung out over a considerable distance. Meanwhile, in some of the JFM and all of the Gujarat FC villages we studied, the population consisted mainly of 'oustees', that is, displaced people, evicted in one JFM case from their original homes in a national park or protected area. In all of the Gujarat FC cases, the oustee communities had been evicted from land that had become submerged by the creation of a reservoir. In some cases the displaced 'community' was relocated together to a new site, while in others it was fragmented, forcing a more difficult restructuring of relationships in a new or changed community.

Finally, the pattern of out-migration that occurred in many villages had created 'communities' where a significant proportion of the adult population was missing for extended periods of time.[1] Whether this debilitated community control or not, could vary from case to case. If men were long-term migrants, women may have gained more influence. In several of our PIM villages, the success of the WUA in managing irrigation had led to decreases in migration. However, where extensive migration occurred because of the inability of the working population to earn adequate incomes at home, the absence of people was likely to affect the growth of a robust CNRM institution.

'Natural resource' seems to be a straightforward concept, but CNRM scholars differ over what a resource is and how natural it may be. We have followed the standard dictionary definition of the term 'resource', which refers to 'a means of supplying what is needed' or a 'stock that can be drawn on' (OED), or 'a source of supply and support' (Webster 2010). Modern usage includes both inanimate and animate resources and thus we have treated fish as a manageable resource. In any case, seemingly inanimate resources such as soil, water and forests are also full of life. How 'natural' a resource is may vary, especially when it is managed by human beings. All three of the resources studied here were natural but they were also manipulated by users, either by building field channels or check dams, or by planting seedlings in a degraded forest or placing fingerlings in a reservoir.

'Decentralization' usually refers to the process of transferring decision-making authority and implementation control from a higher to a lower level governing body. However, decentralization could mean different things in different contexts. Carney views it as a 'shift in the locus of power from the centre towards the

---

[1] Among the villages we selected for research there are also cases where in-migration of a sizable number of agricultural labourers occurs regularly, but this seems to have less of an effect on community dynamics.

periphery' (Carney, 1995: 3). The principle of subsidiarity is the overarching theme in these theories, based on the observation that decisions taken as close as possible to the citizens yield better results than those taken at higher levels. The most discussed context is that of formal governments, either at the national level or the sub-national level, but decentralization may also refer to the processes involved in programmes such as CNRM where the government cedes control to an agency or institution outside its own sphere.

A widely used definition that encompasses this kind of decentralization is the one formulated by Rondinelli:

> [T]he transfer of responsibility for planning, management, and resource-raising and -allocation from the central government (agency) to (1) field unit(s) of central government ministries or agencies; (2) subordinate units or levels of government; (3) semi-autonomous public authorities or corporations; (4) area-wide regional or functional authorities; or (5) Non-governmental Organizations. (Rondinelli, 1981: 22)

This definition captures not only the typology but also the scope for various levels of decentralization.

Other literature on this subject, particularly donor literature, offers a more detailed examination using a three-pronged terminology to examine the processes and impacts of decentralization. The three can be categorized as (a) administrative decentralization, also often described as de-concentration; (b) fiscal decentralization, which means financial/resource decentralization and (c) political decentralization or devolution (Manor, 1999: 5; Rondinelli, 1981: 16). There are other terms with subtle nuances that describe more forms of decentralization–for example, delegation, deregulation and privatization—but in the context of this study, it will suffice to differentiate three main types of decentralization:

> *Administrative decentralization*: This type of decentralization involves very limited transfer of authority to units or sub-units at a subordinate level, such as regional, district or local offices of the central administration or a service delivery organization. These units usually are delegated authority in policy, financial

and administrative matters without any significant independent local inputs. Decentralization involves the transfer of authority for specific decision-making, financial and management functions by administrative means to different levels under the same jurisdictional authority of the central agency. This is the least extensive type of administrative decentralization and the most common found in developing countries. General de-concentration (a term used by Parkor and Manor) occurs to the extent that a variety of tasks are de-concentrated to a horizontally integrated administrative system. Functional de-concentration occurs when specific tasks are de-concentrated to the field units of a particular government body or agency (Parker, 1995: 19). Some authors have questioned the legitimacy of describing de-concentration as a form of decentralization at all, as the process of decision-making happens 'without being subject to local pressures' (Parker, 1995: 6).

Fiscal decentralization: This process refers to downward fiscal transfers, by which higher levels in a system cede control or influence over budgets and financial decisions to lower levels. This authority may be passed on to de-concentrated bureaucrats who are accountable only to their superiors at higher levels, or to unelected appointees selected from higher up. Fiscal decentralization derives much of its advantage from the argument that efficiency improves when government is in closer proximity to the people. Revenue mobilization, innovations in economic activity, accountability of officers and grass-roots level participation in governance are expected to increase through fiscal decentralization (Bahl, 1999: 5). A significant caveat that appears in most of the literature on fiscal decentralization relates to its close link with the devolution process. Based on experience in Africa, Mawhood critiques this form of decentralization using the same argument presented for de-concentration. Fiscal decentralization unattended by any steps towards democratization rarely increases the influence of organized interests at lower levels and therefore, by itself, cannot be regarded as an example of genuine decentralization (Mawhood, cited in Manor, 1999: 7).

Political decentralization: Devolution is the most common way of understanding genuine political decentralization in a unitary state. In both unitary and federal states it refers to the transfer of authority from a central agency to units that are autonomous at a lower level, such as provincial, district and local authorities, legally constituted as separate governing bodies. In the case of a federal state, the units may have existed before the formation of the state and the creation of its central government.

Through devolution, the central government/agency either relinquishes certain functions or creates new units of government that are outside its direct control. Devolution in its purest form has certain fundamental characteristics. First, local units of government or institutions are autonomous and independent and are clearly perceived as separate levels of governance over which central authorities exercise little or no direct control. Second, local governments/institutions have clear and legally recognized geographical boundaries within which they exercise authority and perform public functions. Third, local institutions have the power to acquire resources to perform their functions. Fourth, devolution implies the need to 'develop local governments as institutions' such that they are perceived by local citizens as organizations providing services that satisfy their needs and as governmental units over which they have some influence. They can make and modify rules independently. In Manor's view, the greater the decentralization and grant of autonomy over decision-making, the greater the need for democracy in the institution to which power has been transferred (Manor, 1999).

Decentralization policies for NRM in India fortunately present enough elements of all the three types of decentralization, including the critical element of devolution. The first two forms of decentralization are essential for the third to succeed, since devolution or democratic decentralization on its own is likely to fail. Democratic authorities at lower levels in political systems 'will flounder if they lack powers and resources, meaning both the financial resources and the administrative resources' to effectively carry out governing functions. In other words, political decentralization must be accompanied by some degree of fiscal decentralization and some degree of de-concentration or administrative decentralization (Manor 1999: 7).

The development literature is increasingly focusing on a holistic approach to decentralization. The United Nations Development Programme (UNDP) connects the term 'decentralization' with overall governance, as it firmly believes that decentralization of, say, the public sector, will in itself not be effective unless support is also provided to strengthen local governance, involving the public, private and civil sectors. And, in turn, good governance at the local level will also not be possible without the transfer of powers and capacities through decentralization. The UNDP defines decentralization as 'the systematic and harmonious interrelationship resulting from the balancing of power and responsibilities between central governments and other levels of government and non-governmental actors, and the capacity of local bodies to carry out their decentralized responsibilities using participatory mechanisms' (UNDP, 2005: 3).

With reference to CNRM, decentralization is frequently called 'management transfer', that is, handing over the power and the responsibility to manage a resource by the government to a community-based institution. Despite the fanfare and rhetoric about 'community empowerment' that accompanies the transfer, both de jure and de facto, the actual power to make decisions and implement them may be much less. Decentralization is frequently only partial, and the community rarely ends up with autonomous control. As noted in Chapter 1, very little management transfer had taken place either to forest dwelling communities in the JFM programme, or to fishing communities in the FC programme. Nevertheless, there was an institution to which end-users belonged, where members could voice their grievances and demands, and where they potentially had a role in the management of their resource.

'Institution' was a key concept in our study because if the radical changes implicit in CNRM were not institutionalized, community control over NRM may quickly be lost. Also, if the CNRM institution had been designed to be weak, or if it was designed to be strong but had weakened through neglect, conflict or corrupt behaviour, it was unlikely to endure. To institutionalize, as Samuel Huntington made us understand, is to create 'stable, valued, recurring patterns of behaviour' (Huntington, 1968: 12). In common parlance, institutions have often been described as 'the rules of the game'. The CNRM institutions we are studying were inaugurated in a context where new rules and patterns of behaviour were yet to be established and made legitimate. The new patterns are not universally valued and may be easily destabilized.

After the resource management authority is transferred to a community, it is vital that the institution which takes up the responsibility follows democratic procedures. This requires elections for the officials (usually a President and a Secretary and members who sit on the executive or management committee) and strict adherence to rules regarding nomination, balloting, vote counting, etc. Once elected, the executive/management committee should proceed in accordance with democratic rules and regulations set out in the legislation. During our fieldwork, as will soon become evident, we found many ways in which such rules and regulations could be bent, twisted or got around.

Another important issue for institutions is how they interact with other institutions. CNRM institutions, although self-governing, can never act with complete autonomy as they are 'nested' in relationships with other institutions, most of them governmental. For example, in PIM villages, the WUA did not have full autonomy in irrigation management decision-making because the government owned the reservoir and canal system and its officials controlled the delivery of water to the WUA's outlet. Also, especially in drought years, the WUA may have had to struggle with other institutional competitors for the water it needed. These included not only other WUAs, but also municipalities which had a claim to a share of the water, or industries encroaching upon rural areas that could, with the right political influence, just take it.

'Governance' is a concept we will use to refer to the manner in which the CNRM institution conducted itself. It involves more than 'management', which means the direct handling or manoeuvring required to achieve desired results. Defined as 'orderly rule' (Mitra, 2006: 1), 'governance' also differs from 'government' in that it refers to *the way* in which power and authority are exercised, and not just the exercise itself. According to the UNDP it includes 'the complex mechanisms, processes and institutions through which citizens and groups articulate their interests, exercise their legal rights and obligations, and mediate their differences' (UNDP, 1997: 5). Kaufmann, Kraay et al. go even further: governance refers to 'the traditions and institutions by which authority in a country is exercised for the common good. This includes (a) the process by which those in authority are selected, monitored and replaced, (b) the government's capacity to effectively manage its resources and implement sound policies and (c) the respect of citizens and the state for the institutions that govern economic and social interaction among them' (Kaufmann, Kraay et al., 1999: 1).

In seeking to distinguish between good and bad governance and to assess the quality of CNRM we have focused on various components or aspects of governance that are regarded as crucial to the success of CNRM institutions. These included the levels of participation, transparency, accountability, responsiveness, equitability and respect for rules in an institution. In our research we have aimed to investigate each of these, and relate 'the level of good governance' not only to the effective management of a resource, but also to the inclusion of the 'weaker elements' as participants and recipients in the distribution of its benefits.

In brief, *participation* was measured in terms of the extent of involvement of members in the governance of the institution, including the level of involvement of 'the weaker elements'. Were there indications of the new institution being received enthusiastically or apathetically by the community? Was the willingness to participate confined to a few? Did only members of well-off, elite groups become members of the EC, or were 'the weaker elements' included? *Accountability* refers to the trustworthiness of officials of the CNRM institution to report and explain all their transactions to members. Were true records of decision-making and accounts made public and available to all? Did the members have the ability to reward or punish the office bearers of the CNRM institutions based on their performance? *Transparency* was closely related to accountability and referred to the openness of decision-making. Were true records of decision-making and accounts kept and made available to all? How much did the general membership know about the institution's activities and about their own rights and responsibilities?

Responsiveness referred to the readiness of the institution and its officials to deal with members' demands or grievances. Was the responsiveness exercised only for a few, or for all? *Equitability* referred to the fairness of treatment and of benefit allocation rendered by the institution and experienced by members of the community. Were some of the members systematically excluded? Over time, did the 'weaker elements' get their fair share of benefits? *Respect for rules* takes us to a key aspect of governance, which is also known as 'the rule of law'. Did the laws and rules and not individuals, govern the activities of the institution? Respect for rules applies both to the behaviour of officials and the behaviour and expectations of the community.

'Equity' is often assumed to be interchangeable with 'equality', but this is not the case. Rather, equity connotes the pursuit of fairness in a situation where pursuing complete equality is neither feasible nor achievable. Whereas equality may be an ideal, fairness may be more practicable. With reference to CNRM, equity was usually an issue that had to be dealt with in terms of the involvement and treatment of members of the CNRM institution, and in particular of 'the weaker elements', whether or not they were members of the CNRM institution.

'Impact on income and expenditure' seemed at first glance to be a straightforward concept, one that economists dealt with regularly. However, it was first, difficult to measure changes in household income and expenditures, and second, to separate out the change caused by CNRM from a myriad of other causes of change in income and expenditures.

Measuring changes in household income and expenditures was a complication our project faced due to lack of reliable 'before CNRM' and 'after CNRM' data. Acquiring 'before CNRM' data depended on the memory of informants, many of whom could not remember, for example, how many quintals of various grains they had grown five years earlier, and how much they were worth then. The inability to remember the amount of expenditure on diesel fuel, fertilizers, seeds, pesticides, water, field labourers and credit and debt payments added to the problem. Our field investigators frequently felt that informants were either guessing or inventing data that would please the interviewer.

Separating out the CNRM impact on income and expenditures was an equally difficult, if not futile exercise, referred to here as 'attribution'. Two examples will suffice. Picture a fishing family who were members of an FC. After some bad years their fish catch had increased, and their farming income had also been increasing gradually over the last several years. Moreover, two members of the household had been migrating for four months a year for the last ten years to engage in agricultural labour work in another district. The main reason why their fishing had improved was because two years ago the family put their increased income, garnered from various sources, into buying a better boat and other fishing equipment. They were able to purchase the boat and equipment at a subsidized rate provided exclusively for FC members. Would it be justified for us to say that their subsequent income increased because of the FC and CNRM?

Another example: a family living in a JFM village adjacent to a forest was not allowed to cut wood or graze cattle, although removing NTFP was periodically allowed. The FD encouraged and enabled JFM members' farming outside the forest by levelling land and building check dams to raise groundwater levels. The members contributed labour to these JFM construction projects. The FD also provided grass for cattle and buffaloes, and eventually the beginnings of a dairy operation that could lead to cash earnings for participating villagers. Again, if their poverty had been reduced, how much could this have been attributed to CNRM?

Accurate attribution was virtually impossible in a context where many factors—including good or bad monsoon rainfall, local poverty-reduction projects, the availability of other employment, varying prices on domestic or even international markets—could have had an impact on rural household income and expenditures.

Also, in most rural households there were usually members whose incomes were only partially derived from CNRM activity, as well as those whose incomes came from an entirely non-CNRM source.

All of these complications made the possibility of a clear and unequivocal answer to our central question very difficult: what was the impact of CNRM on income and expenditures? Nonetheless, we were convinced that first, the question was worth asking, and second, that the inductive approach of our research would tell us at least what villagers in the 30 CNRM institutions thought was the impact, if any, of CNRM on their village and on their households. At the end of the research we expected to have information and data derived from a variety of instruments and sources, with the totality of the evidence leading to a convincing analysis.

'Poverty' has been placed at the end of our conceptual discussion, but it is probably the most important concept that we have dealt with in our research. India, notwithstanding its impressive economic growth in the past two decades, is home to the largest number of the world's poor people. The share of India's poor in the global total increased from 22 to 33 per cent during 1980–2005 (Ravallion, 2008). Today, approximately 400 out of the 1.2 billion of the world's poor reside in India.[2] This poses a formidable challenge not only for the poor to sustain a meaningful existence, but also for policymakers to find ways out of the dire conditions in which the poor live. An important characteristic of poverty in India is that much of it is chronic and structural (Mehta et al., 2010). Getting out of poverty, therefore, may require massive restructuring of India's economy, socio-cultural norms and above all political processes. India's constant fear is that if unattended, the consequences of impoverishment may be political instability which could threaten the country's democratic processes.

The poverty issue in India has received significant attention amongst a large number of scholars, policymakers and civil society at large. The poverty debate, focusing mainly on measurement, causation and policy formulation, is by far the most enduring academic discourse in the country (Deaton and Dreze, 2007;

---

[2] http://iresearch.worldbank.org/Povcal-Net/index.htm

Dev, 2007; Manna, 2007; Sen, 2005; Srinivas, 2007; Suryanarayana, 2008). Right since the pre-independence days, thinkers like Dadabhai Naoroji (1901) have discussed at length who should be considered 'poor' in a given context. The debate has continued right to the present. During our research, the controversy over the Tendulkar Committee's attempt to redesign the methodology for drawing a poverty line became headline news and in 2011 the Deputy Chairman of the Planning Commission was asked by the Supreme Court of India to define poverty in the country (GoI, 2009).

As per the official definition, poverty in India is measured in terms of a stipulated level of monthly per capita expenditure (MPCE), below which a person may not be able to meet his/her basic food requirements. This cut-off point actually refers to an income which enables a household of five persons or four adult consumption units (termed as 'nutrition units') in urban and rural areas separately, to obtain the minimum calories required to be alive and productive. The MPCE is calculated by looking into the state-specific food consumption basket separately for rural and urban areas and the prevailing consumer price index at a given time. Essentially, the MPCE takes into account a specific food basket that would enable a person to obtain the prescribed level of calories per capita per day (2,400 and 2,100 calories in rural and urban areas, respectively) deemed necessary for leading a healthy and productive life. In this sense, the poverty line (or the MPCE) is linked to a normative requirement of calories rather than the actual number of calories that an individual consumes. The poverty line, expressed in terms of MPCE, at a given price level is the basis for estimating the number of people living below the poverty line (BPL) in a particular year. The estimate is made on the basis of the consumption and expenditure data provided by the National Sample Survey Organization (NSSO) every five years. Based on the NSSO data, the Planning Commission issues poverty estimates in terms of a head count ratio (HCR), reflecting the proportion of people living BPL.

Thus, the poverty line is defined in terms of expenditure rather than income (which is much more difficult to estimate), and it consists of only some basic requirements as noted above.

Expenditures on health and education have not been included in this calculation until recently, as these services at least in rural areas were expected to be provided by the state free of cost. Of late, the poverty line for rural areas has been revised by making provisions for expenditures on health and education. According to the latest available estimates for 2004–05, the poverty HCR was 41.8 and 25.7 per cent for rural and urban areas respectively. The HCR varies significantly across the states in India (Dev and Ravi, 2008).

The HCR, as noted above, provides estimates of the proportion of the poor population in the country, but it does not help identify which individual is poor. Identification of the individual or household is important for the implementation of policies aimed at reducing poverty. This is particularly so when the focus of anti-poverty programmes is more on individuals/households (often called 'beneficiaries') rather than on the systemic problems that cause poverty and/or define the environment within which the poor try to eke out their living.

By and large, anti-poverty programmes in India have adopted a beneficiary-oriented approach, especially from the late sixties when the slogan of 'Garibi Hatao' (eliminate poverty) was popularized by Indira Gandhi. It became essential to devise a method by which the poor could be identified, and this was done by undertaking separate (Census) surveys under the auspices of the central Ministry of Rural Development (MoRD) to identify BPL households. The identification was based on a mix of assets, employment and income indicators of households living in rural areas. By 2010, four BPL surveys had already been conducted and a fifth is underway. Based on the survey, each household is given a card indicating its ranking in terms of the composite score of indicators used for identifying poor households. Generally, households with a score below a cut-off level are considered BPL households. This may not necessarily align with the poverty estimate using the official poverty line. The poverty estimates prepared by the Planning Commission however, are used as indicators for the transfer of resources from the centre to the state governments for implementing various anti-poverty programmes, typically funded by the MoRD. The BPL status of a household is neither static nor reflective of the level of consumption expenditure, which is used as the basis for estimating poverty at the national, state and regional levels.

Whereas the official definition of poverty in India takes a monolithic view of deprivation by focusing only on food and calorie consumption, there has been increasing recognition of the fact that poverty is multidimensional and therefore should address various dimensions of deprivation including socio-cultural, human, spatial and political as well as economic. In this sense, the approach adopted for the BPL survey is a small step forward as the indicators incorporate a range of economic and also social variables such as social groups, single women, etc. (Himanshu, 2010; Saith, 2005; Sen, 2005).

In this context, attempts have been made to use alternative methods for measuring poverty. The asset-based approach is one such effort (Srinivas and Ray, 2006). Thus, although the official approach has been to consider income/expenditure as an indicator of poverty, the ongoing debate strongly recommends a more comprehensive approach for measuring poverty. Srinavasan (2007), while revisiting the debate, has commended various efforts to develop a minimum needs approach to target poverty. In none of these approaches did the identification of the poor solely rest on the minimum nutrient requirement to fix a minimum living standard. He further notes that all the earlier attempts to identify the poor did consider items like clothing, medical needs and transportation as essential components of any household's expenditure, along with expenditure on a certain basic quantity of essential food items.

One important point that emerges from this debate is the need to look at poverty in a more comprehensive and context-specific manner rather than in a monolithic and static manner. Second, with regard to causation, a plethora of studies has gone into examining the factors leading to poverty (Bhide and Mehta, 2008; Dev and Ravi, 2007; Dhamija and Bhide, 2010; Himanshu, 2007; Patnaik, 2007). First and foremost, poverty in India is more a rural than urban phenomenon. Among the major economic factors associated with rural poverty are: access to land and irrigation, rural infrastructure and availability of non-farm employment. However, poverty is overwhelmingly influenced by social marginalization and hence found to be concentrated amongst the SCs, STs and women. Physical remoteness and lack of entitlement to forest resources are also found to be important correlates of rural poverty. In addition, political instability, conflict and natural disasters also create pockets of highly concentrated poverty in India. In fact, in many cases these multiple factors seem to operate simultaneously, making it far more difficult to reduce the poverty levels at hand.

In sum, it is evident that most of the factors associated with rural poverty pertain to the issue of access to basic factors of production, social stratification and political situations prevailing in a region. All these may require systemic solutions rather than working mainly on supply side mechanisms to provide basic amenities.

Operationalizing the complex concept of poverty for empirical research such as ours posed a formidable challenge, not only in terms of identification and measurement, but more importantly with regard to the specific dimension of human well-being impacted in the many context-specific situations covered by our study. First, it may be noted that identifying the poor and/or measuring poverty using the calorie-based money-metric poverty line was impossible in a situation of 'before-after CNRM' comparisons where base line information was missing and the time gap was five years or more. Collecting information on consumption expenditure/income thus ran the risk of serious errors and approximation. The attempt made here to assess the impact on poverty in a 'before-after CNRM' context thus needs to be seen as using indicative measures to capture the direction and broad magnitude of change rather than any precise estimations.

The second difficulty in operationalizing the poverty concept stemmed from the fact that each of the resource management programmes and the corresponding project interventions dealt with only a sub-set of the poor within a village. Assessing the impact on poverty across our four sets of target groups and across the project interventions therefore required different approaches focusing on those who could be termed as relatively better or worse off within the specific context of the resource policy intervention. For instance, a PIM project, as against a JFM project, was not likely to have as many poor in the target groups. Thus we attempted to identify whether the project intervention had positively impacted those who were relatively worse-off than the rest of the member households, or not. To adopt such a 'relative', rather than an 'absolute' measure of poverty or the poor segment of the population, we resorted to asset-based measures, mainly ownership or not, of land at the household level. Given the diversity of situations and conceptual as well as methodological difficulties in measuring poverty, it was imperative that a flexible approach be adopted while operationalizing the poverty concept within the diverse settings of the field enquiries in the present study. Thus we have emphasized suitability, feasibility and internal consistency within a specific chapter rather than forcing commonality across all the chapters. This, we hope, is viewed as an inevitable limitation of a study such as ours since it encompasses a wide array of situations pertaining to natural resources, policy interventions and poverty.

2. CNRM Research Site Selection

Our first task was to select the CNRM sites in Gujarat and MP where we would conduct our fieldwork (see Figures 2.1 and 2.2 of Gujarat and MP). Each site would technically be the location of a project in which a community of end-users was participating in the management of a resource (either water, forest or fish). In most cases, the CNRM site was a village, but as discussed earlier, there were some CNRM sites that covered more than one village, or a part of a village. The four specialists will explain the particular selection strategies followed by them and the circumstances in which more than one village or part of a village belonged to the CNRM project they studied.

Random selection of villages was unsuitable because a number of criteria were necessary to ensure that the CNRM projects could be adequately studied. First, a selected village would have to have an ongoing CNRM project with a functioning CNRM institution. Eventually, we stipulated that the CNRM project and the institution would have to have been functioning for five years. Only by imposing these criteria would we be able to measure change, if

Figure 2.1

Map of Gujarat: Location of Research Sites

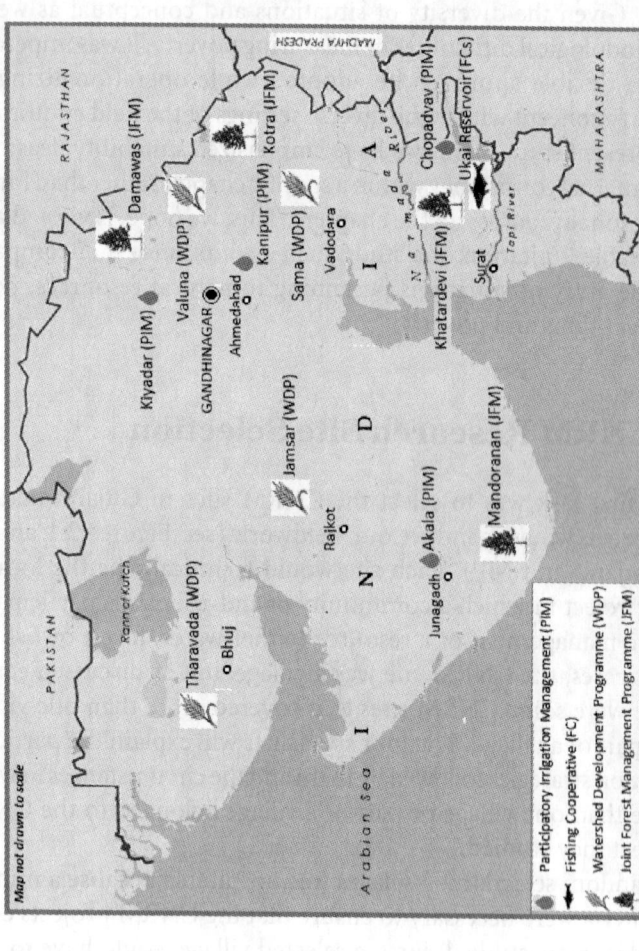

Source: Drawn by authors.

Note: This map does not claim to represent the authentic domestic or international boundaries of any country. This map is not to scale and provided for illustrative purpose only.

Figure 2.2

Map of Madhya Pradesh: Location of Research Sites

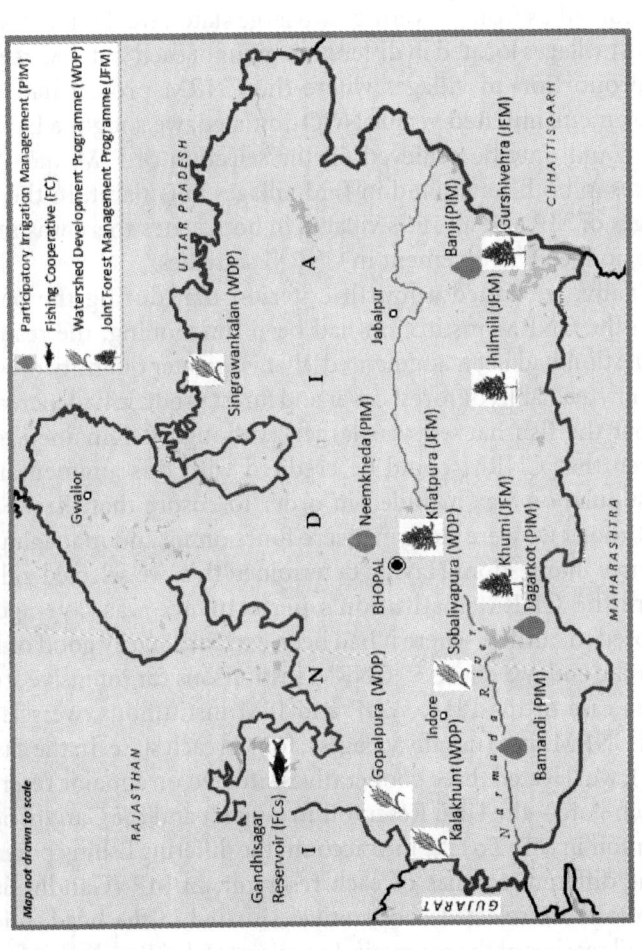

Source: Drawn by authors.

Note: This map does not claim to represent the authentic domestic or international boundaries of any country. This map is not to scale and provided for illustrative purpose only.

any, in various dimensions of the economy of the village and the members of its CNRM institution.

Two additional criteria for selection were geographical spread and the balance of government- versus NGO-initiated projects. As regards geographical spread, although budget limitations constrained us from 'covering' two large states, we did try to select CNRM villages located in different regions of each state. As regards the proportion of villages where the CNRM project had been government-initiated versus NGO-initiated, we sought a balance. This could only be achieved, in the selection of PIM and WDP villages in both states, and in JFM villages in Gujarat. In the JFM villages of MP and all IFCs villages in both states there was found to be no NGO involvement in CNRM activities.

Finally, we added a fourth criterion that during the period when the CNRM institution had been functioning, the resource in question had been augmented, that is, greater quantity of water was now available, or forest cover and forest produce had increased, or that the fish harvest was larger. Although it remained to be proven that CNRM could be credited with this augmentation, the stipulation was included in order to ensure that the CNRM institutions we were studying were functioning and managing the resource in question. Having determined this, we selected villages where the CNRM institution's performance was 'average' as opposed to outliers where it had been extraordinarily good or bad.

In the end, we chose 30 CNRM institutions for intensive study. In the case of the PIM, WDP and JFM institutions, we selected eight CNRM sites (usually villages), four in each state. In the case of IFCs), we selected three cooperatives situated on a major reservoir of each state—the Ukai Reservoir in Gujarat and the Gandhi Sagar Reservoir in MP. To take into account the differing fishing potential of the different reaches of each reservoir, in MP (Gandhi Sagar Reservoir) we selected cooperatives situated in the head, middle and tail reaches of the reservoir. In Gujarat (Ukai Reservoir), for the same reason, we selected three such cooperatives, but these included multiple smaller villages or hamlets, nine in the head reach, eight in the middle and eleven in the tail end of the reservoir.

To sum up the selection process, it must be said that we did not, nor ever could expect that our samples would be representative of all the CNRM activities in the two states, let alone the whole of India. Nevertheless, our research findings do reveal a diversity in village contexts—geographic, demographic, socio-cultural, economic and political—that is suggestive of the much greater level of diversity facing CNRM in the country as a whole. The contrasts in CNRM policies and in the approaches taken by Gujarat and MP in implementing CNRM add another element to the diversity. As Chapters 3–6 will reveal, the range of successes versus failures (and all the gradations in between) of CNRM institutions that we have discovered have proven both challenging and enlightening for analysis.

2.1. Fieldwork

We began the fieldwork with FGDs with the members of the local CNRM ECs in the 30 sites selected for study, focusing on a long checklist of open-ended questions regarding not only the introduction and operationalization of CNRM activities, but also the village economy in terms of sources of income, means of production, credit, productivity, etc. The primary source of income for most households of the villages we were studying was agriculture. It was obviously the main occupation for our informants in PIM and WDP villages. But even in JFM and many FC villages, agriculture was the main source of livelihood. In the JFM villages, we used FGDs to pursue economic information related to forest protection and rehabilitation as well as the harvest of NTFP. In the FC villages, the FGD focus was on fish catch and prices, fishing technology and practice, the leasing system, shipping and marketing and the role of contractors and merchants.

The FGDs were also used to elicit general information on poverty in each village and whether the introduction of the CNRM programme had had any impact on it. The research instrument on the other hand was intended to gather more extensive data on poverty at the household level and this was a household survey of 50 households in each of the 30 research sites. We devised our survey questionnaire as carefully as possible with questions to elicit income and expenditure data from farming households, as well as for those where income was additionally earned from fishing or forest activities or migrant work. To get net income we needed data covering not only a household's entire income, but also its complete expenditure. This was no mean task, as we were asking informants about not only what their income and expenditures had been in 2008–09, but also to compare these with what they remembered their income and expenditures to have been before the CNRM institution was inaugurated in their village. The cost of assets was more easily recalled, and also the year in which they were bought. However, some villagers were reluctant to divulge truthfully how much they had invested in assets like land, vehicles, or valuables like jewellery.

3. Conclusion

The methodologies used in the analysis of each of the four following chapters vary to some extent depending on the resource, resource management and the resource management institution to be studied. The details of each of these will be presented by the authors of Chapters 3–6. We have nevertheless taken the first step to answering our central common question about the impact of CNRM institutions on poverty in rural India by examining here in Chapter 2 the complexity of the central concepts involved and presenting the definitions that we all could agree on. Details of the fieldwork have also been spelt out, including the FGDs and the HHS. We end this chapter listing out a set of questions that guided our research, and which the chapter authors attempt to answer based on data elicited from their case studies. It is to be expected that the answers might vary significantly from author to author. Nonetheless, the similarities and the differences in the answers will be instructive:

1. At the village level, how was the CNRM project and institution introduced?
2. How did the project and institution perform, both de jure and de facto, in terms of CNRM goals?
3. What was the extent of productivity and income increase?

4. How decentralized and inclusive was the governance of the CNRM institution?
5. What has been the impact on the poor members of the village?
6. How integrated was the project intervention and what was the extent of the outreach?
7. How has the project and institution contributed to effective, equitable and sustainable resource management?

3

Participatory Irrigation Management in Gujarat and Madhya Pradesh: When and How Can It Benefit the Poor?

Shashidharan Enarth

1. Introduction

Recorded history indicates that starting from the Chola kings and the Maurya dynasty in 3rd century BC, through the era of invading rulers and colonial governments and right up to the democratically elected governments in India, construction of irrigation dams and canals with the aim to increase irrigation has been a major preoccupation of the state. Chandragupta Maurya built dams, extensive canal systems and introduced irrigation fees in the Girnar region of Gujarat. The trend continued into the 20th century with India investing more than ₹600 billion or US$ 80 billion (at 1980 base prices) between 1950 and 2000 to expand the area under irrigation (World Bank, 1998: 4). This amounted to 90 per cent of all public investments in agriculture during the same period with the result that irrigated area increased by 131 per cent during the same period (Kishore, 2002: 112). Currently, 38 per cent of India's net sown area (NSA) is irrigated by three major sources of irrigation—publicly owned and operated surface irrigation systems, publicly owned groundwater irrigation schemes and predominantly privately owned groundwater wells. Public systems irrigate about 36 per cent of the total irrigated area of India (Brewer et al., 1999: 14). More than 58 per cent of agricultural production in India today comes from irrigated farms. Irrigation for food production uses up the largest share of human managed water supply (estimated at 80 per cent in most South Asian countries).

Thus, irrigation projects have contributed significantly in averting the spectre of a food crisis that was predicted in the early years of independence. Large reservoirs and canal systems are in fact considered to be icons of modernization and the most important means of maintaining food self-sufficiency. Yet there are predictions that at the current rate of population growth (1.68 per cent) and agriculture productivity growth (3 per cent), there will be a food shortage by the year 2050. Estimates by the Planning Commission of India indicate that agricultural productivity must grow at 4.5 per cent per annum to meet the food demand (World Bank, 1998: 8). The scope for increasing the area under cultivation is problematic, given the demand for land for non-agricultural uses. Thus, to achieve this goal, productivity per unit area of irrigation will need to double by 2015 (World Bank, 1998: 8). Simply put, irrigation facilities will have to be optimally utilized to get 'more crop per drop'. While exploring the limited scope of expanding the physical area through new irrigation projects, the main focus has to be on the performance improvement of existing projects through appropriate reforms in management systems and institutions. This is considered a more cost-effective approach to addressing the problem than creating new infrastructure (Lal, 2003: 39–42). For example, improving efficiency in water use by a mere 10 per cent will save enough water to add 14 million ha of land under irrigation (Postel, 1993: 60). Moreover, India has already developed 76 per cent of its ultimate irrigation potential. Developing the remaining 24 per cent will be progressively more difficult and expensive given the fact that the most technically feasible sites have already been exploited (Lal, 2003).

2. Irrigation Institutions in India and the Centralizing Tendency

With a rapidly increasing population and recurring drought and famine conditions, India decided to invest in publicly managed irrigation infrastructure of dams and canals with almost no cost sharing with farmers (Vaidyanathan, 1999). As a result, the increase in irrigation facilities saw a corresponding increase in the size and mandate of irrigation bureaucracy in India. Not only did the state pay for the infrastructure, its agency—the Irrigation Department (ID)—was given nearly complete control over the infrastructure. For reasons described in greater detail in the following sections, the performance of the ID was very poor. Despite a steady decline in the utilization of irrigation facilities during the four decades of state control, water users continued to be passive recipients of inefficient services and had no recourse to claim their entitlements. It is easy to trace the origins of such a lopsided top-down governing system to the Bombay Irrigation Act 1876, which was adopted by all state governments and governs the distribution of authority and functions for irrigation operations. The Act gives complete control of irrigation systems to a government department, then the Public Works Department, but no provision for the water users to either participate or hold the ID to account for the quality of services (Lele and Patil, 1994).

3. Problems with Public Irrigation Systems in India

Even though the achievement of creating physical infrastructure for irrigation appears very impressive in terms of the investment and the number of projects, the performance is far from satisfactory when it comes to delivering water to the fields. Poor efficiency in water use, environmental damage due to improper use and inequitable distribution of irrigation benefits have remained the main areas of concern. Average seepage loss from canals in India is around

45 per cent (Tiwari and Dinar, 2002:103). The Ministry of Water Resources estimated in 1991 that 5.8 million ha of irrigated land were already degraded due to waterlogging, alkalinity and salinity (Lal et al., 2002: 37). On the equity front, water entitlements among the farmers in the irrigation command area have been prone to disruptions due to many systemic and social problems. The two popular notions of equity, namely, prior appropriation (head-enders versus tail-enders) and proportionate equality (small versus large land holders) were both found to be problematic in public irrigation systems (Chambers, 1988: 37). A study of irrigation projects conducted in six states of India has revealed that a farmer in the tail-sections of a canal system is more likely to be deprived of irrigation services than a farmer from the middle and head reaches (Shah, 2003).

There are three broad categories of problems that can explain the unsatisfactory performance of the irrigation programme in India:

1. **Institutional Constraints:**
   The state IDs are a good example of typical government bureaucracy, which has changed little over time. Administration has been overly centralized and lacks accountability, management skills and client focus. It tends to be remote, top-down and has only minimal contact with farmers. The organization is dominated by civil engineers, with limited presence of professionals from other disciplines such as the social sciences or agriculture. Linkages with other government departments, especially agriculture and cooperative development, are weak. In many states in India, the ID has grown in staff strength to be one of the largest state employers. As a result, both politically and administratively the ID staff constitutes a strong interest group. Past attempts at irrigation sector reforms have had to contend with political pressure mounted by the employees. As an institution, they have poor learning mechanisms and therefore poor capacity to respond to changing demands and to adapt to new opportunities.

2. **Financial Constraints:**
Starting right from the very basic water pricing system, incentives for efficient water use have been largely absent. Irrigation fees have been very low, often less than 30 per cent of operations and maintenance (O&M) costs and less than 2 per cent of the crop value (Oblitas and Peter, 1999: 7). Mismanagement and corruption have contributed to a high default rate in the payment of these fees. Construction and major repairs of the physical system have been contracted out centrally and not locally and are poorly monitored, leading to cost over-runs and pilferage. These factors have led to persistently inadequate allocations for the upkeep of the physical system. As much as 70 per cent of the O&M budget goes to staff salaries leaving negligible amounts for actual maintenance works (Joshi, 1999: 108). This is in stark contrast with the situation prior to independence during the colonial rule. For the British administrators, irrigation was a revenue earner. For example, net irrigation revenue made up more than 25 per cent of the total revenue receipts collected by the administration in the province of Punjab during 1927–28 (Paustian, 1968, cited in Shah et al., 2009). Politically, it became increasingly difficult for policymakers to impose financial discipline despite clear evidence that irrigation made for an excellent marginal benefit-cost ratio. As a consequence, pubic irrigation systems were kept alive through massive subsidies. The exact quantum of subsidy is hard to estimate because of the nature of the subsidy. In most cases, the subsidy was implicit in that it was computed as the deficit in recovering irrigation expenses through revenue receipts. In an assessment done for the year 1994–95, out of the total expense of ₹136 billion incurred by all the state IDs, only 5 per cent (i.e., ₹5.4 billion) was recovered and 95 per cent was underwritten by the government as subsidy (Dhawan, 1997: A-72). The Central Water Commission reported in 2006 that only 7.9 per cent of the O&M costs are recovered through water charges.

3. **Physical Infrastructure Constraints:**
   A common physical constraint has been the inadequate maintenance of canals resulting in the steady deterioration of irrigation infrastructures. Physical constraints have often stemmed from design flaws in the project planning and construction phases. Designs for delivery systems have often been carried out with inadequate field level and historical data provided by farmers. The result has been a rapid decline in the physical condition of the system, which in turn, is the main cause for poor utilization and high levels of wastage. Remedial measures, attempted sporadically through one-off grants for repairs and rehabilitations have been fiscally unsustainable due to water pricing policies as illustrated in the previous paragraph.

4. Policy Provisions: A Comparison

The PIM Acts introduced in various states have derived their broad policy contours from the trend-setting Andhra Pradesh Farmers Management of Irrigation Systems Act of 1997. The Act redefined the role of the ID as an enabling and back-stopping support organization. It mandated the creation of formal farmers' organizations that would be empowered to take over management responsibilities from the ID. The Madhya Pradesh Act, which was introduced in 1999, was more or less a replica of the Andhra Pradesh Act. Gujarat however, chose to delay the introduction of its legislation because two of the leading NGOs from the state, the Aga Khan Rural Support Programme (AKRSP) and the Development Support Centre (DSC), made a case for further refinements and changes in the key provisions of the Act. Table 3.1 illustrates the key differences between the Acts of the two states involved in this study.

Provisions pertaining to three management functions deserve special discussion in the context of decentralization. The first deals with the very concept of a farmers' organization. In MP, the secretary of a WUA is a sub-engineer (SE) from the ID as per the

Table 3.1

Significant Differences in the PIM Acts of Gujarat and MP

Key Features/ Provisions	PIM Gujarat	PIM MP
Year of legislation	2007	1999
Applicability	Not notified yet[1]	All projects above 40 Ha
Legal Status of Farmers' Organization	Registered under the Cooperative Societies Act.	Registered under the PIM Act
Provisions for higher level of institutions	No provision for farmer participation in managing distributory canals and reservoirs	Provision for farmer management at all levels.
Composition of farmers' organization	All office bearers of WUA were farmers.	All office bearers of WUA are farmers except the crucial secretary who is an ID-appointed sub-engineer.
Fiscal autonomy	Water rates fixed by WUA Collection by WUA O&M expenses by WUA	Water rates fixed by ID Collection by Revenue Dept. O&M expenses by ID
Operational Autonomy	Water allocation and distribution by WUA	Water allocation and distribution jointly by ID/WUA

Source: PIM Act of Gujarat (2007) and of Madhya Pradesh (1999).
Note: O&M = Operation and Maintenance.

MP Act (1999). When the role and authority vested in the office of the Secretary of a WUA was considered, it became clear that despite the rhetoric of the devolution of authority to farmers, the real control of irrigation and all its attendant functions went right back to the ID through its SE. The second provision deals with decisions pertaining to fiscal matters. Given that delayed maintenance and poor supervision of construction have been two of the main causes for under-utilization, the new arrangement intended to give this responsibility to the WUAs based on the success of farmer-managed pilot projects. For the WUA to be able to function in a financially

[1] The Act was passed in Gujarat State Assembly in 2007. However, the ID had not completed the process of formulating the rules and regulations, without which the Act was ineffective. There were Government Resolutions (GRs) that enabled the ID as well as farmers to initiate PIM in their irrigation command area.

sustainable way, it was imperative that they be given autonomy not only to control revenue but also expenses. However, this objective of decentralization was undermined in the case of MP where revenue generation and expenditures were completely beyond the control of the WUA. The water rates were fixed by the government and the recovery of water charges was carried out by the revenue department. The MP cases evaluated in this study clearly reveal the vulnerability that the WUAs could face in the absence of autonomy. The third aspect was a result of the combined effect of the first two, namely, lack of operational and fiscal autonomy. The motivation and ability of the farmers and the WUA leaders to meaningfully participate in day-to-day irrigation operations was severely compromised due to the continuing dominance of the ID in management functions. MP's was a case where the de jure provisions of the Act, were not only inconsistent with the objectives of decentralization, but also, the de facto implementation was much worse.

The situation in Gujarat was significantly different and better on these counts. Only farmers from the command area could become members of a WUA and its office bearers. Therefore, the authority to frame rules affecting irrigation operations remained with the water users. More importantly, the Act provided the WUA complete authority to decide the water rates and recover dues from farmers directly. This enabled the WUA to be fiscally responsible and therefore made the leaders accountable to the farmers.

5. Irrigation in Madhya Pradesh

The economy of MP, with its population of 60 million and an estimated 44 per cent living BPL, was dominated by agriculture which accounted for 35 per cent of the State Gross Development Product (GDP), and 80 per cent of employment. More than one-third of the population belonged to socially and economically disadvantaged groups consisting of STs (20 per cent) and SCs (15 per cent), one of the highest proportions in India. Approximately 78 per cent of the total state population was engaged in agriculture. In 2005–06, MP had a total irrigation

Table 3.2

Number of MP Irrigation Schemes as per 2005–06 Records

Scheme	Total	Completed	Area Irrigated ('000s Ha)
Major	21	9	941
Medium	114	101	372
Minor	4,296	3,332	659
Total Surface irrigation	4,431	3,442	1,972

Source: Irrigation Utilization Report, Statistical Division, MPWRD.

potential of close to 2.4 million ha, created through nearly 3,500 major, medium and minor surface irrigation schemes. Out of the net sown area of 14.77 million ha, less than 2 million ha (13.5 per cent) could be irrigated through various sources of irrigation (see Table 3.2). This was below the national average to begin with. In reality, it was even worse, with only about 30–40 per cent of this potential being used, as per official data. One of the major reasons for underutilization (as discussed in the earlier sections) was the inadequate or delayed maintenance of irrigation infrastructure (mainly the canal system). The ID was weak in engaging farmers, resulting in an attitude of indifference amongst farmers towards the upkeep of the canals and discipline in using water.

6. PIM in Madhya Pradesh

The introduction of the PIM Act in 1999 may be considered as the formal beginning of policy reform in MP. Unlike states such as Andhra Pradesh and Gujarat that experimented and developed the capacity to manage the transition from bureaucracy to farmer managed systems, MP initiated implementation of the same through administrative orders. As a result, a large number of WUAs were formed with little or no preparatory work to reorient either the farming community or the ID staff to their new roles and the responsibilities of various stakeholders. Thus, for the first four

Table 3.3

Status of PIM in MP

Total No. of Water Users' Association in MP	2,416
Total No. of Distributory Committees in MP	90
Total No. of Project Committees in MP	0
Total no. of Turnout Committee members in WUAs	10,283
No. of women president of WUAs	28 WUAs have Women Presidents
Schemes where elections were held in 2006	All

Source: PIM Monitoring Cell, MPWRD.

years, despite having a large number of formally constituted WUAs (See Table 3.3), the actual irrigation operation and performance in utilizing the irrigation potential saw little change. In fact, general awareness and the willingness on part of farmers to take on new responsibilities was quite low.

Since 1999, over 2,400 farmers' organizations have been formed throughout the state, on secondary and primary-level canal systems. The management of the canal systems including their O&M below the outlet at the minor or sub-minor level has been transferred to the elected WUAs. Official records mention that PIM is being practiced in over 15.05 lakh (150,500,000) ha through farmers' organizations, including WUAs at the primary level and the Distributory Committees (DCs) at the level of secondary canal (PIM Monitoring Cell, MPWRD, 2010). Also, Project Level Committees, intended to be federated bodies of all WUAs and DCs under a project were yet to be formed.

In 2005, the World Bank-funded Water Sector Restructuring Programme lent the state government funds to build the ID's capacity to implement PIM. Prior to that, with the help of funds from the Indo-Canadian Environment Facility (ICEF), a pilot project was established by the state government in 2002 in which NGOs were invited to play a facilitating role in organizing and building the capacity of WUAs. In the same year, a separate PIM Monitoring Cell was formed within the ID to help the learning process. The pilot project lasted for four years from 2004 to 2007.

Two of the four MP case studies in this research are projects that were part of the ICEF-funded initiative.

7. Irrigation in Gujarat

The geography and climate of Gujarat presents a rather unique mix of resource rich regions and resource poor regions. While South Gujarat is bestowed with abundant land and water resources, the regions of Kutch and Saurashtra are known for their arid and desert ecosystems. Since the latter make up for more than 60 per cent of the total area of the state, augmenting water resource supply through water harvesting and conveyance systems has been a top priority for the government. The area under irrigation has steadily increased from 2.4 million ha in 1988 to 3.0 million ha in 1995 (Hirway I et al., 2002: 274).

Water use for agriculture has been an important agenda item for planners and development agencies alike. This can be gauged from the fact that 89 per cent of available water globally is consumed for agricultural purposes (World Bank, 2007: 29).

Gujarat's achievement in creating irrigation infrastructures can be considered truly a representative sample of the country's preoccupation with irrigation. By constructing 18 major, 160 medium and over 1,600 minor irrigation dams and canals, Gujarat state has created a total irrigation potential of 1.48 million ha. When the large multipurpose Sardar Sarovar Project (SSP) was completed, it was expected to add another 1.8 million ha to the area irrigated. Not counting the SSP, Gujarat irrigates 32 per cent of its net sown area through various sources. This was in stark contrast to MP where only 13.5 per cent of the net sown area could be irrigated (NWRD, Government of Gujarat, 2009). Table 3.4 summarizes the achievement of creating irrigation potential in Gujarat.

From Table 3.4, it can be seen that the actual utilization of the potential developed in surface irrigation lagged behind the other major source which was groundwater. These utilization statistics have been found to be incorrect due to flawed methods used to

Table 3.4

Irrigation in Gujarat by Source (000's Hectares)

Source of Water	Potential for Irrigation	Potential Developed	Potential Utilized	% Utilization
1. Major and medium schemes	1,800	1,410	1,094	77
1.1 Sardar Sarovar Project (including conjunctive use)	1,792	25	25	100
1.2 Minor irrigation	348	265	162	61
Total Surface water	3,940	1,700	1,281	75
2. Groundwater (including privately-owned)	2,548	2,035	2,034	99.99
Total (1 + 2)	6,488	3,735	3,315	91

Source: NWRD, Government of Gujarat (2009).

record utilization.[2] As explained earlier, the shortfall in utilization of created irrigation potential was largely due to management problems that the policy reform aimed to address through the transfer of management responsibility to the water users.

8. Contrasting Approaches to PIM

The divergent approaches taken by Gujarat and MP in introducing and consolidating PIM are evident not only in the provisions of the Acts, but also in the key players who participated. While the MP government initiated its programme in 1999 through its own ID from the beginning, Gujarat had introduced the programme much earlier in 1994 as a result of the carefully planned and implemented action research and advocacy work of two NGOs. Later in 2004, the MP government accepted the fact that the ID had serious limitations in implementing a programme that required social organizing skills. They invited a few NGOs to help in the process, but soon it

---

[2] An area is considered irrigated if it receives just one watering during the year, even if the entitlement is for multiple waterings. It is common knowledge that a large number of irrigation projects operate with vastly suboptimal efficiency and there is no method to register this shortfall in utilization.

was evident that the poor start that PIM got in 1999 had made an enduring negative impact on the attitude of ID officers as well as local farmer leaders. The top-down big-bang approach to implementing PIM in MP also made it very difficult to monitor performance and make mid-course corrections. In contrast, two well-known NGOs in Gujarat (DSC and AKRSP) scaled up their PIM implementation programme gradually, constantly improving the process of organizing farmers into a formal institution as well as bringing in policy corrections based on lessons learned from the pilot projects. The Act in Gujarat therefore reflects some of these lessons learned. While the MP Act continues to place the ID as the central player at all levels of its irrigation systems (minor, distributory, branch and project level), the Gujarat Act and practice allows considerable autonomy to WUAs in operational and fiscal matters.

9. PIM and Poverty

Despite the indisputable conclusion that irrigation has increased the agricultural productivity and the income of farmers, the distribution of incremental benefits to various water users has been less clear. The mere fact that private irrigation sources have expanded rapidly in the last six decades indicates that the availability of irrigation improves the economic viability of agriculture. Since the cost of creating irrigation potential is capital intensive, economically weaker farmers are deprived of this benefit. Thus, to improve equitable access to irrigation, large public investments in irrigation infrastructure are justified. However, as described in the earlier sections, the central objective of public irrigation systems of providing an irrigation source to the poor who would otherwise be incapable of making private investments, was not achieved due to the top-down, unaccountable management system of the ID. The idea of decentralizing irrigation management through PIM was shaped by the concern for better utilization and improving access. These objectives appear to have been moderately successful from a resource management perspective. However, there is inadequate evidence to suggest that the benefits of decentralizing irrigation management have indeed flowed to the poor and in turn impacted the levels of poverty.

The adverse impact of water deprivation on the productivity and income of farmers is evident from the fact that rain-fed areas have a much higher incidence of poverty than irrigated areas. A study by Raj Kapila and Uma Kapila showed that rain-fed areas have higher incidence of poverty and therefore investment on irrigation delivers higher marginal benefits in terms of poverty alleviation (Kapila and Kapila, 2006: 220).

However, the true extent to which reliable irrigation can help or hinder income levels is relatively less known. If PIM achieves its purported objective of improving efficiency and equity in irrigation operations, does that make it more likely to enable poor farmers to gain as much as the non-poor farmers? Moreover, since there is more than one approach to decentralization and farmer participation, are some approaches more predisposed to benefitting the poor than others? With these as central guiding questions, a sample of four WUAs from Gujarat and MP each were selected for detailed study.

10. Selection of WUA Case Studies

While arriving at the sample of eight WUAs for this study, particular attention was given to four variables: geographic location, demographic category, size of the irrigation scheme and PIA involved. This is summarized in Table 3.5.

Four of the WUAs received capacity building and social organizing support from NGOs while the remaining four WUAs were promoted and supported by the ID.

11. Analytical Framework/Research Design

Our study aims to explore the relationship between the process of decentralization (management transfer from central authority to end-users), institutionalization of participatory management

Table 3.5

Key Features of the Case Study Villages in Gujarat and MP

State/WUA	Geographic Location	Demographic Category	Size of the Irrigation System	Project Implementing Agency
Gujarat				
Kiyadar	North Gujarat	OBC	Major	NGO
Kanipur	Central Gujarat	Patel and OBC	Major	ID
Chopadvav	South Gujarat	Tribal	Minor	NGO
Ubhen	Saurashtra	OBC	Medium	ID
MP				
Neemkheda	Central MP	Tribal and OBC	Major	ID
Banji	Eastern MP	Tribal and OBC	Medium	ID
Bamandi	Western MP	Patel	Medium	NGO
Dagarkot	Western MP	Tribal	Minor	NGO

Source: Field data summary, (2009).

(democratic WUAs) and performance in terms of delivering sustainable benefits equitably (inclusive of the poor). Therefore, one of our operational hypotheses is that if the management of irrigation was to be devolved from the ID to the WUAs, then benefits accruing to the poor would be far better than if it was controlled by the ID. The research thus involved examining the institutionalizing of the decentralization process and gathering empirical evidence that would help quantify the benefit streams to various segments of stakeholders in an irrigation system.

PIM and the other three decentralized resource management programmes studied in this book shared many common features in terms of policy provisions. At the same time, there were features that were salient to PIM alone. It is useful to enumerate them here so that the data, its analysis and the inferences are discussed keeping in mind the commonality as well as uniqueness of the resources.

Unlike other CNRM programmes, PIM is based on a resource that has clear physical and management boundaries. In other words, it was possible for an irrigation system to exclude access to would-be users by virtue of its physical nature and management

Image 3.1

The Ubhen Reservoir Irrigates Eight Villages

Source: John R. Wood.

Image 3.2

Akala Field Channel

Image 3.3

Haribhai Chowdhury: WUA Secretary, Kiyadar

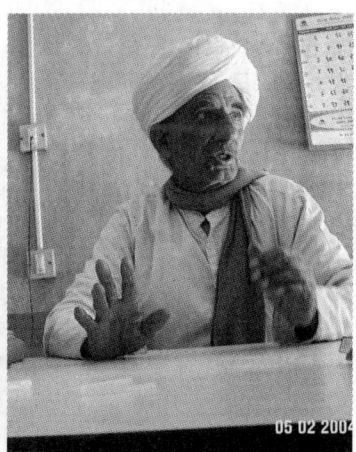

Source: John R. Wood.

Source: Shashidharan Enarth.

Image 3.4

Dagarkot's Tank

Source: John R. Wood.

Image 3.5

Jijibai: Dagarkot, WUA President

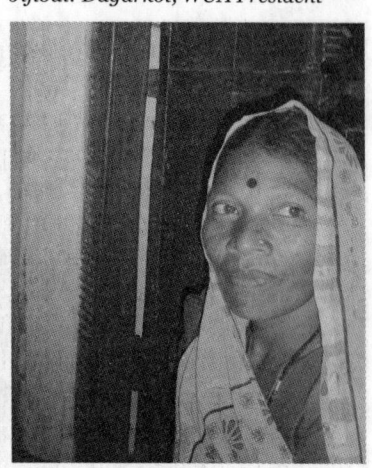

Source: John R. Wood.

Image 3.6

Map of Dagarkot's Irrigation System as Drawn by Farmers

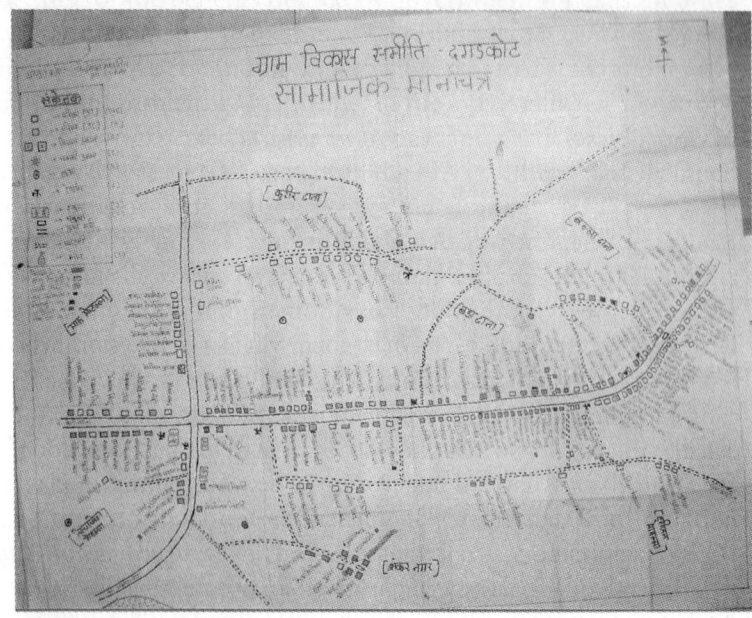

Source: John R. Wood.

controls. PIM requires water users as individuals to make significant contributions as well as join in collective action. For example, individual farmers could derive excludable and measurable benefits based on their decisions related to crop selection, inputs, cultivation practices and post-harvest interventions. In contrast, the quantum and distribution of benefits from other community-managed resources required collective investments, management and benefit appropriation. Therefore, PIM was more predisposed to user participation.

Formal irrigation institutions have a longer history and therefore are more evolved and better organized than other programmes. IDs rank among the largest and arguably the most politically significant public agencies in the country. Therefore, the decentralization process was fiercely resisted, challenged and negotiated by the ID, NGOs and farmers.

12. Introduction to Case Studies

The following sections give descriptive and quantitative narratives on the eight case studies based on data gathered from (a) secondary sources that include records from the ID, NGOs, research institutions and WUA offices (b) primary data from farmers, their leaders, NGO facilitators and ID officials and (c) FGDs with specific interest groups such as the landless and the tail-end farmers.

Household level data was gathered from 50 families who were water users belonging to each of the eight WUAs. The household level data covered topics such as source-wise income and expenditure from agriculture and non-agricultural activities, seasonality in income and expenditure, participation in WUA governance and perception of benefit accrual as a result of PIM. To capture the economic impact of PIM policy on the water users, data pertaining to economic parameters were collected for the period before and after the introduction of PIM. Since the year of introduction of PIM varied across the states and, in the case of Gujarat, within the state too, any spatial comparison of economic data would be fraught with unacceptable errors. To make matters even more challenging, data related to income-expenditures from household interviews were prone to errors due to high recall bias. This was particularly true for data pertaining to agriculture and household expenses and income for time dating back to 1995 (15 years ago). It became evident that the data sets on these parameters were of questionable reliability and therefore hazardous to use for assessing changes over a period of time.

Since the central question in this research pertains to PIM's impact on poverty, it was imperative that alternative sets of empirical data be collected as the basis for analysing the impact of PIM on income levels and thus on poverty. Additional secondary source information was collected and a second round of FGDs was conducted in all eight villages to gather data on changes in incomes and poverty levels. Another serious limitation in gathering relevant data came from the fact that all PIM members were farmers with land in the command area, and only they were respondents to the HHS. As a result, one significant stakeholder in irrigation, namely landless labourers whose livelihoods are integrally tied to the extent of irrigation, could not be included in the interviews. Since irrigation is known to have a direct and significant impact on wage earnings of landless families, separate FGDs had to be conducted to capture this aspect.

It must be mentioned here that secondary data was scarce and difficult to access in MP. This was because WUA records were maintained by an ID SE and rarely kept in the villages. In all four WUAs in MP, the irrigation utilization data for years prior to PIM was unavailable. In contrast, two of the four WUAs in Gujarat had records in the respective villages and the remaining two were available with the ID.

12.1. Case Study 1: Akala Water Users Association, Jetpur Block, Rajkot District, Gujarat

Akala village is about 12 km from Jetpur town on the border of Rajkot and Junagadh districts. Along with the neighbouring village of Chokhi, Akala village comes under the command area served by a minor canal of the larger Ubhen irrigation scheme. The dam, built across the river Ubhen, was constructed in 1979 but the canal network was completed only in 1992. The scheme is designed to irrigate a total area of 2,500 ha with the help of two main canals and an extensive network of minor canals and watercourses spread over eight villages including Akala and Chokhi. Until 2004, the ID managed the irrigation operations almost unilaterally. However, unlike the usual passive role of farmers in irrigation management elsewhere in the state at that time, farmers from these eight villagers were consulted at various stages of the irrigation operations. The initiative came from the ID as part of a pilot project called Joint Irrigation Management by the Government of Gujarat (GoG) in the 1980s and 1990s. Under this initiative however, the farmers had no formal decision-making authority or operational responsibilities.

In 2005, again at the initiative of the ID, there was an attempt to enhance farmer participation in the irrigation operations through a formal WUA in the form of an Irrigation Cooperative Society. To cover the entire 2500 ha in eight villages, eight WUAs were formed. The Akala WUA was one of them. The villagers decided to name their WUA the Kamdhenu Participatory Irrigation Cooperative Society. The WUA has a command area of 228 ha fed by a minor canal and six watercourses. The WUA has a membership of 173 farmers, even though the actual number of families cultivating in the command is higher. This is because land division between heirs of a title owner has not yet been registered with the WUA. Besides, there are farmers who have chosen not to be members of the WUA. Another important factor that has a bearing on canal operations and the motivation for participation is the number of private wells in the village. There are more than 240 open wells or tube wells, which comes to an average of one well per family. Their dependence on the canal is therefore not so acute.

12.1.1. Water Users Association and Participation

Akala, Chokhi and the neighbouring villages were dominated by the Leuva Patels. They made up about 90 per cent of the population. The remaining 10 per cent consisted of members of the Harijans, Khats, Bharwads and Darbar communities. True to popular notion, Patel farmers are more enterprising than most other farming communities in Gujarat. The leadership of most of the local institutions comes from this community. The Akala-Chokhi WUA was no exception. The Executive Engineer and his team from Junagadh provided the leadership role during the initial interaction between farmers and the ID. Early leaders from the village included Jamanbhai Rupapara and Kanjibhai Radadia. Since the Patels are also politically well connected, the ID staff usually responded well to the farmers' demand for water. As a result, the usual trend of antagonistic attitudes towards the ID and its inefficiencies was not seen here. In 2008 and 2009, however, the farmers were upset when the ID delayed the canal cleaning operations before the irrigation season. The delay had in fact resulted in denial of irrigation to some farmers in the mid and tail sections. In the first three years of PIM, the farmers had not felt the need to formally take over management functions from the ID, but after 2008, they started asserting their right to take control of some of the maintenance responsibilities. However, after the formation of WUAs during 2001 to 2004, the engineers delayed transferring these responsibilities by two to three years and this caused some restlessness among the WUA leaders.

In 2006, Jamanbhai and Kanjibhai were elected unopposed as the President and Secretary of the WUA respectively. There is an executive committee consisting of two representatives from each of the five watercourses. The committee meets two or three times a year and the attendance is moderate with about 50 per cent of members attending. While attendance is open to all members, the response from the farmers is lukewarm. Yet, most farmers interviewed for this study (41 out of 50) were aware of the WUA and its role in supporting the ID in irrigation operations. They were quite content with the quality of services and did not appear to be seeking any greater participation. The fact that they had an alternate source of irrigation through private wells also contributed to their low level of motivation to improve canal management. Financial and operational aspects of irrigation continue to be managed by the ID and therefore there is little by way of management information shared with the farmers. The collection of water charges was good (more than 90 per cent).

12.1.2. *Performance and Benefits*

Relative to other minor irrigation projects in Gujarat, the Akala canal network is in good shape due to good construction and sound maintenance by the ID during the early years of the JIM program. However, there are problems of seepage in a couple of places on the minor as well as watercourses which has in turn reduced the irrigated area from 228 ha to less than 200 ha, even though this is not reflected in the official registers. Irrigation utilization has been further reduced due to poor monsoon rainfall and consequently poor storage in the reservoir for many years. Unlike other PIM projects where physical rehabilitation plays an important role in raising the utilization levels, the Ubhen project has required and received very little attention in terms of rehabilitation. Because of this and the fact that the ID has managed the irrigation operations quite well, there has been no notable impact of PIM on irrigation performance, as Figure 3.1 below shows.

The dip in irrigated area in 2008 and 2009 adversely affected the tail-end farmers. There were plans afoot to line the canal system to reduce the seepage, which would also help in inhibiting the growth of wild grass inside the canal. The WUA also plans to take control of the financial aspects and then mobilize funds on their own to invest in upgrading the infrastructure.

Figure 3.1

Irrigation Performance of the Akala WUA (Ubhen Irrigation Project)

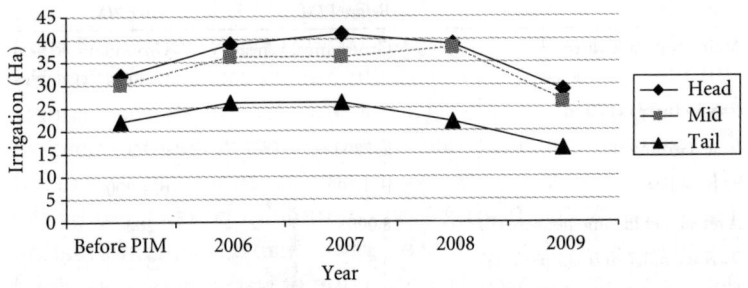

Source: Akala WUA records and ID records.

As mentioned earlier, the Patel farmers are among the most progressive in the state. They have traditionally led the farming community in achieving high productivity and profitability, especially in groundnut and garlic production. The fact that almost every family owns a private well indicates their capacity to invest and optimize production. Expectedly, the introduction of PIM has impacted neither the cropping pattern nor productivity of the crops, as can be seen from Table 3.6 below. In fact, the average net profit/acre from agriculture has registered a marginal decrease, as farmers claim that input costs have gone up and the sale price for cotton and oilseeds has held steady. This decrease, however, is within the margin of error and therefore considered inconsequential. The introduction of cotton and vegetable cultivation was more in response to the lucrative market for these products rather than PIM or the management of irrigation.

12.1.3. Migration, Landlessness and the Poor

Akala appears to be a prosperous village with a much higher proportion of land being irrigated than the state average. The incidence of poverty is low, even though there are some families who are classified as BPL. There are 17 landless families. Unlike most landless families in India, they are not poor because there

Table 3.6

Impact of PIM on Agriculture in Akala Village (Ubhen)

Indicators	Before PIM	After PIM
Main crops cultivated	Groundnut, Wheat	Groundnut, Wheat, Cotton, Vegetables.
Productivity (kgs/acre)		
a. Groundnut	a. 720 kgs	a. 750
b. Wheat	b. 1,200	b. 1,200
Average net income per acre (₹)	8,000	7,200
Average milch animals per family	3.5	3.5
Income from sale of milk	Nil	Nil*

Source: FGDs and household interviews.
Note: *consumed by the households or bartered among neighbours.

is a high demand for labour and availability of high wages during the kharif and rabi seasons. They are also regular sharecroppers who lease land from the Patels for periods ranging from two years to six years. The terms of lease are not exploitative and therefore quite remunerative to the sharecroppers.[3] PIM has had no impact on either the terms of sharecropping or the incidence of it. The demand for agricultural labour can also be gauged from the fact that every year more than 20 tribal families from the Panchmahals and Sabarkantha districts migrate to Akala to fill the demand for labour during the peak season. There is no evidence of migration from the village to any place outside the district or state. Anecdotal evidence, however, points to the high probability of sharecropping and in-migration being on the rise because the second generation Patels are moving away from full-time agriculture and seeking employment opportunities in the non-farm sector, thus putting enormous pressure and hardship on aging parents who are not able to manage cultivation. As shown in Table 3.7, there is no evidence of distress migration from Akala. On the contrary, there is in-migration of about 25 families who sharecrop. This arrangement has become an institution over the last 10 years and shows no signs of reversing

Table 3.7

Impact of PIM on Landless and Poor in Akala

Indicators	Before PIM	After PIM
Number of landless families	17	17
Average annual wage employment days	300	300
Average daily wage (₹)	90	110
Number of share-cropping families	~ 65	~75
Families in-migrating	25	30
Average number of days family in-migrates annually	300	300
Average wage rate earned during migration (₹)	90	110
Source of in-migration	Panchmahals, Sabarkantha	Panchmahals, Sabarkantha

Source: Household interviews and village panchayat records.

---

[3] The most common terms of agreement under sharecropping arrangements are for the landowner to provide land and water for a 50 per cent share of gross produce. The lessee provides all labour and agricultural inputs.

as more and more youngsters from the Patel families are moving away from farming.

In conclusion, Akala's WUA is certainly not a representative case either for PIM or for the political economy of irrigated agriculture. A well-managed canal and a large number of private wells have given farmers a high degree of reliability in terms of cultivating irrigated crops. Yet, less than 50 per cent of the dominant farming community of the Patels relies on sharecropping. This is attributable to their rising standard of living and the unwillingness of their youngsters to pursue agriculture. On the other hand, this has created an opportunity for impoverished tribal families and landless families to move into the village and enter into long term sharecropping arrangements. For this reason, the motivation and level of interest among the landowners in PIM and WUA activities is modest. Even though the progressive Patel farmers are appreciative of the advantages of better management under PIM, their willingness to take on more responsibilities is waning. The physical structure of their canals has been significantly better than that of other government canals. This, the availability of reliable alternatives to canal water (private wells) and declining interest in agriculture among the Patels makes for a situation that is not conducive for strengthening PIM.

Since Akala is a prosperous village with a high proportion of irrigated land, even the poorest families are more secure than those in other regions of the state where irrigation facilities are not so extensive. It can be safely concluded that introduction of PIM, while not unwelcome by the farmers, has not made any significant impact on either the overall irrigation performance or on poverty levels in the village. In other words, water resource augmentation and distribution in Akala, as a consequence of PIM, appears to be insignificant.

12.2. Case Study 2: Kiyadar Water Users Association, Visnagar Block, Mehsana District, Gujarat

Kiyadar village was situated in the middle section of a minor canal which in turn connected to the tail-section of a distributory canal from the Sabarmati Irrigation Project. The irrigation project was often referred to as the Dharoi project because the reservoir was located near the village of Dharoi. In terms of economy and wealth, Kiyadar was markedly poorer than the villages in the neighbourhood populated by wealthier Patidar (Patel) farmers. The Choudharys and Harijans made up about 80 per cent of the population. Compared to the Patels, these caste groups have taken to serious farming only two generations ago. The average landholding in Kiyadar too is less than 2.5 acres compared to 5.5 in the Patel villages.

When the DSC, an NGO actively promoting CNRM programmes, contacted Kiyadar village in 1997, the village had already had a history of collective volunteer work. A religious organization called Swadhyaya was actively organizing villagers in community activities such as tree planting, health and sanitation work and food banks for the poor. Kiyadar also had a very well managed profitable milk cooperative society that served more than 80 households from 1970 onwards. Besides this, the villagers also had the advantage of learning about PIM from other DSC projects in the neighbouring villages, most notably from village Thalota. The two representatives from Kiyadar village who attended the workshop had contrasting personalities. Haribhai Choudhary was a quiet, short, unassuming man, of shy demeanour. Jesing Choudhary, on the other hand, was a vocal, well-known leader in the village. Both of them were associated with the management of the milk society in the village. Haribhai had already put in 20 years of work as Secretary and Jesing was the President and member of the EC for a few terms. Therefore, when a WUA was formally registered in 1998, Jesing and Haribhai were elected as its first President and Secretary respectively.

The canal network that served the farmers of Kiyadar had suffered extensive damage. Out of the combined length of 10.2 km of minor canal and the watercourses, more than 8 km were dysfunctional due to breaches or other hydraulic problems. When irrigation management responsibilities were transferred to the WUA in 1998, the maximum area that was irrigated was 24 ha. This was less than 10 per cent of the total designed irrigation capacity of 315 ha. The canal repair works required an estimated ₹1.32 million and a five-year construction schedule. After considerable negotiation and advocacy work by DSC, in 2008, a MoU was drawn up between the ID and the WUA that gave complete control of repair work as

Figure 3.2

Irrigation Performance of Kiyadar

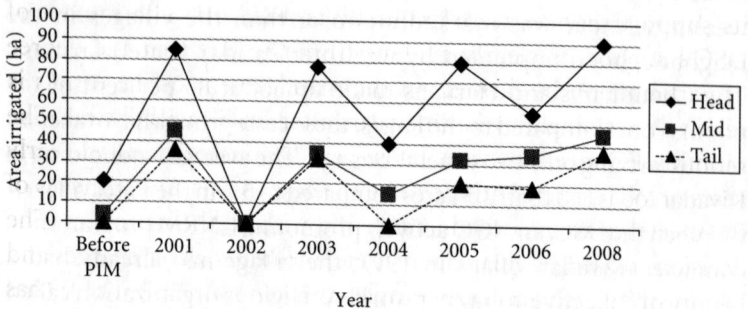

Source: Kiyadar WUA records, (2000–08).

well as irrigation operations to the farmers. During the very first season after PIM was introduced, the area under irrigation went up from 24 to 166 ha. As shown in the graph above (Figure 3.2), the area under irrigation went up and down erratically during the subsequent years, but registered a steady overall increase. Irrigation was not possible at all in 2002 due to poor rainfall and inadequate storage in the reservoir.

Such wide fluctuation in irrigation were caused due to frequent breaches in the canal system that were not repaired during the first phase of the rehabilitation work. Despite such challenges, the WUA outperformed the ID, not only in terms of total area irrigated, but also in providing water to land in the middle and tail sections of the canals. While farmers from the middle section did receive some, even if negligible amount of water before PIM, the tail section received none at all. When the management switched to the WUA, farmers from the tail and middle reach consistently received irrigation. In fact, the WUA mandated equal access to all by adopting a tail-to-head irrigation schedule.

12.2.1. Decentralization and Governance by Kiyadar's WUA

Haribhai Chaudhary and Jesing Choudhary provided leadership right from the inception of the WUA in 1998. As a support NGO, DSC provided community organization support and capacity-building inputs to strengthen the governance of the WUA. From 1997 to 2002, the DSC's involvement was intensive and after this phase, its support services were gradually tapered off. The impact of DSC's support is clearly evident from the fact that the degree of participation by farmers in the management of the canals is relatively very high, even nine years after DSC's withdrawal. The monthly EC meetings were taken very seriously during the early years of WUA and continue to be the case to this day. Minutes of the meetings are recorded and shared with all the members. The decisions regarding financial matters, including water charges and administrative expenses are completely taken by the EC. The ID has no role to play in the irrigation operations or collection of water charges. All maintenance works, big or small, are managed by and paid for by the WUA. As of 2010, the WUA maintained a track record of 100 per cent recovery of water charges from the farmers. Besides an amount of ₹130,000 that was collected from the members towards paying the cost of rehabilitation of the canals, the WUA had generated a surplus of over ₹200,000 from their revenues from water charges.

In terms of decentralization and participation, Kiyadar presents a good case study where the devolution of decision-making powers was institutionalized and the ID had almost no role to play in matters pertaining to irrigation within the WUA command area. Sound mechanisms of transparency and accountability were in place to ensure that information on financial and operational matters was not only made available to every member, but their involvement in management functions was also encouraged. There were effective reward and sanction rules that penalized members and office-bearers for any infringement of discipline or rules. Haribhai served as the Secretary for 11 years except for a period of one year in 2006. In fact, the dependence on Haribhai seems to be quite heavy. In 2010, when Kiyadar brought together 13 other WUAs to form a Federation of WUAs, Haribhai was encouraged by DSC and other WUA leaders to run for the office of President of the Federation. There has been considerable anxiety in Kiyadar over their inability to find a competent replacement, if and when Haribhai moves on to the new position. However, the WUA has transitioned from one president to another quite smoothly.

Table 3.8

Impact of PIM on Economic Indicators in Kiyadar

Indicators	Before PIM	After PIM
Cropping pattern by small and marginal farmers	Millet (Jowar/Bajri), corn (all rain-fed)	Cotton, vegetables, Mustard, Castor, Wheat.
Average net income per ha*	₹2,500	₹8,400
Average Migration days/annum/ adult	30	0
Wage rate for labour work**	₹65/day	₹130/day
Average milk yield/cow	3.0 litres/day	4.8 litres/day
Land price per ha**	₹25,000	₹110,000

Source: FGDs and household interviews, (2009).
Notes: * value of surplus production after providing for household consumption.
  ** adjusted for inflation.

The increase in canal irrigation has had an important secondary impact. The seepage from the canals helped improve the water table in the village. Many farmers who owned shallow wells could irrigate additional land for a winter crop. As shown in Table 3.8, this increase in area under irrigation had a direct and measurable impact on increasing demand for labour and the wage rate. During a good monsoon year, when the irrigation project is operational to capacity, Kiyadar village, in fact, has to seek labour from outside their village. Another indicator of the benefits of WUA management has been the price of land, which went up from ₹25,000 per ha in 1997 to ₹110,000 or more in 2010. While other external factors such as growing urban limits and industrialization have also contributed to the increase in land prices, the arrival of irrigation water has resulted in an increase in land prices in Kiyadar where there were no such external influences. Moreover, other rain-fed land in the village has seen no such increase.

A large share of the increase in the area under irrigation went to the mid-reach and tail-end farmers. This can be seen from the Figure 3.2 where the tail-end farmers and mid-reach farmers could stabilize the irrigated area from under 20 ha per year to over 70 ha. Many of them received water for the first time. Information gathered from local vegetable sellers and in FGDs indicates that local consumption of vegetables increased after the WUA began managing irrigation due to the increase in area under vegetable cultivation. Vegetable cultivation along with the main crops increased because farmers found the irrigation schedule more predictable.

12.2.2. Impact on the Landless and the Poor in Kiyadar

Kiyadar has 21 landless families, 10 of them Harijans and 11 Waghris. Two Harijan families and 10 Waghri families have sharecropping arrangements with farmers in the village. Besides, they also provide agricultural labour during peak seasons. Expectedly, with an increase in the irrigated area, the demand for labour increased proportionately and so did the wage rate. It doubled from ₹65 per day in 1995 to ₹130 in 2008. Before PIM, the landless families and even some farmers without irrigation would seek wage employment in Visnagar, Mehsana and Ahmedabad during the rabi and summer seasons. On an average, the adults worked for 55 days outside Kiyadar, even though this was not considered migration because they could return home every day. This situation changed quite dramatically with the improvements in canal irrigation. Far from seeking wage employment outside the village, as many as 40 labourers come into Kiyadar every year for periods ranging from 30 days to 70 days to meet the demand of agricultural operations.

The absence of an irrigation well was one the biggest constraints faced by small farmers in their quest to break out of poverty. With a steady and increasing income since 1994, 13 families dug new wells and started cultivating rabi crops too.

In conclusion, Kiyadar is a good example of how the devolution of irrigation responsibilities including decision-making about water rates and maintenance functions can, by itself, improve resource utilization. Even before any substantial rehabilitation work could be done, farmer participation resulted in the reduction of waste and excessive irrigation. The emergence of a democratic way of governance also played an important role in institutionalizing certain practices that in turn improved equity and fiscal discipline. With financial responsibility came a sense of responsibility. Every year since 1995, the Kiyadar WUA has balanced its budget by constantly bringing cost effectiveness into its maintenance and fixing water rates so that costs were completely recovered. The secondary impact on the landless and poor has been one of the most remarkable features of Kiyadar's success story.

The role of a support agency (DSC) was very crucial. The social organizers of DSC put great emphasis on a reward and sanction system, mechanisms for transparency and the involvement of women and marginalized groups. This institutionalized the practice of maintaining equitable access to water for traditionally excluded families such as tail-enders and the Harijans.

12.3. Case Study 3: Chopadvav Water Users' Association, Sagbara Block, Narmada District, Gujarat

There are 19 villages covered by the Chopadvav Irrigation project, situated in the Sagbara block of Narmada District. The reservoir, which is located near Chopadvav village (hence the name of the scheme) was built in 1981. However, it took another 11 years before the canals could be constructed. Even after the construction of the canal systems was completed in 1991, irrigation operations were erratic and much of the designed command area of 1,020 ha received no water at all. Even those farmers who managed to get some water chose to cultivate low-risk crops due to the unpredictable operations of the ID. The main cause of this unpredictability was the poor physical condition of the canal. The predominantly earthen canals were poorly designed and the quality of construction was so weak that the canals and embankments would breach frequently.

The canal network consisted of 8 km of a main canal that was cement-lined and a total 38 km of minor and sub-minor canals and watercourses that were unlined earthen structures. The command area of the project comprised of farmland belonging to 557 farmers from 19 villages. Pankhala, the village examined in this study, was one of them and was located in the mid-reach of the main canal. This village was representative of the demographic and land-use pattern observed in the 19 command area villages. Out of 275 households in Pankhala, 95 per cent belong to STs and 5 per cent were Leuva Patels. Among the tribals, the Vasavas and Tadvi tribes were almost equal in number.

During the first three years after completion of the canals, that is, 1991 to 1993, the only irrigation farmers saw came as a result of seepage from the reservoir and main canals. Farms adjoining the canals benefitted from the seepage water initially, but later it turned out to be a curse because of constant waterlogging. Poor quality of work on the main canal, although lined by cement mortar, coupled with poorly designed minor networks meant that water never went beyond the mid-reach of the command area. Much of the irrigation done during those three years was unofficial and unplanned. There were no formal records available that indicated how much irrigation was done during that period. Farmers recollected that the total irrigation during the 1991–93 period never exceeded 30 ha per annum.

In 1993, some farmers from Pankhala heard of the activities of an NGO, the AKRSP. The AKRSP was active in natural resource development projects in the Sagbara block. They had also helped in setting up farmer-managed lift irrigation projects in two neighbouring villages. A few villagers from Pankhala contacted the AKRSP and requested them to explore the possibility of forming a similar WUA for managing the Chopadvav project. Thus began the interaction between the AKRSP and the villages that came under the command area. Dhir Singh Vasava and Fateh Singh Vasava were the early leaders from Pankhala village who interacted with Ashok Patel of AKRSP in 1993. By 1993, many more farmers were aware of the objectives of the PIM programme and by December 1993, a WUA by the name of Sanjivani Piyat Sahakari Mandali was formed. Since there was no legislation to promote PIM in Gujarat at that time, a state government notification was issued to include Chopadvav's project as one of the 13 state-sponsored pilot projects on PIM. This enabled a formal transfer of irrigation management from the ID to the WUA. The farmers and AKRSP jointly assessed the physical condition of the canal system and soon came to the conclusion that the canal networks required substantial repair work before any improvement in irrigation operations could be achieved. The government agreed to fund the repair work in a phased manner, with the farmers' contribution covering 10 per cent of the repair cost. The WUA was registered as a cooperative in 1994 with 157 farmers enrolling as members. Over the years the membership has grown to 460, including 36 women members. Dhir Singh was elected President of the WUA and Dashrat Tadvi the Secretary. While Dhir Singh was re-elected for every subsequent term of four years, Dashrat had to be removed in 2001 when it was discovered that he had misappropriated WUA money. Krishnabhai Vasava is now the Secretary.

12.3.1. Decentralization and Governance by Chopadvav WUA

The decentralization process seen in the Chopadvav project makes it amongst the best PIM projects in Gujarat. Decision-making authority has been truly devolved not only in terms of irrigation operations but also in fiscal matters. The WUA decides the water rates and is responsible for the recovery of dues from members. All members of the EC are farmers and there is no representation from either the ID or the AKRSP. Two of the EC members are women. Under the management of the EC, the WUA has consistently run a surplus budget and ensured 100 per cent recovery of dues for every subsequent year since the launch of the WUA. The EC meets every month to ratify the accounts and monitor the operations. Verification of the records indicates that EC meetings are indeed a regular feature and well attended. There is a reward and sanction system that ensures compliance with the WUA rules and member' rights.

The rehabilitation of the canal system has been a slow and long-drawn-out affair. This has caused friction between the ID and the WUA. The WUA contends that the ID not only undermines the suggestions and contributions made by the farmers in design and supervision of the works, but also fails to appreciate the need for speedy release of funds so that canal networks are repaired completely. At the time of this research (2010), only the main canal and a small part of a minor and a sub-minor canal have seen some repair works. This was grossly inadequate to ensure that farmers at the tail section of the main and minor canals got water. As a result;

the level of participation by the adversely affected farmers is low. The village leaders were also unhappy that the ID was not giving approval to their proposal to line the minor canals with bricks or cement slabs even though it was widely acknowledged that unlined canals contributed to large water loss due to seepage.

The WUA was financially very sound and has no outstanding dues owed by the farmers or to the government. They had a reserve fund of over ₹140,000 accumulated over the years from surplus and cost-saving measures. The secretary, who was paid ₹1,800 per month, was responsible for maintaining the books of account and registers. Two part-time water distributors were hired during the irrigation months to assist the Secretary in day-to-day irrigation operations. The role of the ID was limited to the opening of the main gate and release of water into the main canal. With a commendable track record of successfully managing the canals with minimal external support for more than 10 years, the Chopadvav WUA had established credibility and clout with the ID to ensure that water release was done without any major glitches.

There were no records to indicate the extent of irrigation undertaken prior to PIM. However, from household interviews as well as ID records, it came across beyond doubt that the area under irrigation before 1994 was less than 25 ha. As the canal system got repaired and management operations were transferred to the WUA, the area irrigated registered a steady increase. With the exception of 2000–01 which was a drought year, the area under irrigation increased from 25 ha to 630 ha in 2003–04. The subsequent years did not see any further increase because the canal repair work did not keep pace with the increase in demand for water. In fact, delays in administrative approval for further rehabilitation had started to gradually reduce the irrigated area. In terms of the distribution of water across the head, middle and tail sections, it can be seen that although the head- and mid-reaches consistently got more water than the tail, even ID engineers acknowledged the fact that they never expected the water to reach the tail sections, let alone irrigate 75 ha. The WUA was confident that once the remaining rehabilitation work got completed, tail-end farmers would be guaranteed the same access to water as farmers from the head and

Table 3.9

Impact of PIM on Economic Indicators in Chopadvav

Indicators	Before PIM	After PIM
Cropping pattern by small and marginal farmers	Rain-fed paddy, corn and pigeon pea	Cotton, groundnut, irrigated paddy
Average net income per ha*	Less than ₹2,600	More than ₹6,600
Average migration days/annum/adult	110	23
Wage rate for labour work**	₹15/day	₹55/day
Average milk yield/cow	2.5 litres/day	4.5 litres/day

Source: Field data summary, (2009).
Notes: * value of surplus production after providing for household consumption.
   ** adjusted for inflation.

middle reach. This assurance of entitlement did have a tangible impact on the small and marginal farmers whose land was in the command area.

Until 1993, these farmers raised rain-fed crops of paddy, pigeon-pea and maize. Production was barely enough to meet their household consumption requirements. Out-migration was therefore a common occurrence. With management in the hands of the WUA, the cropping pattern changed dramatically to cotton, groundnut and irrigated paddy. Pigeon pea was often inter-cropped with groundnut to meet household consumption needs. With irrigation available beyond the monsoon period, out-migration came down significantly (see Table 3.9) and the income from agricultural produce increased up to 240 per cent.

12.3.2. Impacts on the Landless and the Poor in Chopadvav

There were 39 landless households in Pankhala village. The improvements in irrigation operations did have a measurable impact on their economic well-being. With the significant increase in the area under irrigation, the demand for wage-labour increased proportionately. As seen from Table 3.9 above, the increase in wage rates reflected this change in demand. Increases in canal irrigation had also had another indirect impact: due to the high rate of seepage from earthen canals, the water table in the wells improved to such an extent that well owners could also increase their area under irrigation, further increasing the demand for labour. Besides increasing the area under irrigation, the assurance of timely supply of water also resulted in increased productivity. The WUA subsequently added agricultural input supply activities for their members, further improving profitability through reductions in input costs.

In conclusion, increases in area under irrigation and the consequent improvements in the economic well-being of Chopadvav WUA members could be clearly and directly attributable to the changes in management responsibilities. The participation of farmers not only in repairing the canal but also in operating the irrigation schedule contributed significantly to reducing water loss and improving access to water for a much larger number of farmers than ever before. Therefore, the increase in the number of farmer-beneficiaries and the area under irrigation after 1994 was clearly directly attributable to the farmers' role in managing it. It can further be inferred that the share of benefits had also reached two categories of households that had traditionally been marginalized from irrigation benefits: the small and marginal farmers who had no access to private irrigation sources and the landless families who relied on migration and wage labour.

Chopadvav is a good case of decentralization policy actually translating into devolution of decision-making powers to the community. Thanks to the consistency in balancing their budget every year by ensuring fiscal discipline and by adhering to good democratic behaviour, the WUA also demonstrated its institutional sustainability. The fact that the poorest (the small landholders and landless families) had received tangible and enduring benefits is evidence that the decentralization policy not only ensured better irrigation, but also improved the livelihoods of the poor.

12.4. Case Study 4: Ganesh Water Users' Association, Kanipur, District Ahmedabad, Gujarat

Kanipur village was approximately 15 km from the outskirts of Ahmedabad city. Two decades ago this was an agriculture-dependent village, but with the rapid expansion of urban limits, the livelihood profile changed quickly from agricultural to industrial and wage-earning activities. More than 60 per cent of households in Kanipur had at least one member earning an income from non-agricultural sources (Field Survey Data, 2010).

Agricultural land in Kanipur and the adjoining villages fell under the command area of the Sardar Sarovar Irrigation Project.[4] Kanipur was a very large village with more than 5,000 ha of land and a population of over 5,000 with over 950 households. More than 450 households belonged to the Thakore community. There were 210 Patel households and the remaining population comprised of Kolis, Chamars and Harijans (Field Survey Data, 2010). Given the proximity to Ahmedabad city and its non-farm employment opportunities, there was a larger percentage of landless wage-earning families in Kanipur. There were no reliable statistics about the actual number of landless wage-earning households, but a rough estimate by villagers put it at 120 families. The village was also home to a large number of transient communities who come from neighbouring districts and live in the village and work in the rice mills.

12.4.1. Decentralization and Participation in Kanipur

In the late 1990s, the GoG decided that the entire command area of the SSP project would be managed through PIM. Unlike rest of the irrigation projects in Gujarat that were administered by the ID, the SSP project had a separate organizational setup called the Sardar Sarovar Narmada Nigam Limited (SSNNL). However, almost the entire staff of SSNNL consisted of engineers and administration personnel from the ID sent to SSNNL on deputation. This fact is significant because the organizational culture and orientation of SSNNL staff towards participatory processes were the same as those of the ID. The process of promoting PIM and the outcomes of their efforts were no different from the experiences seen in other PIM projects that were promoted by the ID.

---

[4] The Sardar Sarovar Irrigation Project, known as SSP, is part of the multi-state, multi-reservoir mega irrigation and power project implemented along the Narmada River that flows from MP and Gujarat into the Arabian Sea. (See Wood, 2007)

Given the large command area of Kanipur, the SSNNL officials promoted three Water Users' Associations. They were called Sardar WUA, Ganesh WUA and JanKalyan WUA. The farmers did not have any clear recollection of the events that led to the creation of these WUAs. From anecdotal accounts it appears that there was no election or even any consultation between SSNNL staff and the farmers prior to the registration of the WUA. In 1997, Jayantibhai Patel, an affluent farmer from Kanipur, was chosen by the SSNNL staff to be the President of the Ganesh WUA, the case profiled for this study. An EC too was nominated. Yet, financial matters and irrigation operations were managed by the field staff of SSNNL, despite the fact that PIM policy required these functions to be delegated to the WUA.

The relationship between SSNNL and the farmers was that of a service provider and recipient rather than an enabling agency and a self-governing farmers' organization. Ganesh WUA had 290 ha of command area under its jurisdiction. Nevertheless such a demarcated command area was inconsequential because the very same field staff of SSNNL managed key irrigation operations, including demand collection and recovery of water charges for all the WUAs in Kanipur and indeed many other adjoining villages and WUAs. Even though the SSP project was touted as a source of reliable irrigation, the actual irrigation benefits to the farmers trickled in at an agonizingly slow pace because of poor construction of the minor and sub-minor canals. Also, there was a standoff between SSNNL and the farmers over the issue of construction of watercourses. From the beginning the GoG took a policy decision to seek 100 per cent cost contribution for construction of structures below the sub-minor canal system. This included watercourses and field channels. However, after considerable delay and much acrimony, the government was compelled to pay for the watercourses. Like the minor and sub-minor canals, the watercourses too were contracted out to bad contractors. This further alienated and frustrated the WUA office bearers, who played little or no role in influencing the quality of construction despite clear provisions in the PIM policy that decision-making responsibilities were to be shared between SSNNL and the WUA.

12.4.2. Irrigation Operations and Management in Kanipur

Erratic and unreliable irrigation operations by the SSNNL meant that rich farmers operated privately owned deep tube wells to irrigate cash crops. Paddy, cotton and potato were the main crops raised in Kanipur. During this study, the investigators made repeated attempts to obtain information about irrigation operations. Since the O&M was done almost entirely by the SSNNL staff, the WUA had little information. Neither was the SSNNL staff forthcoming in providing the information. However, it was evident from field visits and interviews with farmers that less than 110 ha of the 290 ha were actually irrigated by the SSP. Almost all of the tube wells, numbering about 50, were used to provide a safety net during delays and interruptions in SSP schedules.

Jayantibhai Patel was renominated as President of the WUA in 2003. However, at the time of this study, Jayantibhai informed us that he had formally resigned and notified the SSNNL that the WUA no longer had any responsibility for the O&M of the canal systems.

12.4.3. Impact on the Poor in Kanipur

The close proximity to the metropolis of Ahmedabad makes it almost impossible to delve into the relationship between irrigation, PIM and poverty in Kanipur. A significant number of households in Kanipur had at least 33 per cent of their household income coming from non-farm livelihood sources. Because of the high wage rates that prevailed in the area, the landless families were not necessarily poor. An average non-farm wage-earner earned ₹300 per day. This was considered a secure income when compared to incomes of regular farmers, who felt that their livelihood was more vulnerable due to the unpredictable irrigation schedule and the volatile market for their produce.

In conclusion, Kanipur's case study may perhaps be seen as an example of the total failure of PIM. There are some reasons why the WUA withered away and stayed defunct:

1. The process of WUA formation lacked any semblance of participation. The main stakeholders, the farmers, played only a marginal if any role during and after the creation of the WUA.

2. The rapid transition from agriculture-based livelihood to a mix of non-agricultural activities resulted in diminishing interest in improving irrigation operations and indeed agriculture productivity itself. Due to the proximity to an urban area, land prices were seen to be increasing at an unprecedented rate, continually eroding the motivation of farmers to invest in agriculture and hence irrigation.
3. Farmers who cultivated cash crops managed to secure adequate irrigation through their own personal relationships with SSNNL staff in the field. Where that failed, they had their own tube wells to fall back on.

The Kanipur case study highlights the necessary conditions for sustained community participation in resource management. It further re-enforces the importance of initiating and strengthening participatory processes at the formative stages.

12.5. Case Study 5: Neemkheda Water User's Association, District Vidisha, Madhya Pradesh

The WUA for Neemkheda was formed in 1999 as a result of the PIM Act that was introduced by the MP government. The Neemkheda WUA serves farmers from two contiguous villages, namely Neemkheda and Barkhedi. The command area under the management of this WUA is part of the larger command area of the Samrat Ashok Sagar (SAS) Irrigation Project which irrigates more than 27,900 ha of land in two districts of MP: Vidisha and Raisen. The reservoir is built on River Halali. If irrigated to its full potential, the gross command area would be 37,600 ha. Designed as a multipurpose project, the SAS also generates power and provides drinking water for Vidisha town, besides serving as a flood control mechanism.

The total population of Neemkheda village was approximately 1,300, comprising 170 households. Two Brahmin sub-castes, Sharmas and Saxenas, made up for more than 55 per cent of the population. They were also among the largest landowners in the village. In the social and political hierarchy, they were at the top and not surprisingly, therefore, almost all leadership positions in the village were held by members of these sub-castes. Next in the hierarchy were the Lodhis who made up 20 per cent of the population. At the bottom of the ladder were the remaining households: Harijans (8 per cent), tribals (8 per cent) and Kirars (9 per cent). This data was collected by a field survey done in 2009.

The canal network that irrigated the command area in Neemkheda village received water from the Right Bank Canal through a distributory canal. The network was designed to irrigate a total area of 710 ha. However, since the commissioning of the canal network in 1980, the project has never irrigated more than 250 ha (data obtained by FGD with farmers in 2010). The minor canals and the watercourses at the farm level were unlined earthen structures and prone to frequent breaches. The repair and maintenance of these canals by the ID was grossly inadequate. This was the main reason for poor irrigation coverage. To make matters worse, an aqueduct collapsed about 20 years before the time period of the survey, virtually cutting off water to more than 300 ha of the command area. The aqueduct was not repaired until 2003 when it was taken up under the PIM programme.

In 2000, with the help of funds from the ICEF, an NGO named Self-reliant Initiatives through Joint Action (SRIJAN) began working in Neemkheda. A series of training programmes were conducted for the elected leaders of the WUA and field staff from the ID. The first EC was led by President Hari Sharma and had 17 members, including four women. In 2003, SRIJAN managed to collect ₹200,000 from the farmers and buy a fixed deposit maintenance fund. Interest from this fund paid for minor maintenance work for a few years until this arrangement ended in 2006. Not surprisingly, 2006 was the year SRIJAN's involvement in the project also came to an end when ICEF funding ended.

Prior to the implementation of PIM, the entire irrigation management operations were handled by a SE from the ID. Even the formality of consulting farmers for planning the irrigation schedule was unheard of. Since Neemkheda comes in the middle reach of a distributory, excess irrigation and delinquency by farmers in the head reach area was a major reason for poor services here. In any case, almost all Sharma and Saxena farmers had borewells or open wells to supplement irrigation. These farmers, therefore, were able to cope with the risk of erratic and even non-supply of canal water. Less wealthy farmers would either limit their crops to rain-fed varieties or go for an irrigated crop only after tying up with well owners to purchase water, often at an exorbitant price.

The introduction of PIM did have some positive impact for the first four years. The EC played a role, even if just consultative, in the collection of farmers' demands for water, scheduling irrigation cycles and carrying out minor maintenance of the canals. This resulted in a marginal increase in the area under irrigation and more significantly it increased the coverage of irrigation in the mid- and tail-reaches of the canals. However, after 2006, this arrangement withered away following SRIJAN's withdrawal from active community organizing work. The EC rarely met and there were no records at the WUA level. The SE maintained accounts and most of the operational responsibilities were reverted back to the ID. Table 3.10 summarizes the performance of Neemkheda WUA before and after PIM.

12.5.1. Decentralization and Participation in Neemkheda

The first semblance of farmer participation in irrigation came only after community organizers from SRIJAN started interacting with the farmers and the ID. Motivated and sometimes coerced by SRIJAN staff, ID staff made efforts to reach out to the farmers during

Table 3.10

Impact of PIM on Irrigation by Neemkheda WUA

Indicators	Before PIM	After PIM
Command area of Neemkheda	715 ha	715 ha
Maximum area irrigated	315 ha	475 ha
Tail end irrigation	15 ha	75 ha
Farmers'/WUA's involvement in management	None	Minor canal repairs and recovery of dues (until 2006)

Source: Registers for 2007 provided by SRIJAN, and interviews with SRIJAN staff.

irrigation operations. They sought the help of farmers in minor repair works and scheduling of irrigation. However, despite the provisions in the Act, the actual management responsibilities were never handed over to the WUA. The interaction between farmers and engineers did result in focusing the canal repair works on the tail section of the command area. As a result, many farmers from the tail reach received water for the first time in 20 years. Apart from the sporadic collaboration with the ID for repair works during 2000–03, the WUA and its EC had no management responsibilities or role in decision-making. Accounts and records pertaining to irrigation were maintained by the ID and even farmer leaders had no access to this information. For this reason, the extent of decentralization was almost non-existent. Table 3.11 below indicates how the farmers responded to issues of participation and governance.

Table 3.11

Governance and Participation of Farmers in Neemkheda WUA

	Response from Farmers		
Criteria	Positive	Negative	No Response
Awareness of PIM	12	38	0
Attended meetings	2	32	16
Knowledge of financial matters	1	49	0
Incidence of conflict resolution by WUA	0	5	45

Source: Registers for 2007 provided by SRIJAN and interviews with SRIJAN staff.

12.5.2. Performance on Equity in Neemkheda

Figure 3.3 shows the performance of irrigation services since the introduction of PIM. The graphs disaggregate the command area according to the location along the canal—head, middle and tail. Out of the 710 ha of command area land, approximately 240 ha fell in the tail section of the canals.

The tail-reach farmers were amongst the worst affected due to dysfunctional canal operations. The introduction of PIM in 1999 did result in repairs of damaged sections of the canal and this increased water availability to some farmers, notably in the tail sections.

Figure 3.3

Irrigation Performance of the Neemkheda WUA

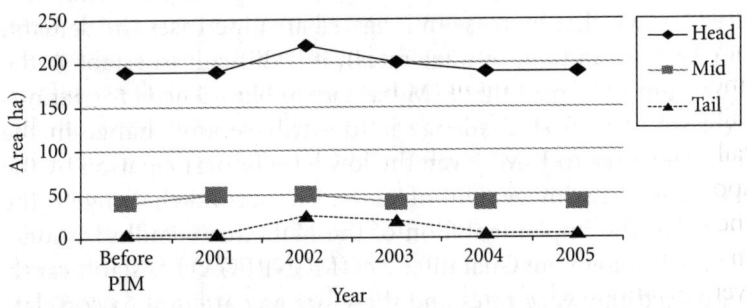

Source: Registers for 2007 provided by SRIJAN, and interviews with SRIJAN staff.

However, this was due to a one-time grant that enabled repair work. To meet recurring maintenance expenses neither the ID nor the WUA had put into place a revenue source. As a result, the benefits of better canals could not be sustained in the subsequent years. Canal conditions went from bad to worse, farmer participation waned and management functions gradually shifted back to the ID.

The denial of irrigation services was found to be unrelated to the landholding pattern or caste divisions. That was because the small landholdings as well as lower caste members had no preponderance about the location of the fields in either head, mid or tail sections of the canal. Therefore, while there was marginal and short term improvement in the performance of irrigation (and hence benefits to all farmers) on the whole, there was no evidence that linked increased benefits to the poor.

12.5.3. Other Impacts on the Poor in Neemkheda

Apart from the lower-caste and small landholding households, landless households were clearly amongst the poorest in the village. There were only eight landless families and their primary source of livelihood was wage labour. It must be mentioned, however, that the landless families were not the only ones who drew a significant proportion of their income from agricultural wages.

More than 40 other households were actively engaged in wage labour within a village and in neighbouring villages. While it is well known that increase in irrigated area increases the demand for labour (and hence wage rates), it is difficult to establish the quantum of impact that PIM has had in Neemkheda for various reasons. The first challenge is to attribute any change in the irrigated area to PIM, given the low level of participation by the WUA in the management of water. The second challenge is the fact that the implementation of the Mahatma Gandhi National Rural Employment Guarantee Act (MGNREGA) has significantly impacted the wage rates and therefore any attempt to correlate wage rate increase with irrigation will not be conclusive. For instance, wage rates increased from ₹40 per day in 1999 to ₹110 per day during 2009, MGNREGA typically pays ₹120 per day.

Irrigation and PIM had had no significant impact on migration levels in the village. There was no distress migration reported. Young men left the village to seek employment in the nearby cities of Vidisha and Bhopal, but that trend was influenced by the growth in non-agricultural employment opportunities in these cities rather than by any improvements in irrigation. Similarly, the incidence and severity of indebtedness showed no correlation with the change in irrigation management. In fact, the level of indebtedness remained constant until 2008 and fell only when labour opportunities increased due to the MGNREGA.

In conclusion, there has been really no decentralization of management, even of the most rudimentary kind, to the Neemkheda WUA and therefore the implementation of PIM policy in Neemkheda can be considered very poor. It is difficult to ascribe to the PIM any change in the benefits accrued to farmers who were members of the WUA. While the role played by an NGO could be credited for the short-lived increase in the area under irrigation, it was clear that farmer participation was not institutionalized and there was neither a real attempt nor any willingness on part of the ID to devolve responsibilities. Therefore, it is safe to conclude that PIM had had no impact, positive or negative, on the economic well-being of the poor or the poorest in Neemkheda.

12.6. Case Study 6: Banji Water User's Association, Bicchia Block, Mandla District, MP

The Banji WUA was formed in 2000 as one of eight WUAs promoted under the Matiyari Irrigation Scheme in Bicchia block of Mandla district. The scheme gets its name from the river Matiyari that feeds the reservoir. The Banji WUA covers a command area of five villages and the town of Anjania. Construction of the reservoir and the canal system took 11 years to complete and the scheme was commissioned in 1986. It was designed to irrigate 10,120 ha of land covering 69 villages including the 945 ha belonging to the six villages covered by the Banji WUA. Acute poverty and poor groundwater yields meant that there were only 45 private wells in the village Banji.

Banji village had a population of 1,343 comprising 190 households. More than half (105) belonged to either the Bairagi or Gaud castes. Another 55 households were from the Jharia and Paradhan castes, and the remaining 30 households consisted of Harijans, tribals and Yadavs. The local leadership was from the Jharia and Paradhan community (this data was obtained from the village panchayat secretary in 2010). Due to their close proximity to Anjania, many families had one or two members employed in the shops and establishments located there. Out of 190 households, 155 owned agricultural land. The main crops were rice, wheat, chickpea and pulses. Altogether, 35 families were landless and relied on agricultural labour as their main source of income. Another 20 families, many of them small farmers, depended on agricultural and non-farm wage opportunities for up to 50 per cent of their income. Of the 15 Harijan families, 9 were landless. The Matiyari irrigation project provided water to about 80 ha of land while 45 ha was unirrigated. There were about 45 open wells.

12.6.1. Water Users Association and Participation in Banji

The Banji WUA was formed in the year 2000 along with seven other WUAs promoted by the ID to cover 69 villages that the Matiyari scheme irrigates. The formation of the WUA was done without any involvement of the villagers and therefore there was little information available in the village about the processes involved or the key players from the village who may have participated. The SE and his team of field staff co-opted some of the village elites and carried out the formalities of an election to the offices of President and Vice President. Mahendra Patel, a farmer from Anjania was elected the president in 2000. In the 2006 election, his relative— Vinod Patel—became the President. Vinod Patel was a merchant who owned a shop trading in commodities. In fact, most of the farmers from Banji ended up buying inputs and selling their produce to Vinod and therefore he had enormous influence in the village.

The role played by the WUA in irrigation management appeared to be minimal, if at all. None of the farmers interviewed was even aware of the role of the WUA in operation and the maintenance of the canals. Even though many farmers voted during the WUA elections, only two of them knew what their WUA was mandated to do under the PIM Act. Most of them did not even acknowledge the existence of a WUA. None was aware of any EC nor heard of any meetings. The President himself acknowledged that there was little scope for him or the EC to play any role when all operational and financial matters were controlled by the SE and water distributors. There were indications from some farmers of collusion between the President and the ID staff in misappropriating the maintenance budget that the WUA received as grants annually. The problem of marginalization was total when it came to women. There was no formal representation of women in the WUA and their participation in any function related to irrigation was absent. Capital grants for major canal repairs too were suspected to be misappropriated by the WUA office bearers and the ID. The farmers who responded to our interviews did not know that a budget of ₹11.6 million was approved and spent on repair works during the years 2003–05.

12.6.2. Banji: Irrigation Performance and Benefits

The operation of the canals has always been erratic. The main canal had three siphons that frequently clogged up, depriving large swaths of the command area of irrigation water for long periods of time. The ID claimed to have repeatedly made budget proposals of ₹11.6 million for major repairs, but funding had been sporadic and unpredictable. In 2008, there was another proposal to use funds available under the MGNREGA to repair parts of the watercourses. Works were indeed taken up now and then in the following years, but the ability of the canals to carry water to all parts of the command area continued to be compromised because of incomplete work and the high rate of seepage due to unlined canals.

Irrigation figures for Banji were hard to come by because the WUA maintained no records of irrigation operations, even though the law required them to. Instead, it was the SE located in Mandla town who kept custody of all the records. Figure 3.4 below gives the performance of the Banji WUA across the years. It can be seen that there was no impact of PIM on the extent of utilization of water from the reservoir. Since 2005, the area under irrigation had also steadily gone down due to big breaches in the main canal and clogging of siphons.

There was neither a pattern nor correlation between performance and the introduction of PIM in 2000. As a matter of fact, utilization had been consistently less than 50 per cent of the command area. Tail-end farmers were the worst affected in terms of access. Large sections of the tail villages had been cut off from the command due to a damaged siphon that the ID and WUA had failed to

Figure 3.4

Irrigation Performance by the Banji WUA

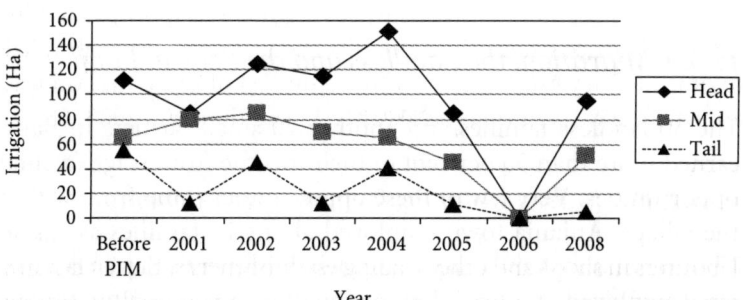

Source: FGD with farmers, (2009).

Table 3.12

Impact of PIM on Economic Indicators in Banji

Indicators	Before PIM	After PIM
Main crops cultivated	Rice, Wheat	Rice, Wheat
Productivity (kgs/acre)		
a. Rice	a. 1,900 kgs	a. 2,000 kgs
b. Wheat	b. 1,100 kgs	b. 1,100 kgs
Average net income per acre (₹)	8,500	8,700
Average milch animals per family	1.2	1.2
Income from sale of milk	NIL	NIL

Source: FGD and HHS, (2009).

repair. With such unreliable canal operations and very few wells in the command area, farmers were averse to taking any risk with high-value crops. As a result, small and medium farmers earned substantially less income from farming than their counterparts in other schemes where they had options to buy water from private well owners if the canal failed.

There was no evidence to suggest that implementation of PIM in Banji had had any impact on the performance of irrigation. By extension, there could be no relationship between PIM, income generation and poverty levels either. As Table 3.12 indicates, productivity and net income registered no noticeable change as a consequence of PIM. The same held true with other allied activities such as animal husbandry.

12.6.3. Migration, the Landless and the Poor in Banji

The 30 landless families and another 20 small farmers in Banji earned more than 50 per cent of their income from wage earning opportunities. Very few of these opportunities came from within the village. Anjania town employed about 15 families as casual labourers in shops and other trading establishments. Eleven families were employed at a brick kiln operated by a few wealthy traders from Anjania. This activity was seasonal and lasted for about

Table 3.13

Impact of PIM on Employment and Migration in Banji

Indicators	Before PIM	After PIM
Number of landless families	12	13
Average annual wage employment days	150	280
Average daily wage (₹)	55	90
Number of families in share-cropping	None	None
Families migrating	95	80
Average number of days family migrates annually	120	85
Average wage rate earned during migration (₹)	70	120
Migration destination	Chhattisgarh and Andhra Pradesh	Chhattisgarh and Andhra Pradesh

Source: FGD and HHS, (2009).

six months a year. During these six months, the wages ranged from ₹65 per day to ₹90 per day, depending on the demand from agricultural operations. Until the year 2007, the landless families as well as an additional 40 to 50 small farmers migrated regularly to Chhattisgarh and Andhra Pradesh for three to four months. The average wage earned at these locations was ₹120 per day. In 2008, the implementation of MGNREGA had a significant impact on the migration as well as wage rates. Table 3.13 shows both indicators of migration, that is, the number of days of employment both locally and during migration as well as the daily wage rate to not have changed as a result of PIM because there had been no notable increase in the area under cultivation.

With no stable increase in the area under irrigation in the last 10 years (1999–2009), the demand for agricultural labour in Banji had stagnated. Unlike many other villages in the western and southern districts of MP where the groundwater table produces better yields, investments in private irrigation facilities had been poor or non-existent in the Mandla district and therefore had not contributed to any increase in demand for agricultural labour. When demand and wage rates did register a notable increase in 2008, it was seen as a result of the introduction of the MGNREGA rather than any change in agriculture.

In conclusion, the process of decentralization and farmer participation was very poorly implemented in the Matiyari Irrigation Scheme as a whole. Even as passive recipients, the farmers of Banji and five other villages served by the WUA had no opportunity to participate in managing irrigation operations. The leadership of the WUA was dominated by one family and the exclusion of other leadership aspirants nearly total. Therefore, there was no element of community management whatsoever in the Banji WUA. In fact, any attempt at an assessment of the impact of PIM in terms of improved irrigation performance or better equity and more focus on the poor was a futile exercise.

The poor were neither better off nor worse off as a result of PIM. The changes in the economic situation of the village in general and the poor and marginalized in particular could be directly attributed to opportunities for wage employment that came from outside of the WUA, such as non-farm activities in nearby Anjania or due to the increase in demand from industrial and agriculture activities in the prosperous regions of Chhattisgarh and Andhra Pradesh.

12.7. Case Study 7: Dagarkot Water Users' Association, Khalwa Block, Khandwa District, MP

Dagarkot is a tribal village in the Khalwa block of Khandwa district in MP. The village population consisted of 255 families of the Korku tribe and eight Harijan families. Unlike tribals in the eastern part of the state, tribals in Dagarkot had practiced sedentary farming for more than 100 years and were thus far less dependent on forest resources. Most (92 per cent) of the families owned land and derived a significant portion of their livelihood from farming. However, the farming systems were quite rudimentary and could be characterized as subsistence farming. All economic indicators such as the quality of dwellings, movable and fixed assets suggested that the village was very poor. Brewing and consumption of illicit alcohol had been a serious problem in the village for many decades.

The level of indebtedness was very high and much of it is caused by the problem of alcoholism.

Dagarkot fell within the programme area of the NGO, the AKRSP. Community organizers from AKRSP visited the village in 2005 to initiate a dialogue with the community to explore the scope of implementing CNRM projects. They promoted a local people's institution called the Village Development Committee (VDC) and made it a forum for planning and implementation of all development activities sponsored and supported by the AKRSP. The idea of rehabilitating the government canal came from the AKRSP and not the villagers. The suggestion was mooted as part of the AKRSP's strategy of promoting PIM in the state. After some persuasion, the villagers agreed to take on some management responsibilities for improving and running the irrigation system. In the year 2000, there was a dysfunctional WUA promoted by the ID that had combined the Dagarkot project along with another minor irrigation project. The AKRSP arranged for the management responsibility of the Dagarkot project to be handed over to an irrigation committee (IC) under the overall management of the VDC. In 2007, an agreement was drawn up between the ID and the VDC for the rehabilitation of the canal and the eventual turnover of management functions to the IC/VDC. Neither the committee nor the VDC was a formally registered body. The WUA in Dagarkot was therefore the VDC/IC.

12.7.1. Dagarkot Water Users Association and Participation

Dagarkot's irrigation project was designed to provide water to 115 ha of land belonging to 85 farmers. The IC consisted of members who represented parcels of land irrigated from 13 outlets off the main canal. The members, in turn, elected the President. The first President was Suraj Ram Vikas. The committee received significant training inputs from the AKRSP during the first two years (2006–07). These included visits to successful farmer-managed irrigation projects in MP, as well as Gujarat. More importantly, the AKRSP managed to secure decision-making autonomy for the VDC. This meant that, unlike other WUAs elsewhere in MP, the Dagarkot WUA (VDC) was given full control over operational and financial decisions. The important functions of fixing and recovering water rates from farmers and scheduling water distribution were done by the VDC, which in turn gave them the authority to introduce incentives for fiscal and operational discipline.

Prior to the formation of and turnover of irrigation management to the Dagarkot WUA, the total irrigation provided by the ID averaged between 25 and 30 ha and never exceeded 45 ha. The reason for poor utilization was the high rate of seepage from the unlined canal which prevented water from reaching the tail sections of the command area. In fact, many farmers in the head-reach would use water that seeped from the canal. At many places along the canal stretch, persistent seepage and waterlogging had resulted in serious soil alkalinity.

An amount of ₹500,000 was spent to bring the canals up to a certain performance level so that water could reach the tail section. To get the idea of participation started, the AKRSP sought and obtained 10 per cent of the rehabilitation cost from the farmers as their contribution. An additional contribution worth 10 per cent of the cost was made through labour and local materials. The VDC and IC held meetings at least four times a year and the attendance was very good. These meetings were open to all members, but mandatory for the committee members to attend. The annual General Body Meeting was also well attended. The water rates were decided and annual budget approval sought at these meetings. The level of awareness about the VDC/IC's mandate, relative to other WUAs in the state, was very good. Out of the 50 farmers interviewed for the study, 35 could describe the role and responsibilities of the VDC and IC in providing irrigation. Financial details were however less well known amongst the farmers, with only 21 having any knowledge of the budgeting processes. A notable feature of the institution was the participation of women. Besides having three women as IC members, the VDC chair was also held by a woman, Jijibai Korku. Women's attendance at VDC/IC meetings was strong compared to the trend in other parts of the state where it was almost non-existent.

Figure 3.5

Irrigation Performance by the Dagarkot WUA

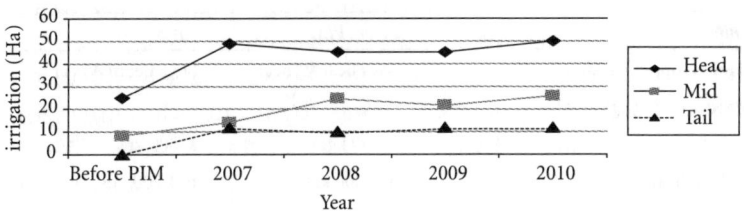

Source: Dagarkot WUA records, (2010).

12.7.2. Irrigation Performance and Benefits in Dagarkot

Figure 3.5 shows the significant increase in the area under irrigation after the management was handed over to the VDC/IC. From a maximum irrigation of 45 ha before PIM, the VDC/IC managed to maintain irrigation between 75 and 88 ha after they assumed responsibilities, showing an increase of over 100 per cent. Equally important was the distribution of the increased area under irrigation. It was seen that the middle and tail sections of the command had improved access as a result the of VDC/IC management. While the canal continued to need major repair work, quick maintenance of minor problems enabled them to keep utilization levels consistently high.

The impact of the VDC/IC's management of irrigation can be seen not only in terms of an increase in absolute area under irrigation, but also in the productivity of crops. Table 3.14 shows that the productivity of two main crops (soya bean and wheat) increased up to 25 per cent as a result of timely and adequate irrigation which was in turn possible due to better management. This translated into a higher quantity of total production as well as a higher sale price. As a result, the net income from agriculture increased markedly. Similarly, the increase in crop residues also motivated many families to keep or even increase the number of milch animals. Since there was no provision for the organized sale of milk, there was no data on the impact of irrigation improvement on income from animals. However, focused group discussions with

Table 3.14

Impact of PIM on Income and Consumption in Dagarkot

Indicators	Before PIM	After PIM
Main crops cultivated	Soya bean/Wheat	Soya bean/Wheat
Productivity (kgs/acre)		
a. Soya	a. 650 kgs	a. 800 kgs
b. Wheat	b. 1,000 kgs	b. 1,200 kgs
Average net income per acre	₹8,000	₹11,000
Average milch animals per family	1.5	2.25
Income from sale of milk	Nil	Nil
Assets and consumption	No motorcycles, 10 mobiles, 25 TVs	10 motor cycles, more than 35 mobiles, 70 TVs
Annual expense on liquor per family	₹2,000	₹5,000

Source: Field survey data, (2010).

animal owners clearly indicated that the consumption of milk by family members had increased.

An unpleasant result of the increased income from irrigated crops in Dagarkot was that many families reported higher consumption of liquor, thereby increasing domestic strife. The number of motorcycles and televisions (TVs) had also registered a significant increase. AKRSP staff candidly admitted that many families had not used the increased prosperity and income surplus to build assets or a resource base for sustained livelihood improvements. Instead, much of the additional income had been squandered on conspicuous consumption of items such as bikes, mobiles, TVs, non-essential clothing and liquor.

12.7.3. The Landless, Agricultural Labour and Migration in Dagarkot

Twenty families in Dagarkot were landless and got their entire income from wage labour. An additional 90 families had small parcels of land, but had to take up wage labour regularly to supplement their income from agriculture. These families had land outside the command area of the irrigation project where they cultivated only rain-fed kharif crops. After the harvest season they sought employment opportunities by migrating to various cities in MP for durations ranging from a month to six months. With the introduction of PIM and the consequent increase in irrigated areas, agricultural wages went up from ₹82 per day to 130 per day during the peak harvest season for rabi crops (Field Survey Data, 2010). Added to this, the implementation of MGNREGA in 2008 led to a further increase in the number of wage-earning days available to these families. However, this did not have any significant incremental impact on the wage rates because the MGNREGA programme employed them during the summer months when there was no irrigation. The impact is more visible in migration data presented in Table 3.15. Traditionally, migration has been a result of distress as well as opportunity for many families in Dagarkot.

The reduction in the number of migrating families and the number of days they migrated could possibly be directly attributable to increase in irrigation due to the VDC/IC's management. The MGNREGA also contributed to this reduction, but only after the year 2008 when it was implemented. The wage rates offered to

Table 3.15

Impact of PIM on Landless Families and Migration in Dagarkot

Indicators	Before PIM	After PIM
Number of landless families	15	20
Average annual wage employment days available locally per family	25	110
Average daily wage (₹)	₹82	₹130
Number of families engaged in share-cropping	2–3	2–3
Families migrating	130	110
Average number of days family migrates annually	140 days	75 days
Average wage rate earned during migration (₹)	₹90	₹200
Migration destination	Akola, Harda, Khandwa	Akola, Harda, Khandwa, Indore

Source: FGD and HHS, (2009).

migrating families were so competitive that many families continued to migrate out of choice.

In conclusion, the level of impoverishment of Dagarkot was worse than that of the three other case study villages in MP. Thus, the impact of any economic growth and income was more marked here than in the other cases. All families in this village were officially BPL. Data on dwellings and other family assets validated this fact implying that any improvements in managing the irrigation project would benefit the poor. Besides increased irrigation as a result of PIM, there was also a marked improvement in the condition of the tail-end farmers who were traditionally the worst affected due to poor canal management. Dagarkot also presents an interesting case of NGO support and its impact on decentralization and quality of governance. In Dagarkot, the level of participation of farmers was the highest amongst the four MP cases. The devolution of decision-making powers for water charges, recovery and maintenance functions amongst others gave the Dagarkot WUA considerable autonomy and therefore a sense of responsibility and motivation to sustain its institutional capacity.

12.8. Case Study 8: Satak Water User's Association (Bamandi), Kasrawad Block, Khargone District, MP

The Satak Minor Irrigation project is also referred to as the Bamandi irrigation project and gets its name from the reservoir near Bamandi village. The cluster of villages that formed the command area of the scheme was dominated by the Kunbi Patel caste who trace their roots to the northern districts of Gujarat from where they emigrated many generations ago. They made up about 45 per cent of the population of the villages. The Rathods made up another 30 per cent, the Nahars and the Balais about 15 per cent and Harijans, tribals and other minor castes constituting the remaining 10 per cent (Data obtained from village panchayat secretary in 2010). Leadership positions in the village panchayat as well as other organized economic and political activities were dominated by the Patels and the Rathods. A milk cooperative society was promoted in 2000 by the state dairy department, but wound up the same year due to leadership conflicts. An agriculture credit cooperative covered seven villages in the cluster, but the operations and the benefits were cornered by the wealthier Patel farmers. There were also deep divisions within the Patel community along party lines. During the time of the study, the BJP held sway and therefore their candidates occupied the elected positions in Panchayat elections as well as other user group-specific institutions, including the WUA.

The Satak irrigation scheme was commissioned in 1966. The project was designed to irrigate 2,757 ha of land belonging to 3,490 families, spread across 17 contiguous villages. The water distribution network consisted of a main canal, distributaries and watercourses totalling approximately 52 km in combined length (Project Office, 2010). Cotton, chilli, wheat and corn were the main crops cultivated in the area. Utilization of the irrigation potential was poor right from the beginning. The poor state of physical infrastructure particularly for watercourses and siphons was the main cause of underutilization. When it became clear to the ID that the canal network was inadequately designed and constructed, the designed command area of 2,757 ha was officially revised to 1,850. Despite this reduction, political compulsions made it necessary to retain the original 17 villages in the command area, making the entire distribution system vulnerable to conflicts.

From 1966 to 1999, the project was managed by the state ID. A team of one SE and three water distributors (*amins*) was responsible for its overall O&M. Bamandi villagers recall that the SE would make only occasional visits to the command area and that he left much of the O&M responsibilities to the water distributors. By 1975, the canal systems were in such a poor state of disrepair that large portions of the command area towards the tail section of the main canal were completely deprived of any irrigation water. There were no records available on actual irrigation during the first 20 years of the project. However, from villager accounts on this matter, it was found that the project never irrigated more than 1,100 ha. In fact, during the decade of the 1990s, total irrigation came down to less than 800 ha. Much of this irrigation was cornered by farmers in the head and middle-reach villages of Bamandi, Salimpura and Regwa. The tail villages of Balgaon and Balkhad received no water at all from the project. Their exclusion was so established a fact that most of the well-to-do farmers from these tail villages went ahead and invested in private open-wells and tube wells. In fact, on an average, every farmer at the time of the survey owned an open or deep tube well in these villages during the time of the study.

12.8.1. PIM and WUA Governance in Bamandi

The Satak Water Users Association was formally registered in 2000. The SE, Mr Abhay Shukla, played an anchor role in promoting the idea of PIM and in seeking farmers' participation. Mr Shukla was enthusiastic about engaging farmers and their leaders in the implementation of the new irrigation rules. However, the SE and his staff did not have adequate social organizing skills to catalyze collective action. In 2002, an NGO called Association of Social Advancement (ASA) was invited by the state government under a pilot programme to strengthen the capacity of WUAs through training and support. The programme was funded by the ICEF. Budget provisions were made not only for capacity-building inputs but also for physical rehabilitation of the canal networks. An initial budget of ₹12.8 million was earmarked for this purpose.

Under the ASA's supervision, the Bamandi WUA leaders were given training in irrigation operations, book-keeping and minor maintenance skills. The SE and his team of water distributors continued to provide technical help. Water charges were fixed and recovered by the ID initially, but after the ASA's intervention, the responsibility of collecting charges for water was delegated to the WUA. Functional committees were formed to oversee water distribution, fee collection and dispute settlement. The first President of the WUA was Babubhai Chaudhary (a farmer from the higher and wealthier Kunbi Patel caste). The District Collector played a part in ensuring that the WUA elections were held democratically and the rehabilitation of the canal done efficiently.

The involvement of the ASA was crucial in ensuring that Bamandi farmers played a role in irrigation management during the years 2003–07. Canal repairs were done by the ID through contractors, but the involvement of farmers did have some effect on the quality of work. Despite significant improvements in the condition of the canals as a result of the repair work, the tail sections of the main canal continued to be problematic. The watercourses there also had serious damages that required repair. Efforts were made to supplement ICEF funds with state government funds to extend the repair works right up to the tail sections. An additional ₹4.75 lakhs was allocated by the state government in 2007 and 2009 for specifically improving the watercourses. However, these efforts were grossly inadequate given the fact that complete repair of the canal network would need a budget of more than ₹300 lakhs. Farmer (and WUA leaders) interest and participation in management functions waned due to persistent problems with the canal operations and erratic fund availability. The support provided by the ASA also came to an end in 2007 when the ICEF funding arrangement was wound up. Since then, irrigation operations, for all practical purposes, reverted back to the SE and his team of two water distributors.

In 2006, Ramesh Mandloi became the Bamandi WUA President and a new EC was formed. The election, supervised by the District Collector, was contested along party lines with the BJP emerging the winner. The WUA EC meetings were rare and conducted as a formality to comply with the provisions of the PIM Act. As of 2011, the WUA EC, headed by Suresh Patel as President, had very few operational responsibilities. The SE, however, believed that the WUA played an important role in conflict resolution and assisting the ID in carrying out water charge recovery.

12.8.2. Irrigation Performance and PIM in Bamandi

From Figure 3.6, it can be seen that there was a significant increase in irrigated area in the year 2000 but the increase could not be sustained over the following years. The surge in irrigation during the year 2000 was due to a government order to provide full irrigation to combat the effect of a severe drought. It can be seen that the benefits of irrigation were cornered by the head and middle sections while the tail section received very little. Due to rehabilitation of the main canal under the ICEF grant

Figure 3.6

Irrigation Utilization by the Bamandi WUA

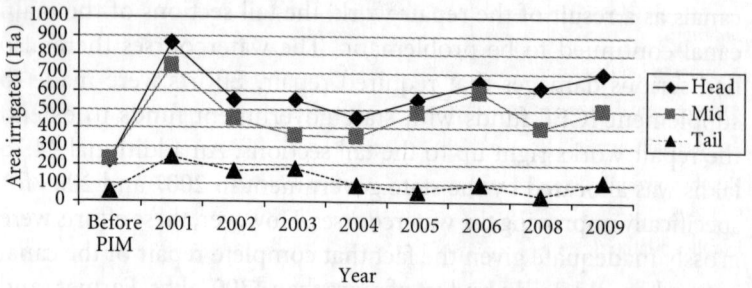

Source: WUA records obtained from ID, (2009).

and the involvement of the ASA during 2003 and 2004, water began to reach the tail sections and thus created a steady increase in irrigation utilization. This time, however, the tail sections did get a significant share of the benefits of improved performance. There is however no evidence to suggest that amongst the farmers who benefitted from this increase were the poor farmers who were targeted as beneficiaries or that they derived special benefits. In other words, poor management did not selectively deprive poor farmers any more than non-poor farmers.

12.8.3. *The Landless and Migration in Bamandi*

The number of landless families was seen to vary significantly across the 17 villages. Regwa village had the highest number of landless families—130 out of 670. However, contrary to expectations, landless families were not amongst the poorest. Wage employment opportunities were not scarce and therefore the wage rates were very competitive. There was seasonal variation in the wage rates which peaked around the harvest time of the kharif season and the beginning of rabi season. The wage rates had held steady for many years until 2007 when the MGNREGA program was implemented in the state. With the prevailing government wage rate at ₹122 per day, the condition of landless families improved further. As seen in

Table 3.16

Impact of PIM on Landless Families and on Migration in Bamandi

Indicators	Before PIM	After PIM
Number of landless families	870	1,000
Average annual wage employment days	210	310
Average daily wage (₹)	76	110
Number of families engaged in share-cropping	Not available	25
Families migrating	600	400
Average number of days family migrates annually	150	110
Average wage rate earned during migration (₹)	110	200
Migration destination	Malwa region for agriculture operations	Malwa region for agriculture and Indore for non-farm activities.

Source: FGD and HHS, (2009).

Table 3.16, there was no discernible change in real wages as a result of the introduction of PIM.

The migration rate out of Bamandi was seen to have come down during the period of 1990 to 2009 for two main reasons: (a) a rapid increase in private irrigation wells in the 1990s and (b) the availability of MGNREGA employment opportunities during the non-peak season of summer. As Table 3.16 reveals, the migration patterns showed a notable reduction, but had not stopped by any means. On the contrary, many families migrated by choice to take benefit of high wage rates in various cities such as Indore and other Malwa destinations. Soya cultivation and processing industry were the main employers of these migrating families. Wage rates averaged around ₹200 per day and went as high as ₹300 per day during the peak seasons of October and February. Therefore, many landless families moved to Indore regularly during the peak seasons too despite employment opportunities locally. Another indicator of the relative well-being of landless families in the command area villages was the low incidence of share-cropping. This can be explained from the risk assessment point of view. When wage-earning opportunities were plentiful, the poor choose to avoid riskier share-cropping arrangements, particularly when the crops required high-cost inputs.

In conclusion, it can be inferred from the data provided, that the enactment of the PIM Act and consequently the formation of a WUA in Bamandi did have some impact on improving the quality of canal rehabilitation, which in turn had some impact on water availability to farmers in the tail sections of the command area. It is, however, highly debatable whether this increase in irrigation could have been attributed to farmer management at all. The participation of farmers in irrigation management was short-lived even prior to the ASA's involvement coming to an end. Even during this period there was no evidence to conclude that the poor and landless were included in sharing any additional benefits due an increase in the command area. With the withdrawal of the ASA, even this incidental benefit to the farmers in general seemed to end. Despite the notable increase in real incomes of the landless and small farmers, the increase was directly related to increased employment opportunities within the village created by the MGNREGA and labour shortages in the Malwa region where poorer families chose to migrate during the lean seasons.

In Dagarkot, the only case in MP where an NGO intervention made it possible for the WUA to assume irrigation management responsibilities, the outcome was dramatically different. Of the four WUAs in MP, Dagarkot was the best performing WUA not only in terms of increasing the area under irrigation but also in addressing equity issues by ensuring irrigation access for tail-end farmers. Similarly, despite the provision in the Gujarat Act for devolution of decision-making powers to WUAs, two of the four cases in Gujarat opted to leave the functions to the ID. The Akala and Kanipur WUAs were promoted by the ID with little or no initiative to build WUA capacity to take over management functions. The performance of these two WUAs contrasted sharply with the other two in Gujarat where WUAs had a higher degree of autonomy and thus were able to deliver water more efficiently and equitably.

13. Decentralization and Community Participation: Did CNRM Deliver the Desired Results? An Analysis

The eight case studies described in the foregoing sections provide a wide range of situation analyses in terms of the processes of decentralization and accrual of economic benefits to the poor. We can see that there were a number of interdependent variables that qualified both the institutional/governance aspects of decentralization as well as the income generation aspects. As expected, these variables combined in a rather complex way to present many contexts that could explain why some WUAs performed well in managing resources, while others did not. Further, we can also draw inferences about why CNRM impacted the poor in varying ways. To analyze the findings and discover patterns of relationships between the decentralization process and the impact on poverty levels, it would be useful to revisit the central research questions and make an attempt to contextualize the findings based on the following questions:

13.1. How was the CNRM Project and Institution Introduced?

The one common factor that shaped the course of the eight CNRM institutions was the approach taken by the two states under study to inaugurate the programme in their respective communities of farmers. The process of introduction and subsequent building of the institutions proved to be very closely related to the de jure policy provisions as well as the presence and pathways taken by the promoting agencies during the early stages of the programme. As described in the introduction about the policy initiatives of the two states, MP can be considered as a case illustrating a top-down rapid legislative approach while Gujarat employed a slower bottom-up approach. This difference in approach by itself set the course for the decentralization process and the consequent influences on enabling participation. Added to this were some major differences in the content of the legislation that defined the extent to which control over resources was actually devolved to the farmers. In MP, the PIM Act allowed the retention of all crucial management decision-making authorities by the ID functionaries. Most crucially, the WUAs got no fiscal autonomy whatsoever. In contrast, the Gujarat Act required that the WUA be given full authority and responsibility to not only decide and collect water charges, but also retain up to 60 per cent of the receipts to meet operational expenses. In MP, the WUAs are completely dependent on the ID for any maintenance functions, while the Gujarat WUAs, having no external administrative processes to comply with, were able to respond to maintenance needs more quickly.

The role played by NGOs in catalyzing collective action and building the capacity of institutions to function democratically was clearly very crucial in institutionalizing participation and democratic behaviour among the leaders. Where this was absent, as in the case of the five WUAs with little or no such support systems, the participation level was poor or even absent as was in the case of Kanipur, Banji and Neemkheda. Therefore, the initial processes that established roles and responsibilities were quite crucial in setting the participatory trend and a culture of sensitivity to equity issues. When these were enabled, either through a support agency such as an NGO or by ID officials, the results were clearly positive. It can safely be surmised that the concern for equity was not only a consequence of early institutionalization of participation, but also the result of a catalyzed process with external help. Tail-end farmers gained access to water in Kiyadar, Chopadvav, Dagarkot, Akala and Neemkheda. However, that gain could be sustained only in the first three, whereas Akala's and Neemkheda's WUAs were soon marginalized by the ID. Soon after, canal maintenance broke down and tail-end deprivation returned. Once the controlling stake of the WUAs (as in the case of Kiyadar, Chopadvav and Dagarkot) or of the ID (in the other five WUAs) got entrenched in the formative years, it became very difficult to reverse the situation later. While the former three WUAs benefitted from this, the latter five found it very difficult to motivate farmers to participate.

Table 3.17

Comparative Analysis of Participation, Decentralization and Governance of WUAs

WUA	Support Agency	Capacity Building Inputs	State of Empowerment of Community
Akala	Department	Modest	Modest
Kiyadar	NGO (DSC)	High	High
Chopadvav	NGO (AKRSP)	High	High
Kanipur	Department	Poor	Very poor
Neemkheda	NGO (SRIJAN)	Modest	Poor
Banji	Department	Very poor	Very poor
Dagarkot	NGO (AKRSP)	High	High
Bamandi	NGO (ASA)	Modest	Moderate

Source: Field data summary, (2009).

The data clearly and unequivocally indicates that community empowerment was a crafted process and not a spontaneous process. The two major factors that undermined any indigenous efforts at the empowerment process were (a) existing local elites and their vested interests and (b) perverse incentives for the ID to sabotage the empowerment process. Given the entrenched position of local elites and the socio-political structure of rural communities in India, it was unlikely that these factors could be dealt with without external catalytic and back-stopping support. Table 3.17 shows the role played by external agencies and its impact in the villages studied.

There was a direct correlation between the involvement of NGOs and the level of participation and empowerment of the community. There were two clear relationships here: first, NGOs were clearly more effective in building the capacity of the WUA to take on resource management responsibilities than was the ID. Secondly, the role of ID officials as promoters of PIM created a conflict of interest situation because empowering a WUA would be possible only if a corresponding disempowerment process happened at the ID level. With much at stake in terms of control over water and finances, the ID had proved itself to be inadequate, either by design or by default, to play the role of a support agency.

13.2. How did the Project and Institution Perform, Both de jure and de facto, in terms of CNRM Goals?

Poverty reduction was never the stated objective of PIM, either de jure or de facto. The policy change was largely justified in terms of the advantages that decentralization would bring in improving efficiency in resource utilization. The distributive dimension of PIM, if any, was considered an incidental benefit. The most tangible benefit in terms of impact on poverty came from the resource augmentation that happened due to better rehabilitation and maintenance of the canals. Better infrastructure made it more likely that tail-end farmers were not excluded from their entitlements. However, as can be seen from Table 3.18 below, mere improvement of the physical system at the time of canal rehabilitation could not yield sustained benefits to tail-end

Table 3.18

Comparative Analysis of the Impact of PIM in the Eight Case Study WUAs

WUA	Change in Irrigation Utilization	Change in Wage Rates Due to PIM*	Change in Number of Days of Employment Due to PIM*	Change in Migration Due to PIM*
Akala	No change	No change	No change	No change
Kiyadar	Sustained increase	Increased by 75%	Increased by 50%	Decreased to zero
Chopadvav	Sustained increase	Increased by 70%	Increased by 30%	Decreased
Kanipur	Decreased	No change	No change	No change
Neemkheda	No change	No change	No change	No change
Banji	Increased marginally	No change	No change	No change
Dagarkot	Sustained increase	Increased by 60%	Increased by 80%	Decreased by 50%
Bamandi (Satak)	Increased marginally	No change	No change	No change

Source: Field data summary, (2009).

Note: * Wage rates and employment opportunities have increased in some of the villagers as a result of the introduction of the MGNREGA programme and also due to non-farm demand for labour. Similarly, the impact on migration is also caused by better earning opportunities rather than distress and therefore increased in-migration is not a negative effect.

farmers unless the WUA retained control over operational as well as fiscal matters.

Whether or not the PIM policy had an implied poverty reduction objective is debatable. There is less ambiguity as to whether a sustained increase in irrigation utilization improved the real wages of landless families and others who relied on agricultural labour for a significant share of their family income. If we can demonstrate that irrigation utilization has indeed improved as a result of the WUAs' active participation, then by extension, it can be concluded that WUAs were more likely to manage irrigation in a manner whereby a surge in agricultural activities leads to an increase in demand for labour and consequently in higher wage rates.

13.3. What Was the Extent of Productivity and Income Increase?

Productivity and income had indeed increased where certain predisposing conditions had been fulfilled. Irrigation benefits were optimized when matching crop husbandry practices were implemented. Scope for such linkages was better in tribal areas because the farmers had a relatively recent history in switching from rain-fed farming to irrigated farming. This could be seen in the Chopadvav and Dagarkot WUAs where the farmers were tribals. The supporting agency bundled agriculture extension activities along with their promotion of PIM and in the process demonstrated that the benefits of well-managed irrigation could be further improved with good agriculture practices. Increased income proved to be a significant motivation for sustaining participation by farmers in the management of the WUA.

The linkage that yielded the most benefits for the WUA was with a capacity-building support agency that had the wherewithal to build the WUA as a democratic farmers' institution. Three out of the four WUAs that received such support were also the three in terms of irrigation performance as well as delivering benefits to the poor. The next crucial linkage was the one with the ID. Despite the turnover of management responsibilities to the WUAs, the ID continued to wield enormous control over irrigation operations. This was true even in Gujarat where operational jurisdiction was completely handed over to WUAs from the outlet where the WUA command began. However, the ID's continued control over water release in the main and branch canals meant that the welfare of the WUA and its famers was quite vulnerable to a stressful relationship with the ID. Linkages with agri-input agencies and the market, while critical for optimal benefits to farmers, were easily established when irrigation improved and became predictable.

13.4. How Decentralized and Inclusive Was the Governance of the CNRM Institution?

The eight cases were a study of contrasts. Table 3.19 below summarizes the nature and extent of participation of farmers in WUA management.

Only three WUAs—Kiyadar, Chopadvav and Dagarkot—had full fiscal autonomy. This gave them a clear advantage on three counts: (a) creating the incentive to be cost-effective, (b) quick

Table 3.19

Nature and Extent of Farmers' Participation in Irrigation Management

WUA	Irrigation Operations	Canal Maintenance	Financial Decisions	Extent of Decentralization
Gujarat				
Akala-Chokhi	Consultation	Consultation	No	Medium
Kiyadar	Full	Shared with ID	Full	High
Chopadvav	Full	Shared with ID	Full	High
Kanipur	No	No	No	None
Madhya Pradesh				
Neemkheda	Consultation	No	No	Low
Banji	No	No	No	None
Dagarkot	Partial	Partial	Full	Medium
Bamandi (Satak)	Consultation	Consultation	No	Low

Source: Field data summary, (2009).

response to repair and maintenance needs and (c) ensuring fiscal and operational discipline among members through reward and sanction systems. Not surprisingly, these three WUAs were the ones that successfully augmented the resource and ensured better access to those who were previously marginalized. The absence of any role in operational and fiscal matters in the remaining five WUAs made them poor cases of decentralization. As pointed out earlier, there is a clause in the MP farmers' Participatory Irrigation Management Act 1999 that undermined the decentralization process by handing over the crucial financial and operational control to a SE from the ID. Against this backdrop, it is commendable that Dagarkot WUA managed, largely due to the intervention of the AKRSP, to negotiate and secure some authority over fiscal matters and to that extent effectively improving performance.

Regarding the devolution of financial decision-making powers to the WUAs, in all the three cases, fiscal autonomy resulted in increased costs to the end-users. Indeed, the water charges increased by as much as 100 per cent over the government rates in some cases. However, the fact that these three WUAs reported the highest recovery of water charges and were the best managed amongst the eight implies that higher water charges (a) made economic sense to the farmers, as they were ensured better returns due to predictable irrigation services (b) timely maintenance and accountable management functions were indeed of higher economic value and therefore cost-effective.

13.5. What Was the Impact on the Poor (Landless, Marginal, Small Land Holder) Members of the Village?

The impact of irrigation on the landless and the poor is debatable. PIM as a policy did little to include landless families. And since irrigation by its very nature excludes landless families, the distribution of benefits to the landless and the poor were only incidental, even though significant in quantum.

However, evidence from all eight studies counters the argument that irrigation only benefitted the landed farmers. The fact that agricultural labour wages peaked during the rabi and summer season clearly indicated the positive relationship between better irrigation management and higher incomes for the landless and poor. It is difficult to isolate this correlation from other incidental developments that further caused an increase in wages. For example, the introduction of non-farm wage employment opportunities through the government-initiated employment guarantee programmes had a significant impact on wage rates in five of the eight cases studied. A similar influence on the wage rate could be seen as a result of increased industrial activity and higher demand for labour that was available for families willing to migrate. While it is difficult to measure the contribution of irrigation towards wage-earning opportunities and wage rate increases, the positive nature of this linkage was established beyond doubt by the evidence seen in cases where such external opportunities were minimal. Dagarkot, Kiyadar and Chopadvav villages reported steep increases in wage rates during the irrigation season even when other opportunities remained the same.

The challenge that persisted however was how to attribute these benefits for the poor to PIM and the institution of CNRM. The correlation held true to the extent that it could be established that an irrigation increase was caused due to the more efficient management of canals and an equity-conscious WUA. This was indeed the case in Dagarkot, Kiyadar and Chopadvav, where the WUA performed markedly better in maintaining the canals systems and ensuring timely water to the tail-enders as compared to the situation when the management was done by the ID.

13.6. How Integrated Was the Project Intervention and What Was the Extent of the Outreach?

Irrigation projects have to deal with the adverse impacts of unsustainable resource management practices. Poor maintenance of canals has led to waterlogging and considerable loss of land due to resulting salinity. When the WUAs maintain the physical infrastructure (canal and outlets), adverse effects are nearly eliminated. This could be seen in Kiyadar and Chopadvav where the WUA was able to arrest the spread of salinity due to seepages. An attendant benefit that came with better maintained canals was the equally dramatic improvement in water use efficiency. Drastic reductions in seepage and other forms of water waste directly and positively impact the area under irrigation. The tendency of marginalizing the tail-enders was reduced as a consequence.

The single biggest challenge that all WUAs faced was the vulnerability of their autonomy to interference and irresponsible actions by the ID. Leaders from all four WUAs in MP had to deal with rent-seeking pressures from ID staff. With the exception of Dagarkot, all of them capitulated. The second most critical challenge that undermined the capacity of WUAs is the perverse influence that local elites try to exert on WUA leaders for narrow self-interest based reasons. Since head-reach farmers had historically derived illegitimate benefits due to poor functioning of the canals, the WUA leaders had to withstand the efforts made by the elites to safeguard their vested interests. With a poor culture of collective action for the common good, rural communities found these pressures unmanageable. This was where the external catalyst role of NGOs could have played an important part in establishing the rule of law and accountability mechanisms that counter elite capture. Successful WUAs found a way to resolve conflicts through reward and sanction systems that applied to all members.

13.7. How Has the Project and Institution Contributed to Effective, Equitable and Sustainable Resource Management?

The relative success of Dagarkot, Kiyadar and Chopadvav and the abject failure of Kanipur and Banji to decentralize resource management responsibilities to resource users was quite stark. In terms of good resource management practices, the evidence suggests that when CNRM institutions have better fiscal autonomy and are able to conduct business in a sustainable way, they were better equipped to invest in maintenance and renewal of infrastructure.

The very fact that the Kiyadar and Chopadvav WUAs and to a lesser extent Dagarkot WUA were able to recover 100 per cent of their operating costs indicated that the resource users were capable of bearing the true cost of the sustainable resource management practice. It also helped that the more farmers had access to water, the more likely they were to generate the revenue required to meet the costs. When equity suffered, as in the case of Neemkheda, Banji, Satak and Kanipur, the involvement in management or in cost-sharing reduced and the process of degeneration of the resource began. When the governing structure was unaccountable to the resource users, as in the case of these four WUAs, the abuse of resources was more likely.

Canal rehabilitation, when done well, as in the case of Kiyadar, Chopadvav, Akala and Dagarkot, reduced the most common environmental damage caused by irrigation, namely, waterlogging and salinization of the land. Government assistance came in the form of capital grants for one-time rehabilitation. When execution was done either by the WUA or under their direct supervision, the quality of work was better and to that extent, WUA management contributed to better resource use efficiency. When rehabilitation and maintenance functions were performed by the ID, the outcome was grossly inadequate in quantum as well as quality.

14. Conclusion

The central question of whether decentralization of irrigation management through the policy of PIM has impacted poverty levels can be answered only by naming the two crucial prerequisites that preceded the delivery of benefits. The first prerequisite is the nature and extent of decentralization possible within the policy framework. The second prerequisite is the integrity of the processes adopted and quality of implementation of the decentralization and democratic institution-building processes. The performance of the eight WUAs on these two criteria would help sum up the answer to the central question.

The first section of this chapter describes the key provisions of the PIM Act in the two states. It could be argued that the Act introduced in MP did not, by design, allow decentralization or devolution of authority beyond the administrative level. The fact that a SE was mandated to do the most crucial management functions, namely water distribution and financial management, in one stroke neutralized any provision the Act had to enhance farmer participation. The lack of motivation and indeed disillusionment and resentment among farmers and their leaders in MP could be directly attributed to this crucial policy flaw that defeats the very objective of the policy of handing over control to farmers. Interestingly, the only WUA in MP that fared well was Dagarkot where the intervention of an NGO made it possible to go beyond what the Act provided and actually gave the operational and financial authority to the WUA. In contrast, the Gujarat Act provided for complete operational and financial management authority to be transferred to the WUA on the signing of the MoU. Ironically, in two of the four Gujarat WUAs, namely Kanipur and Akala, this process was compromised, due to reluctance on the part of ID officials to let go of these powers. These two WUAs did poorly in comparison to the other two where the provision for devolution of operational and fiscal decision making was actually implemented. These two WUAs not only increased the area under irrigation in a sustainable way, but also ensured that the increased area benefitted the tail-end farmers and contributed to wage increases in the village which in turn benefitted the poor.

There were clear patterns observed in the process adopted in promoting PIM and its impact on the capacity of the WUA to function as a democratic participative farmers' institution. The policy change to CNRM recognized that the institution of collective action in rural communities was not a tradition and therefore needed to be catalyzed and facilitated. This required an agency that was sensitive to social organizing dynamics and competent to organize communities that deal with issues of social marginalization and poverty. The ID was not endowed with an organizational structure and culture that was conducive for its staff members to promote participation. Not surprisingly therefore, the three WUAs that were promoted by the

ID—Akala, Kanipur and Banji—were amongst the worst performers when it came to farmers' participation and good democratic governance of the WUA. Among the remaining five that received some capacity-building support from NGOs, Neemkheda and Bamandi, could not sustain the participation of farmers because the NGOs failed to institutionalize participatory practices and strengthen the mechanisms that enabled participation. These two WUAs witnessed a steady decline in farmer participation in irrigation management and a corresponding resurgence of the ID's control over all crucial responsibilities. The three WUAs that were supported by NGOs that focused not only on building the capacity of the WUAs, but also institutionalized democratic behaviour during the initial years, succeeded in having their irrigation operations completely controlled by the farmers even after the NGOs withdrew their involvement.

To sum up, genuine decentralization of irrigation management responsibilities is likely to improve not only resource utilization in terms of benefit generation but also improve equitable access among those who have entitlements. However, the process of decentralization needs to be taken to a level where there is democratic devolution of decision-making rights from the public agency (the ID) to the resource users' institution (the WUA). This requires external support and capacity-building inputs by an agency that has social organizing competency as well as the readiness to proportionately disengage from irrigation operations at the WUA level.

The relationship between decentralization and poverty is evident, even if it is indirect. There is evidence to show that the process of decentralization does result in augmenting the resource and thus in generating more income in a sustainable way. The benefit stream also does reach the poorest, not as a consequence of decentralization per se, but as a result of increased wealth creation and an incipient democratic ethos that influences the way the additional wealth is distributed.

4

Resource Management and Poverty in Gujarat's and Madhya Pradesh's Inland Fisheries: Hopeful Opportunities and Hard Realities

Jharna Pathak

1. Introduction

Fish production in India increased from 2,444 thousand tonnes in 1981–82 to 8,290 thousand tonnes in 2010–11. In 2010–11, inland fish constituted 61 per cent of total fish production while marine sources made up the balance. Over time, the share of fish production from marine sources declined from 59 per cent (1,445 thousand tons of the total production of 2,444 thousand tons) in 1981–82 to 39 per cent in 2010–11 (3,220 thousand tons out of the total fish production of 8290 thousand tons) (provisional figures, GoI, 2005). An upsurge in inland fishing in reservoirs, lakes, ponds, rivers and canals has been witnessed since 1999–2000. Scholars argue that India's marine fisheries' production has reached a plateau and, at best, only a marginal increase can be predicted in the near future (Sinha and Katiha, 2002). They suggest that much of the increase in demand for fish will have to be met by increasing production from the inland sector.

Reservoir fishing, along with riverine fishing and aquaculture, has been the main source of inland fish production. Reservoir fishing lies half way between capture fishing, in which wild fish held in some form of common ownership are caught, and aquaculture, which involves the active rearing of fish held in private ownership. The capture-cum-culture fisheries studied here use varying degrees of resource enhancement and management, usually stocking of fingerlings from hatcheries in water bodies (e.g., reservoirs) which previously did not support fishing activities. Worldwide, large reservoir projects prioritize drinking water followed by irrigation use, industrial use, generating hydropower, flood control and water storage. As a result, fish capture and culture practices in large reservoirs get the least priority. Thus, the productivity of fish production in large reservoirs has been lower than that of small inland water bodies.

Marothia (2012: 163) notes that these multi-use common water bodies constitute an important component of community assets in India and are used as a traditional commons to meet the food and livelihood needs of many communities. In many states, efforts have been made to design efficient policies and governance regimes for sustaining inland fishing. Like other cooperatives, IFCs have been formed in Indian reservoirs to make communities responsible for managing fishing activities in view of the failure of the government to do so. Theoretically, the creation of FCs recognizes the need for direct control by local end-users over the utilization and management of fish resources. The FC as an institution needs therefore to be designed to take care of (a) productivity, (b) equity, (c) sustainability, (d) the need for democratic decentralization and (e) the participation of users in managing reservoir fishing. As these objectives are interconnected, it makes it difficult to study the impact of the FCs. FCs can adapt to their changing environment and devise rules shaped by principles that have evolved over time.

The impact of FCs on poverty depends on the initial level of poverty, the extent of dependence on the fish resource and the size of the resource. The biggest challenge for the FCs that we studied has been to strike a balance between the short-run objective of increasing the income of communities depending on fishing and the long-run objective of maintaining equity and sustainability in the use of the fish resource.

Given this context, the successful management of a reservoir fishery by an FC depended both on the natural rate of regeneration of fish as well as adherence to the rules to be observed by individual FC members in harvesting fish from the reservoir. Also, technological extension services for enhancing production, prohibition against the use of trawl nets, destructive techniques such as the use of explosives and toxins, or the use of electronic locating and positioning devices, prohibition against catching certain sizes of fish in certain seasons for sustainable reproduction and adequate storage, transportation and marketing facilities for selling fish have encouraged fishermen to participate in the activities of their FCs.

The GoI (2005) has given first preference to fishing cooperative societies to lease large scale reservoirs. They can only be leased out to others if the FCs do not bid for leasing in the reservoir. Reservoir fishing in Gujarat and MP has been managed under a cooperative governance structure—an internal institutional structure model with a distributed governance system.[1] In MP, the Madhya Pradesh Fish Federation (MPFF) manages FCs formed in large irrigation projects while the Fisheries Department (FD) is in charge of the FCs for medium and minor water bodies. Traditional fishing communities and Bangladeshi refugees were given preference to form cooperative societies. Gujarat's FD manages the affairs of FCs formed in large irrigation projects while other fishing grounds are managed by the local panchayats. For reservoir fishing, Gujarat has given preference to displaced tribals who form a cooperative society to purchase the lease of the reservoir. This study compares the processes followed in the formation and operation of FCs in Gujarat and MP. While this kind of reservoir fishing research has been neglected, it is vital for assessing the performance of the FCs in managing the resource.

---

[1] Three alternative internal governance structures are associated with fishing cooperative management, namely, self-organizing institution, cooperative management and communal management (Townsend and Pooley, 1995). Institutional arrangements or working rules defined who can control the resource and how the technologies are applied. They also define the extent of the property rights regime over resources (for details see Marothia, 1997).

2. Context and Theory

2.1. Problems in Reservoir Fishing

The physical characteristics of fish and the water body, the socio-cultural environment of users and the institutional arrangements for managing fish production and associated activities are the most important factors in determining the productivity of reservoirs. Jyotishi and Parthasarathy (2007) note that reservoir fishing in India requires special attention because it is often the main source for domestic consumption and provides full-time employment to two million people and part time employment to another four million. The relative importance of inland capture fisheries has been declining along with a corresponding increase in culture fisheries. Only proper institutional, technical and financial support can contribute to the fulfilment of the multiple developmental goals involved.

Though considerable research has been carried out in the marine biological sciences, economic information on various aspects of inland fish cultivation has seldom appeared in the literature. Sinha and Katiha (2002: 65) have shown that medium and large reservoirs have on average a poorer yield compared with smaller ones. Mishra (1987: 41–98) in his studies of fishing in tanks and ponds in West Bengal emphasizes poaching as a major constraint. The erratic and inadequate stocking of quality fish seed or fingerlings, the uncertainties involved in fish production, the existence of middlemen, lack of governmental incentives, the sale of undersized fish and the lack of proper transport and marketing facilities are considered by poor fishermen to be major inhibiting factors. Sinha and Jha (1997: 65) have emphasized the need for effective planning of stocks, community management of the resource and training of fishermen in improved methods of fish rearing, catching and storage.

2.2. Common Property Resource and Fishing

Gordon (1954: 137) believed that fisheries would be plagued by the dual problems of low income among fishermen and overfishing because he thought that (a) individual self-interest would override the best interests of the community as a whole, (b) the environment was limited and (c) the resource was collectively owned and freely open to any user. Bland and Donda (1995) noted that the fisheries sector acts as an employer of last resort with low entry barriers and high exit barriers for people with low opportunity costs. Ecological conditions and locational factors create distributional effects among fishermen (Platteau et al., 1985: 36).

An FAO study (1993: 93) has shown that a small-scale fishery which has regulations laid out for those allowed to fish is often inflexible, costly in terms of monitoring and enforcement, subject to political interference and lacking in communication between resource users and managers. Sultana, Paul and Thompson (2007: 537) point out that if institutional arrangements can be developed with a local flavour, then benefits like greater empowerment of participant communities can be achieved.

Developing community-based management in fishing is not without hitches. Various researchers like Samal and Meher (2003) and Rahim et al. (1992) have over the years highlighted the sorry plight of fishermen and lamented the degradation of CPRs. They have written extensively to point out how powerful special interest groups have marginalized local small-scale fishermen.

2.3. Poverty and Fishing

It has been a common assumption that small-scale fishermen are poor and that development initiatives in small-scale fisheries set in place by governments, donors and NGOs could contribute to the reduction of poverty. But the truth is that the issue of poverty has never been addressed directly (World Bank, 1982 in Bene et al., 2000).

The issue of a single measure for the multidimensional concept of poverty poses a great challenge to understanding the implementation of FC projects. The World Development Report (2001), however, enlarged the traditional conception of poverty (where income/expenditure is below a certain level) by associating low levels of achievement in education, health and nutrition and high levels of vulnerability and powerlessness with low levels of income/expenditure. Irrespective of the definition of poverty used by various scholars, poor households derive less benefit from fishing compared to non-poor households (Reddy, 2001).

It is well documented in the literature that (a) the extent of dependence on the resource by the community (Ballabh et al., 1988), (b) the size of the benefits accruing from the fish resource (ibid.) and (c) the sustainability of the benefits of the FC (Sinha and Jha, 1997: 65) influence the participation of fishermen in FC activities. Although there is strong theoretical and empirical evidence suggesting the conditions for the success or failure of FCs in poverty reduction, designing policies to create local institutions for managing natural resources still remains a challenge (Rahim et al., 1992). Some studies like Gupta et al. (1999) point out that the benefits may be skewed in favour of the wealthier sections of fishing communities and that equity and poverty are largely determined by mediating institutions.

Samal and Meher (2003: 3319–25) have shown that income from fishing is higher for households that are not primarily engaged in fishing than it is for those dependent solely on fishing. Unfortunately for the poor, in almost all studies, the existence of successful common property regimes is shown to be steadily declining (Beck and Nesmith, 2001: 119–33).

FAO (1993) study has pointed out that certain factors may impede the successful establishment and sustainable working of community-based management systems, such as the lack of fishing communities' competence to take on a management role, the difficulties in determining boundaries between different groups of users (including non-fishermen), the unwillingness of politicians to divest power and the already high levels of capitalization of many fisheries.

The remoteness and marginalization of reservoir fishermen suggests that they consumed their produce locally or sell it in the local market, but this is not recorded in government statistics. Also, there have been no studies of poor fishermen being targeted for assistance through projects or programmes. The existing literature contains no systematic and comprehensive study of the extent, nature, causes and dynamics of poverty in fishing communities.

There is very limited understanding of the impact on poverty of FCs and alternative fishery management regimes.

Currently, financial and resource sustainability-related problems are making the GoI realize the importance of community-managed organizations. Some have been formed on the initiative of fishermen, while others have been created by sheer political will or external pressures. The FCs have evolved through various bottom-up[2] and top-down[3] approaches to resource management. Gujarat and MP, two states in western India, have followed these diverse approaches respectively in forming FCs and managing inland fishing in large scale reservoirs. In this context, the present chapter uses case studies of FCs in both states and a FF as a lens through which the impact of community-based institutions on poverty and equity can be viewed and understood.

The remainder of this chapter is organized as follows: section 3 outlines the objectives and framework of analysis while section 4 discusses the methodology and limitations of the study. Section 5 elaborates upon the structure of FCs in Ukai and Gandhi Sagar reservoirs and section 6 presents snapshots of the formation and functioning of the six FCs to be studied. Section 7 examines assets owned as well as the income and expenditure patterns of fishermen's households. Sections 8 and 9 conclude the chapter and discuss the way forward, respectively.

3. Objectives and Conceptual Framework

3.1. Objectives

As with other resource users, the hypothesis that governs the FCs is that increased participation and decision-making by fishermen in the FCs would improve the benefits emanating from the

---

[2] The bottom-up approach implies proactive members as participating in the management of the resource. The advantage of this approach is that it encourages members to become involved in and think more creatively about FC management. Bottom-up project management can also be viewed as a way of coping with the increasing gap between the information necessary to manage resources and the ability of managers to acquire and apply this information.

[3] The top-down approach means that the resources are managed by the government.

resources managed by the FCs. In order to test this hypothesis, this chapter examines: first, the process of decentralizing fish resource management from a central authority to end-users; second, the extent to which FCs have affected poverty and achieved equity in sharing benefits and third the policy implications needed for tapping the full potential of FCs on a sustained basis. Various states in India practice diverse institutional arrangements in managing inland fishing. This chapter examines two such arrangements, namely those practised in Gujarat and MP, at two points of time, that is, before and after the formation of the FC. The empirical realities presented and discussed will serve to create a conceptual framework (such as that used by Bandaragoda and Firdousi, 1992: 28) within which the impact of community participation, poverty and equity can be examined.

Ideally, in FCs, as in other cooperatives, the management and control of the resource along with its benefits vests directly in the hands of the users. The structured behaviour of the FCs is related to all external and internal constraints. Even under these constraints, there are certain controllable variables, which when influenced, could impact the performance of the FCs in terms of increasing incomes, reducing poverty, bringing about equity in benefit sharing and a sustainable fish harvest.

Since the cooperatives in both states were already in operation for five years, we tried to address questions pertaining to the situation before and after the formation of the FC. As in the other studies in this volume, these questions included:

1. At the village level, how was the FC project and institution introduced?
2. How did the project and institution perform, both de jure and de facto, in terms of CNRM goals?
3. What was the extent of productivity and income?
4. How decentralized and inclusive was the governance of the FC institution?
5. What has been the impact on the poor members of the village?
6. How integrated was the project intervention and what was the extent of the outreach?
7. How has the project and institution contributed to effective, equitable and sustainable resource management?

4. Methodology, Sampling and Data Collection

The procedure for selecting sites for the study involved various steps. The first step was to select inland fishing sites in Gujarat and MP having FCs functioning for the past five years (2004–09). Following the Fisheries Policy of the GoG, FCs were mandatorily formed in large scale irrigation projects. Thus, selecting a large-scale irrigation project became a vital step in selecting the site. FCs formed in the Ukai reservoir in Gujarat and the Gandhi Sagar reservoir in MP were selected for study following more or less a similar methodology as adopted by the other studies presented here. Basically an FC having not less than five years' experience in managing the resource was taken as the unit of analysis.

Given the specificity of a fish resource, the location of the FCs was vital for analyzing the dependence on the resource. Keeping this in mind, we distributed the Gujarat and MP samples of 270 households each on the basis of three locations of FCs in the reservoir, that is, 90 households in each of the head, middle and tail portions of the reservoir. We selected the Songadh FC in the head, the Ravjibunda FC in the middle and the Tokarva FC in the tail reach of the Ukai reservoir. Similarly, the Gandhi Sagar, Rampuriya and Sanjit FCs were selected from the corresponding locations in the Gandhi Sagar reservoir for our MP sample households.

One point that requires mention is that unlike the Gandhi Sagar reservoir, where all the fishermen of one village constituted an FC, the FCs formed in the Ukai reservoir included more than one village. Fishermen from the Songadh and Ravjibunda FCs were spread across nine villages each and the Tokarva FC consisted of fishermen from 11 villages. Random sampling of fishing households with the highest number of members in the FC was used for the selection of the households. In the event of a shortage of the required number of households, the village with the second highest number of fishing members was selected and so on. Consequently, in Gujarat we selected the following villages: Juni Bavli, Juna Amalpada and Serula from the Songadh FC, Ravjibunda, Bhitkhurd and Dhaj from the Ravjibunda FC and Tokarva and Aamkuti from the Tokarva FC. Thus, our total sample of 270 fishing households of Gujarat was spread across eight villages in Ukai but only three villages in Gandhi Sagar.

The reference year for our study was 2009 and the performance of fishing management by a community and its impact on poverty was compared with that in the year 2004 when the FD was managing fishing activities in Gujarat and MP, FGDs were carried out prior to the selection of FCs and their villages. A primary survey was carried out to collect information on the socio-economic characteristics of fishermen, fish species and their market rates, cost and related information like the number and size of fishing vessels, gear type, employment days, fishing time, expenditure on fishing and non-fishing assets, income earned from fishing and other economic activities and so on. To understand the impact of the participation of fishermen in FCs on poverty, information was collected on (a) household socio-economic indicators, (b) awareness of fishermen about FCs and their participation in FC-related activities, (c) the attitude of fishermen towards managing the fish resource, (d) problems faced by fishermen and (e) additional support required by fishermen. This list is only indicative of the items of information collected for our study. We also tried to address the extent of dependence of fishermen on fishing activities before and after the formation of the FC. A comparison of their livelihoods with and without the intervention or pre-project and post-project status comparison would have helped in addressing our research questions. However, all of India's large scale reservoirs had already formed FCs. Thus, the non-availability of a reservoir without FCs and the non-availability of base line data pertaining to the pre-project status made us depend on information obtained from different stakeholders based on their memory. It should be noted that there were exogenous variables like soil quality, climate, topography and a number of physiographic parameters that affected the link between the FCs and poverty, but these were outside the scope of this study.

Despite such limitations, the present analysis tries to examine the process of decentralization and its impact on the income and poverty status of communities depending on it. The project in both states, by design, excluded non-FC members, who may or may not

Image 4.1

Ukai Reservoir at Dusk

Image 4.2

High Value Fish: Catla, Rohu, Mrigal and Kati

Source: John R. Wood.

Source: John R. Wood.

Image 4.3

A Fishing Family of Ravjibunda Village

Source: John R. Wood.

Image 4.4

Gandhi Sagar: A Day's Fish Catch

Source: Kairav Trivedi.

Image 4.5

Loading Fish Crates at Rampuriya

Source: Kairav Trivedi.

have constituted a major part of the poor. In Gujarat, the Ukai FC project excluded non-STs and thus opened opportunities for illegal harvesting of fish by non-members of FCs. When the Ukai FCs failed to prevent non-member fishermen from using trawl nets and prohibited fish harvesting practices, the benefits to non-FC members was greater than that for FC members. In MP just as in Gujarat, the project excluded households that were not displaced by the dam and yet were traditionally from the area. These households were allowed to fish in the periphery of the reservoir thereby setting a limit to their fish harvest and income earned from fishing.

5. Structure of the FFs and FCs

5.1. Structure of the FFs: Ukai Reservoir, Gujarat and Gandhi Sagar Reservoir, MP

Across the two states, dependence on the type and extent of fishing carried out varied considerably. For example, only 11 per cent of the total fish production in Gujarat came from inland waters while in MP it was 100 per cent dependent on inland fishing (GoI, 1994). Thus, the use of inland water bodies for commercial production was hardly known in Gujarat, whereas in MP, inland fishing was the sole source of fishing. As the importance of inland fishing in the two states was different, intervention activities by the governments in each state also varied, creating different impacts on the livelihoods of the communities dependent on them. We will be using in-depth analysis of our FC case-studies in the Ukai and Gandhi Sagar reservoirs to show how the two regimes affected the incomes and livelihoods of fishermen in Gujarat and MP respectively.

Ukai, the reservoir selected for study in Gujarat, is the largest reservoir among seven large reservoirs in the state, with an average FRL (full reservoir level) of 20,145 ha. In MP, the Gandhi Sagar reservoir is one of the 13 large scale irrigation projects and the average FRL in Gandhi Sagar covered 41,317 ha, roughly double the size of the Ukai reservoir. This had implications for fish catches and the stakes of the fishermen and governments in managing the resource.

The de jure control of the Ukai reservoir rested with the Gujarat state government. In Gandhi Sagar, FCs formed by fishermen managed the resource under the control of the MP government. The diverse management practices of the two states shaped the structural form of FCs in the two reservoirs. As tribal communities got preference to lease in the reservoir according to the Fisheries Act, tribal fishermen came together to form FCs. In Ukai, the FCs were broadly organized at two levels: the primary level and the secondary level. At the primary level were cooperative societies with individual fishermen as members, while a FF was formed at the secondary level with the FCs as members. The FCs got federated to FFs that were strategically formed to mobilize capital to pay the FD for the lease, increase the bargaining power of fishermen, boost sales, create better marketing services and provide the benefits of economies to scale. At the time of the Ukai FCs formation, how the FCs were to obtain funds to pay the lease amount and address other issues like externalities like illegal fishing were left to be seen.

Over the years, reservoir fishing in MP has witnessed a change in the institutional regime managing the fish resource. Originally, it was managed by the state government and then it was transferred to the Madhya Pradesh Fish Development Corporation (MPFDC). The MPFDC continued to manage fishing in the reservoir until 2005. In 2005, overexploitation of the resource led to a transfer of management from MPFDC to the MPFF. The MPFF was formed as an apex organization federating all the FCs in all the major large scale reservoirs of the state. It was headed by a bureaucrat appointed by the state. The government made the formation of FCs mandatory by enacting a law. Each FC had its own committee including a president and a secretary. The presidents of the FCs became members of the MPFF who then elected the president of the MPFF. Major decisions, such as the selection of the contractor, fixing fish rates, deferred wages and bonuses, were taken by the MPFF and implemented by the FCs.

In both states, the FCs managed the accounts. The FCs in MP paid deferred wages to their members during the monsoon season (July and August), when there was no fishing activity. The MPFF took all the major decisions related to the stocking and distribution of profits in the form of bonuses, choice of contractor to market fish and the fish rates (₹17 per kg was the prevailing fish rate fixed). Out of this, fishermen contributed ₹0.50 per kg of fish catch towards the administrative and maintenance expenditure of the cooperative, ₹1.50 towards deferred wages and so on. To sum up, fishing policy had treated fishing in reservoirs of large scale multipurpose dams as a CPR whose management rested with the tribal communities (Gujarat) or indigenous communities (MP) who were displaced by the dams. Gujarat and MP followed different approaches towards the formation of their FCs. The size of the resource and its relative importance shaped these approaches and the role of each state in managing them.

5.2. Profile of Fishing Cooperatives: Ukai Reservoir, Gujarat

Out of 13 cooperatives formed in the Ukai reservoir, we carried out a detailed study of three FCs. A snapshot of these three cooperatives is given below:

5.2.1. The Songadh Fishing Cooperative

The Songadh cooperative, one of 13 FCs formed in the Ukai reservoir got registered in 1992 (Table 4.1). It was located in the head reach of the reservoir and included fishermen from nine villages namely Juni Bavli, Budhvada, Juna Amalpada, Serula, Chacharbunda, Navi Ukai, Siletvel, Limbdi and Juni Shavkashi. As no individual FC could purchase the lease of the fishing ground from the FD, all the Ukai FCs came together to form an FF named Songadh Matsya Mahasangh under the leadership of elders from Songadh village. However, the FF defaulted in paying the lease to the department and remained non-functional. In 2004, Ukai fishermen made a second attempt to come together to re-form the FCs and created a new FF named Tokarva Matsya Mahasangh under the leadership of Tokarva village.

We studied three villages of Songadh cooperative in detail: Juni Bavli, Juna Amalpada and Serula. The majority of households in these villages belonged to the STs who were 'oustees' displaced from their villages during the construction of the Ukai dam. They fitted the pattern often described in India's burgeoning literature on the alienation of marginalized communities, including STs, from natural resources like land, water and forests on which their livelihoods depended (see Lobo and Kumar, 2009: 112–20). The government had promised to compensate these oustees by allotting 5 acres of land and the right to fish in the reservoir. Households that received land as compensation were dissatisfied with the inferior quality of their new land, which was located in distant places. They chose instead to stay near the reservoir rather than cultivate the land given by the state.

A committee of 11 members, led by a president and secretary managed the affairs of the Songadh cooperative. The president and secretary were unanimously elected by the committee members. Committee members were selected on the basis of their representation of their cluster of residence. Discussions with the president indicated that the fishermen did not cooperate in managing the FC. Their past experience of forming an FC and failing to manage it loomed large in the minds of the Songadh FC fishermen. Rather than trying to correct past errors, they showed an overall lack of interest in the affairs of the FC. They nevertheless followed important FC rules such as stopping fishing during the monsoons and not catching juvenile fish.

The majority of government schemes, such as free housing or subsidies on boats and nets were routed through the FFs. Our discussion with fishermen indicated that since in the past the federation had largely been controlled by fishermen from Songadh village, a large number of households residing in this village received the benefit of such schemes. With the change in leadership to Tokarva village, the Songadh fishermen no longer enjoyed the preferential treatment that they did in the past. Like the other FCs, fishermen of Songadh had to struggle constantly against illegal fishing from within and outside their jurisdiction, mainly by fishermen from Maharashtra. Reduction in benefits for FC members from government schemes and the FC's inability to check unlawful fishing practices led fishermen to defy FC rules. Sensing a loss of control by the FC over reservoir fishing, the fishermen were discouraged from becoming FC members. At the time of the survey there were only 158 members, which was small compared to earlier numbers. Some Songadh fishermen told us that only the lure of subsidized nets and boats made them want to continue with their FC membership. Most of the fishermen complained about the nexus between the contractor and FF committee members. Serula fishermen argued that leaders of the FCs and FF lacked the technical know-how and managerial skills necessary to lead the fishermen. Such discontentment had weakened the cohesiveness within the FCs formed in the FF, having adverse financial implications for their functioning.

5.2.2. *The Ravjibunda Fishing Cooperative*

The Ravjibunda Fishing Cooperative was formed in the middle reach of the Ukai reservoir. It was registered in 1992 (Table 4.1). A general body meeting was called where the leaders explained to the villagers the need and value of forming the FC and FF. The fishermen really had no choice but to agree to the request made by their leaders. This led to the formation of the Ravjibunda FC covering eight villages.

The Ravjibunda FC had a total of 210 fishing members. The number of actual fishermen was greater than the number who were FC members. The president of the Ravjibunda Cooperative was also a committee member of the FF. The challenges faced by the Ravjibunda FCs were more or less the same as those faced by the Songadh FC, such as illegal fishing, illegal selling of fish in the open market, etc.

Members and even committee members in all these villages were irregular in attending meetings of the committee to discuss day-to-day problems related to the functioning of the FCs. Only the lure of obtaining benefits like free housing schemes or subsidies for boats and nets compelled some fishermen to associate with the FC. Discussions with fishermen indicated that there was a need for FCs to pressurize the FD to stock fingerlings of high-valued fish species like Rohu and Catla, which were almost on the verge of extinction. According to Kartha and Rao (1993: 14), there is a strong correlation between the fish yield and stocking density. However, the Ravjibunda FC president noted that lack of information on the stocking of fish, the exploitation of stocked fish and the degree to which stocking rates were adjusted to the natural carrying capacity of the reservoir made the management of fishing difficult.

5.2.3. *The Tokarva Fishing Cooperative*

The Tokarva Fishing Cooperative was formed in the tail reach of the reservoir, close to Gujarat's border with Maharashtra, and was registered in 1992 (Table 4.1). No general body meeting was organized in the village to explain the reasons and procedure for forming the FC and FF. Fishermen who engaged in fishing in the reservoir were enrolled as FC members. The Tokarva FC had a membership of 102 fishermen from 11 villages.

The president of the Tokarva Cooperative was concerned about the general lack of interest of the committee members in the functioning of the FCs and complained about the lack of control of the FF over FC activities. Like the other Ukai FCs, lack of interest of members in FC activities and the inability of the FCs to monitor fishing activity weakened the working capital base. The weak capital base and inability of the FCs and FF to raise funds from external sources made the FF dependent on a contractor for buying the lease of the fishing ground. Potentially, this left the lucrative fishery open for exploitation by any unscrupulous contractor who was neither a fisherman by birth nor by occupation. Table 4.1 is a profile of the study cooperatives of Ukai Reservoir in Gujarat.

To sum up, in the Ukai cooperatives, fishermen showed little interest in the functioning of the FCs. The inability of the Ukai FCs to stop illegal fishing discouraged cooperative behaviour amongst member fishermen. They failed to develop a long term fishery strategy and their lack of credibility added to member indifference. It appears that the routing of government schemes through the FCs was the only attraction for members to continue their membership in the Ukai FCs. This clearly reflected the failure of members to actively participate in the decision-making processes.

Table 4.1

Profile of the Study Cooperatives/Villages: Ukai Reservoir, Gujarat

Detail	Juni Bavli	Juna Amalpada	Serula	Ravjibunda-Haripur	Bhikhurd	Dhaj	Tokarva	Amkuti
Name of the FC	Songadh cooperative			Ravjibunda cooperative			Tokarva cooperative	
Location of the FC	Head			Middle			Tail	
Name of the taluka	Songadh			Uchchal				
Revenue or forest village	Forest	Forest	Revenue	Forest	Revenue	Revenue	Revenue	Revenue
No. of households	110	180	202	230	664	65	310	150
Total population	560	789	910	995	3,096	274	1,150	975
Caste (%)	ST: 91 OBC: 9	ST: 87 OBC: 13	ST: 89 OBC: 11	ST: 88 OBC: 12	ST: 100	ST: 100	ST: 84 OBC: 16	ST: 88 OBC: 12
Nearest town (and distance in km.)	Ukai (13)	Ukai (15)	Ukai (18)	Navapur (6)	Navapur (6)	Navapur (8)	Navapur (9)	Navapur (10)
% of households engaged in fishing	70%	70%	75%	80%	80%	85%	85%	80%
Sources of income (arranged in descending order)	AH; C; AL; Oth; F	AH; C; AL; Oth; F	AH; C; AL; F	AH; C; AL; F	AH; C; AL; F	AH; C; AL; F	AH; C; AL; F	AH; C; AL; F

Source: Field survey, (2009).

Notes: Number in parentheses is the distance (in kms) from the nearest town.

AH = animal husbandry, C = cultivation; AL = agricultural labour, Oth = others (self-employed as carpenter, plumber, shopkeeper, etc.); F = fishing.

5.3. Profile of Fishing Cooperatives: Gandhi Sagar Reservoir, Madhya Pradesh

5.3.1. The Gandhi Sagar Fishing Cooperative

The structure of the Gandhi Sagar reservoir FCs was the same for all cooperatives formed in all major irrigation projects of MP, and hence little scope existed for any individual FC to vary its functioning. The head reach FC formed in the Gandhi Sagar reservoir was called the head-reach FC (Table 4.2). It was formed by fishermen of Gandhi Sagar village located 29 km away from the nearest town, Bhanpura in Mandsaur district. Nearly all (98%) of the households were Bengali Muslims from Bangladesh who took refuge in India and were rehabilitated in this village. They were given the right to fish in the reservoir along with the oustees of the dam. This village was a forest village, but only three months before our survey, Gandhi Sagar reverted to the status of a revenue village. Thus, no fishermen owned or cultivated any land in the village. A majority of the households were dependent on fishing for their primary source of income. It was surprising to find that the initial level of poverty in this village was low compared to the villages of Gujarat.

The Gandhi Sagar dam was constructed in 1960 and fishing here started in 1962. During our FGDs, we learned that villagers were not consulted before the formation of the FC. Fishing in the reservoir guaranteed membership in the FCs. A majority of FC members were unaware about the institutional change that occurred during the switch from MPFDC to MPFF control. However, they were aware about who their contractor was and about FC rules such as the selling price of fish, deferred wages[4] and bonus.[5] They consider themselves more as labourers working for the contractor than as equal partners in reservoir fishing.

The control of operations by the contractor was effective in checking illegal fishing by non-members, restricting the use of small

---

[4] Since no fishing was allowed during the monsoon, fishermen received a deferred payment of ₹0.50 per kg from the state government.

[5] FC committee members and the membership decided on a percentage of the profits of the FC to be paid out as a bonus to all members at the end of each financial year.

nets and explosive devices and confining the sale of fish to the FCs. The fishermen complained that the inadequate release of fingerlings in the reservoir along with the unchecked pressure of the fishing population in the reservoir had led to a decline in high-valued fish. Some of the villagers were unhappy with the nexus between the FD and the contractor which they said had reduced the level of FC control over the resource to only managing accounts and resolving conflicts amongst members. Some members furiously argued that the functioning of the FCs and FFs would only improve if the FD helped fishermen directly by monitoring fishing activities, stocking high-valued fingerlings and providing facilities like cold storage.

The President of the Gandhi Sagar FC was elected unopposed by the members of the FC. The EC consisting of nine members was selected by the members in a general body meeting. Apart from managing the accounts and collaborating with the FD for monitoring its own members and accessing various government schemes, the FC and its EC had no management responsibilities or role in the decision-making processes. Consequently, the FC lacked any long-term strategy for the development of the fishery. This was true for other FCs also.

Deferred wages along with bonuses and small credit were the only links that bound members together. They did generate members' interest in attending the FC meetings and kept them aware about the accounts and queries raised about the functioning of the FC in the general body meeting. Conflicts regarding low fish rates or illegal fishing did arise during these meetings. However, there was no evidence of any interaction between fishermen and the FD about the functioning of the Gandhi Sagar FC. This was true for other FCs also.

5.3.2. *The Rampuriya Fishing Cooperative*

The population of Rampuriya, an FC located in the middle reach of the Gandhi Sagar reservoir was 610. A majority of the FC households (75%) belonged to the SCs and the rest to the Muslim community. This village was a forest village, so members did not own land. Most of the households were mainly dependent on fishing for their livelihood.

As in the Gandhi Sagar FC, the Rampuriya FC fishermen were also not informed about the change in the institutional regime for managing the reservoir. A majority of households were aware of the rules of the FC, including deferred wages but few were aware about the process for selecting a contractor and the role of the FF in managing FC activities.

Like the fishermen of the Gandhi Sagar FC, Rampuriya fishermen were also unhappy about the contractor's interference and complained that the FC must succumb to decisions taken by the FF. They noted that the FD had reduced the stocking of high-valued fish, namely Rohu, Catla and Mrigal. Only their concern for deferred wages and bonuses had retained their interest in attending any meeting about financial transactions.

5.3.3. The Sanjit Fishing Cooperative

Sanjit was a revenue village located in the tail reach of the reservoir. A total of 2,861 persons resided in the village. Nearly 90 per cent of the population belonged to the Muslim community while the rest were STs. Fishing was the major source of household income but the extent of dependence on it was less compared to the two other cooperatives. Apart from fishing, which provided the main source of income, some Sanjit fishermen owned and cultivated land.

Like other FCs formed in the Gandhi Sagar reservoir, deferred wages and bonuses were the major attractions for fishermen to attend the general body meeting. They faced more or less the same challenges as those faced by the other FCs of the Gandhi Sagar reservoir. Table 4.2 presents a comparison of the Gandhi Sagar FCs.

To summarize, the FCs formed in the Ukai and Gandhi Sagar reservoirs faced several common problems, such as (a) weak capacity in technical skills, (b) generally low levels of innovation and flexibility (partly due to their dependency on government officials), (c) limited access to markets, (d) little or no linkages to commercial financial institutions and general weaknesses in accessing credit services, (e) weak commercial linkages with the other FCs operating in the reservoir and across all the large scale

Table 4.2

Profile of the Fishing Cooperatives/Villages: Gandhi Sagar Reservoir, MP

Name of the village	Gandhi Sagar	Rampuriya	Sanjit
Name of the FC	Gandhi Sagar	Rampuriya	Sanjit
Location of the FC	Head	Middle	Tail
Name of the taluka	Bhanpura	Neemunch	Neemunch
Revenue or forest village	Forest/Revenue	Forest	Revenue
No. of households	546	127	472
Total population	2,750	610	2,861
Caste (% of total population)	Muslims: 98% SC: 2%	SC: 75% Muslims: 25%	Muslims: 90% ST: 10%
Nearest town (and distance in km.)	Bhanpura (29 km.)	Neemunch (40 km.)	Neemunch (65 km.)
% of households engaged in fishing	100%	100%	100%
Sources of income (arranged in descending order)	Fishing	Fishing, non-agricultural labour	Fishing, non-agricultural & agricultural labour

Source: Field survey, (2009).

reservoirs of their state and (f) lack of a long-term strategy. Easy access to external sources of credit to pay the lease had prevented FCs in Ukai from operating as member-owned business units, and had also reduced the importance of mobilizing their own resources. In the Gandhi Sagar reservoir, government officials had developed a nexus with unscrupulous contractors who worked to serve their own self-interest by taking advantage of lacunae in the by-laws. All of these problems set the constraints within which the FCs operated.

5.4. Profile of the FC Study Households: Ukai Reservoir, Gujarat and Gandhi Sagar Reservoir, MP

In Gujarat, 270 households were surveyed from the three FCs covering eight villages of the Ukai Reservoir (Junibavli, Juna Amalpada and Serula from the Songadh FCs, Ravjibunda, Bhitkhurd and Dhaj from the Ravjibunda FCs and Tokarva

Table 4.3

Characteristics of the Study FC Households: Ukai Reservoir, Gujarat

Name of the FC	Songadh	Ravjibunda	Tokarva	Total
Name of villages studied	1. Junibavli 2. Juna Amalpada 3. Serula	1. Ravjibunda 2. Bhitkhurd 3. Dhaj	1. Tokarva 2. Aamkuti	
Sample size (N)/ location in reservoir	90/head	90/middle	90/tail	270
Forest/Revenue village	Junibavli and Juna Amalpada are forest villages and Serula is a revenue village	Revenue	Revenue	
Displaced (oustees) community	100.0%	100.0%	100.0%	100.0
Reasons for displacement:				
Construction of dam and reservoir	100.0%	100.0%	100.0%	100.0
Population (N)				
Total population	469	455	476	1400
Average family size	5.2	5.0	5.3	5.1
Caste				
ST	100.0	100.0	100	100.0

Source: Field survey, (2009).

and Aamkuti from the Tokarva FCs). The total population of the villages under study in Gujarat was 1,400 and the average family size was five persons per household (Table 4.3). All of the households were oustees displaced from villages that got submerged during the construction of the Ukai dam and reservoir. Caste-wise analysis shows that 100 per cent of the households belonged to the STs.

The total population of our sample households in the Gandhi Sagar reservoir was 1,712 with an average family size of 6.3 which was higher than their counterparts in Gujarat (Table 4.4). Caste-wise analysis shows that nearly 64 per cent of the Gandhi Sagar reservoir households belonged to the SCs, 34 per cent to Muslims while the rest were STs (Table 4.4).

Table 4.4

Characteristics of the Study FC Households: Gandhi Sagar Reservoir, MP

Name of the FC	Gandhi Sagar	Rampuriya	Sanjit	Total
Name of villages	Gandhi Sagar	Rampuriya	Sanjit	Total
Sample size (N)/location on reservoir	90/head	90/middle	90/tail	270
Forest/Revenue village	Revenue*	Forest	Revenue	
Displaced community	98.9	98.9	100.0	99.3
Reasons for displacement:				
Construction of dam and reservoir	47.2	30.3	37.8	38.5
Bangladeshi refugees from 1971 war	52.8	69.7	62.2	61.6
Population (N)				
Total population of sample households	532	600	580	1712
Average family size	5.9	6.7	6.4	6.3
Caste (%)				
ST			1.1	1.9
SC	7.8	76.7		64.4
Muslims	92.2	23.3	98.9	33.7

Source: Field survey, (2009).
Note: * Three months from the date of the survey the village was declared a revenue village.

6. The Formation and Functioning of FCs

6.1. FCs in the Ukai Reservoir, Gujarat

As the foregoing FC snapshots reveal, the fishermen of the Gandhi Sagar reservoir were better organized, and as will be detailed below, better off compared to those of Ukai. The question is whether the differences in income and livelihoods could be attributed to the functioning of the FCs, and to what extent.

To answer this question, one has to look closely at the processes that were underlying the formation of the FCs in both the states. FC formation in India was earlier characterized as following a 'top-down' versus a 'bottom-up' approach and it will be shown here that MP followed a top-down approach to fish management while Gujarat adopted a more bottom-up approach. While the government possesses the de jure right to the resource in reservoir fishing, the two states have used this right differently in creating their FCs.

6.2. Comparing the Formation of FCs

Ukai: The functioning and effectiveness of the Ukai FCs usually depended on the process of their evolution. It was clear that the FCs and FF were formed to mobilize capital to pay the lease amount to the FD. However, an improved level of awareness and participation by Ukai fishermen in FC activities could have improved FC management of the fish harvest. Unfortunately, the decision to form an FC was usually made at a meeting attended by the village leaders who were supposed to disseminate information about the FCs to the fishermen. When asked about FC formation, only 44.5 per cent (39.3 + 5.2) of Ukai households said they were informed by the President or/and the Secretary of the FC (Table 4.5). A majority of the rest were informed by friends, neighbours or relatives (55%). This reflects the weak role played by FC leaders in motivating the fishermen. Moreover, where women participated in fishing activity, the proportion of women members in the FCs was almost negligible. Thus, gender did not play an important role in the formation of FCs.

Awareness regarding the Ukai FCs was high amongst the communities. Greater awareness occurred because it was through the FCs that benefits were distributed in the form of providing housing facilities, free nets and loans for boats and so on. As the Ukai FCs were unable to mobilize their own capital for leasing in the fishing ground, they had to explore external sources of borrowing. This was stated by 33 per cent of the households (Table 4.5). Another 43 per cent doubted the intentions of the FCs. They felt that their need for funds to pay the lease amount to the federation was seized as an opportunity by the contractor to secure fish catch at a predetermined price. This response was uniform across the FCs. Inadequate motivation and consultations amongst the fishermen led the latter to doubt the intentions of the FCs. All this would in turn have had considerable bearing on the level of participation.

Table 4.5

Formation of the FCs and Level of Awareness: Ukai Reservoir, Gujarat and Gandhi Sagar Reservoir, MP

Details	Ukai				Gandhi Sagar			
FCs	Songadh	Ravjibunda	Tokarva	Total	Gandhi Sagar	Rampuriya	Sanjit	Total
Awareness about FCs								
Yes*	100.0	100.0	100.0	100.0	68.9	72.2	80.0	73.7
Who informed about the FCs?								
Villagers/relatives	65.6	38.9	61.1	55.2	18.9	23.3	27.8	23.3
President	25.6	54.4	37.8	39.3	8.9	14.4	21.1	14.8
Secretary	8.9	5.6	1.1	5.2	15.6	25.6	33.3	24.8
Others		1.1		0.4	56.6	36.7	17.8	37.1
Why/how was the private contractor hired?								
No idea	34.5	18.4	20.1	24.2	6.7	1.1	11.2	6.3
To mobilize the capital to pay for the lease	23.0	35.7	41.3	33.3				
To properly manage fishing activity					22.2	25.6	21.1	23.0
FF invited the contractor; FC has no control over it					52.6	48.2	47.9	49.6
Nexus with the contractor	42.5	45.9	38.6	42.5	18.5	25.1	19.8	21.1

Source: Field survey, (2009).
* *Note:* The rest were not aware about the FCs.

Gandhi Sagar: The Government of MP had made the granting of fishing rights to FCs mandatory and the FCs were mandated by the FF. Awareness regarding the FCs was quite high amongst the Gandhi Sagar reservoir community members. Table 4.5 shows that the greater awareness (74%) may have been due to benefits accrued from the FCs in the form of bonuses, deferred wages and so on. Our research shows that while some villagers learned about their FC's formation from the President (15%) or the Secretary (25%), an equally high percentage of the households (37 per cent) learned about it from government staff or the contractor. Another 23 per cent received information from their neighbours, relatives and friends. This throws some light on the poor quality of motivational activities carried out in the villages.

Discussions with fishermen indicated that the MP government had only a limited understanding of the principles of cooperatives and had preconceived notions about what was good for the FCs. In its quest to maximize returns from the reservoir, the government marred the democratic process in the FCs and FF by inviting contractors to monitor and market the fish catch. Nearly 50 per cent of the Gandhi Sagar households (see Table 4.5) indicated their negative feelings about this. Another 23 per cent reported that past experience of the FCs' failure to manage fishing encouraged the FF to invite the contractor to take over. Fishermen complained that the government allowed the contractor to restrict the FCs to simple functions like paying bonuses and deferred wages, rather than training and facilitating them to monitor the reservoir, operate a cold storage facility, explore new markets for fish or sell the harvest at a better price and so on. Encouraged by positive relations with officials, a contractor could make a substantial investment to monitor the reservoir and make sure that fishermen honoured their commitment of selling their fish to him. In doing so, the real control rested with the contractor and not the fishermen. The nexus between the government and the contractor was perceived as a problem by 21 per cent of the households. This was true for all the Gandhi Sagar FCs. With the MP government controlling the resource through the contractor, the ability of the FCs to help their members was a question that called for thorough examination.

6.3. Comparing Conformity to FC Rules

Conforming to the rules of the FCs is the first step in promoting the incentive for responsible behaviour in fishermen for achieving the collective outcome. FCs in both states used operational rules in an effort to increase the income of fishermen and promote a sustainable fish harvest. Some of these rules included closure of fishing during the monsoon for two months and the prohibition of catching juvenile fish, using a trawl net or using explosive devices to catch fish. In both states it was necessary to become a member of an FC as well as to sell fish only to the FC (Table 4.6). Most of the rules found common in the FCs formed in both the states, were devised to assure sustainability along with productivity of the fish harvest.

Ukai: Table 4.6 shows that only 27 per cent of the Ukai households reported having sold their fish to the FCs. More or less a similar trend was observed across FCs in the Ukai reservoir. As the monsoon was the breeding season for fish, FCs stopped their members from catching fish from June to August. This was confirmed by 99 per cent of the households. Moreover, 98 per cent said that they did not catch juvenile fish. This suggests that the fishermen were trying to improve the sustainability of the resource. Over 35 per cent of the Ukai households were aware of the reasons for the closure of the reservoir and endorsed it saying that they were going to benefit by a larger fish harvest. The majority of these informed households were in Songadh and Ravjibunda. However, although a majority of the households obeyed the rule of abstaining from fishing during the monsoon, nearly 37 per cent of the households, mainly from the Ravjibunda and Tokarva FCs, did not understand the reason for doing so. This ignorance clearly reflected the poor quality of FC motivational activity.

Even though the use of trawl nets was prohibited in the Ukai reservoir, 27 per cent of the fishermen (100–72.9) used them. The use of trawl nets was marginally higher in Songadh compared to the other two FCs. This indulgence in short-term gains by fishing illegally spoke volumes about the apathy of members and the lack of motivational activity carried out by the FCs. Discussions with fishermen across the Ukai FCs indicated that the FCs lacked the

Table 4.6

Conformity to FC Rules: Ukai Reservoir, Gujarat and Gandhi Sagar Reservoir, MP

Details	Ukai				Gandhi Sagar			
FCs	Songadh	Ravjibunda	Tokarva	Total	Gandhi Sagar	Rampuriya	Sanjit	Total
N	90	90	90	270	90	90	90	270
What is the process of election?								
Nomination					2.2	10.0	15.6	9.3
Unanimous				100.0	97.8	90.0	84.4	90.7
Do you abide by the rules of the FC (% to total N)?								
Do not catch small fish	98.2	98.6	95.6	97.8	98.4	99.8	96.3	97.8
Do not use trawl net	68.2	78.5	79.7	72.9	100.0	100.0	95.6	98.6
Sell fish only to FC	30.0	22.2	28.9	27.0	99.7	98.3	97.5	98.8
Do not catch fish during monsoon	98.7	99.7	99.2	98.8	100.0	100.0	99.2	99.7
Do you stop fishing in monsoon season (%)?								
Yes	100.0	100.0	100.0	100.0	100.0	100.0	100.0	100.0
Why is fishing in the reservoir stopped during the monsoon?								
Do not know	27.7	45.8	37.2	37.1				
Alternative employment available in agriculture	28.9	20.5	33.7	27.8	4.3		2.2	1.7
Fish breeding time/seedlings released by department	43.4	33.7	29.1	35.1	95.7	100	97.8	98.3

	100.0 (31.1)	100.0 (33.9)	100.0 (35.1)	100.0 (100)	100.0 (29.1)	100.0 (34.6)	100.0 (36.3)	100.0 (100)
Total (% to total N)								
Benefits of FC?								
Availability of fish for longer period	100	100	100	100	59.9	43.3	53.3	52.2
Bonus earned					31.1	44.4	34.4	36.7
Insurance					8.9	12.2	12.2	11.1
Challenges faced by FCs: Illegal fishing?								
Does not exist	30.0	13.3	40.0	27.8	62.2	63.3	63.3	62.9
Low	15.6	22.2	16.7	18.2	32.2	34.4	25.6	30.7
High	54.4	64.4	43.3	54.1	5.6	2.2	11.1	6.3
Political Interference?								
Does not exist	1.1		1.1	0.4	6.7	1.1	11.1	6.3
Low	3.3		1.1	1.5	62.2	67.8	71.1	67.0
High	95.6	100.0	98.9	98.2	31.1	31.1	17.8	26.7
Conflict between groups?								
Does not exist	42.2	34.4	17.8	31.5	46.7	51.1	56.7	51.5
Low	31.1	23.3	22.2	25.6	32.2	42.2	25.6	33.3
High	26.7	42.2	60.0	43.0	21.1	6.7	17.8	15.2

Source: Field survey, (2009).

authority to stop illegal fishing by non-members. Over 72 per cent of the households reported that illegal fishing was taking place in the reservoir (Table 4.6). Discussions with fishermen in the Songadh and Ravjibunda revealed that in addition to members, fishermen from the neighbouring villages of Maharashtra were also involved in illegal fishing, over which the FCs had no control. This encouraged members to break FC rules, lowered their morale and, coupled with the lack of proper monitoring and the low rate for fish offered by the FCs, discouraged them from participating in FC activities.

Though elections were inherent in the design of the Ukai FCs, they were hardly ever conducted. The selection of the President by unanimous choice was more prevalent in these FCs. Interestingly, political interference was reported to be high in all the Ukai FCs (98%).[6] Such interference led some fishermen to sell their catch in the open market rather than to the FC, thereby further weakening their ties with the FC. The prevailing lack of interest showed that the process of decentralization and fishermen' participation had been very poorly implemented in all the Ukai FCs.

Gandhi Sagar: Compared to their counterparts in Ukai, a majority of the households of the Gandhi Sagar reservoir followed the FC rules closely (Table 4.6). Nearly 98 per cent of households reported that they do not catch small fish. This was more or less true for all the FCs. Virtually all households sold their fish to their FC, because of the strict monitoring by the contractor, who made fishermen conform to the FC rules. A majority of the households knew why the fishery was closed during the monsoon and almost

---

[6] In 2009, during our research, a trader, Ishaq Maradia, moved the Gujarat High Court and accused Purshottam Solanki, a powerful Koli community leader who influenced several assembly seats in coastal Saurashtra and was then the Minister of Fishery in the GoG, of having given away fishing contracts for 58 reservoirs in the state, each spread over at least 200 ha (2 sq. km), without any tendering processes and at rates below the price fixed in the previous contract. According to Maradia, contracts worth ₹40 crore per annum were awarded for ₹2.36 crore. This cost the government ₹400 crore. The contracts were renewed at such low rates for 10 years (*The Indian Express*, 2012). At present, the special anti-corruption bureau (ACB) court in Gandhinagar which is hearing the plea against Solanki is deciding whether to hear a request for handing over the case to the Central Bureau of Investigation, or to monitor by itself. For details, see Meera Ahmed, 'The Curious Case of Purshottam Solanki' at www.truthofgujarat.com/the-curious-case-of-Purshottam Solanki/#.UgaloJKKpET (accessed on 11 June 2013).

all claimed to have discontinued fishing then. Better knowledge about the rules and strict monitoring helped in explaining this more responsible behaviour amongst the fishermen of the Gandhi Sagar reservoir.

Besides improving the sustainability of the fish resource, fishermen of all three FCs formed in Gandhi Sagar also reported that spot insurance[7] and bonuses earned from the FCs were added advantages of having the FCs (Table 4.6). Discussions with fishermen revealed that some of the rules on the amount of bonuses and deferred wages paid were revised by members in their meetings.

Monitoring of the fishing ground by the contractor, who had a stake in the fish harvest, is believed to have reduced illegal fishing (as reported by 63% of households) and thereby increased incomes for Gandhi Sagar fishermen. Another 31 per cent reported some extent of illegal fishing, while 6 per cent, mainly from Sanjit, reported frequent occurrences of illegal fishing. Discussions with fishermen suggested that lack of proper monitoring encouraged non-members to defy FC rules. Similarly, 67 per cent of the households reported low levels of political interference in the functioning of the FCs while 27 per cent noted the existence of high levels of such interference. Amongst the FCs, fishermen from Sanjit reported a higher degree of political interference than their counterparts in Gandhi Sagar and Rampuriya.

The large size of the reservoir and greater number of fishermen created a challenge for the proper functioning of the Gandhi Sagar reservoir FCs. Despite their common dependence on reservoir fishing, cohesiveness amongst members had not grown. This was evident from the fact that 33 per cent of the households reported some degree of conflict while 15 per cent reported a high degree of conflict amongst members. In addition to this, nearly 81 per cent of the households reported the increase in population pressures as a problem. This was felt by households of all three FCs in general and Rampuriya and Sanjit in particular.

Interestingly, most (67%) Gandhi Sagar fishermen regard political interference as minimal even when the whole structure of

---

[7] Spot insurance, provided by the government, paid fishermen ₹50,000 in case of any physical disability and ₹100,000 in the case of death.

the FF involves political interference by the government. Fishermen are under the impression that their FC President and Secretary have been ineffective in bargaining for a raise in fish rates. All these challenges clearly point towards the need to diversify the economic activity of fishermen in favour of non-fishing activities. However, the lack of alternative employment in non-fishing activities, and ownership of land and animals may have put additional pressure on fishing.

6.4. Comparing Collective Choice Decisions

Collective property rights over reservoir fishing by FCs include the right to manage, exclude and alienate. A comparative analysis of the Ukai and Gandhi Sagar FCs throws light on the extent to which they could jointly manage fishing resources.

Ukai: All the FCs formed in Ukai had the potential to regulate the fish harvested. This was unlike Gandhi Sagar, where the government-controlled MPFF managed the harvest and the FCs were reduced to harvesting fish and selling them to the contractor. Though the Ukai FCs enjoyed a de jure right to fish in the reservoir, they did not enjoy the right to sell or lease out the reservoir to a third party. On the other hand, they had to purchase the reservoir on lease, failing which the reservoir would be left unmanaged. This practice compelled the Ukai FF to borrow funds from a private contractor in order to purchase the lease of the reservoir. However, the borrowing contract required FC members to sell their fish to the private contractor, which most fishermen argued was the result of a deal made between the contractor, a politician and the FF leaders. The dependence on the contractor weakened the bargaining power of the Ukai FF and FCs when it came to negotiating fish rates.

Gandhi Sagar: Unlike as in Ukai, the FF in Gandhi Sagar (which had fishermen representatives but was headed and controlled by a government official) had granted fishermen de jure rights of access and withdrawal of the fish harvest but had retained formal rights of management, exclusion and alienation. The Gandhi Sagar fishermen, in turn, only cooperated and exercised rights to management and exclusion by defining the rules of harvesting the fish. Thus, fishing in the two states was affected by a conglomeration of de jure and de facto property rights which may have overlapped, complemented or even conflicted with one another. From the above discussion, it is clear that the two states had adopted diverse institutional arrangements, and devised operational rules to suit their physical and economic conditions.

6.5. Comparing Awareness about and Participation in FC Activities

Participation of members in FC-related activities is vital for successful decentralization; without it, the potential benefits from local experience and information cannot be realized. While participation in different FC activities shows the extent of involvement, it is essential to understand the extent of awareness amongst the members about FC-related activities.

Ukai: Table 4.7 shows that 100 per cent of Ukai fishermen were aware of the formation of their FC and its functions. This was true for all the Ukai FCs. Nearly 74 per cent of the Ukai households were aware that their cooperative's accounts were managed by their secretary, while the rest believed that it was the president who did this work. Similarly, 91 per cent of the Ukai households were aware that minutes of the meetings were prepared by the secretary. Compared to the level of awareness, the level of participation of members in almost all the activities of the Ukai FCs was lower, most of it simply being to assist friends and relatives who were also committee members or the President of the FCs. It had nothing to do with the FC. For example, only 14 per cent of the Ukai households, mainly from Ravjibunda and Tokarva, had asked their FC questions about financial accounts and government schemes. The low level of participation might have been due to lack of knowledge (as only 24% households in the Ukai FCs believed that they were entitled to see the financial records of the FC) or due to lack of interest (nearly 74% households) in FC activities. The low contribution of fishing to income, the inefficient ways of managing

Table 4.7

Functioning of FCs and Level of Awareness: Ukai Reservoir, Gujarat and Gandhi Sagar Reservoir, MP

Details	Ukai				Gandhi Sagar			
FCs	Songadh	Ravjibunda	Tokarva	Total	Gandhi Sagar	Rampuriya	Sanjit	Total
Awareness about the management of FC								
No Idea	64.4	88.9	82.2	78.5	24.4	14.7	22.2	21.0
Collect fish and sell to contractor, manage accounts	35.6	11.1	17.8	21.5	44.4	56.2	43.3	49.4
Non-functional FC					31.1	29.1	34.4	29.6
Awareness about functions of FCs								
Yes*	100.0	100.0	100.0	100.0	68.9	72.2	80.0	73.7
Involvement in FCs activities?								
Yes*	12.2	42.5	23.3	24.9	58.6	46.9	38.4	48.9
Involved in which activities?								
Not interested	89.9	66.5	64.5	73.6	25.6	36.7	23.3	28.5
Not informed about any activity					15.6	1.1	10.1	8.9
Work on request of president/secretary	7.8	21.2	25.5	18.2	44.4	38.9	43.3	42.2
Advised fishermen to stop using trawl nets and to sell fish to FCs	2.3	12.3	10.0	8.2	14.4	23.3	23.3	20.4

Who manages the accounts?								
Secretary	62.1	100.0	82.5	73.6	76.5	67.4	71.4	71.7
President	37.9		17.5	26.4	23.5	32.6	28.6	28.3
Who writes the minutes of meetings?								
Secretary	88.5	100.0	91.9	91.0	78.8	67.4	69.4	71.7
President	11.5		8.1	9.0	21.3	32.6	30.6	28.3
Can all members see the financial books of accounts?								
Yes	47.8	7.8	17.8	24.4	67.8	35.6	7.8	39.1
No	52.2	92.2	75.6	73.3	26.7	63.3	87.8	57.2
No idea	1.1		6.7	2.2	5.6	1.1	4.4	3.7
Did you ask FC about benefits and other financial transactions of FC? Yes = 1****	1.1	19.8	12.2	13.6	63.3	32.2	18.9	48.1

Source: Field survey, (2009).

Notes: 1. * the response of the remaining households was negative.

2. ** the rest have not asked about FC benefits or financial transactions.

FCs and the prior experience of failure in forming an FC and FF may have discouraged fishermen of all FCs in general and in Songadh in particular from participating in FC activities.

Gandhi Sagar: As against 100 per cent households in the Ukai reservoir in Gujarat, nearly 74 per cent of the households in the Gandhi Sagar reservoir were aware about the functioning of the FCs, with a majority of them being from Sanjit (80%) and Rampuriya (72%). Nearly 72 per cent of households in the Gandhi Sagar reservoir know that their FC secretary managed the accounts while a similar percentage of the households recognized that the secretary wrote the minutes of FC meetings. There was little variation in the levels of awareness about FC functioning across the FCs. Nearly three-fifths of the households in the Gandhi Sagar reservoir assumed that they were not entitled to see the financial records of their FC. A majority of these respondents were from Rampuriya and Sanjit. However, 48 per cent of households, mainly from Gandhi Sagar and Rampuriya, raised questions about FC financial matters in FC meetings. The advancing of loans and giving of bonuses motivated these members to raise questions on financial accounts.

When asked about the method adopted by the FCs for managing the fish harvest, nearly 21 per cent of households in Gandhi Sagar did not have any idea about it. Another 49 per cent of households reported that the FC collects fish and sells them to the contractor, while the rest (30%) believe that the FC is not functioning. A similar trend was witnessed across the FCs. Given the high level of dependence on fishing and its contribution to the income of Gandhi Sagar reservoir households, it was assumed that fishermen would enthusiastically participate in FC activities. Table 4.7 shows that nearly 29 per cent of the Gandhi Sagar reservoir households indicate a lack of interest in FC activities while 9 per cent report that they have no information about the work of the FC. Like Ukai, a majority of households who have reported their involvement in FC activities do so only to assist the president or committee members who also happen to be their relatives or friends. Discussions with several fishermen suggested that the Gandhi Sagar FCs are reduced to managing books of accounts and paying bonuses and deferred wages, and that it is their personal friendship with the president that motivates them to get involved. This kind of involvement, more or less similar to that observed in Ukai, seems unlikely to create a favourable environment for democratic decentralization.

7. Income and Employment Patterns

7.1. Comparing Major Sources of Income and Employment Patterns

In order to understand the extent of dependency of the households on different occupations, each household was asked about its various sources of income during the year prior to the survey. The household was also asked to indicate the sources of income of all its earning members. Any household that reported more than one source was asked to rank the different sources of income in order of their importance to the household.

Ukai: Of the total population surveyed in the Ukai reservoir, 55 per cent were engaged in one or more economic activity (Table 4.8). The remaining persons were outside the labour force such as students, housewives, the very young and old or disabled and sick persons.

Our HHS revealed that the primary source of income for 33 per cent of the Ukai households was animal husbandry, followed by cultivation (24%). Only 12 per cent of households reported fishing as their primary income source. In addition to this, nearly 77 per cent of workers were engaged in some secondary economic activity. Fishing was the secondary source of income for nearly 51 per cent of Ukai households. Across FCs, most Ravjibunda and Tokarva FC households that were primarily engaged in animal husbandry and agriculture supplemented their incomes by fishing. Agricultural labour supplemented the income earned from cultivation for the Songadh FC households. Songadh fishermen indicated that their unsuccessful attempts at forming an FF in their not-so-rich resource base and the incapacity of the present FF in managing the resource had discouraged them from taking active part in the functioning

Table 4.8

Major and Secondary Sources of Income and Status of Ownership of Assets by FCs: Ukai Reservoir, Gujarat

Details	Ukai Reservoir: Gujarat			
1) Name of the FC	Songadh	Ravjibunda	Tokarva	Total
2) Total workers				
a. Workers	57.8	54.4	54.1	55.4
b. Non-workers (student, housewife and retired)	42.2	45.6	45.9	44.6
Occupational status:				
3) Major Source of Household Income (%)				
a. Cultivation	17.8 (16)	32.2 (29)	22.2 (20)	24.1 (65)
b. Animal husbandry	45.6 (41)	22.2 (20)	30.0 (27)	32.6 (88)
c. Fishing	5.6 (5)	20.0 (18)	10.0 (9)	11.9 (32)
d. Agricultural labour	22.2 (20)	15.6 (14)	33.3 (30)	23.7 (64)
e. Non-agricultural labour	3.3 (3)	3.3 (3)	2.2 (2)	3.0 (8)
f. Other (self-employment as plumber, carpenter, shopkeeper, etc.)	5.6 (5)	6.7 (6)	2.2 (2)	4.8 (13)
4) Secondary Source of Household Income				
a. Cultivation	38.9 (28)	18.3 (11)	20.0 (15)	26.1 (54)
b. Fishing	38.9 (28)	55.0 (33)	60.0 (45)	51.2 (106)
c. Agricultural labour	9.7 (7)	16.7 (10)	13.3 (10)	13.0 (27)
d. Non-agricultural labour	2.8 (2)	3.3 (2)	4.0 (3)	3.4 (7)
e. Other (self-employed as plumber, carpenter, shopkeeper, etc.)	9.7 (7)	6.7 (4)	2.7 (2)	6.3 (13)
f. Total	100 (72)	100 (60)	100 (75)	100 (207)
[% to total household]	80.0	66.6	83.3	76.7
5) Size of landholding owned (N)				
a. > 2.5 acres	2	21	10	33
b. 2.5–5.00 acres	2	6	5	13
c. Total	4	27	15	46
6) Status of ownership of land **				
a. Own land	4.4 (4)	30.0 (27)	16.7 (15)	17.0 (46)
b. Cultivate forest land	44.4 (40)	22.2 (20)	45.6 (41)	37.4 (101)
c. Do not cultivate land	51.1 (46)	47.8 (43)	37.8 (34)	45.6 (123)

(contd...)

(contd...)

Details	Ukai Reservoir: Gujarat			
7) % of animals owned to total				
a. Small animals (goat, sheep and hen)	51.1	58.8	54.3	54.5
b. Large animals (cow, buffaloes, ox)	48.9	41.2	45.7	45.5
c. Total animals (N)	370	102	210	682
[% to total animals]	[54.3]	[15.0]	[30.8]	[100.0]
8) Total assets owned (N)	90	90	90	270
a. Households owning net alone (% to N)	12.5	43.8	28.9	36.3
b. HHs owning net (% to N)	100.0	100.0	100.0	100.0
c. HHs owning net and boat (% to N)	22.2	47.8	23.3	31.1
d. HHs owning net, boat and land (% to N)	1.1	0.0	1.1	0.7
e. HHs owning net and land (% to N)	7.8	31.1	16.7	18.5
f. HHs owning animals (% to N)	82.2	56.7	77.8	72.2

Source: Field survey, (2009).
Note: Figures in parentheses indicate number of observations and figures in brackets [ ] indicate % to total animals.

of the FC. On the whole, fishing may not have been an assured source of income but it certainly provided a supplementary source of livelihood to many households.

Even in Ukai, where animal husbandry and agriculture were major sources of livelihood, fishermen possessed only a small asset base for these land-based activities (Table 4.8). Perhaps poverty had discouraged them from investing in physical assets like big animals or land (only 17 per cent of the households owned land which were mainly marginal tracts). This emphasizes clearly the importance of fishing as an additional source of income for households with poor asset bases. However, poverty and the low stock of fish in the reservoir could be the reasons why only 31 per cent of households owned a boat and net that enabled them to go for deep reservoir fishing. This was true for all the FCs.

The poor economic condition of fishermen and probably the size of the fish population in the reservoir discouraged them from investing in physical assets like animals, boats or land, let alone assets like education which had the potential to increase the income of the households.

Gandhi Sagar: In contrast, in Gandhi Sagar, fishing was a major source of livelihood for 85 per cent of the households (Table 4.9). As the women folk did not go out to fish in the reservoir and households did not possess livestock, the percentage of female workers was less as compared to that in Ukai. During our field visits, we saw women preparing bait, repairing nets and rolling *bidis*, but most of these tasks went unreported. Greater dependence on fishing had fuelled the expectation of fishermen for increased incomes from fishing which in turn had led to investments in boats and nets (68%).

Table 4.9

Major and Secondary Sources of Income and Status of Ownership of Assets by FCs: Gandhi Sagar Reservoir, MP

Details	Gandhi Sagar Reservoir			
1) **Name of the FC**	Gandhi Sagar	Rampuriya	Sanjit	Total
2) **Total workers**				
a. Workers	50.8	55.2	49.6	51.9
b. Non-workers (students, housewife and retired)	49.2	44.8	50.4	48.1
3) **Occupational Status/Primary Source of Income (% of HHs)**				
a. Cultivation	1.1		4.3	2.2
b. Fishing	92.2	93.3	71.3	84.5
c. Agricultural labour	1.3	1.1	11.2	4.8
d. Non-agricultural labour	3.3	4.4	13.2	7.4
e. Other*	2.2	1.1	0.0	1.1
4) **Secondary Source of Income (% of HHs)**				
a. Cultivation			21.1 (8)	14.0 (8)
b. Fishing			2.6 (1)	1.7 (1)
c. Agricultural labour			15.8 (6)	10.5 (6)
d. Non-agricultural labour	100.0 (2)	100.0 (17)	60.5 (23)	73.7 (42)
Total	100.0	100.0	100.0	100.0
[% of total households]	3.5 (2)	29.8 (17)	66.7 (38)	21.1 (57)

(contd...)

(contd...)

Details	Gandhi Sagar Reservoir			
5) Size of landholding owned (N = 11)				
> 2.5 acres			11	11
6) Status of ownership of land				
a. Owned land			12.2	4.1
b. No land/do not cultivate forest land as well	100.0	100.0	87.8	95.9
7) Total households owning animals			6	6
8) Assets owned (N)	90	90	90	270
a. Households owning net alone (% to N)	44.4	8.9	33.3	28.9
b. Households owning net (% to N)	100.0	100.0	100.0	100.0
c. Households owning net and boat (% to N)	55.6	91.1	57.8	68.1
d. Households owning net and land (% to N)			5.6	1.9
e. Households owning net, boat and land (% to N)			3.3	1.1

Source: Field survey, (2009).
Note: Figures in parentheses indicate number of observations.

Only 11 households, all from Sanjit, owned land (size less than 2.5 acres). Unlike the FCs of Gujarat, landless households, particularly of the Gandhi Sagar and Rampuriya FCs, did not cultivate forest land while very few (six households) owned animals. When asked about secondary income sources, only 57 households (21%) supplemented their incomes mainly from non-agricultural labour. These households belong to the Sanjit (23) and Rampuriya (17) FCs. This clearly indicated the lack of alternative avenues of employment. Moreover, low investments in education or physical assets like animals or land, signified the weak financial condition of fishermen. In such a situation, greater dependence on fishing had encouraged fishermen to invest in boats and nets (68%) with the expectation of earning higher incomes (Table 4.9).

Such an investment by fishermen in an area highly dependent on fishing and one that discouraged exit, necessitated proper management of the available fish resource that could ensure a sustainable fish harvest.

7.2. Comparing Fish Catch and Income from the Reservoirs

The amount of fish caught per year in Ukai (156,972 kg/year in Table 4.10) was significantly less than that caught in Gandhi Sagar (924,561 kg/year in Table 4.11). A comparison of fish production in both the states was difficult as yields in reservoirs were typically not proportional to their size. The productivity of a reservoir typically depended on natural factors beyond human control and interventions. Owing to paucity of data, we were not able to isolate natural factors affecting productivity. However, it was hypothesized that the livelihood of fishermen could have been better provided for had the FCs/FF been better managed.

Ukai: After the formation of the FC, fish production increased by 1.3 per cent and 5.7 per cent in Ukai and Gandhi Sagar respectively (Table 4.10). However, further analysis showed that the quantity of low-valued fish (like Kati and local species) was higher (72%) in Ukai than high value fish (like Rohu, Catla, Mrigal). Fish catch of high valued fish had reduced drastically in Ravjibunda and Songadh. The failure of the department to maintain a reserve stock of high valued fish had led to a decline in the quantity and quality of fish in general and high valued fish in particular. In addition fishermen complained about the inability of their FCs to prevent poaching of high-valued fish.

Gandhi Sagar: In MP however, the catch of high valued fish like Catla and Mrigal had increased after the formation of FCs (Table 4.11). Apparently, a reserve stock of high value fish was maintained here and the contractor kept an eagle's eye out to avoid pilferage. Another important reason for the increase in catch was that in the absence of other viable sources of livelihood, more and more people took up fishing.

Table 4.10

Species-wise Fish Catch and Incomes Earned by Fishermen in FCs: Ukai Reservoir, Gujarat

Fish Variety	Before the FC (Constant Terms in 2009 Prices)				After the FC			
	Songadh	Ravjibunda	Tokarva	Total	Songadh	Ravjibunda	Tokarva	Total
Fish Catch (kg/year)								
Rohu	12,020	12,866	13,834	38,719	10,797 (−10.2)	8,435 (−34.4)	12,970 (−6.2)	32,202 (−16.8)
Catla	13,347	13,791	15,774	42,912	10,350 (−22.5)	7,832 (−43.2)	14,189 (−10.0)	32,370 (−24.6)
Mrigal	12,195	10,316	13,707	36,219	10,123 (−17.0)	10,289 (−0.3)	13,495 (−1.5)	33,907 (−6.4)
Kati	3,852	3,845	3,792	11,489	3,484 (−9.6)	7,823 (103.5)	2,523 (−33.5)	14,484 (26.1)
Minor produce[1]	6,606	12,450	6,582	25,638	11,641 (76.2)	18,954 (52.2)	14,092 (114.1)	44,009 (71.7)
Total	48,020	53,268	53,689	154,977	46,395 (−3.4)	53,333 (0.1)	57,269 (6.7)	156,972 (1.3)
Total income of fishermen (₹/year)*								
Rohu	453,394	485,300	523,260	1,461,954	388,680 (−10.2)	303,675 (−34.4)	466,922 (−6.2)	1,159,276 (−16.8)
Catla	503,444	520,214	598,248	1,621,905	362,239 (−22.5)	274,114 (−43.2)	496,610 (−10.0)	1,132,963 (−24.6)

(contd...)

(contd...)

Fish Variety	Before the FC (Constant Terms in 2009 Prices)				After the FC			
	Songadh	Ravjibunda	Tokarva	Total	Songadh	Ravjibunda	Tokarva	Total
Mrigal	441,617	373,576	506,003	1,321,197	354,307 (−17.0)	360,110 (−0.3)	472,320 (−1.5)	1,186,737 (−6.4)
Kati	85,379	104,741	53,005	243,126	89,899 (−9.6)	80,622 (103.5)	64,775 (−33.5)	235,296 (26.1)
Minor produce[1]	94,212	261,853	82,202	438,266	298,781 (76.2)	709,471 (52.2)	331,973 (114.1)	1,340,225 (71.7)
Total	1,578,046	1,745,684	1,762,718	5,086,448	1,493,905 (−3.4)	1,727,992 (0.1)	1,832,600 (6.7)	5,054,497 (1.3)
Total income of Fishermen (₹/year/capita)								
Total	11,689	12,123	11,521	11,774	4,256	4,683	4,966	4,641

Source: Field survey data, (2009).

Notes: 1. Rohu, Catla and Mrigal are high-valued fish and minor produce include low-valued indigenous species.
2. Figures in parentheses indicate percentage change after the formation of FCs.

Table 4.11

Species-wise Fish Catch and Income Earned by Fishermen in FCs:: Gandhi Sagar Reservoir, MP

Fish Variety	Before the FC (constant terms in 2009 prices)				After the FC			
	Gandhi Sagar	Rampuriya	Sanjit	Total	Gandhi Sagar	Rampuriya	Sanjit	Total
Fish Catch (kg/year)								
Rohu	72,028	50,567	75,006	197,601	86,887 (20.6)	46,637 (−7.8)	52,559 (−29.9)	186,083 (−5.8)
Catla	66,501	58,547	77,774	202,821	121,129 (82.1)	118,168 (101.8)	68,655 (−11.7)	307,952 (51.8)
Mrigal	63,738	61,236	63,933	188,907	106,703 (67.4)	85,906 (40.3)	59,070 (−7.6)	251,679 (33.2)
Kati	22,861	15,682	13,085	51,629	16,915 (−26.0)	44,629 (184.6)	14,303 (9.3)	75,847 (46.9)
Minor produce[1]	65,423	97,483	59,095	222,001	16,132 (−75.3)	59,613 (−38.8)	1,791 (−97.0)	77,537 (−65.1)
Total	295,132	283,554	296,004	874,690	360,860 (22.3)	359,612 (26.8)	204,089 (−31.1)	924,561 (5.7)
Total income of fishermen (₹/year)*								
Rohu	1,412,812	991,858	1,471,212	3,875,881	1,477,077 (4.5)	792,829 (−20.1)	893,501 (−39.3)	3,163,408 (−18.4)
Catla	1,304,403	1,148,375	1,525,506	3,978,284	2,059,192 (57.9)	2,008,856 (74.9)	1,167,142 (−23.5)	5,235,191 (31.6)

(contd...)

(contd...)

Fish Variety	Before the FC (constant terms in 2009 prices)				After the FC			
	Gandhi Sagar	Rampuriya	Sanjit	Total	Gandhi Sagar	Rampuriya	Sanjit	Total
Mrigal	1,250,198	1,201,133	1,254,033	3,705,364	1,813,947 (45.1)	1,460,410 (21.6)	1,004,182 (-19.9)	4,278,538 (15.5)
Kati	379,431	260,275	217,179	856,885	253,729 (-33.1)	669,432 (157.2)	214,548 (-1.2)	1,137,709 (32.8)
Minor produce[1]	1,085,837	1,617,925	980,808	3,684,569	241,985 (-77.7)	894,195 (-44.7)	26,868 (-97.3)	1,163,048 (-68.4)
Total	5,432,681	5,219,565	5,448,737	16,100,983	5,845,930 (7.6)	5,825,722 (11.6)	3,306,241 (-39.3)	14,977,893 (-7.0)
Total income of fishermen (₹/year/capita)								
Total	26,245	41,425	28,829	30,845	18,559	20,881	10,496	16,477

Source: Field survey, (2009).

Notes: 1. Rohu, Catla and Mrigal are high-valued fish and minor produce include low-valued indigenous species.
2. Figures in parentheses indicate percentage change after the formation of FCs.

Table 4.12

Active Fishermen and Number of Fishing Months and Price Before and After FC Formation: Ukai and Gandhi Sagar Reservoirs

	Average no. of Active Fishermen Per Household	Average no. of Fishing Months Per Year	Price (in 2009 prices)	Average no. of Active Fishermen Per Household	Average no. of Fishing Months Per Year	Price
FCs	*Before the FC*			*After the FC*		
Ukai	1.6	5.4	32.9	4.0 (150.7)	5.9 (9.2)	32.0 (−2.5)
Gandhi Sagar	1.9	7.8	18.4	3.4 (77.0)	9.9 (27.8)	16.2

Source: Field survey, (2009).
Note: Figures in parentheses indicate percentage change after FC formation.

All of them also chose to increase the number of days on which they fished (Table 4.12). Despite the increase in the amount of fish caught in Gandhi Sagar, however, incomes declined by 7 per cent. Thus the increase in the fish catch was not reflected in an increase in incomes. It could be inferred that the benefits that should have accrued to the community by maintaining a reserve stock of fish had been misappropriated by the contractor.

7.3. The Contribution of Fishing to Total Income

Ukai: In order to understand the contribution of fishing to total income, we attempted to analyse the total income of households in Ukai from all economic activities. Table 4.13 shows that fishing contributed to 26 per cent (₹14,280) of the total average income (median) of Ukai households (₹55,534). This was lower than that earned from other sources of employment like carpentry, shopkeeping, etc. (₹21,314) signifying that fishing was not a primary source of income for most households there. Income from cultivation and animal husbandry had decreased over these years. The bad monsoon in the year of the survey probably resulted in poor returns from cultivation. All these findings reinforce the point that fishing, though not a primary income source, does supplement income earned from other sources of livelihood.

Table 4.13

Average (Median) Household Income, Contribution of and Difference in Income after FC Formation, by MJSI: Ukai Reservoir, Gujarat

Fishing Cooperatives	Sources of Income (in ₹/year)						
	Cultivation	Animal Husbandry	Fishing	Agricultural Labour	Non-agricultural Labour	Others¹	Total
Before FC formation							
Songadh	4,712 (45)	7,912 (78)	15,142 (90)	8,555 (61)	7,654 (32)	15,160 (5)	38,895 (90)
Ravjibunda	6,066 (42)	5,719 (46)	13,241 (90)	8,935 (61)	5,703 (32)	13,688 (5)	43,146 (90)
Tokarva	3,699 (48)	5,018 (68)	12,386 (90)	9,268 (60)	6,844 (33)	15,209 (11)	39,762 (90)
Total	5,059 (135)	6,611 (192)	13,374 (270)	8,555 (169)	6,844 (97)	15,209 (21)	40,199 (270)
After FC formation							
Songadh	2,473 (42)	5,957 (74)	13,215 (90)	9,591 (47)	9,591 (34)	25,577 (5)	53,818 (90)
Ravjibunda	6,783 (47)	7,226 (51)	15,048 (90)	10,444 (68)	10,231 (34)	19,183 (5)	62,672 (90)
Tokarva	2,223 (54)	6,293 (70)	14,717 (90)	11,510 (63)	8,526 (35)	24,511 (11)	52,567 (90)
Total	3,489 (143)	6,468 (195)	14,280 (270)	10,231 (178)	9,591 (103)	21,314 (21)	55,534 (270)

Share to total income: Before the formation of FC

Songadh	10.4	17.9	34.5	10.4	8.5	18.3	100.0
Ravjibunda	8.1	7.1	38.3	15.5	6.5	24.5	100.0
Tokarva	6.6	8.5	34.5	15.0	5.5	30.0	100.0
Total	8.3	11.1	35.6	13.6	6.8	24.5	100.0
After the formation of FC							
Songadh	5.4	13.8	22.4	9.8	19.7	28.9	100.0
Ravjibunda	8.9	8.8	26.7	15.3	6.7	33.6	100.0
Tokarva	4.9	9.5	29.4	16.3	6.7	33.2	100.0
Total	6.4	10.7	26.1	13.5	11.5	31.8	100.0
% change after FC formation							
Songadh	−47.5	−24.7	−12.7	12.1	25.3	68.7	38.4
Ravjibunda	11.8	26.4	13.6	16.9	79.4	40.1	45.3
Tokarva	−39.9	25.4	18.8	24.2	24.6	61.2	32.2
Total	−31.0	−2.2	6.8	19.6	40.1	40.1	38.1

Source: Field survey, (2009).

Notes: 1. Others include shopkeeper, carpenter, plumber, etc.
2. Figures in parentheses indicate number of observations.
3. MJSI: Major Source of Income.

Over the years (2004–09), fishing income has increased by only 7 per cent. This increase was reported to have been higher in the Tokarva and Ravjibunda FCs. However, in per capita per year terms, income from fishing had actually declined from ₹11,774 before the formation of the FCs to ₹4,641 after the formation of the FCs (Table 4.13). The apathy and ineffective management of the FCs may have been responsible for this poor showing. It could also have been due to increasing population pressures on the resource (Table 4.13).

Gandhi Sagar: Unlike as in Ukai, Table 4.14 shows that fishing contributed to 76 per cent (₹38,870) of the total average annual income (median) of the Gandhi Sagar households (₹53,360). This was much higher than that earned from all other sources of employment signifying that fishing here was a primary source of income for most households. After the formation of FCs, the income from fishing increased by 37 per cent. Across the FCs, income from fishing increased in Gandhi Sagar and Rampuriya but declined in the Sanjit FCs. Reductions in fish catch and hence incomes for fishermen in Sanjit led to a decline in their incomes by 18 per cent after FC formation. Thus, the location of the FC was a major determinant of the fish catch.

However, in per capita per year terms, income from fishing had actually declined from ₹30,845 before the formation of FCs to ₹16,477 after the formation of the Gandhi Sagar FCs from 2004 to 2009 (see Table 4.11). One of the reasons for this decline was an increase in population pressures on the resource (as shown in Table 4.12). Overexploitation in the form of increases in the number of months of fishing and active fishermen per household also contributed to this anomaly.

The Gandhi Sagar reservoir enjoyed better fish resource than Ukai and that perhaps explained its larger contribution of fishing to total income here. However, the price that the fishermen earned from their catch had gone down substantially after the formation of FCs whereas in fact it should have been the other way round. Lower prices were obviously beneficial to the contractor but not to the fishermen. To compensate for the lower prices, most of the additional income was generated by over-exploiting the resource.

Table 4.14

Average (Median) Household Income, Contribution of and Difference in Income After FC Formation, by MJSI: Gandhi Sagar Reservoir, MP

Fishing Cooperatives	Cultivation	Fishing	Sources of Income (in ₹/year)		Others*	Total
			Agricultural Labour	Non-agricultural Labour		
Before FC formation (constant terms)						
Gandhi Sagar	7,695 (1)	29,818 (90)		8,978 (2)	27,702 (1)	31,614 (90)
Rampuriya		26,535 (90)	9,234 (1)	7,695 (6)		26,663 (90)
Sanjit		32,742 (90)		12,825 (1)		32,743 (90)
Total	7,695 (1)	28,407 (270)	9,234 (1)	7,695 (9)	27,702 (1)	30,742 (270)
After FC formation						
Gandhi Sagar		46,000 (90)		17,825 (34)	18,400 (9)	56,925 (90)
Rampuriya		39,100 (90)	26,450 (2)	17,825 (46)	27,600 (3)	55,085 (90)
Sanjit	18,630 (9)	26,910 (90)	14,720 (22)	20,700 (47)	23,000 (5)	49,680 (90)
Total	18,630 (9)	38,870 (270)	14,720 (24)	18,400 (127)	23,000 (17)	53,360 (270)
Share to total Income before FC (%)						
Gandhi Sagar	0.15	98.96		0.4	0.5	100.0
Rampuriya		98.25	0.2	1.6		100.0
Sanjit		99.75	0.1	0.3		100.0
Total	0.05	98.99		0.7	0.2	100.0

(contd...)

(contd...)

Fishing Cooperatives	Sources of Income (in ₹/year)					
	Cultivation	Fishing	Agricultural Labour	Non-agricultural Labour	Others*	Total
After FC						
Gandhi Sagar		85.6		11.6	2.8	100.0
Rampuriya		80.5	0.8	17.4	1.4	100.0
Sanjit	5.8	58.0	10.0	24.5	1.8	100.0
Total	1.6	76.0	3.1	17.3	2.0	100.0
% change after FC formation						
Gandhi Sagar	−100.0	54.3		98.6	−33.6	80.1
Rampuriya		47.4	186.4	131.6		106.6
Sanjit		−17.8		61.4		51.7
Total	−100.0	36.8	59.4	139.1	−17.0	73.6

Source: Field survey, (2009).
Notes: *Others include shopkeeper, carpenter, plumber, etc.
Figures in parentheses indicate number of observations.

7.4. Comparing Inequalities Amongst Fishermen

Following Coudouel et al. (2002), the MPCE has been used as a proxy variable for household income. For the subsequent analysis, the MPCE is compared with official poverty lines (₹501.58 in 2004 and ₹1,109.76 in 2009 in Gujarat and ₹408.41 in 2004 and ₹902.82 in 2009 in M.P) that were used as cut-off points to separate the poor from the non-poor (State Planning Commission, Government of MP, 2009). We attempted our poverty analysis using these categories of households. For the household level analysis, we used the monthly consumption expenditure (MCE) of the household (derived from the product of the MPCE and household size). The conventional view is that a society's welfare can be measured in a twofold manner, namely the level of income and the extent of inequality in the distribution of income. The notions of poverty and inequality are closely related—for a given median income, the more unequal the income distribution, the larger the population living in poverty. In order to get a clearer picture of the well-being of a community before and after the formation of the FCs, it was therefore necessary to further examine the distribution of income amongst the households.

Ukai: Table 4.15 shows that nearly 49 per cent of households in Ukai were poor and could not afford to buy the basic basket of goods for their subsistence. There was little variation in the percentage of poor across the FCs. Poverty is a dynamic condition, with large numbers of people moving into and out of poverty during a given time period. When compared with the situation before FC formation, the incidence of poverty as measured by the head count index (HCI) was found to be higher after formation of the FC. Table 4.15 shows that nearly 19 per cent of the Ukai households had experienced a worsening of poverty after the formation of the FC, a majority of them belonging to the Songadh and Ravjibunda FCs. Another 13 per cent, mainly from Songadh, reported an improvement in their poverty status. This increase was evident for households who were poor before the formation of the FC but had successfully come out of poverty after the formation of the FC. On the other hand, the FC programme failed to push 29 per cent of households above the poverty status. Of these FC households who

Table 4.15

Head Count Ratio and Change in Poverty Status After FC Formation: Ukai Reservoir, Gujarat

Fishing Cooperative	Before FC Formation			After FC Formation			Change in Poverty Status (% of total)			
	Poor	Non-poor	Total	Poor	Non-poor	Total	Always Poor	Worsening	Never Poor	Improvement
Songadh	37.8 (34)	62.2 (56)	100.0 (90)	44.4 (40)	55.6 (50)	100.0 (90)	22.2 (20)	22.2 (20)	40.0 (36)	15.6 (14)
Ravjibunda	42.2 (38)	57.8 (52)	100.0 (90)	51.1 (46)	48.9 (44)	100.0 (90)	30.0 (27)	21.1 (19)	36.7 (33)	12.2 (11)
Tokarva	47.8 (43)	52.2 (47)	100.0 (90)	50.0 (45)	50.0 (45)	100.0 (90)	35.6 (32)	14.4 (13)	37.8 (34)	12.2 (11)
Total	42.6 (115)	57.4 (155)	100.0 (270)	48.5 (131)	51.5 (139)	100.0 (270)	29.3 (79)	19.3 (52)	38.1 (103)	13.3 (36)

Source: Field survey, (2009).

Note: Figures in parentheses indicate number of observations.

are chronically poor, nearly 36 per cent were from Tokarva, another 30 per cent from Ravjibunda and the rest from the Songadh FC.

When compared to Planning Commission (2012) statistics, the numbers presented above show that the incidence of poverty in the Gujarat FCs was as low as 27 per cent and that in the MP FCs it was 42 per cent. There are ample studies (GOGb, 2005; Lobo and Kumar, 2009) which show that the tribal communities displaced by the Ukai dam were amongst the most backward communities of Gujarat insofar as education, health and economics were concerned. Our study area had an exceptionally high incidence of poverty as it fell in the area that experienced a major displacement of population when the Ukai reservoir was constructed. Moreover, the FC project, by design, had excluded non-members of the already marginalized area who would probably have been poor people. Illegal fishing by them may have contributed to an increase in their incomes while reducing the fish catch (hence incomes) of member fishermen. In the absence of data on non-members, our study of poverty was restricted only to FC fishermen who faced the negative externalities of illegal fishing. Consequently, our limited data failed to show any improvements in the condition of member fishermen.

7.5. Ukai Reservoir: Who were the Poor?

7.5.1. Participation in Activities of the Ukai FCs

In an attempt to clarify the profile of poor FC households, we made attempts to enquire about the major sources of income, participation in the activities of the FC, ownership of land and other assets, total income earned and income earned from fishing by such households. From the above discussion, it is clear that the low dependence on fishing and the low contribution of fishing to incomes made most fishermen indifferent to participating in FC activities. Those who did participate, mainly in the Ravjibunda and Tokarva FCs, belonged to the non-poor category of households or had experienced improvements in their poverty status (Table 4.16). Improvements in the benefits from fishing, to a limited extent, must have encouraged

Table 4.16

Profile of Poor Households in Terms of Access to Land, Participation in FC Activities and Change in Their Poverty Status: Ukai Reservoir, Gujarat

Details	Songadh	Ravjibunda	Tokarva	Total
1. Participated in the activities of the FC				
Always poor			1.1 (1)	0.4 (1)
Worsened	1.1 (1)	1.1 (1)	2.2 (2)	1.5 (4)
Not poor	3.3 (3)	5.6 (5)	14.4 (13)	7.8 (21)
Improvement in economic condition	2.2 (2)	8.9 (8)	10.0 (9)	7.0 (19)
Total	6.7 (6)	15.6 (14)	27.8 (25)	16.7 (45)
2. Access to land: Poor households (N = 131)				
Cultivate own land	5.1 (2)	31.9 (15)	15.6 (7)	18.3 (24)
Cultivate forest land	48.7 (19)	27.7 (13)	40.0 (18)	38.2 (50)
Do not cultivate	46.2 (18)	40.4 (19)	44.4 (20)	43.5 (57)
Total	100 (39)	100 (47)	100 (45)	100 (131)
3. Access to land: Non-poor households (N = 139)				
Cultivate own land	3.9 (2)	27.9 (12)	17.8 (8)	15.8 (22)
Cultivate forest land	41.2 (21)	16.3 (7)	51.1 (23)	36.7 (51)
Do not cultivate	54.9 (28)	55.8 (24)	31.1 (14)	47.5 (66)
Total	100 (51)	100 (43)	100 (45)	100 (139)
Total (N = 270)				
Cultivate own land	4.4 (4)	30.0 (27)	16.7 (15)	17.0 (46)
Cultivate forest land	44.4 (40)	22.2 (20)	45.6 (41)	37.4 (101)
Do not cultivate	51.1 (46)	47.8 (43)	37.8 (34)	45.6 (123)
Total	100 (90)	100 (90)	100 (90)	100 (270)
4. Status of poverty and dependence on fishing				
Poor + fishing dependent households	2.5 (1)	4.3 (2)	4.4 (2)	3.8 (5)
Non-poor + fishing dependent households	8.0 (4)	25.0 (11)	13.3 (6)	15.1 (21)
Poor + non-dependent on fishing	97.5 (39)	95.7 (44)	95.6 (43)	96.2 (126)
Non-poor and non-dependent on fishing	92.0 (46)	75.0 (33)	86.7 (39)	84.9 (118)
Total	100 (90)	100 (90)	100 (90)	100 (270)

Source: Field survey, (2009).

Note: Figures in parentheses indicate percentage to total observations, that is, N = 90 each for all FCs.

fishermen from Ravjibunda to participate in the activities of their FCs. Surprisingly, in Tokarva, even when income from fishing failed to push households above the poverty line, FC members reported greater participation in FC-related activities. Perhaps, as the FF was formed under the leadership of the Tokarva village, some hope of better prospects encouraged fishermen to participate in FC activities.

7.5.2. Ukai: Status of Poverty and Ownership of Land

Surprisingly, Table 4.16 shows that a majority of the poor Ukai households were dependent on non-fishing activities. Fishing provided fishermen the cushion to withstand inadequate and fluctuating incomes from non-fishing activities. In the earlier sections, we had analysed the ownership of assets like land, animals as well as fishing assets to understand the reason for the high incidence of poverty. Table 4.16 also shows that only 17 per cent of the households owned land and another 46 per cent did not cultivate any land. In the face of landlessness, another 38 per cent of households cultivated forest land. Land constraints in the region compelled people to diversify their sources of income by working as agricultural or non-agricultural labourers, or in other activities. Landlessness and a lack of profitable alternative employment opportunities could have also forced poor households to fall back on forests for cultivation. During discussions, fishermen narrated numerous cases of harassment by forest officials which in turn adversely affected their incomes. However, lack of ownership of land and the risk associated with cultivating forest land had prevented any improvement in their poverty status.

7.5.3. Ukai: Status of Poverty and Major Source of Income

From the discussions presented in earlier sections and Table 4.17, the incidence of poverty in Ukai was found to be high for households depending on non-fishing activities, mainly those engaging in agricultural labour (54.7%), followed by households dependent on animal husbandry, cultivation, other activities and fishing. A similar

Table 4.17

Head Count Ratio and Change in Poverty Status, by MJSI: Ukai Reservoir, Gujarat

MJSI	Total (% to its Total)	Before the FC (% to Total)		After the FC (% to Total)		Change in the Status of Poverty (N)			
		P	NP	P	NP	AP	W	NP	Imp
Songadh Fishing Cooperative									
Cultivation	17.8 (16)	31.3	68.8	43.8	56.3	2	5	6	3
Animal husbandry	45.6 (41)	24.4	75.6	43.9	56.1	7	11	20	3
Fishing	5.6 (5)	60.0	40.0	20.0	80.0	1	0	2	2
Agricultural labour	22.2 (20)	45.0	55.0	55.0	45.0	7	4	7	2
Non-agricultural labour	3.3 (3)	33.3	66.7	0.0	100.0	0	0	2	1
Others (shopkeeper, carpenter, etc.)	5.6 (5)	100.0	0.0	40.0	60.0	2	0	0	3
Total	100.0 (90)	36.7	63.3	43.3	56.7	19	20	37	14
Ravjibunda Fishing Cooperative									
Cultivation	32.2 (29)	48.3	51.7	48.3	51.7	8	6	9	6
Animal husbandry	22.2 (20)	40.0	60.0	65.0	35.0	7	6	6	1
Fishing	20.0 (18)	33.3	66.7	33.3	66.7	4	2	10	2
Agricultural labour	15.6 (14)	57.1	42.9	78.6	21.4	7	4	2	1
Non-agricultural labour	3.3 (3)	0.0	100.0	0.0	100.0	0	0	3	0
Others (shopkeeper, carpenter, etc.)	6.7 (6)	33.3	66.7	50.0	50.0	1	2	2	1
Total	100.0 (90)	42.2	57.8	52.2	47.8	27	20	32	11
Tokarva Fishing Cooperative									
Cultivation	22.2 (20)	40.0	60.0	55.0	45.0	6	5	7	2
Animal husbandry	30.0 (27)	51.9	48.1	48.1	51.9	10	3	10	4
Fishing	10.0 (9)	55.6	44.4	55.6	44.4	3	2	2	2
Agricultural labour	33.3 (30)	46.7	53.3	43.3	56.7	11	2	14	3
Non-agricultural labour	2.2 (2)	100.0	0.0	100.0	0.0	2	0	0	0
Other (shopkeeper, carpenter, etc.).	2.2 (2)	0.0	100.0	50.0	50.0	0	1	1	0
Total	100.0 (90)	47.8	52.2	50.0	50.0	32	13	34	11
Total									
Cultivation	24.1 (65)	41.5	58.5	49.2	50.8	16	16	22	11
Animal husbandry	32.6 (88)	36.4	63.6	50.0	50.0	24	20	36	8

(contd...)

(contd...)

MJSI	Total (% to its Total)	Before the FC (% to Total)		After the FC (% to Total)		Change in the Status of Poverty (N)			
		P	NP	P	NP	AP	W	NP	Imp
Fishing	11.9 (32)	43.8	56.3	37.5	62.5	8	4	14	6
Agricultural labour	23.7 (64)	48.4	51.6	54.7	45.3	25	10	23	6
Non-agricultural labour	3.0 (8)	37.5	62.5	25.0	75.0	2	0	5	1
Other (shopkeeper, carpenter, etc.)	4.8 (13)	53.8	46.2	46.2	53.8	3	3	3	4
Total	100.0 (270)	42.2	57.8	48.5	51.5	78	53	103	36

Source: Field survey, (2009).
Notes: 1. Figures in parentheses indicate number of observations.
2. P = poor (households); 3. NP = non-poor; 4. AP = Always poor; 5. W = Worsening; Imp = Improvement in economic condition after FC formation.

trend was observed in Songadh and Ravjibunda. Fishermen in Tokarva mainly relied on fishing for their livelihoods and were poor, followed by those mainly dependent on cultivation, other activities, animal husbandry and agricultural labour. The situation had actually worsened for those engaged in animal husbandry and cultivation. This was evident from the number of households that were chronically poor or became worse off following FC formation. Moreover, those engaged in fishing largely belonged to non-poor households (14 out of 32 households). After the FC formation, eight households (out of 32 dependent on fishing) remained chronically poor while another four households became poorer. This suggested that given the small contribution of fishing activity to poor households, non-fishing activities failed to offer workers a decent livelihood in an area already facing employment problems. This suggests the need to carefully address policy issues in non-fishing activities, which were outside the scope of our work.

7.5.4. Ukai: Status of Poverty and Income from Fishing

Not only was the dependence of poor Ukai households on fishing low, but the net income earned from fishing was also low compared to their non-poor counterparts (Table 4.18). With nearly 26 per cent of household income contributed by fishing, this contribution was

Table 4.18

Average Income from Fishing and the Proportion of Income from Fishing to Total Income by Poverty Status: Ukai Reservoir, Gujarat

FCs	Poor			Non-poor			Total		
	Fishing	Total	% of fish income	Fishing	Total	% of Fish Income	Fishing	Total	% of Fish Income
	Net Income (₹/year)								
Songadh	13,982 (40)	57,015	23.9	13,215 (50)	47,283	21.1	13,428 (90)	53,818	22.4
Ravjibunda	13,385 (46)	66,550	23.9	18,245 (44)	58,869	30.1	15,048 (90)	62,672	26.7
Tokarva	15,154 (45)	55,033	26.6	14,280 (45)	47,871	33.4	14,717 (90)	52,567	29.4
Total	14,077 (131)	61,768	24.8	15,000 (139)	51,409	27.5	14,515 (270)	55,534	26.1

Source: Field survey, (2009).

Note: Figures in parentheses indicate number of observations.

marginally higher for non-poor households (28%) as compared to poor households (25% of income). Barring Songadh, the same trend was observed for the other FCs. This showed that even though the relative benefits of fishing were higher for non-poor households, the benefits to poor households helped in filling the gaps and complemented income earned from other sources.

From the above discussion, it becomes clear that the area around the Ukai reservoir, marginalized in terms of its remoteness from urban centres, limited by its fragile and low productive resource base and inadequate human and other capital assets like access to land, animals or fishing assets faced low income earning from non-fishing sources. The FC households' dependence on non-fishing activities was induced by the marginality of this area. Given the uncertain returns earned by the FC members in non-economic activities, the potential of fishing to provide a safety net to these households was significant in terms of providing a subsistent but important supplementary source of income. However, as has been noted earlier, the initial conditions of the fish resource and the exploitative ways of harvesting it harmed the potential of fishing to provide such a safety net to FC households. One of the arguments explaining this was the characteristics of the resource *per se*. Uncertainty about the fish catch, sharp fluctuations in the resource, inadequate stocking and over-harvesting of fish resulted in high costs, low returns and a lack of control over fishing activities of non-FC members—all in turn negatively affecting the incomes of the Ukai FC members. They also point towards the imperative need of properly managing this resource, without which these communities cannot sustain themselves. As the benefits emanating from fishing were not significant, the alienated communities posed a great challenge to the government in managing this vital resource.

7.5.5. Inequality among Fishermen: Gandhi Sagar Reservoir, MP

In MP, only 11 per cent of the households that were interviewed were found to be poor while the rest were better off (i.e., non-poor, see Table 4.19). Our research has led us to conclude that unlike

Table 4.19

Head Count Ratio and Change in Poverty Status: Gandhi Sagar, MP

Fishing Cooperatives	Before FC Formation (in percentage)			After FC Formation			Status of Poverty		
	Poor	Non-poor	Total	Poor	Non-poor	Total	Always Poor	Never Poor	Improvement
Gandhi Sagar	14.4 (13)	85.6 (77)	100.0 (90)	4.4 (4)	95.6 (86)	100.0 (90)	4.4	85.6	10.0
Rampuriya	13.3 (12)	86.7 (78)	100.0 (90)	7.8 (7)	92.2 (83)	100.0 (90)	7.8	86.7	5.6
Sanjit	30.0 (27)	70.0 (63)	100.0 (90)	21.1 (19)	78.9 (71)	100.0 (90)	21.1	70.0	8.9
Total	19.3 (52)	80.7 (218)	100.0 (270)	11.1 (30)	88.9 (240)	100.0 (270)	11.1	80.7	8.1

Source: Field survey, (2009).
Note: Figures in parentheses indicate number of observations.

the high state level of poverty (48%), the Gandhi Sagar reservoir fishermen had low initial levels of poverty (data obtained from field survey done in 2008–09). After the formation of the FC, the incomes of Gandhi Sagar households generally increased across all the FCs with a greater increase experienced by the non-poor households. For example, approximately 81 per cent of households experiencing an increase in incomes reported that they had never been poor while another 8 per cent of households reported an improvement in their poverty status. A closer look at the poverty ratios revealed that FC formation had been able to push nearly 22 households above the poverty line.

Conceivably, low initial levels of poverty and strict monitoring by the contractor created a higher fish catch for the FC beneficiaries. However, the extent to which the FC management aided in reducing the poverty of the communities dependent on reservoir fishing is yet to be examined. Incidentally, there was a high probability that the excluded communities (non-traditional communities) were worse off than those who enjoyed the right to fish in the reservoir. Unfortunately, the limitation of our

Table 4.20

Profile of Poor Households in Terms of Access to Land, Participation in FC Activities and Change in Poverty Status: Gandhi Sagar Reservoir, MP

Change in the Status of Poverty	Gandhi Sagar	Rampuriya	Sanjit	Total
1. Participation in the activities of FCs				
Always poor	10.0 (9)	7.8 (7)	4.4 (4)	7.4 (20)
Non-poor	32.2 (29)	34.4 (31)	47.8 (43)	38.1 (103)
Improvement	16.7 (15)	20.0 (18)	14.4 (13)	17.0 (46)
Total	58.9 (53)	62.2 (56)	66.7 (60)	62.6 (169)
2. The extent of dependence on fishing activities				
Poor + dependent on fishing	100.0 (4)	100.0 (7)	73.7 (14)	83.3 (25)
Non-poor + dependent on fishing	93.0 (80)	91.6 (76)	76.1 (54)	87.5 (210)
Poor + dependent on non-fishing			26.3 (5)	16.7 (5)
Non-poor + dependent on non-fishing	7.0 (6)	8.4 (7)	23.9 (17)	12.5 (30)

Source: Field survey, (2009).
Note: Figures in parentheses indicate number of observations.

selection of sample households to only FC members precluded any such analysis.

7.6. Gandhi Sagar Reservoir: Who are the Poor?

7.6.1. Participation in Activities of the FCs

As discussed earlier, fishing was a vital economic activity for both poor and non-poor households in the Gandhi Sagar reservoir area. Table 4.20 shows that households who participated in FC activities belonged mainly to the non-poor category. The level of participation was less for households who had always been poor than for their counterparts in other categories.

Out of 30 poor households, nearly 83 per cent were dependent on fishing for their livelihood while the rest earned their living from non-fishing activities such as agricultural labour. A majority of them belonged to Sanjit.

7.6.2. Gandhi Sagar: Status of Poverty and Major Sources of Income

Table 4.21 shows that the incidence of poverty was high for households relying mainly on cultivation and agricultural labour for their livelihoods. A similar trend was observed across all Gandhi Sagar FCs. Out of a total of 87 per cent of households engaged in fishing, nearly ten per cent were poor while the rest were non-poor. Only 23 households were chronically poor. FC-wise analysis reveals that the majority of fishing-dependent households were from the Gandhi Sagar FC and the Rampuriya FC was the incidence of poverty in these households being low. The above findings signify that income and locational advantage of the FCs had contributed significantly to the welfare of the households for all the FCs in general and the Gandhi Sagar and Rampuriya FCs in particular. It is here that the functioning of the FC became relevant in addressing the careful distribution of resource benefits. The heavy dependence on fishing, the lack of alternative employment opportunities and the rich productivity of the fishery called for proper management of the resource to enable it to contribute to the welfare of the households depending on it.

When this was viewed along with the economic conditions of these households before the FC formation, it was clear that the low incidence of poverty in the study area, the lack of alternative sources of employment and greater productivity of the resource had increased pressures on the resource. This was also evident from the increasing size of the fish catch from the reservoir. Despite a decline in real prices of fish, more and more fishermen were harvesting fish for a greater number of days. This in turn raised the question of the capacity of the FF to ensure the sustainable use of the resource.

7.6.3. Gandhi Sagar: Status of Poverty and Income from Fishing

At the time of the survey, fishing contributed 76 per cent of the total income earned by the Gandhi Sagar reservoir households (Table 4.22). The contribution from fishing was highest for households in the Gandhi Sagar FC (86%) followed by that of

Table 4.21

Head Count Ratio and Change in Poverty Status by MJSI: Gandhi Sagar Reservoir, MP

MJSI	Total (% to its total)	Before FC Formation (% to total)		After FC Formation (% to total)		Change in Poverty Status (N)		
		Poor	Non-poor	Poor	Non-poor	Always Poor	Never Poor	Improved
Gandhi Sagar								
Animal Husbandry	1.1 (1)	100.0			100.0			1
Fishing	93.3 (84)	14.3	85.7	4.8	95.2	4	72	8
Non-agricultural labour	3.3 (3)		100.0		100.0		3	
Other (shopkeeper, carpenter, etc.)	2.2 (2)		100.0		100.0		2	
Total	100.0 (90)	14.4	85.6	4.4	95.6	4	77	9
Rampuriya								
Animal Husbandry	1.1 (1)	100.0			100.0			1
Fishing	93.3 (84)	9.5	90.5	6.0	94.0	5	76	3
Non-agricultural labour	4.4 (4)	50.0	50.0	25.0	75.0	1	2	1
Other (shopkeeper, carpenter, etc.)	1.1 (1)	100.0		100.0		1		
Total	100.0 (90)	13.3	86.7	7.8	92.2	7	78	5
Sanjit								
Animal Husbandry	5.6 (5)	20.0	80.0	20.0	80.0	1	4	
Fishing	75.6 (68)	30.9	69.1	20.6	79.4	14	47	7

(contd...)

(contd...)

MJSI	Total (% to its total)	Before FC Formation (% to total)		After FC Formation (% to total)		Change in Poverty Status (N)		
		Poor	Non-poor	Poor	Non-poor	Always Poor	Never Poor	Improved
Agricultural labour	4.4 (4)	50.0	50.0	50.0	50.0	2	2	
Non-agricultural labour	14.4 (13)	23.1	76.9	15.4	84.6	2	10	1
Other (shopkeeper, carpenter. etc.)	100.0 (90)	30.0	70.0	21.1	78.9	19	63	8
Total								
Animal Husbandry	2.2 (6)	33.3	66.7	16.7	83.3	1	4	1
Fishing	87.4 (236)	17.4	82.6	9.7	90.3	23	195	18
Agricultural labour	1.9 (5)	60.0	40.0	40.0	60.0	2	2	1
Non-agricultural labour	7.4 (20)	25.0	75.0	15.0	85.0	3	15	2
Other (shopkeeper, carpenter, etc.)	1.1 (3)	33.3	66.7	33.3	66.7	1	2	
Total	100.0 (270)	19.3	80.7	11.1	88.9	30	218	22

Source: Field survey, (2009).
Note: Figures in parentheses indicate number of observations.

Table 4.22

Average Income from Fishing and Share of Income from Fishing to Total Income by Poverty Status: Gandhi Sagar Reservoir, MP

	Average (Median) Net Income (₹/year)								
	Poor			Non-poor			Total		
FCs	Fishing	Total	% of Income From Fishing	Fishing	Total	% of Income From Fishing	Fishing	Total	% of Income From Fishing
Gandhi Sagar	95,220 (4)	112,470	92.0	45,425 (86)	54,395	85.2	46,000 (90)	56,925	85.6
Rampuriya	85,100 (7)	140,300	69.6	39,100 (83)	48,760	82.2	39,100 (90)	55,085	80.5
Sanjit	18,400 (19)	45,540	52.5	28,520 (71)	51,520	59.3	26,910 (90)	49,680	58.0
Total	34,385 (30)	55,545	66.6	38,870 (240)	51,635	77.3	38,870 (270)	53,360	76.0

Source: Field survey, (2009).

Note: Figures in parentheses indicate number of observations.

Rampuriya (81%) and Sanjit (58%). Barring the Gandhi Sagar FC, the contribution of fishing to total income was higher for non-poor households (77%) than their counterparts in poor households (67%). Such a difference in contribution to income between poor and non-poor households was more significant for the Rampuriya FC households than the rest.

To sum up, the FCs excluded some households and benefitted only STs (in the case of Gujarat), the traditional communities and the Bangladeshi refugees (in MP). However, our decision to survey only FC members limited us from knowing more about other fishermen, their levels of dependence on fishing, the quantity of fish they harvested and the income that they earned from fishing. This might have in turn helped us to explain the low productivity of FC fishing.

FC advocates have argued that cooperatives were a response to reducing externalities arising out of the high transaction costs of monitoring fishermen. Our case studies reveal how the original concept of the cooperatives was twisted and then made to work in both states. Unlike cooperatives formed for the benefit of members, the cooperatives in MP in particular bred a form of crony capitalism in which the control and distribution of resources were based on close government-contractor relationships rather than on economic fundamentals. This occurred in Gujarat also. This therefore brings forth the ways in which the state tinkered superficially with the institutional framework of cooperatives without modifying the social structure in which the FF and FCs were rooted. Our overall findings suggest that such a coercive cooperative structure would collapse in the absence of coercion.

8. Comparative Questions and Answers

In order to summarize our findings we return to the questions raised at the end of section 3.

1. How was the FC project and institution introduced?

Both the top-down and bottom-up approaches to the FF and FC formation were merely used as tools to assist the governments to meet their goal of controlling the resource. By doing so, the dependency of the FCs was not replaced by self-reliance but was further perpetuated by the new organizational frameworks set up by the governments. Irrespective of the approaches adopted, member participation and community empowerment were nowhere emphasized as a central feature of the FCs. In fact, both strategies were employed to exert FD control over the fish resources. This was done by strategically replacing the FF+FC model of fishing management with the dubious FF+contractor+FC model. Both states, in effect, created an institutional straightjacket. The FCs formed by the top-down approach in MP filtered in the government's structural biases and reinforced its associated powers, while the bottom-up approach in Gujarat revealed the apathy of the government towards FC problems. Whatever might have been the initial conditions of poverty and dependence on fishing for livelihoods, the attitude of the governments towards the FCs resulted in limited participation by members in FC-related activities.

While the governments of both states claimed that the FC+FF model was based on mutual benefits, our case studies indicate that this was often not the case. In both states, the government possesses de jure rights to the resource. It used these rights to devise strategies depending on the level of reliance of a community on the resource and its contribution to the incomes of fishermen. In Gujarat, as fishing income was only a supplementary source of income for FC households, coercive cooperation[8] was used as a strategy whereby a fishing ground was leased to a tribal community only if they formed a cooperative. The FC thus became trapped between the government's apathy towards the difficulties of FCs in mobilizing capital for purchasing the lease and the contractor's willingness to lend money under tight conditions. Fishermen were also bribed by offers of home loans, free boats and nets under the fishermen' welfare schemes implemented only through the FCs. The reservoir was regularly stocked with fingerlings by the FD. Thus, many FCs were formed and were functioning, not because members had created an institution to pursue collective action, but because

---

[8] Coercive cooperation occurs when the state stipulates that individuals can get access to certain benefits/resources only through cooperatives.

of the government-provided benefits that accrued to members. Limited motivational activities by the FCs and personal rapport with the leader got translated into limited levels of participation by the fishermen.

The coercive cooperative method, along with bribed cooperation (as observed by Shah in her 1998 study) was also used by the Government of MP when it made the FC and FF mandatory. The MPFF was supported by revenues collected from a contractor. The rich reservoir fishing in MP probably led to this strategy, which was different from that of Gujarat. In MP, the state government maintained a cooperative monopoly by using contractors to keep non-members out of the fishing ground. Fishermen were bribed by providing benefits under various welfare schemes like those in Gujarat. Given the government's control of the FCs and the limited decentralization of harvesting rights, the increase in the fish harvest and incomes of fishermen in MP had little to do with the participation of fishermen in FC activities but could be attributed to entry barriers faced by non-members and the strict monitoring of the fishing ground by the contractor.

2. How did the project and institution perform, both de jure and de facto, in terms of CNRM goals?

To recapitulate, in Gujarat, the government leased out the reservoir for fishing to an FC by charging ₹150 thousand per year. This meant that the state acted as the custodian of the reservoir. Although the tribal community had the right to fish, the de jure control over fishing in the reservoir remained with the government. Moreover, the lease amount made it mandatory for the fishermen to come together and form a cooperative. To mobilize capital to purchase the lease of the fishing ground, the FF in 2004 approached a private contractor who agreed to pay the lease amount. In turn, the members had to sell their fish to the contractor at prices determined by him. He then sold them in the open market. This showed that the government had divided the functions of ownership and management of the Ukai fishery between itself and the FCs, with the latter involved in harvesting and managing the resource. However, not only were the FCs unable to take the reservoir bed on lease for fishing purposes, they also could not monitor the reservoir and prevent illegal fishing. In reality, they lacked the capacity to control the behaviour of their own members, let alone manage the fishery of a 150 km-long reservoir.

In Gandhi Sagar, an FF was created to manage fishing in the reservoir and this body was headed by a bureaucrat appointed by the state government. One could identify positive aspects of this structure of governance. As the contractor was driven by profit motive, it was in his interest to monitor fishing activities and thereby check illegal fishing activities in the reservoir. When viewed closely, one found that the choice of contractor, and any possible increases in fish rates were controlled by special interest groups which actually impeded the functioning of the federation of FCs. This reduced the role of the FCs to distributing deferred wages and bonuses and managing conflicts amongst fishermen.

3. What was the extent of productivity and income increase?

The declining per capita production of the Ukai FCs points to a fragile resource base that had failed to withstand the intensity of the harvest in both states. In Gujarat, the small contribution of fishing to household incomes explained why fishermen supplemented their income from fishing and did not depend entirely on this source for their livelihood. Fishing supported a low level of subsistence in the Ukai fishing communities. The inherent characteristics of the resource, the pressure of population growth and the commercialization of fishing activity led this resource base to cross a threshold limit after which production per fisher dropped. A sudden shock in the form of a failed monsoon could reduce the water supply in the reservoir, thereby making the whole fishery and its dependents collapse.

In MP, in the absence of alternative sources of employment, fishing provided an assured source of livelihood. Over time, extraction of fish may have resulted in declines in productivity and thereby a decline in fishermen's incomes. Due to the FCs' marginality in terms of its remoteness from urban centres, fragile resource base and inadequate human and other capital assets like access to land, the income earned from non-fishing sources became unfavourable to these communities. The government, facing limited production and income-generating potential in an area constrained by lack of other resource endowments and socio-economic characteristics, realized that fishing was a potential poverty alleviation tool. It stocked the reservoir with fingerlings to raise productivity levels. However, it failed to provide other necessities such as monitoring or marketing facilities, or the training that would have enabled the FCs to take up these tasks.

The marginality of these areas reduced the ability of the fishermen to benefit from the market. Rather than treating the constraints faced by the fragile area with care, the governments in both states treated the FCs as liabilities and outsourced the marketing of fish to contractors. The low price of fish in constant terms, compared to the situation before FC formation, suggested that outsourcing of fishing management, particularly in MP, was not benefitting the fishermen. Consequently, fishing households, particularly in Gujarat, were compelled to look for alternative sources of income, mainly as non-agricultural labourers. Proper management by FCs has the potential to increase fish harvests, and increase income and consumption for fishermen. But the sustainable use of this fragile resource is a major challenge and increasingly a matter of urgent relevance.

4. How decentralized and inclusive is the governance of the CNRM institution?

As stated above, though the approaches to the formation of FCs varied in the two states under study, the indifference of the governments towards decentralizing resource management control to FCs was palpable. In MP most key decisions, like fixing the rate for fish or the choice of contractor, were taken at the FF level, while fishing communities played only a minimal role in managing the resource. The president and the secretary largely managed the books of accounts and resolved conflicts among fishermen. The presidents of the Gandhi Sagar and Rampuriya FCs were fortunate enough to obtain help from their friends and relatives in managing FC-related tasks, but this should not be confused with participation by members. In Gujarat, as they were bound by their contract with the contractor, FCs and FFs had to succumb to the fish rates set by the latter. Thus, whatever approach to FC formation was taken, the absence of decentralization was quite evident in the twisted versions of cooperatives in both states.

Fishing was basically a male-dominated activity and thus in the Gandhi Sagar reservoir females played only a limited role in fishing activity as well as in the FCs. As females did not engage in fishing, they did not participate in any FC activities. Tasks carried out by females like sewing torn nets were unreported. In the Ukai reservoir, the level of women's participation in fishing was higher, but overall low household dependence on fishing and the general indifference towards FCs failed to encourage fishermen, male or female, to actively participate in FC-related activities.

5. What has been the impact on the poor members of the village?

Unlike those in MP, for a majority of the FC households studied in Gujarat, fishing supplemented the income earned from animal husbandry, cultivation and as agricultural or non-agricultural labour. This dependence on non-fishing activities was induced by the marginality of this area, with its fragile and low productive resource base and inadequate human and other capital assets resulting in low income from fishing. In this context, it is clear that whatever fishing contributed to the total income of an Ukai household, it did act as a buffer against risks faced from non-fishing activities. This points clearly towards the need to better manage reservoir fishing, without which Ukai communities would cease to sustain themselves. However, one has to bear in mind that it was the non-fishing activities that failed to provide households with adequate incomes to purchase the basic necessities of life. If any impact on poverty was to be made it would be through various programmes in non-fishing activities rather than through fishing activities. Though limited convergence of FC activities with various schemes devised for fishermen was evident, the latter had only a limited impact on the participation of members in FC-related activities. As the primary source of household income emanated from non-fishing activities like cultivation or animal husbandry, the merging of FCs with schemes promoting land and forest-based activities like JFM could lead to improving the participation of members in FC-related activities.

In MP, as the majority of FC members were non-poor, there was very little impact of the FCs on poverty. Marginality in terms of remoteness from urban centres and the lack of profitable avenues for employment made communities depend heavily on fishing for their livelihoods. The increasing population pressures and declining stocks of fingerlings by the government reduced fish resource productivity and hence fishermen incomes. Having drawn these conclusions though, it is also true that our limited data restricted our scope for rigorously analysing the impact of the FCs in reducing poverty.

Our main finding is that the FCs were not sufficient on their own to combat poverty. However, FCs could definitely be viewed as one strategy that could be applied with other strategies in tribal areas including improved animal husbandry practices, better distribution of land rights, improved agricultural practices and so on. Many different kinds of measures could be used to improve the government's service delivery to poor fishermen. One important measure is simplifying procedures and making them transparent to fishermen. This would improve poor fishermen's confidence in their FCs and plug leakages (illegal fishing, government-contractor nexus or sham elections) in the system. Other important measures could include disseminating information about the choice of the contractor and creating effective monitoring and sanctions that could be used by members to protect the fishing ground. Such measures would empower the FC community and enable it to hold the government accountable, thereby reducing inefficiency and corruption.

6. How integrated was the project intervention and what was the extent of the outreach?

There is no evidence to suggest that the FCs had developed any consciousness of community empowerment on their own or with the support of NGOs. The empowerment of the community through FC activities was constrained by the nexus between local leaders, the contractor and the government. The linkage of the contractor with politicians was reported by fishermen in almost all the FCs. This either undermined FC control of the resource (as in MP) or led to questionable selection of contractors (as in Gujarat). Such interference weakened the ties of members with the FCs, making fishermen want to sell their catch in the open market and not to the FCs. Thus, irrespective of the approaches followed in either state, the FCs had degenerated into institutions that were maximizing profits for the contractor and the government rather than for empowering the community. For the latter to happen, efforts should have been made to train the community to monitor the reservoir, sell fish, manage their own affairs as well as help in scaling-up membership. Unfortunately, both governments failed altogether to provide such kinds of support.

7. How had the project and institution contributed to effective, equitable and sustainable management of the resource?

In MP, there existed a strong inclination within the government to make FCs and the FF appear as if they were formed for purposes of social reform. But in reality they had degenerated into institutions for harvesting fish on a large scale, as well as distributing deferred wages, bonuses and managing conflicts amongst fishermen. Such a model may have increased the fishermen's incomes in the short run, but in the long run the sustainability of the fish harvest was a major concern for reservoir fishing in both states. The signs of resource over-exploitation were quite visible in MP

The MP government forced fishermen to sell their harvest to the contractor rather than strengthen their skills in FC-related activities. Meanwhile, the dependence of FC members on fishing and their inability to resist the control of officials and private parties had made the FCs vehicles for economic exploitation. Aligned with government officials, the contractor made substantial investments in terms of monitoring the reservoir to ensure that FC members sold their catch only to him. In turn, the fishermen become concerned only with earning their livelihoods. They suffered from limited education and meekly obeyed the instructions of the government to participate in a system that benefitted the contractor at the cost of fishermen. Buckling under his control, they become resigned to working in a system that created minimum advantages for them rather than trying to change the larger structures of the system (Scott, 1985: 92).

Our discussions with fishermen revealed that they felt robbed of their autonomy and were only labourers engaged in catching fish from the reservoir. They felt that they had become puppets that the government used to execute its strategies but were powerless to make the government accountable for such manipulation. In the absence of any decentralization of power, the FCs functioned as instruments for overcoming managerial problems rather than as new platforms that allowed fishermen to participate in the management of their resource. Some talked about the need for NGOs to train fishermen in managing the FC, to establish respect for rules, devise accountability measures to counter corruption and market fish so as to benefit those who caught them. In view of the hard realities discussed here, extraordinary measures and extraordinary leadership will be the need of the hour to unlock the potential of India's fishing cooperatives.

The degradation of the fish resource in both study areas constituted a serious environmental risk predicting the disruption of biophysical functions and the fish harvest. The process of stocking the reservoir with fingerlings and efforts made to renew the resource by stopping fishing operations during the monsoon, not catching juvenile fish, using fishing nets of particular sizes etc. did help the regeneration of fish. But intensive harvesting of fish exposed reservoir fishing in fragile areas to grave degradation. The increase in the population dependent on fishing, market-induced demand and the resource-extractive policies of governments, particularly in MP, resulted in overly intensive fish harvesting.

The lack of strict supervision in Gujarat (where there was no check on illegal fishing or selling of fish catch outside the FCs) resulted in similar overexploitation and degradation of the fish resource in the long run. In sum, the policies of the governments in both states revolved around resource extraction without any sensitivity towards the imperatives of sustainable fish management.

9. The Way Forward

The foregoing analysis of the functioning of the FCs and poverty in the context of Gujarat and MP indicates that the FCs had varying potential in terms of enhancing livelihoods in communities (varying from low dependence on fishing in Ukai to high dependence in Gandhi Sagar) that were at the margin of the development process. Given the multiplicity of the causes of poverty, it was not surprising that the FCs, however set up, were not panaceas for poverty reduction. Yet the potential of the FCs in contributing to household incomes and in reducing poverty had been reduced with the alienation of fishermen from the processes of planning and implementation. The main lacunae in fishery reform started from the conceptual and implementation levels. At the conceptual level, it was naive to expect a group of fishermen to purchase the lease of the fishing ground of the reservoir. The implementation of FCs, moreover, required motivation of members, training in record keeping and the setting up of an effective monitoring and sanctions system. It also called for support during the post-implementation stage and assistance for the FCs in marketing their catch.

Properly launched FCs may impact poverty better if they are part of a larger package of interlinked and complementary strategies that combat poverty at different levels within a national framework. Within such a framework, the FCs can play an important role as an additional strategy for supporting livelihoods in marginalized tribal/rural areas. Real decentralization of management to FCs will assign decision-making control regarding the resource to fishing communities that have the knowledge and incentives to make decisions best suited to their long-term needs. This will require adequate support and safeguards from both state and central governments to ensure enough autonomy and fiscal control for the FCs, as well as training in public administration, financial management, communications, community relations and marketing. With strong administrative capacity and accountability mechanisms the FCs can reduce the current scope for corruption. To translate this potential into reality, FCs as institutions will have to overcome the current lack of fisher interest, lack of participation and lack of elections to ensure that the FCs function in a democratic way. Building and strengthening these institutions may take time, but if inland fishing is to continue to be productive in India, they will be worth the effort.

5

Participatory Watershed Development Projects in Gujarat and Madhya Pradesh: Do They Impact Poverty?

Amita Shah*

1. Introduction

1.1. The Context and the Complexities

From isolated efforts for soil and water conservation and drought relief, the WDP has emerged as a key intervention for promoting sustainable livelihoods among a large number of rural households across different agro-ecological regions in India. Over time, watershed development has come to be looked upon as part of an integrated approach to development, rather than as merely a project or a scheme for regeneration and management of natural resources, especially land, water and vegetation. The approach, ideally, seeks to establish and reinforce integration in terms of natural resources, economic activities, social groups, administrative entities and financial resources (Shah, 1998). Put simply, the WDP seeks to attain productivity enhancement by simultaneously addressing the issues of resource sustainability and equity in benefit sharing among different categories of households.

* with Hasmukh Joshi, H. Shiddhalingaswamy and Dipak Nandani.

This essentially implied a wider arena of objectives that will focus on five larger concerns: (a) productivity enhancement and economic viability; (b) equity in access to resources and benefit sharing; (c) environmental sustainability; (d) community participation and (e) deepening of decentralized democracy (Joy et al., 2004: 13–28). Of these, the objectives pertaining to productivity, equity, sustainability and democracy relate mainly to outcomes whereas community participation is seen mainly as a means to achieve the desired outcomes. This obviously suggests a fairly complex web of interconnectedness among the multiple objectives set up for the project.

The participatory approach for watershed development initiated during the mid-1990s represented the highest level of financial as well as administrative devolution in the context of the policies for NRM in India. According to the guidelines prepared for watershed development in 1994, the fund once sanctioned was deposited directly in the bank account of the watershed development committee (WDC), the key institution for the programme (GoI, 1994). This was the first ever policy to provide almost a complete devolution of financial resources to a community-based organization (CBO) at the village (micro-watershed) level (Farrington et al., 1999: 3).[1] The burgeoning literature on watershed development is testimony to the expanding boundaries and promises that watershed development holds, especially for areas and people facing special disadvantages in terms of the quality of, access to, and depletion of natural resources. At the same time, the multi-functionality of the project makes it difficult to assess its impact and monitor the outcomes. It is perhaps this feature of watershed development that has attracted significant attention among researchers as well as policymakers and practitioners.

---

[1] As precursors to this, a number of watershed projects adopting the participatory approach were initiated, though on a smaller scale, with support from various donor agencies and involving NGOs as PIAs. Their experience, by and large, suggested that the approach could work on a larger scale, provided an adequate space was created for the processes of institution building and the institutions themselves.

The WDP is not without its critics. They include ecologists who have argued that WDP projects did not pay adequate attention to the harmful effects of rainwater harvesting interventions on both the upstream catchment and downstream areas of a given basin. They also warned that changes in land use associated with WDP affected a watershed's hydrology, which in turn affected social, economic and environmental objectives (Kumar et al., 2006, 2008). A larger group of scholars and donor agencies have been concerned about equity issues in the distribution of WDP projects' benefits (Joy and Paranjpe, 2004; Kerr et al., 1998; Ramchandradu, 2007; Reddy, 2003; Shah, 2001; Shah, Samuel and Joy, 2011; Turton 2000). In keeping with the overall theme of this book, the impact of WDP on the poor and marginalized members of eight villages of Gujarat and MP is the central focus of this chapter.

1.2. Equity and Poverty Reduction in WDPs

The issue of equity (if not poverty reduction) poses one of the most difficult challenges in the implementation of watershed projects. This occurs primarily because of the complexities in the planning, execution and benefit-sharing mechanisms involved in watershed projects. These complexities arise primarily due to the various trade-offs involved, such as: (a) private vs. social benefits; (b) short term vs. long term gains and (c) scientific (i.e., 'ridge to valley' and integrated) approach vs. crop productivity-centric approach for resource management. Thus, the WDP aims at enhancing both private (through increased productivity of land) as well as long-range social benefits (by ensuring improved land quality, sustainable water use and enhanced restoration of biodiversity) (Shah, 2004: 6–8). This poses a serious challenge of striking a balance between its multiple objectives.

A major conflict may arise mainly between productivity enhancement and the rest of the four objectives noted earlier. For, productivity enhancement is often found to be associated with increased use of water for irrigation, use of inputs rather than skill and labour intensive crops and farm practices, and a depletion of groundwater in the treated watershed. What is of greater concern is that such gains in productivity are confined to a small sub-set of households, particularly the landed households, who often are able to access additional water resources produced by project intervention.

In fact, poverty reduction is intrinsically linked to the issue of who benefits from the increased water resources as well as the fodder, fuel and minor forest produce that may be obtained from the development of pastures and community land/forests within the watershed. Prima facie, therefore, the issue of equity plays a critical role in determining the outcome of conflict or convergence among the five broad objectives. Equity in resource access brings with it an emphasis on the limited, efficient and environmentally sustainable use of water and also a special focus on the development of CPRs. Attaining these objectives would necessitate participation of various stakeholders, which eventually may strengthen the process of deepening decentralized democracy.

Conversely, inequitable access to resources and benefits may lead a small set of beneficiaries to undertake input-intensive farming, following business-as-usual practices, which in turn may not be environmentally conducive. Moreover, the absence of an equity focus could also undermine the interests of the poorer stakeholders in the community, thereby becoming detrimental to democratic norms (Shah, 2001: 4).

There are two major constraints in establishing a direct link between watershed development and poverty reduction. The first refers to the inequitable sharing of benefits from water, which in most cases, leaves out a large proportion of poor communities. The second refers to the observed neglect of CPRs such as pastures and community land/forests owing to a number of limitations that are legal (access to forest land for treatment), socio-political (feasibility of encroachment on CPRs) and ecological (excessive use and degradation) (Shah et al., 2011).

As mentioned earlier, the policy objective emphasized in watershed projects is equity rather than poverty reduction (Crase and Gandhi, 2009: 333; Farrington et al., 1999: 77; Shah et al., 2011).[2] In the mid-1990s, the stated objectives of the MoRD guidelines following the Hanumantha Rao Committee Report (1984) had placed special emphasis on 'improving economic and social conditions of the resource poor and the disadvantaged sections of the watershed community such as the asset-less and women'.[3]

The available evidence does not present a very encouraging picture about the equity and poverty reduction aspects of WDPs, at least until the mid-2000s.[4] There are, however, a few shining

---

[2] For instance, the new Common Guidelines effective from April 2008 lay special emphasis on the equity aspect of watershed development. In fact, equity and gender sensitivity have been recognized as important Guiding Principles for project implementation (GoI, 2008). The Common Guidelines envisage that: 'Watershed Development Projects should be considered as the levers of inclusiveness. PIAs must facilitate the equity processes such as (a) enhanced livelihood opportunities for the poor through investment in their assets and improvement in productivity and income, (b) improving access of the poor, especially women to the benefits, (c) enhancing the role of women in decision making and (d) ensuring access to usufruct rights from the CPRs for the resource poor' (p.7). The other guiding principles such as decentralization, community participation and capacity building are dovetailed to the larger objectives of equity. Also see Joy et al., 2006.

[3] Subsequently, the revised guidelines (2011) made it mandatory to form User Groups (UGs) and Self-help Groups (SHGs), which included women and also recommended special groups comprising only of women. The promotion of income-generating activities through training, credit and marketing support was envisaged as the main plank for addressing the issue of equity in these guidelines. Besides these, membership of women and the landless was made mandatory in village watershed committees. Similarly, special emphasis was laid on technology for reducing drudgery and extending support mechanisms through Mahila Mitra Kisan in the Guidelines for NWDPRA prepared by the Ministry of Agriculture (MoA). Targeted budgetary allocations were made for the promotion of income generating activities focusing specifically on women and the asset-poor.

[4] For details see Shah et al. (2011a). A study conducted by Ramchandradu (2007) observed that of the 55 micro watershed projects, 25 had made some efforts for identifying poor households in the initial stages of project implementation. The number, however, got reduced to 11 in the subsequent stages of evolving institutions for the poor and planning; only seven projects sustained their focus on poor households at the time of execution. Further, whereas inclusion of members of the weaker sections and women was an important criterion while setting up the watershed committee, the focus got diluted at the time of planning. Moreover, consultation, if any, was limited to the dominant section of the village. Participation was low in 40 per cent of the sample watersheds. What is more striking is that while setting the priorities or activities to be included in the action plan, a strong bias was found, usually towards the better-off families of the village or convenience of implementation in terms of availability of funds, labour etc. Use of labour was often given lower priority under the guise of its non-availability locally.

examples of good practices, such as Hivre Bazar and Ralegaon Siddhi, where strong local leadership led to ensuring equity and sustainability in the use of water and other CPRs (Menon et al., 2007: 13). Some of the flagship programmes supported by National Bank for Agriculture and Rural Development (NABARD) and Danish International Development Agency (DANIDA) have had similar results (Shah et al., 2011).

1.3. Community Participation and Institutions as the Vehicle for Change

As noted earlier, with equity at the centre of watershed development along with the three other objectives/outcomes (i.e., productivity, sustainability and decentralized democracy), community-based institutions operate as a critical means or vehicle to attain these outcomes.

The institutional arrangements envisaged by the policy guidelines have been presented in Figure 5.1. It may be noted that the institutional arrangements varied over time and also across different programmes which were supported by different state ministries as well as the GoI. What we have presented below depicts some of the common features found in most of the programmes.

As seen in Figure 5.1, the nature and quality of institutional processes holds the key to determining the bio-physical/ environmental and socio-economic impact, including poverty reduction, resulting from watershed projects in a given setting. The basic hypothesis is this: other things being equal, the more intense and broad-based the processes, the better is the impact in terms of environmental sustainability, economic viability and equity. There are, however, important caveats to this hypothesis and these are discussed below. Participatory processes are likely to be fairly weak and more rhetorical than real and rigorous as found in the case of most of the participatory NRM projects in India and other developing economies (Hickey and Mohan, 2004: 159–75).

According to the guidelines (2008) the WDC should have at least 10 members, of which five should be from the SHGs/UGs; one

Figure 5.1

Watershed Development Projects: Institutional Processes

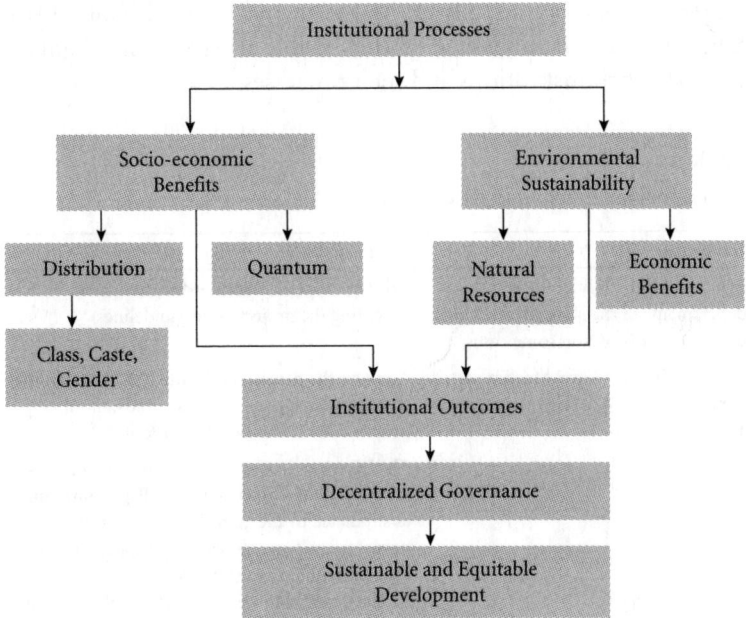

Source: Author's own.

each from the watershed development team and representatives from SCs, STs, the landless and women. Also, as per the guidelines, the Gram Sabha constitutes the WDC and nominates/selects the president and secretary of the WDC. It meets annually in an AGM. In this sense, the Gram Sabha plays a critical role in the formation of the WDC and the appointment of its key functionaries.

One may find that the policy space for creating CBOs, especially WDCs, UGs and SHGs is fairly well spread over the time span of any project. For instance, WDCs are formed right at the first stage and continued until the completion of the project. After this, the WDC formally gets dissolved and usually hands over its tasks to the village panchayat. Thus the WDC does not have much of a formal role to play in the post-project phase. In fact, two other institutions, that is, the UGs and the SHGs may take over some of the activities initiated during the project implementation phase in the post-project period. Experience, however, indicates that the UGs are seldom formed and/or activated and that the SHGs also tended to die out gradually in the post-project period (DSC, 2010; Shah et al., 2009; Singh et al., 2011).[5] Table 5.1 sheds some light on the watershed institutions and their processes.

Table 5.1

Watershed Institutions and Processes: A Profile

Institutions	Specific Role
PIA: consists mainly of the line departments of the state governments or DRDA, or NGOs in some cases	Primary responsibility for designing and executing the project as per guidelines
District and State Level Machineries: Department of Rural Development and DRDA	Approve the project, select the PIA, sanction the technical work plan as well as funds, monitor project activities as per the work plan
WDC	The EC consists of elected/nominated members from different segments of the village community as stipulated by the guidelines. Also sets up the norms for resource development allocation and use across different segments of the communities. All the financial powers are vested with the WDC
Gram Sabha: generally not involved beyond holding annual general meetings (AGMs)	Selects/elects the WDC and approves the work plan
UGs and SHGs: Not mandatory, hence seldom formed and/or operational	UGs are responsible for taking care of structures created during the project and working out the norms for the use, distribution and future management of resources. SHGs are generally formed around income-generating activities for the poor/women as part of the project activities.
Village Panchayat and PRIs: often a sheer formality	Future management of the project is handed over to PRIs, along with the watershed development fund (WDF).

Source: Author's own.

---

[5] There is a dearth of studies that have looked into the sustenance of watershed institutions in the post-project period. Most of the existing studies have tried to look into the institutional processes during or immediately after completion of the project implementation. It is therefore difficult to find a causal link between the institutions and project outcomes in the post-project context.

To a large extent, the weak institutional base of a watershed project hinges on the fact that the project has a fixed duration of about four–six years, which since 2008 has been extended to a seven-year period. This essentially grants a temporary and also instrumental role to the WDC formed under the projects. The short and fixed time perspective for the CBOs in watershed projects also impinges on the very process through which the committees are formed. The general experience is that the committees are formed within the first few weeks of the project duration and generally through nomination, which in most cases reproduces the existing power structures obtaining in the villages.

Conversely, PIAs assume a critical role in spearheading the processes of institution building and their actual functioning. The CBOs therefore started taking a back seat right from the beginning, at least de facto if not de jure. A study by WASSAN (Watershed Support Services and Activity Network) from 1995 to 2005 has captured the dynamics of the institutional processes across a typology of watershed projects (Ramchandradu, 2007). The study observed that the initial attempts at awareness generation were not sustained till the last phase of the project in a majority of the GoI-funded and NGO-facilitated projects. The focus on involving the poor in these institutions was relatively minimal in this category of projects. Projects where NGOs were involved as PIAs and those which had been funded by donor agencies, demonstrated better performance in terms of institutional processes.

More recently, a study covering 200 micro watersheds in Gujarat (Shah, 2001), MP, Andhra Pradesh and Rajasthan has suggested that there was hardly any institutional support in the post-project period as the WDCs were expected to discontinue once the project implementation was over. A similar case was observed with respect to the presence of the PIAs after the project is completed.[6] A somewhat similar observation was also obtained by a rapid

---

[6] For details, see DSC (2010: 7).

assessment of about 1,000 micro watersheds in MP, Maharashtra and Karnataka.[7]

This suggests a peculiar situation and some caveats, somewhat different from the rest of the three cases presented in this volume, in which the poverty outcomes were shaped by two overarching constraints emanating from (a) the nature of the resources (or intervention), which tended to exclude a large part of the poor and also had limited scope for influencing those who were covered under the project and (b) the institutional mechanisms envisaged by the project guidelines, which allowed only limited opportunities for the CBOs to impact project outcomes beyond the limited duration of project implementation. In this context, the role of the PIA assumed critical importance in shaping the nature of the institutional processes and their actual functioning during and after the project period. Thus, the agency for the poor rests mainly with the PIA rather than the community, and this in turn tests the PIA's commitment, prior experience and more importantly, continued presence with the community in the post-project period. Another caveat was that the PIA had limited space in terms of time and project intervention, much of which was determined by the technical protocols of treating a watershed in a scientific manner.[8]

Thus the central propositions in this analysis include: (a) the poverty impact in a typical micro watershed hinges mainly on the role played by the PIAs; (b) most of the poor (the landless and those with poor quality of land) may tend to gain only marginally from the project and (c) the CBOs could help ensure that limited benefits reach the relatively poor farmers, but the impact on poverty

---

[7] A large scale enquiry into the techno-economic and institutional aspects of watershed projects was carried out adopting a common methodology for sampling and data collection instruments in the three states. The study was conducted by three organizations: Gujarat Institute of Development Research (GIDR) in MP, Society for Promoting Participative Ecosystem Management (SOPPECOM) in Maharashtra and Centre for Interdisciplinary Studies in Environment and Development (CISED) in Karnataka. For details see, Lele et al., 2009; Shah et al., 2011b.

[8] For instance, technical considerations like ridge-to-valley procedures, ground water balance, biodiversity, land capability and environmental protection are generally followed by the CBOs along with the PIAs while preparing an activity plan.

will only be marginal. Moreover, local dynamics matter significantly in terms of shaping the success of the project in a technical and procedural sense; its impact on the poor and poverty reduction, which may be only at the margin.

1.4. Examining the Interface: Moderate Scope for Poverty Reduction?

From the discussion above, we can identify five essential pre-conditions (or proximate causes) through which community participation and institutions may effectively influence equity and perhaps reduce poverty. These include:

1. The nature and coverage of the activities carried out by the project.
2. Inclusion of the landless and poorer communities in the activities carried out by the project.
3. Anticipated spill-over effects (in terms of employment generation, or increased wages) that help the poor in an indirect yet sustained basis.
4. Anticipated size of the benefits that could flow, directly (through inclusion in the project) or indirectly (through wage/employment generation).
5. Anticipated sustenance of benefits in the post-project period.

As argued earlier, participatory processes and community-based institutions, de jure, did have a fairly critical role in deciding all of these parameters. Nevertheless, poverty outcomes were governed largely by structural factors such as the property rights regime, agro-ecological potential, agrarian structures and administrative processes, as well as the local socio-political dynamics. Therefore, the core issues to investigate are:

1. Whether or not participatory (community-based) institutions (as against those enforced merely by statutory requirements) had been created. This would capture the issue of decentralization.

2. Whether or not these institutions were broad-based and had scope for protecting the stakes of the poor against elite capture. This would address equity and democratization.
3. How effective the participatory institutions have been in terms of three important dimensions, that is, transparency, accountability and the rule of law.
4. Whether the institutions endured after the projects or got handed over to other organizations like the PRI. This would capture the sustainability aspect.
5. What role the PIA played after the project implementation was over? This would highlight the role of an external agency.

The subsequent analysis addresses the two sets of issues listed above, namely: (a) what were the nature and coverage of the activities carried out by the project and (b) what was the larger socio-economic milieu obtaining in the study region.

2. Approach and Methodology

2.1. Selection of Micro Watershed and Households

The analysis presented here is based on case studies of four micro watersheds, covering different agro-ecological contexts, in each of Gujarat and MP. The selection of the micro watersheds was based on the following qualifying criteria:

1. The project implementation was to be completed by 2004–05, that is, about three–four years prior to conducting the study.
2. The project needed to be perceived by informed persons at the district level as reasonably successful, thus, avoiding non-successful and the best performing projects.
3. The average number of households within the project villages needed to be around 300 so as to avoid selecting very small or large villages.
4. The projects needed to capture a mixed pattern of involvement of NGOs and government as the PIA.

5. The community in the village should have a substantial stake in and dependence on agriculture; this was ensured by avoiding villages on the fringes of a major urban centre.

The selection procedure involved the following steps: the first step was to select four districts in each state, where watershed projects had a reasonably good presence. The districts were also selected in a manner so that they covered different socio-economic and/or agro-ecological contexts within the state. The second step was to select one micro watershed in each of the eight districts across the two states. The specific projects were selected using the qualifying criteria noted above. The next step was to conduct a complete house listing of all the households within the village by collecting information on a small set of household indicators as well as on the interface with the project. This was also followed by a FGD in order to capture the overall perceptions about the project among different segments of the village community.

The house listing and the initial FGD were used for selecting a sample of households using two major criteria, namely ownership of land and irrigation. In all, 1,926 households were covered through the house listing in the eight study villages—1,011 in Gujarat and 915 in MP. A sample of about 50 households was selected from three different categories, namely landless (24); land without irrigation (13) and land with irrigation (13). A total of 400 households were selected from eight villages covered under the study (see Table 5.2).

Besides the primary surveys of households, including the house listing, project-related information was collected through (a) secondary data from the records of the watershed committees; (b) village transects and (c) detailed discussions with some of the informed persons within the study villages.

The analysis, however, was limited by the fact that due to the short project duration, in most cases the local WD institutions were more or less dormant. Also, the PIAs did not have much direct involvement in the project area. Since the investigation took place after a gap of about five years or longer, villagers, by and large, had lost track of and perhaps interest in the intervention, which was officially deemed to be completed. Hence, much of the information

Table 5.2

Identification of the Study of Micro Watersheds in Gujarat and MP

S. No.	Village	Taluka (District)	Year of Commencement	Year of Completion	Number of Households	Name of PIA Govt/ NGO	Resource Augmentation through Check dam and Well Recharge	WDC
						Gujarat		
1	Valuna	Meghraj (Sabarkantha)	2004	2008	202	Development Support Centre (IWDP 1)	Yes	Yes
2	Jamsar	Wankaner (Rajkot)	2004	2006	200	Sarvodaya Seva Sangh (DDP1)	Yes	Yes
3	Tharavada	Bhuj (Kachchh)	1999	2001	362	SRDT DDP 2	Yes	Yes
4	Sama	Kalol (Panchmahal)	2000	2006	366	DRDA	Yes	Yes
						MP		
1	Kalakhunt	Jhabua (Jhabua)	2003	2005	250	ASA (RGMWM)	Yes	Yes
2	Sobaliyapura	Bagali (Dewas)	2002	2007	350	Samaj Pragati Sansthan (RGMWM)	Yes	Yes
3	Gopalpura	Ratlam (Ratlam)	2002	2007	450	SDO FD (IWDP)	Yes	Yes
4	Singrawankalan	Nawgaon (Chhatarpur)	2002	2007	404	Haritka (DPIP)	Yes	Yes

Source: Field survey, (2008).

Notes: ASA: Action for Social Advancement (an NGO); DDP: Desert Development Programme; DPIP: District Poverty Initiative Programme; DRDA: District Rural Development Agency; IWDP: Integrated Watershed Development Programme; RGMWM: Rajiv Gandhi Mission for Watershed Management.

Image 5.1

Valuna Watershed Map on the Wall of DSC Village Headquarters

Source: John R. Wood.

Image 5.2

Contour Bunding Arrests Monsoon Run-off

Source: John R. Wood.

Image 5.3

Check dam at Gopalpura

Source: John R. Wood.

Image 5.4

Village Tank at Kalakhunt

Source: John R. Wood.

we gathered for the analysis of the institutional aspects came from group meetings, transects to the physical structures constructed under the project and discussions with PIA informants. Usually the most important informant in the village was the person who had served as secretary of the WDC.

2.2. Identification of the Poor and the Poverty Impact of Watershed Projects

The analysis of the poverty impact has been based on a specific set of outcome indicators covering important aspects like access to alternative resources, income and employment, assets and indebtedness and participation in community-based institutions. However, before identifying the specific outcome indicators of our study watershed projects, it might be useful to specify those whom we considered as poor and how they were identified in the specific context of watershed projects in the study regions.

3. Who are the Poor?

The issue of identifying the poor is fairly complex, as already noted in Chapter 2. The official approach is to identify households that are BPL by using multiple indicators. But this approach has certain inherent limitations. We may nonetheless recapitulate some of the important issues involved in the identification process with specific focus on watershed projects in the two states covered under the study. These issues include:

1. BPL status was not a reliable indicator because of the high degree of variability in the administrative processes in identification and the issuing of BPL cards.
2. There was an absence of base-line information prior to the project intervention.
3. Poverty was likely to be transient in nature, especially in dry land/rain-fed areas where the WDPs are likely to be located.

4. The WDPs, in most cases, left out landless communities who often constitute a large proportion of the poor.
5. The economic benefits were likely to taper down over time and in the process, some of the initial impacts and the beneficiaries may get overlooked in a post-project assessment.
6. The direct economic impact of watershed development, unlike that in the case of irrigation, forestry and fishery, was somewhat small and not so certain. Thus, the impact, if any, may not necessarily have led to reductions in poverty (measured in terms of the official cut-off of MPCE). Rather, it may have helped in improving livelihood status in terms of income, employment and access to basic amenities.

According to primary data collected through our house listing, about 45 per cent of the households in the study villages in Gujarat and 38 per cent in MP had a BPL card. This was somewhat strange as overall, Gujarat had a much lower incidence of poverty as compared to MP. This issue will be discussed later in section 3. Given these limitations, we adopted an asset-based index to gauge the impact of watershed projects on the poor.[9] Since the idea was to understand the impact of these projects on relatively poor households (in an equity sense), we worked out a hierarchy of relative poverty using different combinations of ownership of the three basic assets of land, water and livestock. Accordingly, 14 categories were identified across the scale of relative poverty. For instance, a household not having land, water or livestock was considered to be the most poor, whereas those having more than 2.5 acres of land, with irrigation and also livestock were considered the least poor in the scale of relative poverty.

---

[9] In fact, land and irrigation also constituted one of the five exclusionary criteria for identifying BPL households was adopted by GoI in 2010. These include: (a) families who own double the land (this clause would not be applicable to STs because of the problem of land alienation) of the district (if a state so desired, this could even be calculated at the block level) average of the agricultural land per agricultural household if partially or wholly irrigated (three times if completely un-irrigated); (b) families who had three- or four-wheeled motorized vehicles, such as jeeps, SUVs, etc.; (c) families who have at least one mechanized farm equipment such as tractor, power tiller, thresher, harvester etc.; (d) families who had any person drawing a salary of over ₹10,000 per month in non-government/private organizations or was employed in government on a regular basis with pensionary or equivalent benefits and (e) income tax payers.

4. Watershed Projects in Gujarat and MP: A Snap Shot

Watershed development has emerged as an important developmental programme supported by various ministries and programmes such as Agriculture, Irrigation, Rural Development, Environment and Forests, Panchayati Raj and more recently the MGNREGA.[10]

According to the Working Group on Natural Resource Management for the 11th Plan, about 51 million ha of land were treated under various watershed projects by the end of the 10th Five Year Plan.[11] This worked out to be about one hundred thousand micro watershed projects (at about 500 ha per watershed) already implemented in different parts of the country. Of these, the three major projects, namely the DPAP, the DDP and the IWDP implemented through the MoRD had contributed funding to about 62 per cent of the treated area.

4.1. Extent and Coverage of WDPs in the States

Gujarat and MP have been two major states where watershed projects have been implemented on a large scale. An important feature that distinguishes the two states, is that while the WDP in Gujarat has had a significant influence from NGOs, the one in MP has been driven through a special purpose vehicle under mission mode. In MP, the projects supported by the MoRD were being implemented by the RGMWM, the only agency of its kind in the country. In what follows we present a snapshot of the watershed projects in the two states.

Over time, watershed projects have made significant inroads into Gujarat and MP It may, however, be noted that the database for the WDPs was far from satisfactory, partly because the projects

---

[10] At the time of this study (2010), systematic efforts had been made to attain greater convergence between watershed projects and the MGNREGA as 80 per cent of the works under the latter was fairly similar to watershed projects.

[11] For details see, Report of the Working Group on Natural Resource Management (2007), Planning Commission, New Delhi.

Table 5.3

Watershed Development Projects in Gujarat and MP: 2007–08

Main Features	Gujarat	Madhya Pradesh
No. of Completed WDPs (approx.)	8, 163	12,000
Total Area Covered by the Completed WDPs (ha)	4,566,000	5,008,000
WDPs created by MoRD (%)	36.6	33.3
WDPs created by MoA (%)	8.7	9.9
% of NSA	46.3	34.1
Districts with Larger Concentrations of WDPs	Kachchh, Rajkot, Surendranagar, Jamnagar, Panchmahal, Dahod, Banaskantha	Jhabua, Ratlam Chhindwada, Bhind, Seoni, Dhar.

Source: Amita Shah, 2007.
Notes: WDP: Watershed Development Project; MoRD: Ministry of Rural Development; MoA: Ministry of Agriculture; NSA: Net Sown Area.

were being implemented through various organizations. Lack of coordination has marred systematic planning of these programmes at the central and state levels.[12] Table 5.3 presents a snapshot of the WDPs in Gujarat and MP.

The details presented above highlight the fact that the WDPs, unlike the other three programmes covered in this book, had a significantly larger coverage nationally and also within the two states. In this sense, the study of eight WDPs at best may be treated as carefully selected case studies rather than being representative of the programme and/or the states.

4.2. The Study Regions: Districts and Villages

The study areas covered a wide range of socio-economic contexts in the two states. It may be noted that three out of the four districts in each state selected for the study also represented those where a large number of watershed projects were already being implemented. The

---

[12] The NRAA (National Rain-fed Area Authority) and the Common Guidelines are the most important result of this planning.

exceptions were Sabarkantha in Gujarat and Chhatarpur in MP The selection of these two districts was guided by the consideration of avoiding another district (i.e., Banaskantha that appears in the list presented in Table 5.3) with fairly similar agro-climatic conditions such as Kachchh in the case of Gujarat; and including one of the most backward districts, that is, Chhatarpur in the case of MP. Tables 5.4 and 5.5 present basic profiles of the villages selected for the study.

Compared to Gujarat, the study regions in MP were better endowed in terms of rainfall with an average of close to or more than 1,000 mm per year. The proportion of irrigated area in the districts was somewhat in the same range. This, prima facie, could be due to the relatively lower importance of commercial crops and/ or the limited ability to invest in groundwater extractions among village communities in MP The major crops grown in the study areas in MP were subsistence crops like maize, *jowar*, gram and other pulses, as well as wheat.

Another important difference was with respect to the substantially higher proportion of SC/ST populations in the MP

Table 5.4

Profile of the Study Villages: Gujarat

Village (District) Details	Jamsar (Rajkot)	Valuna (Sabarkantha)	Tharavada (Kachchh)	Sama (Panchmahal)
Name of Taluka	Vankaner	Meghraj	Bhuj	Kalol
No. of Households	127	187	406	366
Total Population	729	1,070	1,845	1,860
Female/Male Population Ratio	88.3	92.4	91.9	86.7
Land ('00 acres)	15.23	12.58	45.06	13.81
NSA ('00 acres)	7.19 (47.2)	4.02 (31.9)	13.10 (29.1)	11.51 (83.3)
% Irrigated area to NSA	47.2	Approx. 40–50	29.1	83.3
% of Major Caste	Koli: 90	ST: 100	Patel: 40 Muslim: 50	OBC: 85
Main Crops	Cotton, Til, *Jowar*, Mung	Maize, *Jowar*, Gram, *Tur*, Til	Cotton, Mango, Cumin, Wheat	Wheat, Rice Mung, Maize, *Bajri*, Gram

Source: Village records from *Talatis*, fieldwork 2009.

Table 5.5

Profile of the Study Villages: MP

Village (District) Details	Singrawankalan (Chhatarpur)	Kalakhunt (Jhabua)	Sobaliyapura (Dewas)	Gopalpura (Ratlam)
Taluka	Nawgaon	Jhabua	Bagali	Ratlam
Households	312	156	230	339
Total Population	1,729	1,122	1,428	1,939
Male Population	85.7	1.0	97.5	1.0
Total Land ('00 Acre)	13.83	10.10	21.64	21.82
NSA	8.27 (59.8)	6.07 (60.1)	13.70 (63.4)	12.02 (55.1)
% Irrigated to NSA	62.4	24.4	55.5	34.1
% of Major Caste	SC: 33 Kushwaha: 25 Brahmin: 20	ST: 100	ST: 50 Yadav: 50	ST: 100
Main Crops	Gram, Peas, Wheat, Mustard	Maize, *Jowar*, Gram, *Tur*, Til	Maize, *Jowar*, Mung, *Tur*	Maize, *Jowar*, Gram, *Tur*, Til

Source: Village records from Talatis, 2009.

districts and also the villages covered by the study. For instance, the ST population constituted as large as 87 per cent of the population in Jhabua as against 26 per cent in the case of Ratlam. Meanwhile, the SC population accounted for 23 per cent of the population in Chhatarpur and 18 per cent in Dewas. Strangely, the ratio of female to male population was found to be fairly favourable in three out of the four villages in MP (except for Chhatarpur). This could be taken to imply the possibility of migration by both males and females, as one often observes in the case of migrants from Jhabua and other districts bordering Gujarat.

4.3. Profile of Households in the Study Villages

Our house listing in the study villages covered a total of 1,926 households; 1,011 in Gujarat and 915 in MP. Of these, about 36 and 20 per cent of the households were landless in the two states respectively. This was fairly substantial. It may, however, be noted that those who reported having no land may also have included some of those whose father or brother owned the land, so that the household may have had some share. This issue is also difficult to ascertain beyond a point as reporting 'no land' helped the households to attain BPL status and therefore entitled them to a number of subsidies under the various government schemes for poverty reduction and rural development. Table 5.6 presents the distribution of households by ownership/access to land, irrigation and livestock among the study villages.

4.3.1. Ownership of Land, Irrigation and Livestock

Table 5.6 shows the distribution of households across broad categories of asset ownership and indicates that of the 647 households with land studied in Gujarat, 444 had access to irrigation, that is 69 per cent of the landed households. The situation in MP was quite different. Whereas 80 per cent (i.e., 735 out of the total 915) of the households had land, only about 58 per cent of the households reported access to irrigation. About 75 per cent of households in the study villages reported ownership of at least one livestock.

This indicates that a substantially large proportion of the households, especially those having livestock but no land, may have

Table 5.6

Ownership of Land and Livestock and Access to Irrigation

S. No.	Household by Ownership	Gujarat (% of all HHs)	Madhya Pradesh (% of all HHs)
1	Landless	364 (36.0)	180 (19.7)
2	All Households with Land	647 (64.0)	735 (80.3)
2.1	Land without Irrigation	203 (20.0) (31.3)*	312 (34.1) (42.4)*
2.2	Land with Irrigation	444 (43.9) (68.7)*	423 (46.2) (57.6)*
	Total (1 and 2)	1,011 (100)	915 (100)
3	No Land with Livestock	188 (51.6)**	65 (36.1)**
4	Land with Livestock	591 (91.4)**	586 (79.7)**
5	All Households with Livestock	779 (77.0)	660 (72.1)

Source: Field survey, (2009).
Notes: Based on the house listing in the study villages.
* Per cent of landed households.
** Per cent of landless and landed households.

had critical dependence on pasture land for their livelihood. For instance, Tharavada village in Gujarat presented a situation where more than 80 per cent of the households had livestock but only 47 per cent of the households had land. A pro-poor watershed project would need to therefore pay special attention to pasture land and the increased availability of fodder. A similar situation was observed in the case of Sobaliyapura in MP The village-wise information presented in Table 5.7 suggests significant variations in ownership of assets within and across states.

Table 5.7

Land, Irrigation and Livestock Among Households in the Study Villages

Villages	Landless	Land without Irrigation	Land with Irrigation	Land with Livestock	All Households
		Gujarat			
Valuna	09	96	97	194	202
(2.33)*	(4.4)**	(47.5)	(48.0)	(96.0)	
Jamsar	38	34	108	146	180
(5.67)	(21.1)	(18.9)	(60.0)	(81.1)	
Tharavada	193	33	136	291	362
(6.27)	(53.3)	(9.1)	(37.6)	(80.4)	
Sama	124	40	103	148	267
(1.94)	(46.4)	(15.0)	(38.6)	(55.4)	
Gujarat Total	364	203	444	779	1011
(4.01)	(36.0)	(20.0)	(44.0)	(77.0)	
		Madhya Pradesh			
Singrawankalan	32	23	167	168	222
(10.4)	(14.4)	(10.4)	(75.2)	(75.7)	
Kalakhunt	55	113	55	161	223
(3.37)	(24.7)	(50.7)	(24.7)	(72.2)	
Sobaliyapura	63	68	60	139	191
(8.29)	(33.0)	(35.6)	(31.4)	(72.8)	
Gopalpura	30	108	141	192	279
(5.41)	(10.7)	(38.7)	(50.6)	(68.8)	
MP Total	180	312	423	660	915
(6.74)	(19.7)	(34.1)	(46.2)	(72.1)	
Grand Total	544	515	867	1,439	1,926
	(28.2)	(26.7)	(45.0)	(74.7)	

Source: Primary survey, (2009).
Notes: * Mean landholding.
** Per cent to total households in the village.

Table 5.8

Categorization of Poverty at the Household Level

Category of Households by Poverty Levels	Details
Poverty 1	Landless without Livestock
Poverty 2	Landless with Livestock
Poverty 3	Marginal Farmers without irrigation, without livestock
Poverty 4	Marginal Farmers without irrigation, with livestock
Poverty 5	Marginal Farmers with irrigation, without livestock
Poverty 6	Marginal Farmers with irrigation, with livestock
Poverty 7	Small Farmers without irrigation, without livestock
Poverty 8	Small Farmers without irrigation, with livestock
Poverty 9	Small Farmers with irrigation, without livestock
Poverty 10	Small Farmers with irrigation, with livestock
Poverty 11	Medium Farmers without irrigation, without livestock
Poverty 12	Medium Farmers without irrigation, with livestock
Poverty 13	Medium Farmers with irrigation, without livestock
Poverty 14	Medium Farmers with irrigation, with livestock

Source: Author's own.
Notes: With regard to landholding, Marginal means less than 2.5 acres, Small means 2.5–5 acres and Medium means more than 5 acres.

4.3.2. *Poverty among Households: An Asset-Based Index*

In what follows we present the basic information on how the households in the study villages were distributed across 14 categories of a relative poverty index by considering the ownership of three sets of assets (land, water and livestock). Table 5.8 presents the 14 categories developed by combining (a) ownership (or lack thereof) of land, irrigation and livestock and (b) size of landholding.

Table 5.9 indicates that about 31 and 21 per cent of all the households in Sama village in Gujarat and Sobaliyapura village in MP respectively, were in the category of the most poor. On the other hand, Jamsar village in Gujarat and Singrawankalan in MP had the highest proportion of households (42.8 and 55.4 per cent, respectively) in the highest category of the asset-based index. The distribution of households across the 14 categories varied significantly across the study villages. In MP, the extent of poverty was the highest in

Table 5.9

Index of Relative Poverty (% of Households)

States		Gujarat					Madhya Pradesh			
Ownership of Land	Ownership of Livestock	Valuna	Jamsar	Tharavada	Sama	Singrawankalan	Kalakhunt	Sobaliyapura	Gopalpura	Total
Landless	1) No	0.5	13.3	18.2	31.8	6.8	16.1	20.9	8.6	15.1
	2) Yes	4.0	7.8	35.1	14.6	7.7	8.5	12.0	2.1	13.1
Marginal Farmers		4.5	21.1	53.3	46.4	14.5	24.6	39.9	10.7	28.2
<1 acre Un-irrigated	3) No	1.5	–	0.3	4.5	–	1.3	0.5	2.1	1.3
	4) Yes	18.8	1.1	1.7	6.7	1.8	3.1	0.5	2.9	4.4
<1 acre with irrigation	5) No	–	1.1	–	4.1	0.4	–	–	1.1	0.9
	6) Yes	11.9	2.2	0.6	12.7	0.9	0.4	–	1.4	3.7
Small Farmers		32.2	4.4	2.6	28.0	3.1	4.8	1.0	7.5	10.3
1–2.5 acres un-irrigated	7) No	1.5	–	–	1.1	–	4.9	–	3.9	1.4
	8) Yes	16.3	4.4	3.9	1.9	0.9	21.0	4.7	8.2	7.3
1–2.5 acres with irrigation	9) No	–	0.5	0.3	2.2	1.3	1.8	–	1.8	1.0
	10) Yes	17.8	10.6	5.0	11.2	3.6	5.4	–	5.0	7.1
Medium Farmers		35.6	15.5	8.2	16.4	5.8	28.2	4.7	18.9	16.8

2.5 > acres un-irrigated	11) No	–	1.1	0.3	0.4	2.2	1.3	4.2	6.8	2.0
	12) Yes	9.4	12.2	3.0	0.4	5.4	18.8	25.7	14.7	10.2
2.5 > acres with irrigation	13) No	0.5	2.8	0.6	0.4	13.5	2.2	1.6	6.8	3.4
	14) Yes	17.8	42.8	31.2	7.9	55.4	14.8	29.8	34.4	28.9
		27.7	47.8	35.1	9.1	76.5	37.1	61.3	62.7	44.5
All		100.0	100.0	100.0	100.0	100.0	100.0	100.0	100.0	100.0
n*		202	180	362	267	222	223	191	279	1926

Source: Field survey, (2009).
Note: *No. of observations.

Kalakhunt, followed by Sobaliyapura and Gopalpura at more or less the same level and lowest in Singrawakalan. Overall, 55.5 per cent of households in the study villages could be regarded as poor if we were to go by the criterion of landholding size. How this tallied with other indicators of poverty is probed subsequently in this section.

Overall, these observations indicate that the ownership/access to land and irrigation were basic indicators of a household's economic status, whereas livestock ownership was, by and large, linked to the ownership of land. This also substantiates our choice of criteria for selecting the sample households in the study villages.

4.3.3. Household Income from All Sources

The average annual income of households in the selected villages was found to be about ₹32,000 in Gujarat and ₹32,600 in MP.[13] Table 5.10 shows that the average annual income in the study villages of both states was substantially higher than the poverty lines for rural areas in the two states. As expected, the average income amongst those with irrigation was significantly higher than that among the landless and also among those without any access to irrigation (Table 5.10). In fact, the average annual income among the households without access to irrigation worked out to

Table 5.10

Average Annual Income by Landholding Categories (2007–08)

	Gujarat			MP		
	Mean	N	%	Mean	N	%
Landless	21,719	364	36.0	16,502	150	23.6
Households without Irrigation	23,628	203	20.1	23,555	204	32.1
Households with Irrigation	44,264	444	43.9	47,704	282	44.3
All	32,033	1,011	100.0	32,599	636	100.0

Source: Field survey, (2009).

---

[13] Information on basic food consumption among households revealed yet another dimension of poverty in the study villages.

be fairly similar, that is, around ₹23,000 per year in the two states. The landless households, especially in MP, had the lowest average annual incomes.

4.3.4. Percentage of Households Having Incomes below the Official Cut-off Line

We also tried to work out the proportion of poor households based on household annual income during the reference year as a proxy for consumption expenditures. Using the official cut-off of MPCE of ₹501.58 and ₹408.41 in Gujarat and MP respectively, (Street Planning Commission, Government of MP, 2011), we tried to identify households below and above the poverty line. According to this calculation, 57.5 per cent of the households in Gujarat and 65 per cent of the households in MP had per capita monthly incomes BPL cut-off in these states. This was significantly higher than the revised poverty HCR of 39.1 per cent in Gujarat and 55.6 per cent in MP during 2004–05. A part of the explanation for the relatively higher poverty count by income criteria could be attributable to three main reasons: (a) a part of the food consumption from home production was not included in the income estimate; (b) crop failure and (c) under-reporting of income from various sources. While these are the known limitations of any income-based estimate of poverty, the specific point that we want to emphasize is its link with ownership and size of landholdings. Table 5.11 shows the poverty by ownership of land criteria in the two states.

Table 5.11 suggests that with the exception of only Kalakhunt in MP, the landless had the largest proportion of households with incomes lower than the poverty cut-off. The proportion varied from 60 per cent in Kalakhunt to 84 per cent in Sobaliyapura. The proportion of households with incomes lower than the poverty cut-off was fairly small among the small and medium farmers as compared to the landless and marginal farmers. There were a few exceptions to this larger pattern. For instance, the larger proportion of income poor among the medium landholding size was prima facie due to crop failures and drought-like conditions faced in the villages. Whereas the landless and marginal-small farmers may have

Table 5.11

Poverty by Ownership of Land Criteria (% of Households)

Landholding Size	Gujarat					Madhya Pradesh			
	Valuna	Jamsar	Tharavada	Sama	All	Singrawankalan	Kalakhunt	Sobaliyapura	All
Landless	77.8	65.8	73.6	75.0	73.4	81.2	60.0	84.1	74.7
	(7)	(25)	(142)	(93)	(267)	(26)	(33)	(53)	(112)
Marginal	78.1	44.4	59.5	63.6	67.0	70.0	64.7	90.9	68.1
	(107)	(16)	(25)	(75)	(223)	(14)	(55)	(10)	(79)
Small	68.2	32.7	27.7	38.9	41.6	77.8	71.2	74.1	74.4
	(30)	(17)	(13)	(7)	(67)	(49)	(42)	(43)	(134)
Medium	50.0	18.5	8.8	16.7	15.8	54.2	75.0	27.1	48.4
	(6)	(10)	(7)	(1)	(24)	(58)	(18)	(16)	(92)
All	74.2	37.8	51.6	66.2	57.5	66.2	66.4	63.9	65.6
	(150)	(68)	(187)	(176)	(581)	(147)	(148)	(122)	(417)

Source: House listing survey, (2009).

compensated themselves for their losses by working outside the village, farmers in the medium category of landholdings may have refrained from doing so for socio-economic reasons. In Kalakhunt, the higher proportion of poor among the farmers with medium size landholdings was mainly due to their undivided landholdings with larger family sizes (seven per household).

By and large, the pattern of poverty across the villages confirms the one derived by using the landholding criteria in Table 5.9 earlier. It may, however, be noted that as the poverty categories by income were based on the income levels at the time of the survey; it was quite likely that several of the non-poor in the post-project period were poor. Ascertaining this was difficult owing to the difficulty in collecting income-related information with a time lag. This was particularly difficult given the multiple sources and uncertain nature of income from most of the income sources.

A somewhat similar pattern could be seen in the link between land and the BPL status of households. With a few exceptions, the proportion of BPL households was found to be the highest amongst landless households. There were a number of households in the large farmer categories also having BPL status. This reiterated the aberrations in the manner in which the BPL status was being given to rural households. The problem seemed to be more acute in MP as compared to Gujarat.

4.3.5. Caste and Landholding

Another important aspect of the households in the study villages was their caste/social group characteristics as presented in Tables 5.12 and 5.13. Percentages are given for caste categories.

In Gujarat, 45 per cent of the SCs were landless as compared to 18.5 per cent in the case of MP Conversely, only 7 per cent of the ST households were landless in Gujarat as compared to about 25 per cent in the case of MP. There were, however, variations across villages in each state.

Overall, the analysis of households in this section brings home three important observations. First, poverty conditions were widely prevalent in most villages under study; on an average, however, the

Table 5.12

Caste-wise Landholding Size in the Sample Households: Gujarat

Ownership of Land and Landholding Size (Acres)	SC	ST	OBC	Other	All
Landless	86 (45.3)*	02 (7.1)	247 (39.1)	29 (17.9)	364 (36.0)
< 2.5	83 (43.7)	12 (42.9)	217 (34.4)	22 (13.6)	334 (33.0)
2.5–5.0	18 (9.5)	10 (35.7)	95 (15.1)	38 (23.5)	161 (15.9)
> 5.0	03 (1.6)	04 (14.3)	72 (11.4)	73 (45.1)	152 (15.0)
Total	190 (100.0)	28 (100.0)	631 (100.0)	162 (100.0)	1,011 (100.0)

Source: Field survey data, (2009).
Note: *Figures in parenthesis indicate % to total number of households.

Table 5.13

Caste-wise Landholding Size in Sample Households: Madhya Pradesh

Ownership of Land and Landholding Size (Acres)	SC	ST	OBC	Other	All
Landless	25 (18.5)*	56 (24.8)	69 (28.3)	–	150 (23.6)
< 2.5	11 (8.1)	85 (37.6)	20 (8.2)	–	116 (18.2)
2.5–5.0	54 (40.0)	61 (27.0)	62 (25.4)	3 (9.7)	180 (28.3)
> 5.0	45 (33.3)	24 (10.6)	93 (38.1)	28 (90.3)	190 (29.9)
Total	135 (100.0)	226 (100.0)	244 (100.0)	31 (100.0)	636 (100.0)

Source: Field survey data, (2009).
Note: *Figures in parenthesis indicate % to total number of households.

villages in Gujarat fared better in poverty terms than those in MP. Second, there were substantial inter-village differences in poverty conditions within each state, which could have been due to various factors–resource access, climatic conditions, spatial and social characteristics and also developmental interventions that had taken place in the past. And third, though varied, the pattern of poverty across villages was more or less in conformity where the landless, by and large, were poorer than those with relatively larger landholdings (i.e., > 2.5 acres). Given this pattern, we focus more on the land-based criterion for poverty analysis in the remaining part of this chapter.

5. Impact on Poverty: Coverage and Benefits

This section presents the main findings from an analysis of the primary data on two major aspects of the impact of the watershed projects:

1. the kind of activities that were undertaken by the watershed project and the extent to which these reached out to households across different economic strata, and
2. the nature and magnitude of the benefits received by the households, especially those identified as relatively worse-off within the village communities.

These aspects have been addressed mainly in light of the information collected through house listing and also FGDs with the project functionaries and other informed members of the communities.

5.1. Activities Undertaken and Coverage of the Households

We assessed the level of participation (ascertained at the household level by asking the question: did you participate/were you involved in any of the project activities? yes/no) among different categories of households by enquiring into the nature of activities taken up by the watershed projects in the study villages. At the outset, we found out the distribution of households that reported membership in watershed groups/committees and the various activities undertaken throughout the project. This information was based on the house listing survey conducted in the study villages. We grouped the activities in four major categories related to (a) membership groups/committees formed by the project, (b) inputs and information related to land and agriculture, (c) irrigation facility and (d) employment on the project site. The idea was to find out the extent to which relatively poorer households were involved in the project. In a sense, this was a fairly

Table 5.14

Coverage of Households by Broad Groups of Benefits from WDPs by Poverty Categories: Gujarat

Category of Poor (n)	Group/WDC Membership	Agriculture-related Benefits	Irrigation-related Benefits	Employment-related Benefits
Landless 100.0 (364)	1.1 (4)	0.3 (1)	0.8 (3)	9.9 (36)
Poor 1 (188)	(2)	(1)	(2)	(22)
Poor 2 (176)	(2)	–	(1)	(14)
Marginal 100.0 (157)	3.8 (6)	30.6 (48)	15.9 (25)	21.0 (33)
Poor 3 (16)	–	–	(1)	(1)
Poor 4 (64)	(3)	(14)	–	(14)
Poor 5 (13)	–	(5)	(5)	–
Poor 6 (64)	(3)	(29)	(19)	(18)
Small 100.0 (177)	12.4 (22)	54.8 (97)	29.9 (53)	29.4 (52)
Poor 7 (6)	–	(1)	–	–
Poor 8 (60)	(5)	(21)	(3)	(18)
Poor 9 (8)	(2)	(5)	(2)	–
Poor 10 (103)	(15)	(70)	(48)	(34)
Medium 100.0 (313)	17.6 (55)	51.4 (161)	62.0 (194)	18.8 (59)
Poor 11 (4)	–	(1)	–	–
Poor 12 (53)	(8)	(22)	(4)	(10)
Poor 13 (9)	(2)	(5)	(4)	(2)
Poor 14 (247)	(45)	(133)	(186)	(47)
All (1,011)	100.0 (87)	100.0 (307)	100.0 (275)	100.0 (180)
All Beneficiaries as % to Total HHs	8.6	30.4	27.2	17.8

Source: Based on house listing survey, (2009).
Note: Figures in parentheses indicate number of households.

robust indicator of inclusion of the landless and marginal-small farmers in a watershed project, an issue already highlighted earlier.

Tables 5.14 and 5.15 present the distribution of households that reported some kind of participation in the project. Only a small sub-set of households in both states reported membership in any kind of committees or groups formed by the watershed project in

Table 5.15

Coverage of Households by Broad Groups of Benefits from WDPs by Poverty Categories: MP

Category of Poor (n)	Group/WDC Membership Related	Agriculture Related	Irrigation Related	Employment Related
Landless 100.0 (180)	6.67 (12)	–	–	29.4 (53)
Poor 1 (83)	(8)	–	–	(21)
Poor 2 (97)	(4)	–		(32)
Marginal 100.0 (41)	7.3 (3)	4.9 (2)	2.4 (1)	17.1 (7)
Poor 3 (10)	–	–	–	(2)
Poor 4 (20)	(1)	(1)	(1)	(4)
Poor 5 (04)	–	–	–	–
Poor 6 (07)	(2)	(1)	–	(1)
Small 100.0 (149)	1.3 (2)	9.4 (14)	7.4 (11)	21.5 (32)
Poor 7 (22)	(1)	(1)	–	(5)
Poor 8 (81)	(1)	(6)	(4)	(12)
Poor 9 (12)	–	(2)	(2)	(6)
Poor 10 (34)	–	(5)	(5)	(9)
Medium 100.0 (545)	12.5 (68)	15.4 (84)	21.3 (116)	26.2 (143)
Poor 11 (35)	(2)	–	–	(7)
Poor 12 (144)	(14)	(21)	(25)	(47)
Poor 13 (57)	(7)	(3)	(9)	(12)
Poor 14 (309)	(45)	(60)	(82)	(77)
All (915)	100.0 (85)	100.0 (100)	100.0 (129)	100.0 (235)

Source: Based on house listing survey, (2009).
Note: Figures in parentheses indicate number of households.

their villages. These included 87 (out of 1,011) and 85 (out of 815) households in Gujarat and MP respectively.

1. The number of households reporting agriculture-related benefits was fairly close to those reporting irrigation-related benefits in both states. In MP the number of households with irrigation benefits was larger than those with agriculture-related benefits. In most cases, these households were likely to overlap.

2. Employment benefits were somewhat limited in the case of Gujarat (17.8 %) as compared to MP (25.7 %).
3. Overall, benefits of agriculture and irrigation combined were found to be tilted in favour of relatively better-off farmers, especially those with a medium size landholding and access to irrigation.
4. Conversely, a large proportion of households did not seem to have been covered by any of the benefits.

Overall, we could therefore infer that except for employment, watershed benefits were tilted mainly in favour of farmers with medium landholdings. The pattern was found to be more or less the same across the two states.

The pattern of benefit sharing was not entirely unanticipated in the context of watershed projects, where much of the project-related activity was land based, and also driven by the location of one's land within a watershed.

However, before looking into this aspect, it may be noted that a substantially large number of households reported no direct involvement (or participation) in any of the activities undertaken by the project. The households reporting no involvement accounted for 46.4 per cent of the total households covered by the survey. Further analysis reveals that almost 78.3 per cent of the landless and 43.7 per cent of the farmers with marginal landholdings did not participate in the project, and 27–30 per cent among the small and medium households covered under the survey did not participate (Figure 5.2).

A village-wise picture is presented in Figure 5.3. It shows that the proportion of households which did participate in any WDP activities was as high as 70.4 and 57.7 per cent in Sama and Tharawada in Gujarat. In MP, 61 per cent did not take part in the project activities in Kalakhunt and 48.2 per cent in those of Singrawankalan.

5.2. Treatment-wise Benefits

Tables 5.16 and 5.17 provide information on the number of households that had obtained some kind of benefits from different types of treatments carried out under the watershed projects. It

Figure 5.2

Non-participating Households by Landholding Size

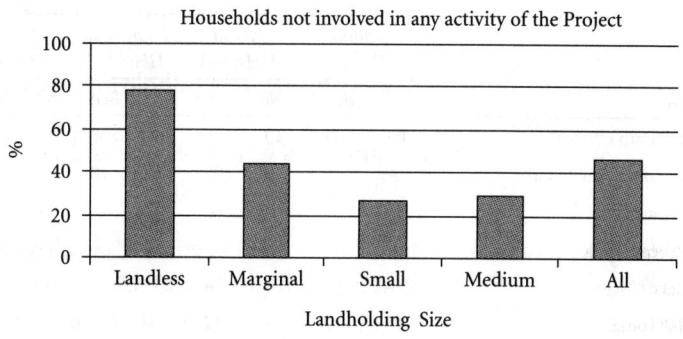

Source: Field survey data, (2009).

Figure 5.3

Lack of Participation in WDP Projects (% of Village Households)

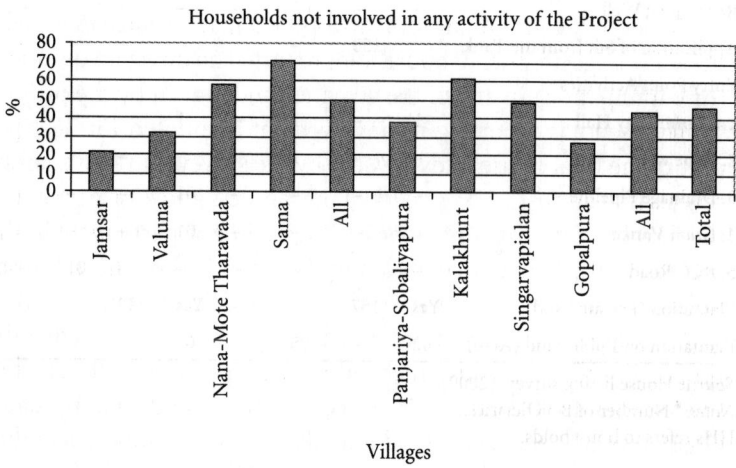

Source: Field survey data, (2009).

appears that in Gujarat the treatments carried out in Jamsar and Tharavada (both in drought-prone districts of the Saurashtra–Kachchh regions) were relatively more broad-based and also covered a fairly large number of households under major treatments like check dams, village tanks, field bunding (in the case of Jamsar) and plantation (in the case of Tharavada). Compared to these two,

Table 5.16

Type of Project Activities and Number of Beneficiaries: Gujarat

Village	Valuna HHs: 202		Jamsar HHs: 180		Tharavada HHs: 362		Sama HHs: 267	
	No.	Bene*	No.	Bene	No.	Bene	No.	Bene
Check dam (Pucca)	08	30	13	135	04	60	03	50
Check dam (Kachcha)	–	–	19	38	09	18	–	–
Stop dam	–	–	–	–	–	–	–	–
Overhead Tank	–	–	–	–	–	–	–	–
Toilets	–	–	–	–	–	–	–	–
Nullah plug	15	15	19	19	–	–	–	–
Field Bunds (% of land)	70	163	60	100	–	–	40	40
Village Tank	–	–	–	–	09	35	–	–
Deepening of Village Tank	–	–	01	NA	02	15	02	–
Farm Pond	23	23	05	05	04	08	–	–
Recharging Well	–	–	02	–	–	–	–	–
Application of Silt from the Tank		150	–	–	–	–	–	–
Entry Point Activities								
1. Community Hall	1	–	1	–	1	–	–	–
2. Tube well	–	–	1	–	–	–	–	–
3. Drainage Pipeline	–	–	–	–	01	–	–	–
4. *Gram Vatika*	–	–	–	–	01	–	–	–
5. RCC Road	–	–	–	–	–	–	01	–
Plantation (Private Land)	Yes	157	–	–	Yes	112	–	–
Plantation on Public land (Acre)	02	–	05	–	03	–	–	–

Source: House listing survey, (2009).
Notes: * Number of Beneficiaries.
HHs refers to households.

the coverage of beneficiaries through the major treatments was somewhat limited in the case of Valuna and Sama.

The situation in MP was somewhat different; the WDP treatments in MP appeared to be minimal in Kalakhunt and Sobaliyapura, but fairly good in the case of Singrawankalan. Another important difference pertained to entry point activities, which were almost

Table 5.17

Type of Project Activities and Number of Beneficiaries: MP

Village	Singrawankalan HHs: 222		Kalakhunt HHs: 223		Sobaliyapura HHs: 191		Gopalpura HHs: 279	
	No.	Beneficiaries	No.	Beneficiaries	No.	Beneficiaries	No.	Beneficiaries
Check dam (*Pucca*)	05	82	–	–	09	63	06	90
Check dam (*Kachcha*)	02	04	–	–	32	–	–	–
Stop dam	04	46	–	–	–	–	–	–
Overhead Tank	03	404	–	–	–	–	–	–
Toilets	40	40	–	–	–	–	–	–
Nullah plug	–	–	–	–	–	–	32	32
Field Bunds (% of land)	–	–	50	107	–	–	20	–
Village Tank	–	–	–	–	–	–	–	–
Deepening of Village Tank	–	–	03	72	1	26	–	–
Farm Pond	–	–	–	–	–	–	19	19
Recharging Well	10	–	–	–	18	–	–	–
Application of Silt from the Tank		72		16	–	–	–	–
Entry Point Activity								
1. Community Hall	–	–	–	–	–	–	–	–
2. Tube well	–	–	–	–	–	–	–	–

(contd...)

(contd...)

Village	Singrawankalan HHs: 222		Kalakhunt HHs: 223		Sobaliyapura HHs: 191		Gopalpura HHs: 279	
	No.	Beneficiaries	No.	Beneficiaries	No.	Beneficiaries	No.	Beneficiaries
3. Drainage Pipeline	–	–	–	–	–	–	–	–
4. Gram Vatika	–	–	–	–	–	–	–	–
5. RCC Road	–	–	01	–	–	–	–	–
Plantation (Private Land)	–	–	–	–	Yes	54	–	–
Plantation on Public land (acres)	–	–	–	–	02	–	96	–

Source: Field survey data, (2009).

absent in three out of four villages in MP. This may have had significant implications for the involvement of local communities in the project. This issue will be discussed at a later stage in this chapter.

5.3. Change in Irrigation: Before and After the WDP

As noted earlier, close to 70 and 60 per cent of the landed households in Gujarat and MP respectively reported access to irrigation at the time of the survey. How many of them already had access before the project was implemented? The data from our house listing suggests that a large majority of these households that reported having access to irrigation at the time of the survey also had access prior to the project. In fact, only 12 households in Gujarat were added to the list of those already having irrigation. On the other hand, six households in Valuna did not report access to irrigation at the time of the survey, though they did have the access prior to the project. These six households belonged to the category of medium land-holders (i.e., > 5 acres). In MP, 23 households not having access to irrigation prior to the project reported such access at the time of the survey.

In all, 35 households in the two states taken together (12 in Gujarat and 23 in MP) were added to the list of farmers having access to irrigation in the post-project period. Of these, three were marginal farmers and 19 and 13 were small and medium farmers respectively. The 35 households were mainly from Jamsar (11), Kalakhunt (6) and Gopalpura (13).

Overall, the irrigated area showed an increase by about 18 and 9 per cent over the pre-project area in Gujarat and MP respectively. The area under additional irrigation in Gujarat was 766 acres and that in MP was 246 acres (see Table 5.18). It is important to note that any decline in irrigated area could have been a fluctuating phenomenon influenced by variations in rainfall.

What was important, however, was the substantial increase in the number of groundwater sources (wells and borewells) in most of the villages, as shown in Table 5.19. The increase in irrigated area therefore, may not have been attributable *entirely* to the project interventions.

Table 5.18

Change in Irrigated Area by Village: Before and After WDP (in Acres)

Villages	Before Project	After Project	Difference	% Change
Gujarat				
Valuna (Sabarkantha)	398.61	394.79	–3.82	–0.97
Jamsar (Rajkot)	540.48	741.51	201.03	27.11
Tharavada (Kachchh)	2,034.45	2,507.84	473.39	18.86
Sama (Panchmahal)	444.92	540.75	95.83	17.72
Total	3,418.46	4,184.89	766.43	18.31
Madhya Pradesh				
Singrawankalan (Chhatarpur)	1,605.90	1,656.64	50.74	3.07
Kalakhunt (Jhabua)	110.0	138.05	28.05	20.32
Sobaliyapura (Dewas)	496.26	577.68	81.42	14.09
Gopalpura (Ratlam)	336.5	422.3	85.8	20.32
Total	2,548.60	2,794.67	246.07	8.80

Source: House listing survey, (2009).

Table 5.19

Change in the Sources of Irrigation by Village: Before and After the WDP

State/Village	Wells		Bore/Tube Wells		Check Dams		Tanks/ponds	
	Before	After	Before	After	Before	After	Before	After
Gujarat								
Valuna	64	64	15	26	6	14		
Jamsar	90	80	40	50	4	17		
Tharavada	15	15	70	150	8	21	07	16
Sama	25	25	–	–	6	10	02	02
MP								
Singrawankalan	96	100	–	–	12	17	–	–
Kalakhunt	24	24	5	19	–	–	4	4
Sobaliyapura	42	42	5	5	4	20	1	1
Gopalpura	105	155	10	13	1	6	1	6
All	461	505	145	263	41	105	15	29

Source: House listing survey, (2009).

5.4. Changes in Income: Before and After the WDP

We tried to trace the changes in income from different sources. The information on income was obtained through direct probing and hence was indicative in nature. Also the income estimates were used as a proxy for household expenditure as the idea was to gauge the changes in net earnings from different sources or economic activities, especially agriculture. The information on income, before and after the project, was at constant prices (2004–05) and thus adjusted for inflation. It may be noted that real income had increased from almost all the sources in all the study villages (Table 5.20). What was noteworthy was the variation in incomes per household amongst villages within and across the state. For instance, agricultural income was found to be fairly high (> ₹40,000) in Tharavada village in Gujarat and in Sobaliyapura village (> ₹50,000) in MP Against this, the lowest income from agriculture was found in Valuna and Kalakhunt in the two states respectively. While this was fairly impressive, the increase was reported by all kinds of households, irrespective of their association with watershed projects.

We have tried to pursue this issue by comparing the changes in income among those who participated and those who did not participate in the project. Table 5.21 presents details about the increases in income from agriculture amongst project-participants versus the rest of the farmers in the village. While agricultural income increased amongst both sets of farmers, the increase was relatively higher among the participating as compared to the non-participating farmers in all the Gujarat villages.

The picture in MP was somewhat mixed. Overall, the project participants had attained relatively higher gains in agricultural incomes as compared to the non-participants. There is, however, a small caveat to this observation. The information in Table 5.21 suggests that the participants had also reported a higher initial income as compared to non-beneficiaries in most cases. This suggests a possible selection bias in favour of the relatively better-off households and/or a reporting bias among the farmers in both categories. The beneficiaries may have over-reported

Table 5.20

Average Annual Household Income from Various Sources in Rupees/Year

Villages		Agriculture	Livestock	Service	Labour Work	Business	Other	Total
Valuna	After	9,054 (194)	4,565 (176)	63,816 (19)	8,347 (159)	21,600 (5)	–	25,781 (202)
	Before	7,161 (192)	3,766 (131)	56,235 (17)	6,404 (144)	12,500 (2)	–	18,671 (202)
Jamsar	After	17,067 (135)	7,356 (117)	27,200 (5)	22,834 (156)	10,409 (11)	5,000 (1)	38,790 (180)
	Before	11,924 (131)	5,074 (92)	17,500 (4)	15,061 (139)	7,083 (6)	5,000 (1)	23,686 (179)
Tharavada	After	44,443 (168)	5,924 (216)	21,500 (2)	16,552 (223)	26,000 (17)	12,289 (38)	37,192 (360)
	Before	35,583 (167)	3,991 (198)	17,000 (1)	11,973 (220)	23,467 (15)	9,095 (37)	27,978 (360)
Sama	After	14,482 (131)	8,973 (130)	50,273 (11)	13,193 (212)	29,889 (9)	9,333 (3)	25,228 (266)
	Before	10,391 (129)	7,480 (126)	42,000 (10)	10,140 (210)	21,222 (9)	5,667 (3)	18,949 (266)
Singrawankalan	After	21,261 (186)	6,455 (11)	32,214 (14)	10,661 (144)	13,000 (17)	8,000 (4)	30,111 (222)
	Before	15,897 (185)	3,773 (11)	46,857 (14)	6,598 (146)	10,533 (15)	6,000 (3)	21,522 (222)

Kalakhunt	After	10,888 (165)	3,875 (4)	45,000 (2)	9,921 (215)	–	22,315 (64)	24,454 (223)
	Before	7,277 (164)	2,333 (3)	28,000 (2)	6,386 (214)	–	15,618 (64)	16,244 (223)
Sobaliyapura	After	54,679 (125)	9,667 (3)	29,700 (10)	9,096 (141)	43,333 (7)	11,500 (2)	45,002 (191)
	Before	28,734 (123)	4,333 (3)	15,125 (8)	6,291 (140)	7,000 (1)	7,500 (2)	23,723 (191)
All	After	23,560 (1,104)	6,432 (657)	50,833 (63)	13,062 (1,250)	20,718 (62)	17,707 (112)	32,252 (1,644)
	Before	16,396 (1,091)	4,884 (564)	41,000 (56)	9,060 (1,213)	16,156 (48)	12,645 (110)	21,945 (1,643)

Source: House listing survey, (2009).

Notes: Numbers reflect prices in 2004–05, at which time the poverty line was estimated by the Planning Commission. Numbers of households reporting income from sources are in parentheses. Income information was not collected in Gopalpura village.

Table 5.21

Changes in Agricultural Incomes among Beneficiaries and Non-beneficiaries

	Beneficiary				Non-beneficiary			
Villages	After	Before	(A–B)	% Over Before	After	Before	(A–B)	% Over Before
				Gujarat				
Valuna	10,478	7,805	2,673	34.2	5,875	5,712	163	2.9
Jamsar	17,537	12,231	5,306	43.4	13,000	9,357	3,643	38.9
Tharavada	50,701	40,316	10,385	25.8	19,779	16,364	3,415	20.9
Sama	18,711	13,093	5,618	42.9	9,477	7,185	2,292	31.9
All	25,323	19,356	5,967	30.8	10,569	8,678	1,891	21.8
				Madhya Pradesh				
Singrawankalan	22,245	16,192	6,053	37.4	20,116	15,558	4,558	29.3
Kalakhunt	12,641	8,494	4,147	48.8	9,316	6,201	3,115	50.2
Sobaliyapura	45,834	25,254	20,580	81.5	73,475	36,231	37,244	102.8
All	27,021	16,840	10,181	60.5	25,725	15,521	10,204	65.7

Source: Field survey data, (2009).

their incomes, whereas the non-beneficiaries may have under-reported their incomes from agriculture, both before as well as after the project.

5.5. Change in Per Capita Income

The above observation is further substantiated by the finding on per capita income for the entire village community under study (see Table 5.22). The average per capita income from all sources was fairly lower than the stipulated MPCE as mentioned earlier (please note that income was taken as proxy for expenditures mentioned above). For instance, the poverty line based on per capita annual income in Gujarat was about ₹6,019 and for MP it was ₹4,901. The average per capita annual income was found to be lower in the case of Valuna and Kalakhunt villages in Gujarat and MP respectively. This suggests a somewhat limited impact on poverty reduction in the study villages.

Table 5.22

Change in Per Capita Annual Income after the Watershed Project

Villages		Per Capita Annual Income from All Sources
Valuna (202)	After	4,899
	Before	3,549
Jamsar (180)	After	8,360
	Before	4,953
Tharavada (362)	After	8,343
	Before	6,265
Sama (266)	After	7,224
	Before	5,474
Singrawankalan (222)	After	5,112
	Before	2,730
Kalakhunt (223)	After	3,565
	Before	4,103
Sobaliyapura (191)	After	7,106
	Before	3,953
Total (1,646)	After	6,588
	Before	4,549

Source: Field survey data, (2009).

5.6. Changes in Income of the Poor at the Village Level

The data pertaining to changes in income suggest that an overwhelmingly large (i.e., about 92 per cent) proportion of the households in the study villages experienced an increase in income from the beginning of the WDP project. This proportion was fairly high as compared to the proportion of households that reported some kind of involvement (Figure 5.2). While there could have been a difference in the degree of increase in income, what emerged was an overall improvement in the incomes of the village communities, irrespective of the sources thereof. We tried to examine the remaining 8 per cent of the households who did not report any increases in their incomes.

Table 5.23

Households Reporting a Decline in Income: Gujarat

Size Class	Negative Income HHs	% to Total HHs	Total HHs	Negative Income HHs	% to Total HHs	Total HHs
				Gujarat		
		Valuna			Jamsar	
Landless	0	0.00	9	6	15.79	38
< 2.5 Acre	17	12.41	137	3	8.33	36
2.5–5.0 Acre	7	15.91	44	2	3.85	52
> 5.0 Acre	2	16.67	12	4	7.41	54
Total	26	12.87	202	15	8.33	180
		Tharavada			Sama	
Landless	9	4.66	193	11	8.87	124
< 2.5 Acre	4	9.52	42	15	12.61	119
2.5–5.0 Acre	6	12.77	47	3	16.67	18
> 5.0 Acre	9	11.25	80	0	0.00	6
Total	28	7.73	362	29	10.86	267
Gujarat Villages	98	9.72	1,008			

Source: Field survey data, (2009).

The information presented in Tables 5.23 and 5.24 suggests that the landless and marginal farmers were not particularly discriminated against in the scenario of widespread improvements in incomes. It may be reiterated that the income data were subject to estimation errors but what was of importance, however, was the shared perceptions about the improvements in economic status. It is likely that these perceptions were influenced by the fact that the field enquiry was linked directly to a project intervention which people looked at favourably and with the hope that another intervention of such kind might come to their village!

5.7. Overall Changes

Overall, the area under irrigation had changed substantially in six out of the eight villages; the exceptions being Valuna (Gujarat) and Singrawankalan (MP). The increase in irrigated area was

Table 5.24

Households Reporting a Decline in Income: MP

Size Class	Madhya Pradesh		
	Singrawankalan		
	No. of HHs	% to Total HHs	Total HHs
Landless	3	9.38	32
< 2.5 Acre	0	0.00	20
2.5–5.0 Acre	2	3.17	63
5.0 > Acre	9	8.41	107
Total	14	6.31	222
	Kalakhunt		
Landless	0	0.00	55
< 2.5 Acre	3	3.53	85
2.5–5.0 Acre	0	0.00	59
5.0 > Acre	0	0.00	24
Total	3	1.35	223
	Sobaliyapura		
Landless	10	15.87	63
< 2.5 Acre	1	9.09	11
2.5–5.0 Acre	3	5.17	58
5.0 > Acre	2	3.39	59
Total	16	8.38	191
MP Villages	33	5.19	636
All Villages	131	7.97	1,644

Source: Field survey data, (2009).

mainly due to the increased number of wells and borewells. The net increase in irrigated area per household was fairly small and was spread over all types of landholding size. Along with irrigation, the cropping pattern and yields may also have changed over time, resulting in substantial increases in incomes from agriculture and livestock.

To what extent was the change in incomes attributable to the watershed project? This issue will be examined in the next section in the light of our HHS results.

6. Impact on Poverty: Evidence from a Sample Survey of Households

This section draws on the evidence collected from a sample survey of 400 households, 50 in each of the study villages in Gujarat and MP. The sample, consisting of both landless and landed households, was based on a stratified random sampling method. Of the total sample, about 50 per cent of households were landless and the rest were landed with or without access to irrigation. In fact, the sample in each village was broadly distributed as follows: 24 landless and 13 each in the categories of landed without irrigation and with irrigation (Table 5.25). There was, however, a slight variation in the number of sample households across villages owing mainly to inaccurate or inadequate information at the time of drawing the sample. The 50 per cent weight for landless households reflects the poverty focus of the present enquiry.

Table 5.25

Distribution of Sample HHs Across the Main Categories and BPL Status

(Number of Households)

Villages	Landless	Landed without Irrigation	Landed with Irrigation	Total	BPL % (no.)	Short Term Migration (%)
			Gujarat			
Valuna	24	13	13	50	22.0 (11)	3.5
Jamsar	24	13	13	50	45.7 (21)	3.9
Tharavada	24	13	13	50	46.0 (23)	–
Sama	24	13	13	50	45.7 (21)	0.7
Total	96	52	52	200	39.58 (76)	1.6
			Madhya Pradesh			
Singrawankalan	24	13	13	50	66.0 (33)	23.4
Kalakhunt	24	13	13	50	60.5 (26)	85.7
Sobaliyapura	24	13	13	50	75.6 (34)	2.1
Gopalpura	24	13	13	50	64.6 (31)	47.3
Total	96	52	52	200	66.7 (124)	38.8

Source: Field survey data, (2009).
Note: Figures in parentheses indicate number of households.

Table 5.26

Sample Households by Social Groups

Village	SC	ST	OBC	Other	All
			Caste		
Valuna (Sabarkantha)	20.0 (10)	10.0 (5)	68.0 (34)	2.0 (1)	100.0 (50)
Jamsar (Rajkot)	–	–	100.0 (50)	–	100.0 (50)
Tharavada (Kachchh)	12.0 (6)	2.0 (01)	50.0 (25)	36.0 (18)	100.0 (50)
Sama (Panchmahal)	22.0 (11)	8.0 (04)	48.0 (24)	22.0 (11)	100.0 (50)
Gujarat Total	13.5 (27)	5.0 (10)	66.5 (133)	15 (30)	100.0 (200)
Singrawankalan (Chhatarpur)	40.0 (20)	–	54.0 (27)	6.0 (03)	100.0 (50)
Kalakhunt (Jhabua)	–	100.0 (50)	–	–	100.0 (50)
Sobaliyapura (Dewas)	2.0 (01)	74.0 (37)	18.0 (09)	6.0 (03)	100.0 (50)
Gopalpura (Ratlam)	–	100.0 (50)	–	–	100.0 (50)
MP Total	10.5 (21)	68.5 (137)	18.0 (36)	3.0 (6)	100.0 (200)
All	12.0 (48)	36.75 (147)	42.25 (169)	9.0 (36)	100.0 (400)

Source: Field survey data, (2009).
Note: Figures in parentheses indicate number of households.

Whereas in Gujarat the sample was dominated by other backward castes (OBCs), the dominant group in MP were the STs. Both accounted for roughly two-thirds of the sample households in their respective states (Table 5.26).

6.1. Benefits Received from the WDP: Gujarat and MP Households

Tables 5.27 and 5.28 present the profiles of direct benefits received by the sample households, especially the landed, who happened to be the main recipients of project activities. It was observed that while the outreach of the project activities was fairly substantial in most of the villages in Gujarat, the same was not true in case of MP with the exception of Singrawankalan. This in turn, may have cast its influence over the nature and extent of direct benefits obtained by the sample households.

Table 5.27

Direct Benefits Received by Sample Households from WDPs in Gujarat (% of Households)

Benefits Received	Valuna	Jamsar	Tharavada	Sama
Farm Bund	15	26	01	10
Pond/Farm pond	02	01	03	03
Check dam	05	04	17	08
Plantation	02	01	–	–
Nullah plug	03	–	–	–
Entry Point Activity	02	02	–	02
Soil Development	–	02	–	–
Fertilizer Use	–	–	–	–

Source: Field survey data, (2009).

Table 5.28

Direct Benefits Received by Sample Households from WDPs in MP (% of Households)

Activities	Singrawankalan	Kalakhunt	Sobaliyapura	Gopalpura
Farm Bund	09	03	09	04
Pond/Farm pond	–	01	02	01
Check dam	13	–	–	–
Stop Dam	06	–	–	–
Plantation	02	–	–	–
Nullah plug	–	–	–	–
Entry Point Activity	–	–	–	–
Soil Development	–	–	01	–
Fertilizer Use	–	–	–	–
Well Recharge	04	–	02	–

Source: Field survey data, (2009).

The above observation was reflected in some of the important indicators capturing the impact of the project activities, especially among the landed households. Table 5.29 presents the findings with respect to the observed changes in irrigated area among the landed households within the sample. It is evident that with respect to net cropped area (NCA) and irrigated land, only a marginal

Table 5.29

Change in Average Cultivated and Irrigated Land amongst Sample Farmers (in Acres)

Village/ (District)	Before			After		
	Irrigated	Un-irrigated	NCA	Irrigated	Un-irrigated	NCA
Gujarat						
Valuna (Sabarkantha)	4.25 (10)	4.14 (23)	5.30	2.43 (13)	2.41 (23)	3.35
Jamsar (Rajkot)	2.61 (17)	6.87 (22)	7.52	2.50 (13)	7.17 (23)	7.59
Tharavada (Kachchh)	5.91 (12)	4.13 (16)	5.26	5.92 (13)	4.00 (15)	5.27
Sama (Panchmahal)	5.34 (7)	2.92 (22)	3.06	3.56 (13)	2.14 (15)	3.01
Total Gujarat	4.25 (46)	4.27 (83)	5.29	3.60 (52)	4.11 (76)	4.80
Madhya Pradesh						
Singrawankalan (Chhatarpur)	6.39 (26)	1.90 (13)	7.34	6.45 (26)	2.77 (12)	7.72
Kalakhunt (Jhabua)	1.53 (11)	2.40 (23)	2.77	1.56 (13)	2.36 (22)	2.78
Sobaliyapura (Dewas)	5.25 (12)	4.32 (17)	5.25	5.82 (13)	3.59 (16)	5.12
Gopalpura (Ratlam)	1.41 (06)	1.95 (22)	1.96	2.06 (11)	1.15 (23)	1.89
Total MP	4.63 (55)	2.62 (75)	4.34	4.54 (63)	2.32 (73)	4.38
All	4.57 (101)	3.49 (158)	4.87	4.11 115)	3.23 (149)	4.59

Source: Field survey data, (2009).

Notes: Figures in parenthesis indicate number of households. Information on NCA is based on the total area owned by 26 landed households in each village.

improvement had occurred, especially in the case of MP. An important difference was that whereas in Gujarat the impact was found mainly in terms of a small increase in the average NCA, the impact in MP was witnessed mainly in terms of an increase in the average irrigated area.

This could have been partly due to the fact that the increase in irrigation was achieved mainly through recharging of groundwater by constructing small water harvesting structures or reducing soil-water erosion by way of farm bunds. Both of these may have had a limited impact in terms of increased area under irrigation or cultivation; in most cases the impact would have been realized in terms of increased intensity of irrigation to the land already put under cultivation or irrigation. This, in turn, may have helped change the cropping pattern as is shown subsequently. To some degree, the extent of involvement (or participation) of households in project activities was linked to the nature of the PIA, an issue to be discussed later.

The positive changes in the NCA and irrigated areas, however, were fairly small, perhaps statistically insignificant. Prima facie, this may have been due to two important reasons: (a) the limited outreach of project activities among the sample farmers and (b) the sub-normal rainfall situation prevailing during the reference year.

It is important to note that the increase in the average irrigated area was found to be favourable for marginal and small farmers (i.e., those with < 5 acres of land) in three out of the four villages in MP (except Sobaliyapura where the farmers with > 5 acres of land had also benefited). In Gujarat, the increase in the mean irrigated area was found to be limited only to the small farmers in the case of Sama (Table 5.30).

The above observations indicate the impact (especially regarding land use and irrigation) over time, as well as the influence of changes

Table 5.30

Irrigated Area Before and After the WDP (Area in Acres)

Village	Landholding	Before WDP		After WDP	
		Irrigated	Unirrigated	Irrigated	Unirrigated
Valuna	< 2.5	1.47 (3)	2.86 (9)	1.38 (3)	1.28 (8)
(Sabarkantha)	2.51–5.0	3.63 (4)	5.17 (13)	2.38 (7)	2.94 (13)
	> 5	7.86 (3)	5.5 (1)	4.19 (3)	4.25 (2)
	Total	4.25 (10)	4.14 (23)	2.43 (13)	2.41 (23)
Jamsar	< 2.5	2.4 (2)	1.48 (5)	1.65 (2)	1.50 (4)
(Rajkot)	2.51–5.0	2.14 (10)	3.12 (10)	1.66 (7)	3.15 (13)
	> 5	3.64 (5)	16.09 (7)	4.4 (4)	32.27 (6)
	Total	2.61 (17)	6.87 (22)	2.50 13)	7.17 (23)
Tharavada	< 2.5	–	2.0 (4)	–	2.0 (4)
(Kachchh)	2.51–5.0	4.14 (7)	3.71 (7)	4.14 (7)	3.71 (7)
	> 5	8.4 (5)	6.4 (5)	8.0 (6)	6.5 (4)
	Total	5.92 (12)	4.13 (16)	5.92 (13)	4.00 (15)

(contd...)

(contd...)

Village	Landholding	Before WDP		After WDP	
		Irrigated	*Unirrigated*	*Irrigated*	*Unirrigated*
Sama (Panchmahal)	< 2.5	2.43 (2)	0.92 (16)	1.39 (7)	0.88 (10)
	2.51–5.0	3.79 (2)	3.42 (3)	3.85 (3)	3.14 (2)
	> 5	9.0 (3)	5.71 (3)	9.0 (3)	5.71 (3)
	Total	5.34 (7)	1.92 (22)	3.56 (13)	2.14 (15)
Singrawankalan (Chhatrapur)	< 2.5	4.33 (15)	–	4.53 (15)	–
	2.51–5.0	5.61 (7)	2.11 (5)	5.96 (7)	2.53 (4)
	> 5	15.79 (8)	2.83 (3)	15.54 (8)	5.80 (3)
	Total	6.39 (36)	1.90 (13)	6.45 (26)	2.77 (12)
Kalakhunt (Jhabua)	< 2.5	1.71 (3)	1.77 (10)	1.48 (5)	1.71 (9)
	2.51–5.0	1.26 (7)	2.38 (11)	1.42 (7)	2.28 (11)
	> 5	2.85 (1)	5.71 (2)	2.85 (1)	5.71 (2)
	Total	1.53 (11)	2.40 (23)	1.56 (13)	2.36 (22)
Sobaliyapura (Dewas)	< 2.5	2.0 (2)	1.94 (8)	2.28 (2)	1.94 (8)
	2.51–5.0	4.22 (5)	3.88 (5)	3.77 (5)	2.74 (5)
	> 5	7.59 (5)	9.64 (4)	8.70 (6)	9.43 (3)
	Total	5.25 (12)	4.32 (17)	5.82 (13)	3.59 (16)
Gopalpura (Ratlam)	< 2.5	1.01 (4)	1.41 (16)	1.39 (7)	0.80 (18)
	2.51–5.0	2.22 (2)	2.51 (5)	3.24 (4)	1.11 (4)
	> 5	–	7.70 (1)	–	7.70 (1)
	Total	1.41 (6)	1.95 (22)	2.06 (11)	1.15 (23)

Source: Field survey data, (2009).

that may have taken place in the villages due to similar interventions other than the WDP's and/or private investments.by the farmers.

6.2. Change in Crop Yields

Increased irrigation was expected to lead to a corresponding increase in agricultural incomes, as already discussed. To a large extent, the increase in agricultural incomes may have been contributed by increased crop productivity. This has been examined in the light of the responses obtained from the sample farmers (Table 5.31).

Table 5.31

Change in the Area and Yield of Major Crops

	All					
	Area in Acre		Yield (Kg./Acre)		Change	
Crops	Before	After	Before	After	Area	Yield
Maize	146.1	109.8	399.3	427.0	−36.3	27.7
Tur	57.1	31.9	208.8	162.1	−25.2	−46.7
Cotton	123.5	164.5	387.7	939.5	41.0	551.8
Wheat	142.8	161.9	374.5	583.8	19.1	209.3
Jowar	73.3	79.6	NA	615.1	6.3	NA
Groundnut	91.6	77.5	277.7	336.2	−14.1	58.5
Bajari	93.1	85.6	378.7	394.7	−7.5	16.0
Till	30.9	17.9	223.9	89.5	−13.0	−134.4
Soyabean	40.8	55.9	297.9	558.7	15.1	260.8
Pulses	87.7	100.1	119.7	128.9	12.4	9.2
	Gujarat					
Maize	81.0	60.6	490.1	524.8	−20.4	34.7
Tur	35.5	14.6	203.9	163.8	−20.9	−40.1
Cotton	77.8	109.2	481.4	1,033.4	31.4	552.0
Wheat	97.2	83.5	360.9	439.8	−13.7	78.9
Jowar	66.2	73.9	NA	635.1	7.7	NA
Groundnut	82.4	68.8	276.9	347.7	−13.6	70.8
Bajari	93.1	85.6	378.7	394.7	−7.5	16.0
Till	19.5	17.9	149.7	89.5	−1.6	−60.2
Pulses	66.0	49.1	84.5	103.4	−16.9	18.9
	Madhya Pradesh					
Maize	65.1	49.2	286.3	306.4	−15.9	20.1
Tur	21.7	17.3	216.6	160.7	−4.4	−55.9
Cotton	45.7	55.3	227.8	753.9	9.6	526.1
Wheat	45.6	78.4	403.5	737.2	32.8	333.7
Jowar	7.1	5.7	434.0	355.0	−1.4	−79.0
Groundnut	9.2	8.7	284.2	245.1	−0.5	−39.1
Till	11.4		350.9		−11.4	
Soyabean	40.8	55.9	297.9	558.7	15.1	260.8
Pulses	21.7	51.0	227.0	153.4	29.3	−73.6

Source: Field survey data, (2009).
Note: Excludes households which did not report production and also sample households from Gopalpura, MP.

The area under cotton underwent a significant increase during the project period. Other crops that gained in terms of area were wheat, jowar and soyabeans. Overall, this suggested an increase in the area under irrigated and high-valued crops as compared to subsistence crops like tur, *bajri* and maize. The pattern was more or less similar in both the states.

There was an increase in yield for most of the major crops, except for maize, tur and jowar. The increase in yield was particularly high in the case of cotton, wheat and soybeans. A number of factors may have contributed to the increases in yield including increased access to irrigation, increased use of chemical fertilizers and also favourable rainfall during the post-project period in parts of Gujarat and MP.

6.2.1. Perceived Impact: Post-project Context

Setting aside the issue of attribution, it may be useful to understand how the sample households perceived the various changes that took place in terms of three important sets of indicators, namely: (a) land use and agriculture; (b) employment, income and assets and (c) social status and any other indicators. Tables 5.32 and 5.33 present detailed information based on perceptions about changes in the post-project period. It should be noted that these perceptions may refer to the entire phase of the post-project period rather than the specific reference year for which the data were presented in the previous tables. It should also be noted that these questions were asked to all the sample households though the questions pertaining to the first set of indicators may have been responded to particularly by the landed households.

The observations from Gujarat suggest that:

1. Whereas an increase in groundwater and soil moisture was perceived by roughly 25 per cent of the sample households, those reporting an increase in irrigated land were only a few. Similarly, very few respondents indicated a reduction in fallow land. Those reporting an increase in the water table ranged from 6 to 13 per cent.

Table 5.32

Perceived Impacts of the Watershed Project: Gujarat (Number of Households)

Perceived Impact	Villages			
	Valuna	Jamsar	Tharavada	Sama
a) Land use and Agriculture				
Increase in cultivable land	–	–	–	1
Increase in irrigated land	–	4	3	5
Decrease in fallow land	9	7	2	5
Increase in groundwater	12	9	13	12
Change in cropping pattern	13	8	10	10
Increased soil moisture	14	14	3	13
Increase in fallow land	2	1	–	–
Increase in water table	8	13	7	6
Increase in availability of fodder and fuel wood from community land	3	3	3	2
Increase in availability of fodder from own land	8	9	3	4
Increase in availability of fuel wood from own land	8	8	4	2
Increase in use of chemical fertilizers	14	16	17	17
Change in source of drinking water	39	49	19	18
Increase in use of HYV seeds	23	17	19	21
Increase in use of pesticides	21	15	20	19
b) Labour and Income Assets				
Reduced migration	3	2	3	3
Increase in labour work and wage rate	36	48	42	30
Increase in disposable income for women	–	4	2	1
Purchase of silver, utensils, clothes	28	48	42	36
Purchase of livestock	33	20	13	2
Repair/Purchase of house	13	18	11	9
Purchase of other assets	6	13	12	8
Repayment of debt	11	7	3	8
Increased expenses on social events	32	33	38	34
Increase in consumption of cereal, pulses, oil (kg/month)	42	47	47	43

(contd...)

(contd...)

Perceived Impact	Villages			
	Valuna	Jamsar	Tharavada	Sama
Increase in consumption of milk, vegetables, fish, egg, meat (quantity/month)	43	47	44	39
Increase in educational expenses (₹/year)	32	29	33	30
Improvement in health care	44	45	43	48
c) Social Status and Other				
Increase in transport facility	48	49	5	48
Increase in hired labour for domestic chores	2	1	–	1
Improvement in social status	15	12	11	14
Savings in bank	1	7	17	10
Increase in land prices	24	27	19	19
Increased expenditure on liquor; tobacco etc.	15	8	11	4

Source: Field survey data, (2009).

2. Close to 20 per cent of the Gujarat households reported a change in cropping patterns and a shift to High Yielding Variety (HYV) seeds and greater use of chemical fertilizers and pesticides. It was thus likely that much of the increase in crop yields was driven by the increased use of modern inputs, in addition to increased irrigation that may have been obtained through sources other than the WDP interventions.[14]

3. About 8–10 respondents (out of the 50 per village) reported an increase in the availability of fodder from agricultural land; only two reported an increase from common property land. A similar pattern was observed in the case of fuel wood.

4. As large as 50 per cent of the sample Gujarat households in Valuna and Jamsar reported an improvement in the

---

[14] This kind of a situation is often observed in a comparative 'with-without' analysis. It is particularly so when the major source of increased irrigation is groundwater, which is provided mainly through private investments and/or similar schemes like those for check dams in Gujarat, independent of watershed projects. A recent study of 91 micro watershed projects, covering all four districts under this study in Gujarat, supports this evidence. For details see, Shah et al., 2012.

Table 5.33

Perceived Impact of Watershed Project: Madhya Pradesh (Number of Households)

	Villages			
Perceived Impact	*Singrawankalan*	*Kalakhunt*	*Sobaliyapura*	*Gopalpura*
a) Land use and Agriculture				
Increase in cultivable land	5	–	3	1
Increase in irrigated land	12	5	3	5
Decrease in fallow land	3	4	2	5
Increase in groundwater	15	1	4	5
Change in cropping pattern	NA	5	9	5
Increased soil moisture	9	4	10	4
Increased fallow land	–	–	–	–
Increase in water table	20	1	8	5
Increased availability of fodder and fuel wood from community land	0	1	7	3
Increased availability of fodder from own land	11	3	3	1
Increased availability of fuel wood from own land	7	3	9	5
Increase in source of drinking water	37	22	33	24
Increase in use of chemical fertilizers	20	15	22	23
Increase in use of HYV seeds	13	13	21	22
Increase in use of pesticides	N.A.	10	22	23
b) Labour and Income Assets				
Reduced migration	–	–	–	–
Increase in labour work and wage rate	35	40	37	3
Increase in women's disposable income	12	–	4	–
Purchase of silver, utensils, cloth	25	33	33	27

(contd...)

(contd...)

Perceived Impact	Villages			
	Singrawankalan	*Kalakhunt*	*Sobaliyapura*	*Gopalpura*
Purchase of livestock	3	4	6	2
Repair/purchase of house	13	1	1	3
Purchase of other assets	4	1	5	3
Repayment of debt	11	4	8	8
Increase in expenses for social events	12	33	33	27
Increase in consumption of cereal, pulses, oil (kg/month)	14	48	37	46
Increase in consumption of milk, vegetables, fish, egg, meat (quantity/month)	9	49	34	46
Increase in educational expenses (₹/year)	17	28	33	39
Improvement in health care	15	48	48	48
c) Social Status and Other				
Increase in transport facility	11	47	50	49
Increase in hired labour for domestic chores	9	–	3	–
Improved social status	9	9	14	12
Savings in bank	9	2	3	1
Increased land prices	12	21	21	21
Increased expenditure on liquor; tobacco etc.	3	1	20	1

Source: Field survey data, (2009).

availability of drinking water; in the remaining two Gujarat villages the proportion was close to half of this.

5. Notwithstanding the relatively limited impact on irrigation and access to fuel/fodder from common property land resource (CPLRs), the responses with respect to wage rates, income and assets were fairly positive. Whereas only a few households reported a change in the extent of migration, a

substantially large number of sample households (ranging from 30 to 42) reported an increase in employment and wage rates. In the case of Jamsar and Tharavada, it was likely that a part of this increase was due to the availability of non-farm employment. Overall, the increase in wage rates may also have been linked to the phenomenally high rate of growth in agriculture and the overall economy since the early part of 2000.

6. The village communities in the Gujarat study villages reported improvements in a number of indicators of economic well-being including consumption of basic food. The purchase of livestock was also reported, especially in Valuna and Jamsar. Sama village was an exception to this pattern.

Overall, the sample households reported a positive change in terms of various amenities such as access to health care, increase in transport facilities and social status (the number of households reporting the last ranged from 11 to 15).

The pattern in MP was more or less like that observed in Gujarat. This was mainly because the policy guidelines for the WDP were the same across the two states and the constraints faced in terms of time frame, legal hitches in taking up development of pastures and other common land, presence of other schemes like drinking water supply, tank renovation, plantation etc. outside the watershed projects also remained more or less similar across the states.

1. A very small number of MP households (up to five per village) reported an increase in cultivated land and a decline in fallow land. Compared to these, a larger number reported an increase in soil moisture, irrigation and changes in cropping patterns (up to 12, 10 and 9 respectively). All these went hand in hand with the increased use of modern inputs.

2. Access to drinking water was reported by 22 to 37 MP households. However, the availability of fodder and fuel from community land was seen to be almost negligible. Interestingly, the impact on the purchase of livestock in MP was found to be almost negligible, unlike that in the case of Gujarat.

3. There was an improvement in amenities like transport and health care services. Ownership of assets had also increased, and so had food consumption.
4. Overall, about 20–25 per cent of the households in MP perceived an improvement in their social status, perhaps due to the improved economic status of their households.
5. Over the period of 2003 to 2010, as many as 29 households per MP village reported increased wage rates (see Table 5.33).

What do these perceptions add up to? How much did the poor benefit from the increases in incomes? Can the positive changes in economic as well as social status be mainly (if not entirely) attributed to the watershed projects? These questions cannot be answered conclusively from an empirical study such as this, where the watershed treatments, including water harvesting structures, did not directly provide irrigation by lifting the water from these structures. In this sense, even the irrigation benefits were indirect in nature.

6.3. The Issue of Attribution

An important check for addressing the issue of attribution was to look for changes in the sources of irrigation that had taken place in each village. Table 5.34 presents information collected through the FGDs on the sources of irrigation before and after the project. It is important to note that changes did take place in project-related interventions such as check dams and tanks, but one also found a substantial increase in the number of wells and borewells in the study villages. In fact, the number of borewells increased significantly in Gujarat. While a part of the increased groundwater use could be attributed to water harvesting structures created by the project, the change in the number of borewells cannot be entirely linked to the improved groundwater table as seen in Table 5.34. Also it may be noted that there was an increase in the number of borewells as compared to open wells in villages like Valuna, Tharawada, Sama, Kalakhunt and Gopalpura. This was in

Table 5.34

The Number of Functional Water Sources in the Study Villages

		Before				After			
State	Village	Tank/ Canal	Well	Bore Well	Check dam	Tank/ Canal	Well	Bore Well	Check dam
Gujarat	Valuna	–	08	04	02	–	15	20	10
	Jamsar	–	10	35	–	–	50	40	06
	Tharavada	–	–	70	02	–	–	150	13
	Sama	02	10	–	03	02	20	10	07
Madhya Pradesh	Singrawankalan	–	95	–	05	–	99	–	10
	Kalakhunt	01	08	05	–	04	12	19	–
	Sobaliyapura	–	08	05	01	01	19	05	15
	Gopalpura	01	11	–	01	06	11	10	06

Source: Primary survey, (2009).

spite of a perceived increase in the groundwater table. This is not to deny that the project had not contributed to the development of groundwater irrigation; rather the point here is one of attributing the entire change to the WDP project intervention. Linking the impact with WDP institutions thus, becomes somewhat more difficult.

The next section dwells on the central question of whether, and in what manner, community management in watershed projects helped tilt the benefits in favour of the relatively worse off, if not the poor.

7. To What Extent Have CNRM Institutions Mattered?

7.1. Community Institutions and Processes

Given the above caveats, we now discuss the processes as well as functioning of the WDP-driven community-based institutions with a view to understanding whether and to what extent these influenced the poverty reduction outcomes of the projects. The analysis in this section draws on the FGDs and also the household level information collected through the primary survey of households.

In Section 1, we postulated prima facie that institutional processes and their functioning were at the centre of influencing the size as well as distribution of the benefits that may have arisen from a watershed project in a village. These were realized through two important means: (a) implementation of the watershed treatments (i.e., the technology) and (b) changing the norms for accessing and sharing the resource. All these, eventually, were set within the overall constraints exerted through structural aspects such as the property rights regime, on the one hand, and external factors that may have influenced the overall efficacy of the project and the institutions, on the other.

Given this backdrop, we present some of the important features of the institutions, the processes that were followed for forming and also for implementing the projects in each study village.

As noted earlier, watershed projects, unlike the other three initiatives covered in this volume, created multiple institutions. These included a watershed development team (WDT), a WDC, UGs and SHGs especially for the landless and the poor. Of these, the WDC being the executive body, assumed critical importance. Unfortunately, the WDCs did not have to continue in the post-project phase, as the project management, in most cases, was handed over to the village *panchayat*. In practice, however, most of these institutions remained dormant, including the PRI.

It is important to note that the PIA played a significant role in forming the community-based institutions and, invariably, in shaping the norms as well as the actual functioning of these institutions, at least during the project phase. The PIA could be a government or a NGO, as already noted. The procedures for forming the institutions were clearly laid down in the respective guidelines, which in most cases were followed ritualistically.

In what follows, we present some important features of the processes followed in forming the institutions and decisions making about the nature of the watershed treatments as well as the norms for resource use and benefit sharing.

7.2. Institutional Profiles

Table 5.35 presents a broad profile of the institutional set-up in the study villages in Gujarat and Madhya Pradesh.

The following observations deserve special attention:

a. Gujarat

1. All the project villages in Gujarat formed a WDC. The WDCs had a stipulated number of members, up to 11, mostly in consonance with the provisions made in the Guidelines. Generally, the WDCs had representatives from marginalized communities and also women. In all of them at least some of the WDC members were drawn from the village *panchayat*.[15]

2. In Valuna and Jamsar the PIA approached village leaders and informed them about the possibility of the project to be initiated in their respective villages. In Sama, the initiative was undertaken mainly by the local leader, whereas in Tharavada a group of village communities, mainly farmers, approached the PIA.

3. At the time of the study, the WDC was still functioning where the PIAs had a long term presence and continuity in terms of watershed-related work. Nevertheless, the WDCs were more or less non-functional; meetings seldom took place and the records were generally kept with the Secretary of the WDC. This was evident because no one, except the WDC secretary, was in a position to represent the WDC as a live and/or relevant institution in the post-project period.

4. The WDF was used in the case of Jamsar and Tharavada. For Valuna and Sama the procedure for obtaining the permission was underway during the time of this study.

5. In all the Gujarat villages, project-specific activities were selected through a village meeting organized by the PIA, in the presence of government officials. Caste-based leadership

---

[15] This was a fairly common practice adopted by a large number of WDCs in Gujarat. The idea was to keep a balance between the different centres of CBOs so as to avoid likely friction among them. In a sense this suggested a co-option mechanism.

Table 5.35

Institutional Set-up: Gujarat

Village	Valuna	Jamsar	Tharavada	Sama
Name of PIA	Development Support Centre	Sarvodaya Seva Sangh	Sahajanand Rural Development Trust	DRDA
PIA's presence in the post-project phase	Strong (periodical visits and new interventions)	Strong (Frequent interactions as the NGO has a local base)	Moderate (the NGO keeps in touch with some members of the community to serve its long-term interest in the area)	Low (No interaction; officers were transferred and the project file is closed)
Project Type	IWDP	DDP	DDP	IWDP
Year of Commencement	1997	1995	1997	2002
Year of Completion	2002	2000	2001	2006
How was the project initiated in the village?	Through the initiative of the DSC which wanted to have hands-on implementation experience.	Sarvodaya Seva Sangh held a meeting. Villagers understood the project and the project was started.	Kachchh, being a desert prone area facing severe problem of water and irrigation, had been a major thrust area for WDP in the state. The villagers approached the PIA, who in turn, approached the Government officials in the district.	A local leader using his political clout with the then ruling party got the project sanctioned for the village (getting a WDP approved was a competitive process as there were many claims for the same.)

(contd...)

(contd...)

Village	Valuna	Jamsar	Tharavada	Sama
How was the WDC formed?	In a village meeting called by the PIA.	In a village meeting called by PIA.	PIA's discussion with local leaders.	PIA's discussion with local leaders.
Utilization of Watershed Fund	Approval from PIA and DRDA still in progress	Used for repair of check dam	Used for repair of check dam	Approval from PIA and DRDA still in progress
No. of WDC members in Gram Panchayat	4	2	4	1
WDC members by caste and gender	ST 11(M-7, F-4)	OBC 11(M-9 F-2)	SC 2(M-1 F-1) Muslim 5(M-3 F-2) Patel 4(M-3 F-1)	SC 6(M-4, F-2) OBC 5(M-4 F-1)
Whether WDC is still functioning?	Yes	Yes	No	No
Meeting	When needed	When needed	When needed	When needed
Who decided the activity and plan?	WDC, UG and PIA	WDC, UG and PIA	Village leaders and PIA	WDC, UG and PIA
No. of SHGs	12	4	2	0
Presently functioning SHGs	8	1	0	0
Members	96	48	24	0
Main Activity	Saving and Credit	Saving and Credit	–	–
Selecting the site of check dam	WDC and UG member and PIA	WDC and UG member and PIA	WDC and UG member and PIA	WDC and UG member and PIA

How did the PIA start the project?	PIA organized a meeting of village leaders. Put up a poster exhibition, rally and worked through personal contacts	Village meeting organized by the PIA in the presence of government officials. Following this, the PIA started an office near the village. Project-related information was distributed and exposure visit was organized.	PIA, village leader and representative of GO (Government organization) held a meeting in village, selected activities.	PIA, village leader and representative of GO held a meeting in village, selected activities
People's Participation	Labour contribution 15%	For agriculture equipment and horticulture plants 50% contribution and other work 10% labour contribution.	Horticulture plants 50% contribution and other work 10% labour contribution	Only labour contribution.
What activity was carried out and how was it decided?	Check dam, Nullah plug, Bori Bandh, community hall and plantation activities carried out. Caste and other leaders decided.	Check dam, loose border, contour bandh, tank, distribution of agricultural equipment, vaccination of animal activities carried out. One person from every family met at a common place and decided.	Check dam, deepening of tank, plantation, farm pond, formation of SHG and community hall were decided in a meeting in presence of government officials and PIA.	Check dam, contour band, deepening of tanks and plantation activities carried out. Village leader and dominant person selected the activities.

Source: Field survey data, (2009).

Note: IWDP—Integrated Watershed Development Project; DDP—Desert Development Project.

in the villages influenced the decision-making process significantly. However, the selection of other leaders in the villages played a major role in the decision-making processes. The selection of the site for check dams, the most important project intervention, was generally made by the PIA, WDC members and potential beneficiaries or/UGs. The work plan was then sent to the DRDA for approval. There was not a single instance where the approval was not granted.

6. None of the villages reported any instance of conflict of interest or disagreement with the decisions taken at the planning stage or during the process of implementation. If there were any such instances, they were not reported to our team of investigators despite repeated probing.

7. A nominal contribution, usually in the form of labour, was reported in all four villages. Additionally, a contribution was also collected for the horticulture plantations in Jamsar and Tharavada.

8. SHGs had been formed in three villages, except for Sama. The number of SHGs formed was 12, 4 and 2 in Valuna, Jamsar and Tharavada respectively. However, only eight and two SHGs were operating in Valuna and Jamsar respectively at the time of the survey. None of the villages reported any formation of user groups separate from the SHGs.

9. The PIAs had a continued presence in Valuna and Jamsar, where the NGOs had undertaken a number of developmental interventions other than the watershed project. These activities, subsequent to watershed project, were done through the WDP institutions.

It may be recalled that the intensity of treatments carried out and the beneficiaries covered were found to be on a larger scale in Valuna, Jamsar and Tharavada as compared to Sama (Table 5.16). It is significant that all these three micro watersheds were implemented by NGOs.

b. Madhya Pradesh

The situation with respect to the processes of forming WDP institutions in MP was somewhat similar to that in Gujarat

(Table 5.36). Most of the PIAs followed the provisions in the guidelines regarding the formation, number of members and composition of WDCs. The WDCs were reported as functioning in two villages, Singrawankalan and Gopalpura. However, the WDCs reportedly met in all four MP villages in case a meeting was required.

An important difference from the cases studied in Gujarat was that one WDC in MP continued to involve a Sub-divisional Officer (SDO) of the state Forest Department, who implemented the project in Gopalpura. Also, in Kalakhunt, a leading NGO had undertaken implementation of the project, but could not complete it owing to intra-village conflicts over the selection of WDC functionaries, the giving out of work contracts and disbursing of funds to local leaders. As a result, WDP activities carried out in Kalakhunt were very few.

Singrawankalan was yet another interesting case where watershed-related work was undertaken through a special scheme, namely the DPIP where special thrust was given to the development of groundwater resources.

While the project activities in MP were decided through village meetings in the presence of the PIA and government functionaries, the sites of the important water harvesting structures seem to have been selected mainly by the PIA. This, in fact, was the larger reality in most of the cases. Thus, the type of PIA mattered more in deciding the type of watershed treatments, and perhaps not that much in terms of the sharing of benefits from the given technical interventions—this issue will be discussed again in the last section.

SHGs had been formed in all of the villages. The number of SHGs that had survived into the post-project phase ranged from five in Singrawankalan to one in Kalakhunt. All of the villages also reported labour contributions, although the cost-sharing for a village tank was found to be an additional feature in the case of Singrawankalan.

Overall, Singrawankalan and Gopalpura experienced better coverage of watershed treatments and beneficiaries, closely followed

Table 5.36

Institutional Set-up: MP

Village	Singrawankalan	Kalakhunt	Sobaliyapura	Gopalpura
Name of PIA and its presence	Haritika; Strong	ASA; Moderate	Samaj Pragati Sansthan; Low	SDO Forest Department; Low
Project Type	DPIP	RGWDP	RGWDP	IWDP
Year of Commencement	2002	2003	2002	2002
Year of Completion	2007	2005	2007	2007
How was the WDP initiated?	PIA organized a meeting of village leaders, followed by an exposure tour. Planning in the presence of DRDA officials.	PIA organized a meeting with the village leader.	PIA and village leaders and DRDA officials met to decide the activities	PIA in consultation with local leaders
Formation of WDC	Yes, formed by PIA	Yes, formed by PIA	Yes, formed by PIA	Yes, formed by PIA
Number and composition of WDC members	11 (SC; OBC; Women reps.)	11; (SC; OBC; Women reps.)	11; (SC; OBC; Women reps.)	11; (SC; OBC; Women reps.)
Utilization of a Watershed Fund	Yes	No	No	No
Members of WDC also are on Gram Panchayat (GP)	3	4	3	2
WDC still functioning	Yes	No	No	Yes
Meeting	When Needed	When Needed	When Needed	When Needed
Who decided activity and plan?	PIA and govt. functionaries through village meetings.	PIA and village leaders in a village meeting.	Gram Sabha.	Mainly by the PIA in a meeting with the village community

No. of SHGs (+ Common Interest Groups)	05 (SHGs) + 21 (UGs)	06	05	05
Members	60	73	61	63
Members presently functioning	5	1	2	3
Main Activities of SHGs	Income generation activity and link with the bank Income generation like vegetable production, pipeline for irrigation, diesel engine for lift irrigation etc.	Saving and credit	Saving and credit	Saving and credit
Selecting the site of the check dam	Farmers and PIA	PIA	PIA and villagers	PIA and villagers
What activity was carried out and how was it decided?	Stop dam, check dam, well recharge, contour bund, construction of toilet and soak pit, seed and agricultural equipment distribution, village water tank construction. WDC decided.	Pond deepening work and contour bund. PIA and WDC member decided.	Check dam, well recharge, plantation, village tank. PIA and WDC member decided.	Check dam, pond deepening, contour bund and plantation. PIA and WDC member decided.
People's Participation	Each household contributed ₹1,000 towards construction of the village tank and ₹30 per month for the maintenance. For other work 10% of the wages earned from labour work was collected.	10% of labour contribution was collected from the from beneficiary	5–10% labour contribution from beneficiary.	5–10% labour contribution from beneficiary.

Source: Field survey data, (2009).

by Sobaliyapura (Table 5.16). This was also substantiated by the fact that their WDCs continued to operate in the post-project phase.

The institutional profiles for the two states presented above indicate more or less similar features, as most of the features were governed by the project design (guidelines) and the time frame of the project, which was fairly short (i.e., for five years). For instance, the formation of WDCs in all cases had been mainly done by nomination. Whereas WDCs were reported to have been in existence in four out of eight villages, in reality these committees had very little operational role in the post-project phase. The records were kept with the PIAs, and the secretary was involved as and when there was any matter related to record keeping. This was mainly because the project fund got exhausted at the time of completion of the project, and any activity that took place thereafter, was generally dependent on the PIA's initiative in accessing additional funds from other schemes.

At the same time, there were some finer differences across the projects. These mainly pertained to the manner in which the project was introduced and the initial processes put into place. By and large, the projects with NGOs as PIA had adopted a more broad-based perspective to watershed development, beyond the technical interventions. Also these PIAs continued their presence in the region, though not directly in the village itself.

7.3. Participation in WDP Institutions: Evidence from Sample Households

The net result of the WDP institution building exercise was the limited involvement of the village community in the functioning of the CBOs in most cases. We have tried to capture these aspects through the survey of sample households in the villages. Tables 5.37 and 5.38 present responses from the sample households on the various aspects of the formation and functioning of the institutions.

The information presented above suggests that awareness of the WDC, its functionaries and opportunities for participation was

Table 5.37

Awareness of and Participation in WDP Institutions Among Sample Households: Gujarat

Details of Awareness/Participation	Valuna			Jamsar			Tharavada			Sama		
	Yes	No	DK	Yes	No	DK	Yes	No	DK	Yes	No	DK
Who was the Chairman of the WDC?	12		38	11		39	9		41	10		40
Who was the Secretary of the WDC?	29		21	14		36	10		40	14		36
Were you aware of the formation of the WDC?	11	39		4	46		6	44		6	44	
Were you present in the meeting where the WDC was formed?	6	44		1	49		1	49		3	47	
Were you involved in any of the meetings or activities of the WDC?	4	46		2	48		2	48		1	49	
Did you ever raise any issue in the WDC?	1	49		2	48			50		3	47	
Was any member of your family part of the PRI or WDC?	6	44		3	47			50		4	46	
Were you consulted about the work carried out on/or near your land?	19	4	1	19	5	1	7	8	7	12	6	3
Was your opinion/suggestion for the work considered while deciding the work plan?	18	1		18	1		7			12		
Who maintained the WDC accounts?	7		43	13		37	1		49	7		43
Who kept the records of the WDC?	7		43	4		46			50	4		46
Were the WDC accounts/records made available to the community?	14	25	11	4	45	1	4	33	13	4	32	14
Did you ever ask for any information regarding the WDC records or beneficiary list etc.?	4	46		2	48			50				50
Can you use part of the WDF?	7	6	37	3	2	45	2	5	43	2	3	45
Were ever denied access to use the WDF?		48	2		50			44	6		34	16
Is there any amount with WDF?	15	18	17	4	22	24	6	11	33	2	16	32
Was any member of the WDC penalized/rewarded?		16	34		10	40		8	42		24	26

Source: Field survey data, (2009).

Table 5.38
Awareness of and Participation in WDP Institutions Among the Sample Households: MP

Details about Awareness/Participation	Kalakhunt			Sobaliyapura			Gopalpura		
	Yes	No	DK	Yes	No	DK	Yes	No	DK
Who was the Chairman of the WDC?	–	16	34	3	14	33	–	11	39
Who was the Secretary of the WDC?	3		47			50	12		38
Were you aware of the formation of the WDC?	1		49			50	11		39
Were you present in the meeting where the WDC was formed?	1	49		8	42		1	49	
Were you involved in any of the meetings or/activities of the WDC?	2	48		7	43			50	
Did you ever raise any issue in the WDC?	2	48		1	49			50	
Did any family member serve on the PRI/or WDC?	2	48		1	49			50	
Were you consulted about the work carried out on/or near your land?	2	48		3	47			50	
Was your opinion or suggestion considered in deciding the work plan?	2	6	8	11	2	2	3	4	3
Who maintained the WDC accounts?	2			11			3		
Who kept the records of the WDC?	2		48			50	6		44
Were the WDC accounts/records made available to the community?	3		47	1		49	2		48
Did you ever ask for any information regarding the WDC records or beneficiary list etc.?	2	43	5	3	28	19	39	11	
Can you use part of the WDF?		50		2	48			50	
Were you ever denied access to the use the WDF?	2	8	40	1	9	40		8	42
Is there any amount with the WDF?		44	6		31	19		40	10
Was any member of the WDC penalized/rewarded?		17	33		16	34		15	35

Source: Field survey data, (2009).

fairly limited in the case of most of our study villages. The major exceptions are Valuna and Jamsar in Gujarat and Singrawankalan in MP. Even in Valuna and Jamsar, less than 10 out of the 50 sample households reported being aware about how the WDCs were formed in their villages. Similarly, not more than 12 respondents in these two villages could recall the name of the president of the WDC. The number of households reporting this in other villages was fairly low. Only in Valuna could 29 out of the 50 sample households identify the secretary of the WDC.

The number of households reporting awareness about the work carried out on their fields was about 18–19 in both Valuna and Jamsar. This was fairly consistent with the coverage of beneficiaries in these two villages. When it comes to information about who kept the accounts and whether the records were made available to the community, very few households could respond. The situation in MP was found to be even more discouraging, except in the case of Singrawankalan.

Overall, it can be concluded that whereas the WDCs were formed in most of the villages, there was hardly any democratization and far less democratic decentralization. All the villages showed a fairly low score on transparency in terms of the maintenance and availability of accounts and records. It was, of course, likely that many of the respondents did not recall several of the events and processes due to the lapse of time. This was probably because the WDC ceased to function formally in the post-project period. The situation was found to be relatively better, however, where a local NGO worked as the PIA and continued to have a presence in the area.

In any case, our field observations suggested that these institutions had had fairly limited influence on the inclusion of the landless and the poor in the benefits of the project, largely because of the technical-legal considerations used for deciding project interventions. For instance, the treatment of pastures or CPLRs was decided mainly by the legal access to such land for development under the project. Also, the number and location of water harvesting structures such as check dams and village tanks was decided mainly according to their technical and financial feasibility. But invariably, the more powerful individuals influenced such decisions, directly or indirectly. Our observations confirm the widely-shared evidence on elite capture in the case of most of the participatory institutions for watershed development (DSC, 2010: 6–8; Kumar, 2007: 24–26; Shah et al., 2011b: 44–45).

The major differences that the institutional process could make include (a) designing a more broad-based and comprehensive treatment within the micro watershed and (b) emphasizing the involvement of local labourers for project activities. It is in this context that the overarching limitations associated with the nature of the resource, the intervention and the institutional design for a time-bound and instrumental role for the WDP institutions seemed to exert their influence — a point that was also noted in the initial part of the analysis in this chapter. The limitations, plausibly, were reflected in the fact that any conflict of interests, during or after the project, was not reported in most of the case studies, except for one in MP This is not to say that there were no real conflicts. For instance, offering contracts for transportation or material supplies was generally a difficult issue. Also, there were general perceptions about misappropriation of funds by some of the functionaries of the PIA or WDC. Most acute was the problem of deciding the sites and the size of the major water harvesting structures from which most of the project benefits flowed. The WDP institutions may or may not have addressed these issues in an upfront manner.

The critical point here is that in either case, this may not have changed the stake or share of the poor in the overall benefits from the project, which were invariably related to privately owned or/ accessed land and water.[16] In what follows we try to examine the central question empirically: How do the community-based institutions bear out on the final outcomes with respect to (a) the size/quantum of the benefits flowing from the project and (b) the impact on the poor?

---

[16] Recognizing this, the recent policy guidelines issued in 2008 have laid out specific measures for including the poor's stake in WDP projects. It will take some time before the outcomes of the new policy realize its full impact.

7.4. WDP Institutions and Poverty: Is there any Systematic Linkage?

The framework presented earlier in section 2 (see Figure 5.1) highlighted the central argument about institutional processes determining the outcomes of watershed projects. However, the framework also struck a note of caution regarding the limited impact of WDP interventions on poorer households, not to speak of poverty reductions per se. It also indicated the outer limit of the poverty impact set by the structural and external factors.

The impact analysis carried out in the subsequent sections suggests certain positive changes at the village level and also among the sample households. For instance, we noted earlier (in Tables 5.12 and 5.13) that the landless and other households in the higher levels of poverty ranking had received only marginal benefits from the project. Similarly, the evidence from the sample households (in Tables 5.30 and 5.31) suggested that the change in irrigation was reported by a number of farmers, but in terms of area, the benefits were quite small and not particularly received by the marginal farmers.

We however report positive changes in real income among a large proportion (92%) of farmers. Also, there were perception-based responses on positive changes since the project period. While there were issues of attribution, it may nevertheless be useful to see whether these positive impacts (if not on poor households per se) could be linked to the institutional processes in place in the eight study villages. This is examined in the subsequent analysis.

7.5. Coverage of Beneficiaries by Village

Earlier we had noted (in Tables 5.14 and 5.15) that the coverage of beneficiaries from different types of project activities was limited to only a sub-set of households in the villages. Beneficiaries here meant participants and all others involved in or touched by the project. In what follows we try to gauge the project outreach across the study villages (Table 5.39). It is clear that Valuna had a relatively

Table 5.39

Benefits from the Watershed Development Project

Benefits From the Watershed Project	Gujarat					Madhya Pradesh			
	Valuna	Jamsar	Tharavada	Sama	All	Singrawankalan	Kalakhunt	Sobaliyapura	All
Group Related	17.8 (36)	22.8 (41)	0.8 (3)	2.6 (7)	8.6 (87)	20.3 (45)	5.8 (13)	14.1 (27)	13.4 (85)
Agriculture Related	50.0 (101)	62.8 (113)	8.8 (32)	22.8 (61)	30.4 (307)	14.4 (32)	15.7 (35)	17.3 (33)	15.7 (100)
Irrigation Related	25.7 (52)	34.4 (62)	34.5 (125)	13.5 (36)	27.2 (275)	23.9 (53)	17.9 (40)	18.8 (36)	20.3 (129)
Employment Related	41.6 (84)	31.7 (57)	8.0 (29)	3.7 (10)	17.8 (180)	34.2 (76)	28.7 (64)	49.7 (95)	36.9 (235)
None of the Benefits	21.6 (39)	32.8 (65)	55.8 (202)	70.4 (188)	49.5 (501)	38.2 (73)	60.9 (136)	48.2 (107)	42.9 (393)

Source: Field survey data, (2009).

better coverage of households under the project activities. Only 21 per cent of the households in the village reported that they had not been involved in any of the project activities. This was fairly high as compared to Sama village in Gujarat where about 70 per cent of the households reported non-involvement in any of the project-related activities. In MP, Singrawankalan had better outreach and Kalakhunt had the lowest coverage of households under the project. Incidentally, both Valuna and Singrawankalan had NGOs as the PIAs.

Further we have tried to examine the link between the institutions and the project impact by juxtaposing an index (based on a sum of the number of households responding positively) of households reporting positive changes in income (Tables 5.27 and 5.28) with the institutional profile that we discussed in this section (see Tables 5.35 a and b).

Tables 5.40 and 5.41 suggest several important observations:

- **Gujarat:** Jamsar and Valuna had the highest overall scores of the perceived impact of watershed project, followed by Tharavada and Sama. When we looked into the relative scores across the three categories of impact, we found that whereas Valuna had received a higher impact in the case of land and agriculture, Jamsar scored higher with respect to employment, assets and income.

Table 5.40

Index of Perceived Impact: Gujarat

| Perceived Positive Impact* | Gujarat Villages | | | |
	Valuna	Jamsar	Tharavada	Sama
a) Land use and agriculture	204	194	145	161
b) Labour and Income Assets	320	359	330	288
c) Social Status and Other	105	104	63	96
Total	629	657	538	545
Ratio of positive responses in category a) to all households in a village	1.0	1.07	0.4	0.6

Source: Field survey data, (2009).
Note: *Based on multiple responses.

Table 5.41

Index of Perceived Impact: MP

	MP Villages			
*Perceived Positive Impact**	*Singrawankalan*	*Kalakhunt*	*Sobaliyapura*	*Gopalpura*
a) Land use and agriculture	178	105	177	152
b) Labour and Income Assets	170	289	279	252
c) Social Status and Other	53	80	111	84
Total	401	474	567	488
Ratio of positive responses in category a) to all households in a village	0.8	0.47	0.92	0.54

Source: Field survey data, (2009).
Note: * Based on multiple responses.

A priori, the above picture appears to be fairly consistent with our understanding of the institutional processes and also the external forces influencing the outcomes.

For instance, Valuna's and Jamsar's micro watershed projects were implemented by two of the leading NGOs in the field of watershed development in Gujarat. They both had prior presence in the area and/or long experience in the field of capacity building for watershed development. This, as we noticed earlier, was reflected in their relatively better activity plan and larger coverage of beneficiaries as compared to the other two study villages. Jamsar also had the additional advantage of access to non-farm employment, which in turn may have got reflected in the highest score in terms of employment-income-assets. On the other hand, the micro watershed project in Sama was initiated by a powerful local leader, but did not perform so well in terms of technical planning and coverage of beneficiaries. Nevertheless, Sama farmers also got access to canal irrigation, which may have diverted their interest from the watershed project. Tharavada scored last in all three sets of indicators. This could be due to a combination of factors like drought-proneness, a high incidence of landlessness and the absence of an experienced NGO or powerful local leader.

- **Madhya Pradesh:** The results from MP present a somewhat different picture. For instance, Sobaliyapura had the highest overall score, and also in terms of two out of the three sets of indicators of assets (land, water, livestock). This project, once again, was implemented by one of the leading NGOs in the field of watershed projects and also capacity building. However, unlike in Jamsar, the other NGO-led projects in MP (i.e., in Singrawankalan and Kalakhunt) could not come on par with Sobaliyapura, in spite of the NGOs' institutional strengths. This was perhaps due to two reasons. On the one hand, in Kalakhunt, the external factor of village level conflicts pushed the project to a standstill and as a result, the land-agriculture related score went down very badly. On the other hand, in Singrawankalan, the land-economics related indicators showed the highest scores, almost on par with Sobaliyapura. Nevertheless, the scores on the other two sets of indicators were not so good; this could have been due to the fact that the Singrawankalan project intervention had a specific focus on irrigation, farm productivity and incomes, but not so much on the other aspects of livelihood or employment enhancements. Also, the area had much less agronomic potential as compared to the other three sites in the state. Interestingly, Gopalpura seemed to have performed better across all the three aspects. It may be noted that the project in Gopalpura was implemented by the Forest Department, with a fairly dynamic team of field officers who had continued presence in the village, especially for activities related to forest development.

The above analyses suggest that the inter-linkages between project impacts, institutional processes and poverty/equity outcomes, despite many complexities, were falling into some kind of pattern. Hence, it almost sounds like a happy ending! But it may or may not have been so, for the analysis based on Tables 5.40 and 5.41 is entirely dependent on perception-based impacts and the responses were likely to be influenced by the intervention and continued presence of a good NGO/ PIA. While it is hard to get to the finer truth; nevertheless, the *overall* findings do suggest that the institutional processes did matter so far as project outcomes were concerned.

To sum up, we recapitulate some of the important observations in terms of the key questions raised in the initial part of this book:

1. *How was the project introduced?* This was done mainly by the PIAs. The project was described as a state-supported intervention for soil conservation and water harvesting and also for the formation of SHGs. The main objective was to improve agriculture in dry land areas. The PIA would implement the project by forming WDCs and UGs.

2. *How did the project perform in terms of CNRM objectives (de jure vs. de facto)?* The actual implementation was in compliance with the project guidelines, though much of the implementation process was carried out as a matter of fulfilling a requirement, rather than creating awareness and ownership among the village communities.

3. *What was the extent of productivity/income increase?* Productivity had shown an increase in a majority of the main crops grown by the sample farmers. These, by and large, included irrigated and high-value crops like cotton, wheat and also maize. Income from agriculture had also shown an increase for a large majority of the farmers; the reported increase was mostly higher among the project beneficiaries as compared to the non-beneficiaries. The income among the former category of households was already higher before the project.

4. *How inclusive was the governance?* The WDCs had members from different categories of the village community including the SCs and STs, the landless and women. But, decisions were taken mainly by the dominant members who belonged to the landed communities as the projects were by and large perceived as a means for enhancing the availability of water/ irrigation for their fields. In the villages where NGOs were involved as PIAs, the process of forming committees was relatively more elaborate, which was further followed by

a more challenging planning process and thereby a more extensive action plan for watershed treatment.

5. *What was the impact on poor members of the village (landless/ marginal/small farmers)?* The project, by design, excluded most of the landless, who constituted a major part of the poor. Among those having land, the distribution of benefits was somewhat mixed. There was no evidence of any special efforts to include the marginal-small farmers in most of the villages; the inclusion was mainly driven by the technical plans for watershed treatments, given the geo-hydrological character of the micro watersheds. Development of CPRs such as pasture land and village tanks was fairly scattered and limited in terms of coverage. To the extent that the project covered marginal-small farmers as beneficiaries, the project did help in mitigating part of their poverty; but the income gain was not limited only to the project beneficiaries.

6. *How integrated was the project intervention and what was the extent of the outreach?* The project covered only a small sub-set of households as direct beneficiaries; the non-beneficiaries may have gained from their own efforts and/or other schemes already implemented in the village.

7. *Had the project contributed to effective, equitable and sustainable resource management?* The projects, in most cases, had led to increased availability of groundwater resources for irrigation. There was some evidence of regeneration of public land under plantations where the forest department was the PIA. How far the project had helped in improving the groundwater table after extraction for irrigation was difficult to gauge in the absence of any systematic monitoring of groundwater resources. There was, however, an overall positive perception that the project had helped in the harvesting of rain water, thereby recharging the water table in the project areas.

A comparison of our interstate findings suggests that the WDP impacts were more or less similar in Gujarat and MP. Any minor differences were mainly attributable to the nature of the PIAs in a specific project. Gujarat had a better presence of NGOs, which seems to have resulted in a more extensive process of planning and institution building than in the case of other PIAs. In this sense, the policy focus on NGOs in Gujarat could be viewed as more favourable to the inclusion of the relatively poorer communities in project activities. Beyond this, one did not find any significant difference across the two states as the project guidelines adopted in Gujarat and MP were more or less the same. It may therefore be concluded that more than the policy guidelines, it was the involvement of agencies with prior experience and/or commitment to implementing participatory natural resource development programmes, that assumed critical importance in the inclusion of the poor. In this sense our findings corroborate the widely held notion about the relatively better performance of NGO-implemented projects as compared to the rest.

How do these findings play out with respect to poverty outcomes? This is a difficult question to address, especially in a situation where the quantum of actual economic benefits was fairly small and also variable according to rainfall. The one thing one could derive from the analysis is that a large proportion of farmers in tribal areas were likely to be marginal land holders, and any benefits reaching them may have contributed to improving their economic status. Similarly, watershed projects may have partly contributed to the reported increase in wage rates in the study villages. Finally, it can be asserted that in the absence of the project interventions, several of the non- or semi-poor households may have slipped into poverty.

8. The Way Forward

The foregoing analysis of CNRM and poverty in the context of watershed development in India indicates complex yet potentially positive outcomes. One of the most important messages emerging from the analysis, perhaps, is that WDPs open up avenues for enhancing livelihood support for marginal and small farmers, who often are on the fringes of being poor. But, WDP projects, by themselves, may not directly lead to poverty reductions in a significant manner as they leave landless households out of their ambit. Again, the project in isolation from other supplementary interventions or support (known as watershed plus) may have had a limited impact on the livelihoods of the poor. In the absence of this, even the SHGs did not find a base for sustenance. And the withdrawal of support agencies (i.e., the PIA) made it difficult to carry forward the agenda of 'watershed plus'. The analysis suggests that the presence of an experienced NGO ensures better sustenance of the SHGs in the post-project phase.

Of course, our analysis was based on empirical evidence from only eight WDP projects of different vintages. Hence, it was difficult to generalize on a larger scale. Also, most of the case studies belonged to the initial phase of implementing the participatory approach for watershed development, that is, 1995–2001. Notwithstanding these limitations, the analysis strongly supports the widely shared need for strengthening the following:

1. The initial processes for setting up a broad-based activity plan that goes beyond the sheer rhetoric of inclusiveness in membership of various institutions.
2. A comprehensive plan for watershed treatment, with special emphasis on CPRs to reach out to the poor.
3. Supplementary interventions that support resource- (water-) use efficiency (if not access), thereby increasing the size of the benefits and their sustenance over a longer period of time.
4. Continuation of the WDCs with a clear mandate to look after the maintenance of the assets created, manage the WDF and mobilize supplementary investments to ensure sustenance and possibly enhancement of benefits in the post-project period.
5. The long-term presence of a support agency in the post-project period.

The newly-adopted Common Guidelines take care of these aspects to some extent. Also, they bring in a specific focus on equity and institutional support. There is a need for both discipline and vigour to ensure that the goals of the Guidelines are realized in spirit and not just the semantics of the implementation processes and institution building. Convergence with initiatives through some of the rights-based programmes such as the MGNREGA or the JFM programme may help in strengthening the processes of democratic decentralization. This, ultimately, holds the key to realizing the full potential behind a pro-poor CNRM in the context of watershed-based development in India.

6

Poverty Reduction and the Community Management of Forests: The Experience of Joint Forest Management Institutions

Madhu Verma*

1. Introduction

The concept of JFM was brought to India through the National Forest Policy of 1988. Its national guidelines were introduced through the GoI circular of 1 June 1990 with the intent of reducing the growing conflict over forest resources between FD officials and local villagers dependent on the forest. The concept of JFM may be defined as, 'the sharing of products, responsibilities, control and decision-making authority over forest lands between the FD and local user groups'. It involved a contract specifying the distribution of authority, responsibilities and benefits (MoEF, 1990). The basic objective behind it was to make local people aware that they were owners of the forests collectively and the FD was the manager. It was important for the forest people to realize that they had a stake in the protection and improvement of forests, and that their social and economic life became enriched by tangible and intangible benefits flowing from well-protected and well-managed forest tracts near their habitation.

Thus the JFM programme promotes the participatory management of Indian forests and aims to encourage forest regeneration by the

*with Munish Sikka and field support of Manish Mishra.

involvement of those with the most at stake, those most affected by forest degradation. They are assigned the major role of assisting the FD in the management of forests through active participation in planning, implementation and monitoring activities. The guidelines clearly mention that the rights of indigenous communities are to be considered as the first charge on forest produce. This was done to motivate these communities and ensure their participation in sustainable forest management activities including the development and protection of forests from which they derived benefits (MoEF, 1990). The circular also envisages the involvement of NGOs and other voluntary agencies with a proven track record to help in the organization of indigenous communities under the JFM. The GoI issued an instruction that state governments must establish usufruct rights for local communities in exchange for their participation. Almost all Indian states have implemented some form of policy that allows for local villager participation in forest management. Some of the early adopters of the JFM included the states of Gujarat, MP and West Bengal. In Gujarat and MP the first resolutions to implement the JFM were passed as early as 1991.

2. The Evolution of the JFM Strategy through the National Forest Policy

The MoEF, GoI, issued instructions to all states on 1 June 1990 that the rights of tribals and other villagers living in and around forests would have priority in terms of forest use. Accordingly, since then, the cooperation of the local people has been sought through the system of JFM. This strategy provides a broad framework for the involvement of local communities in forestry development activities. It provides them rights and concessions to meet their requirements of forest products. Holders of customary rights and concessions in forest areas were to be motivated to identify themselves with the protection and development of the forests from which they derived benefits. In addition to the tribals, due consideration was also given to the involvement of the SCs and poor people.

The JFM concept is not new to India. It is a reinvention or crystallization of successful forest management practices of the past. Forests in India have been managed with multiple sets of objectives at different points of time. Forest management in India has been undergoing steady change since the 19th century. From absolute state control under the colonial regime to participatory forestry in recent times, the management system has been periodically experimented with by the government. During the second half of the 19th century, the forests of rural communities were steadily reserved and nationalized, while the rights of villagers were eroded through a series of legal actions. Lopsided management of forests was prevalent under the old imperial forest policy of 1894 in which the British government laid emphasis on commercial profits from forests and the development of agriculture. The people's interests were made subservient to commercial interests during the colonial rule. The local subsistence needs of people living in and around forests were met by 'minor forests'[1] that yielded only inferior quality timber, fuel wood and fodder while 'value forests' were solely meant for timber logging by commercial interests.[2]

In the first National Forest Policy (1952) of independent India, that is, it was decided that one-third of the country's area should be under forest cover owing to reductions in the annual demand for forest products. Forestry was thus extended beyond forest areas to meet commercial and local people's requirements. Village communities were not permitted to use forests as this would hinder the national interest of maximizing the annual income for the states from timber sales. Extraction of valuable timber from the village commons and involvement of locals in the

---

[1] According to the Imperial Forests Policy of 1894, the British administration classified forests into four types:

1. Hill slope forests: forests under complete protection to check soil erosion.
2. Value Forests: forests solely used for generating revenue. India's best timber species were in this category.
3. Minor Forests: Forests meant for meeting the subsistence needs of forest dwellers.
4. Pasture and grazing grounds.

[2] For further information, see http://www.nlsenlaw.org/forest/law-policy/old-forest-policy-october-1894.

management and protection of forests were completely prohibited in state-owned forests.

Along with these two forest policies, the recommendations of the old Royal Commission on Agriculture, 1926 and the Forest Act, 1927 were also implemented by the federal government with only slight variations from the previous policy. Little effort was made to improve the conservation and management of forests. The emphasis was on revenue generation from timber plantation for the national economy as a whole, and the interests of forest dwellers were ignored. The major move from production forestry to conservation forestry came with the inception of the 'Chipko' Movement in 1972.[3] This movement resulted in the remarkable achievement of checking the persistent degradation of forests and developed initiatives for their efficient and sustainable management.

Subsequently, a significant recommendation by the National Commission on Agriculture (NCA) was given in 1976 to begin a social forestry programme to meet the subsistence requirements of local communities by maintaining a balance between ecological and human needs. This social forestry phase (1976–88) was promoted by the NCA as a programme which would ease the pressure from industrial and commercial forestry and divert attention towards conservation-oriented forestry. Villagers were encouraged to grow for their own consumption tree species for fuel wood, small timber and fodder on village commons and private farmlands. Briefly, the objectives of the social forestry programme were: (a) increasing firewood, fodder, small timber and minor forest product supplies for the rural population, (b) restoring a proper ecological balance and (c) ensuring optimum utilization of land, water, livestock and human resources. These were primarily aimed at meeting the biomass needs of the rural population and restoring ecological balance. Though the programme was largely

---

[3] *Chipko* means 'embrace'. The Chipko Movement emerged in a remote Himalayan hill village at the end of 1972. It was started by a group of villagers in the Uttarakhand region of India who opposed commercial logging. The movement is best known for its tactic of hugging trees to prevent them being cut down. This gave rise to the term 'tree hugger' for environmentalists.

aimed at meeting the biomass needs of the local communities, their involvement in it was marginal or absent. India's forests thus continued to be degraded.

In 1976, with the 42nd Amendment of the Constitution, forests were brought under the Constitution's concurrent list which made it mandatory for the states to take central government approval before diverting any forest land for non-forestry purposes. Later, with the enactment of the Forest (Conservation) Act in 1980, the subjects of forestry and wildlife were shifted from the MoA to the MoEF for providing more focused attention to emerging forestry issues. The MoEF was created in 1984.

Until the early 1970s, forest officials followed customary management practices with little involvement of the local people, apart from meeting their recorded rights and involving them in firefighting. However, due to India's excessive growth in human and livestock population and the subsequent increasing pressures on forests for fuel wood, fodder and NTFP, serious damage was evident. Consequently, conflicts between local people and FD staff cropped up. The government felt the need to protect the forests strategically by regenerating degraded natural forests, increasing biomass and improving biodiversity. This would only be possible if communities living in the fringe areas were assigned the responsibility of protection in return for economic returns from the forests as compensation for their lost livelihoods. Pilot projects were undertaken in villages such as Sukhomajiri (Haryana) and Arabari (West Bengal) during the 1970s and 1980s that got people involved in forest protection as well as in sharing forest produce. Such efforts resulted in an increase in biomass, genetic diversity and forest productivity, as well as in an equitable distribution of forest products and generation of employment and income for local villagers.

Considering similar achievements in other states, the government issued common guidelines for sustainable management of forests across the country in the National Forest Policy of 1988. This initiated a process of reform for forest management at the local policy and operational levels by ensuring that the FD developed close collaborations with local stakeholders for the protection and sustainable management of forests. The important objectives of the National Forest Policy, 1988 were (a) maintenance of environmental stability, restoration of ecological balance and soil and water conservation, (b) increasing productivity of forests to meet first local and subsequently national needs, (c) creating a massive people's movement to protect forests and increase tree cover to achieve the objective of reducing pressure on existing forests and meeting people's needs sustainably and (d) subordinating economic benefits to these principal aims. This led to a paradigm shift in the approach from government-controlled policies and centralized management to decentralized management; from revenue orientation to resource orientation; from production motive to sustainability motive and target orientation to process orientation for the management of the forest resources of the country (SPWD, 1992: 78).[4]

The GoI Resolution of 1 June 1990 laid down JFM procedures for the involvement of people in forest conservation and management through appropriate village level institutions to be known as Joint Forest Management Committees (JFMC). Whereas in earlier policies people and forests were seen as antagonistic, now local people were recognized as potential players in overcoming the plight of India's forests. Khare et al. (2000: 111) have rightly remarked that the 1988 policy was a policy for both 'forest and people'.

Under the institutional mechanism of JFM, three types of committees were constituted, depending upon the nature of forest sites. Forest Protection Committees (FPCs) were constituted in all villages situated within 5 km from the forest block boundaries of dense forests. VFCs were constituted in all other villages situated within 5 km from the forest block boundaries of degraded forests. EDCs were constituted for securing the cooperation of people evicted from villages situated inside national parks and sanctuaries and also in villages outside the protected areas that were situated within a 5 km boundary of these areas and which influenced the protected area.

---

[4] SPWD: Society for the Promotion of Wasteland Development.

3. Making JFM Effective in India

The effectiveness of JFM mainly depends on the stability and continuity of the collaborative efforts between the FD and a local community where this can be achieved with sustainable forest management. According to the definition of the United Nations Commission on Sustainable Development (UNCSD, adopted in 2002 at the World Summit on Sustainable Development, Johannesburg, South Africa), sustainable forest management is 'management (that meets) the social, economic, ecological, cultural and spiritual needs of present and future generations'. It is a multidimensional concept with four main intersecting angles: economic, ecological, social and spiritual. In view of this ideal, the JFM programme has led to several positive and negative outcomes since its inception. The major qualitative indicators to gauge the success of JFM in the country include:

1. A change in attitude and relationships: One of the most significant impacts of the JFM programme has been to change the attitude of local communities and forest officials towards each other and towards forests. Training and orientation exercises carried out in different states have also contributed to a positive change in attitude.

2. Improvements in the condition of the forests: Remote sensing data have shown an improvement in the quality and area of forests. Due to the successful implementation of the JFM programme, including intense protection, the closure of forested areas and the ban on felling and grazing, there has been an increase in the tree population. Overall, the forest cover of the country has increased by 3,896 sq. km. and dense forest cover by 10,098 sq. km. In the area under JFM, incidents of illicit felling have sharply declined. Also, the prolific growth of understorey vegetation has led to increased biodiversity and a relatively rapid increase in wild herbivores. Along with the increase in tree density, species diversity has also increased. Some of the economically important species available in forested areas include Teak

(*tectona grandis*), Mahua (*Madhuca indica*) and Tamarind (*Tamarindus indica*).

3. Reductions in encroachments: At many places JFM has helped in reducing the area under illegal encroachments and the rate of fresh encroachments. For instance, in Andhra Pradesh, nearly 12 per cent of the encroached forest land has reportedly been vacated since the JFM programme was initiated.

4. Employment generation and increase in incomes of local people: The direct impact of JFM has been in employment generation. It has resulted in an increase in the income of participating communities at several places. The JFMCs have benefited from employment generated under the JFM projects, through micro planning, sale of NTFP, etc. It has also helped many FPCs to build up substantial levels of community funds to be used for local development activities.

5. Increase in the availability of fodder and fuel wood: In the state of Haryana, a study was conducted in Aravalli where there was an increase of about 24.4 per cent and 35.9 per cent in the availability of fodder and fuel wood respectively in the sampled villages, as compared to the period before the commencement of the project. Villagers were being permitted to collect fuel wood only from dead, dying and diseased trees, whereas previously they were felling green trees also to meet their fuel wood requirements.

6. Involvement and support of NGOs: Before the introduction of JFM, NGOs were not involved in forest management, but at the time of the study, they were found to be useful to act as a bridge between the FD and the people. They were also found useful in promoting awareness, motivation and transparency into the JFM programme. The latest data (2010) from six states reveals that there were 1,061 NGOs actively participating in JFM in India. In MP and Uttar Pradesh, NGOs have been working together with the FD at the field level.

7. Ecological impact: JFM has led to manifold ecological impacts. It has resulted in improvements in the number of plant species (biodiversity), the status of wildlife, the productivity of trees and NTFPs, water availability and micro-climate change in

forest areas, and the extent of root stocks through soil works and protection. It has led to reductions in siltation, flooding and landslides. It has also resulted in lower incidence of forest fires, illicit grazing and illicit felling. One immediately visible ecological effect of JFM has been the recovery of fodder resources in forest areas. Under JFM protection there has been an increase in 26 new plant species in Nalgonda district of Andhra Pradesh alone. In some sites of MP and Andhra Pradesh a remarkable increase in growing stock has been noticed (Jha, 1998). The soil and moisture conservation work under the JFM programme has enhanced the moisture regime, which is likely to have had a positive impact not only on the forest but also on nearby agricultural fields (ibid.). There has been an appreciable increase in water table levels in Tamil Nadu due to various water harvesting measures undertaken in the forest watersheds. Under community management, the regeneration and growth of biomass, accumulation of litter and organic matter in the soil of degraded forest and pasture land, have led to an increase in carbon stock in land under the JFM programme (Ravindranath et al., 2000).

4. The JFM–Poverty Connection

Poverty is usually measured as either absolute or relative poverty. While absolute poverty indicates an absence of basic life amenities and resources, relative poverty measures inequality in a specific social context. The persistence of poverty is called chronic poverty which describes the number of households remaining poor over a given period of time. The movement of poor people to the non-poor category and vice versa is described as transitory poverty. It is often used for households that were previously not poor but had moved into the category of poor at some later stage. One study (Bhide and Mehta, 2005) tracks rural poverty in India by examining the patterns of movement of rural households across poverty groupings based on a unique panel data set covering a period of three decades (1970–98). It also reports various factors such as social barriers, household composition and village level infrastructure and employment opportunities that are important determinants of the probability of poverty's persistence or reduction.

At the all-India level, the poverty line is based on an expenditure level of ₹356.30 in rural areas and ₹538.60 in urban areas per person per month (Planning Commission, 2010). According to Planning Commission estimates, in MP a family spending ₹327.78 per person per month in a rural settlement is considered to be poor. In the urban context, the expenditure level is ₹570.15 per person per month. According to these estimates, 37 per cent of the population of MP lived BPL, which was significantly higher than India's overall average of 27 per cent. The estimated annual per capita income of those living BPL in the state is $90. MP also ranks low in terms of the human development index (2008), which was at 0.394, as against the national value of 0.472. The state of Gujarat had a slightly higher poverty line for rural areas and a lower poverty line for urban areas compared to MP in the year 2008. In Gujarat a person was considered poor in an urban area if he earned ₹541.16 a month or less while in rural areas the figure was ₹353.93 a month (The Acorn, 2009).

The dependence of poor households on CPRs is reflected in the study carried out by Jodha (1995) covering 80 villages located in 20 districts of six states in India. The study discusses the causal factors leading to the decline of CPRs and the government interventions put into place to improve them. It concludes that common resource degradation may have resulted in the elimination of vital biophysical processes of nature's regenerative activities. This situation may not have been inevitable, but positive policies and alternative options for the poor were needed in order to regulate the usage, enhance the regeneration and raise the productivity of CPRs.

A CIFOR study by Angelsen and Wunder (2003) presents different definitions of poverty and forests' contributions to poverty alleviation. It asks whether forest products act as gap-filling 'safety nets' or 'poverty traps', that is, whether the forest provides relief to the poor by addressing their various needs including food, housing and energy, or provides an 'employment of last resort' for those dependent on forests for their needs and for those with no other livelihood alternative. The study suggests measuring the causes of poverty through a 'Sustainable Livelihood Approach' (SLA) while distinguishing three main benefit categories namely NTFPs, timber and ecological service payments.

Another study (Davies and Richards, 1999) describes three approaches for assessing stakeholder incentives in participatory forest management. These include: (a) the economic analysis and cost-benefit approach, (b) the environmental economics approach and (c) a combination of neoclassical economics with participatory research methods. The study concludes that out of these three approaches, the neoclassical approach combined with participatory research methods satisfactorily addresses wider issues by tackling both the qualitative and the quantitative aspects of economic values. The study also proposes an 'economic stakeholder analysis methodology' by combining methods from all three methodological approaches.

5. The Sustainable Livelihoods Approach (SLA) and Forest–Poverty Linkages

We have chosen the SLA as a conceptual and methodological framework because it provides a useful way of thinking about the linkages between the context, vulnerability, poverty and access to forest resources. It is grounded and contextual, looking at how different people pursue a range of livelihood strategies given particular contexts, combinations of assets, sets of opportunities and constraints presented by institutional structures and processes. The focus is dynamic and enables the consideration of cause and effect at various levels. Finally, the framework is comparative across different national contexts and its diagrammatic presentation makes it relatively easy to understand.

Any particular benefit being derived from forests depends partly on the other assets available to the household and the community.

For instance, artisanal use of forests will need the human capital resources of skill; deriving fodder benefits entails having livestock and forest management may require social capital assets. An analysis of how different assets are linked and how certain combinations of assets affect the pursuit of different livelihood strategies is critical for an appreciation of the forest–poverty linkages. These factors affect the stake that people have in forests as well as their capacity and willingness to take part in sustainable forest management (Baumann, 2006).

A working paper published by the Livelihood Support Programme (LSP 2002) of the FAO reviews how with renewed international commitment to poverty reduction and appreciation of the importance of natural resources for this objective, there have been significant advances and innovations in methodologies for examining environment poverty linkages (Baumann, 2006). These methodological innovations are in part a response to two realizations in development policy. The first is a broad consensus about the multidimensional and dynamic character of poverty which is now defined not only as a lack of material assets but also as exposure to risk and a lack of power. In order to capture this complexity, poverty studies have become increasingly multidisciplinary and multisectoral, involving causative factors ranging from the level of intra-household relations to the national and even global economy. The second realization is that poverty reduction policies have to be people-centred; that is, they will be most effective if they are based on the needs, and the experiences of poverty that are voiced by the poor people themselves.

International experience has shown that there are no simple causal links between forest management and poverty reduction. Despite the evidence of the crucial role that forest resources play in the livelihoods of the poor, the relationship between forest resources and poverty alleviation is far from straightforward. While forests are relatively important to the livelihoods of the poor, their use of the forest either leads to forest degradation (for instance through overgrazing) or becomes a temporary stop-gap measure with little potential as a long-term poverty-reducing strategy. Table 6.1 illustrates some possible livelihood options and alternatives. Of these option D is the only one

Table 6.1

Poverty and Forest Linkages: A Matrix

	Poverty Increase	*Poverty Reduction*
Forest	**A**	**B**
Reduction	The poor do not benefit from unsustainable use of forest resources.	Poverty reduction due to higher household level income from farming or pasture development on forest land (conversion of common access forest land to private access farming land).
Forest	**C**	**D**
Increase	The poor are affected by reduced access to forests, for example through closure for national parks and afforestation.	Less pressure on forests and reduced poverty due to, for example, employment in sustainable forest management and agricultural intensification.

Source: Adapted from Myers (1996).

that could contribute towards both sustainable forest management and poverty reduction.

Taking note of these poverty–forest linkage possibilities and the win-win condition achieved in box D through reducing pressures on forests and creating alternative livelihood opportunities, the present study examines eight villages through the SLA and puts forth possible livelihood strategies that can be implemented across all the villages. The SLA for the present study is presented in Figure 6.1.

Various proposals implemented in the different villages under study were related to infrastructure development and extension of credit facilities. Infrastructure development activity was largely perceived as temporary employment generation activity and its long-term benefits (e.g., check dams and stop dams) were not equally shared but benefitted landholders whose fields were situated close to the structure. Similarly, poor repayment of loans rate had so negatively affected JFMC credit facilitation that providing direct income to all the members was considered to be a better alternative. Almost invariably, the decision-making power lay in the hands of the dominating subgroup in the village and/or the

Figure 6.1

Analysis of JFM in Selected Villages through a Sustainable Livelihoods Approach (SLA) Framework

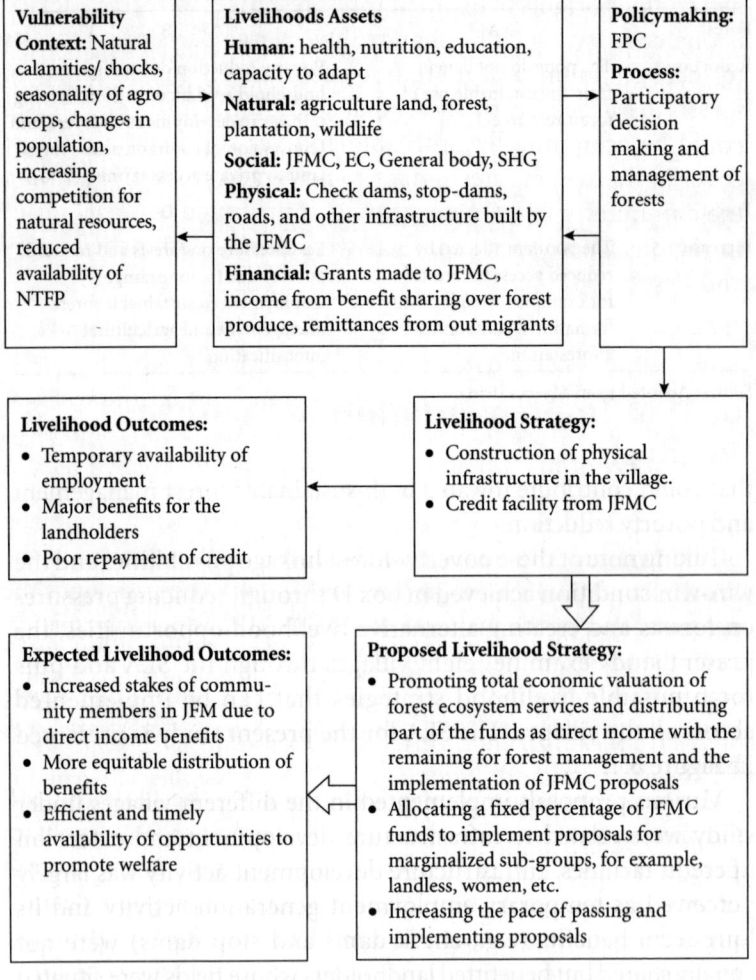

FD. The poor and marginalized tended to become mere followers rather than equal partners in decision making. Thus allocating a fixed percentage of JFMC funds for implementing proposals for marginalized sub-groups, for example, the landless, women, etc. could have countered the dominance of powerful subgroups and possibly raised the stake of the marginalized to take interest in the functioning of JFMC in the village.

Instances of community forest management where communities had complete rights to use their forest resources were few. Mexico is one country which has handed over large parts of its forests to local communities. A study of community management of forests in Mexico clearly shows that community forest enterprises could be economically profitable and yet still maintain forest cover in the area at rates similar to protected areas. In addition, the community forest management contributed to social peace in regions where social conflicts were deeply entrenched (Bray and Perez, 2002).

6. JFM Implementation in Madhya Pradesh

After the GoI directives were issued in in 1991 MP became one of the first states to adopt JFM. With financial assistance of the World Bank, the JFM programme in MP took the lead. Since the promulgation of the mandate of JFM in MP, as per information from the Madhya Pradesh Forest Department (2010), 14,428 JFM committees, including 9,137 VFCs, 4,470 FPCs and 821 EDCs have been constituted as of 2010. About 59,468 ha of forest area was being protected in 2010.

In view of the principles laid down by the GoI, the MP Government passed a Resolution on 10 December 1991 to obtain people's cooperation in areas considered sensitive from the point of view of forest protection. The Resolution prescribed a detailed procedure for the same. JFM aimed to empower local people to actively participate as partners in the management of forest resources and in sharing the benefits derived from its protection and management. It emphasized that JFMCs ensure equitable distribution of the benefits derived from the allocated forest area and village resources among its members. The JFM programme was reviewed from time to time. To make the provisions of the 1991

Resolution more effective, in 1995 a revised Resolution was issued by the state government, which included elaborate arrangements to ensure participatory micro-planning for the protection and management of forests and a clear approach for an integrated Village Resource Development Programme (VRDP). It was amended again in years 2000 and 2001 to make JFM more participatory, demand-driven and empowering for the local people.

The World Bank extended support for the implementation of JFM in MP through the World Bank Madhya Pradesh Forestry Project which was launched in 1995 and ended in 1999. It aimed at assisting the Government of Madhya Pradesh (GoMP) for developing the forestry sector, with the Madhya Pradesh Forestry Department and the GoMP as the implementing agencies. The total cost of the project was estimated at around USD 67.3 million, with a contribution of USD 58 million from the World Bank. The main objective was to strengthen participatory systems for NRM and marketing to improve and sustain the livelihoods of forest-dependent people. The main beneficiaries of the project were expected to be the forest dwellers and forest fringe villagers who were to become equal partners in forest management. In January 2000, the project was pulled out of the state because of several protests by local communities which were of the view that the extent of decentralization and benefit sharing was not done as initially visualized.

Further, in the 10th Five Year Plan of India, four centrally sponsored schemes were merged to form the National Afforestation Programme in order to increase forest cover in degraded forests and adjoining lands including national parks and sanctuaries. This programme was implemented through the Forest Development Authorities (FDAs) established as confederations of selected JFM committees. The FDAs followed a participatory project management approach with the aim of holistic development of the ecosystems, which included the forest and habitations under the Forest Committees. Currently, the operational parts of FDA include components like building community awareness, micro-planning, entry point activities, soil and water conservation, plantation, monitoring and evaluation and social fencing. All of these were to ensure active participation of forest committees. MP constituted 25 FDAs with 856 JFMCs to which ₹27.53 crores were released by the GoI in June 2011(www.mpforest.org, accessed in June 2011).

7. JFM Implementation in Gujarat

In Gujarat, efforts by the FD to protect the forest resource in isolation resulted in conflicts with local communities and damage to the forest resource, leading to the degradation of land resources. Realizing the possible danger, the FD tried to involve local people in the protection and regeneration of forests in south Gujarat, especially in the Vyara and Rajpipla forest divisions in 1986–87, based on the principle of care for usufruct benefits. The results were encouraging not only for the protection and regeneration of the forest resource but also in reducing conflicts between locals and FD personnel.

Based on the National Forest Policy, 1988 and the guidelines issued by the GoI in June, 1990 regarding the involvement of local communities and voluntary agencies in forest protection, management and regeneration to rejuvenate degraded forest lands, the JFM programme was launched in Gujarat by a government resolution in March 1991. Since then the activity of involving local people in the protection and regeneration of forests has been expanded to other areas. Thus a decentralized approach of participatory management based on the broad principle of 'care and share' was adopted and increasingly gained acceptance as a major strategy for the eco-restoration of degraded forest land in the state.

But unlike in MP, JFM in Gujarat is applicable to degraded forest areas only. Its institutional mechanism comprises of a state-level Working Group for policy-level inputs, which is constituted by officials, NGOs and academic institutions. It generally meets once in six months. District-level working committees involving officials, NGOs and Village Level Organizations (VLOs) meet once every two months to solve operational problems and resolve local conflicts. A specially created VLO seeks to build community participation at the village level. A minimum of 60 per cent of the families of a village must join the VLO in order to make it eligible for creating a functional unit of JFM, which is to be registered as a cooperative society under the Madhya Pradesh Society Registration Act 1973. The *Gram Panchayat* of a village may also act as a VLO. The EC of the VLO should have at least two women members and a representative of the concerned *panchayat*, one representative of the NGO (where an NGO is facilitating) and one representative of the funding agency (if any). NGOs are mainly required to extend Human Resources Department (HRD) support and organize the VLOs, and in the absence of an NGO, the FD is required to extend HRD support.

An Action Plan as well as the working scheme before harvesting prepared by the VLO is approved by the Deputy Conservator of Forests (DCF). An agreement known as an *adhikar patra* (letter of rights) is signed between the FD and the VLO and there is a provision for the cancellation of such an agreement or for disqualifying the VLO by the DCF without any compensation in case of non-fulfilment of the agreed conditions. In case of disputes, there is a provision for appeal against the decision of the DCF to the Conservator of Forests. The benefits to the members of the VLO comprise of 100 per cent of the usufruct benefits of intermediate products (i.e., non-wood products), a 50 per cent share of wood products between the FD and the VLO and a 50 per cent share of the net proceeds at the final harvest. No monitory benefit is given to the NGOs.

According to an update from the Gujarat Forest Department (March, 2010), since the inception of JFM in Gujarat, 1,734 *Van Kalyan Samitis* (Forest Welfare Committees, VKS), that is, the VLOs, have been created and registered with the DCF to cover 238,242 ha of forest area, of which 1,355 VKSs were given *adhikar patras* and 488 VKSs were registered as Societies. The benefits provided to the JFM units comprised of works in the form of entry point and support activities carried out in the villages which included land development works like land levelling, creation of minor irrigation and drinking water facilities, promotion of energy-saving devices such as bio-gas plants, solar cookers and solar lights, improved stoves and improved crematories; distribution of grafted fruit trees, construction of school buildings and *anganvadis* (nurseries for children), construction of *van talavadis* (village ponds), check dams, fish rearing, construction of link roads, distribution of community utensils and leaf cup machines. The grass and fire wood available due to protection is allowed to be taken out of the forest free of cost. In more than 20 per cent of the villages covered under JFM, some secondary economic activities have also started, of which the main activity is animal husbandry due to increased fodder availability. In about 20 villages, the bamboo crop on the forest land managed under JFM has been harvested and the benefits distributed to the members.

In addition to JFM in the forest areas, the Gujarat FD also developed a project for villages outside of forests, up to a limit of 5 km from the forest fringe, with the objective of promoting afforestation under a special drive involving the local people. The villagers are organized in their VLOs so as to create a shelter belt through afforestation to reduce pressure on the forest. The benefits from such a drive are shared with the VLO like the sharing mechanism followed in case of social forestry plantation. All this expansion requires legal and policy support. With a view to promoting the programme, the FD has designed a project amounting to ₹250 crore for different activities. Further, to promote the integrated development of villages with afforestation activity and to make people more responsive, FDAs have been created in Gujarat as per the direction of the GoI. As in 2011, FDAs have been formed in the 22 Forest Divisions of the State.[5]

8. Comparing the MP and Gujarat JFM Structures and Processes

The JFM programmes in the two states had both similarities and dissimilarities, which are noted in Table 6.2.

---

[5] For further information, visit www.gujaratforest.org (Accessed in June 2011).

Table 6.2

Comparison of JFM Programmes in MP and Gujarat in 2010

Particulars	MP	Gujarat
Types of JFM	VFC, FPC, EDC	VFC, FPC, EDC
Membership	All adult members who have voting rights	All adult members who have voting rights
Approach in handing over of forests	Villagers form the committee and approach DFO for JFM project	Applicable to degraded forest areas only
Role of forest officials in JFMC formation	Facilitator (as per Gram Sabha Act)	Facilitator
Attendance requirement	At least 50% of adults	50% of adults
EC membership formation	As per the Gram Sabha Act (2001)	Minimum 60% of families of a village must join a VLO to make it eligible for JFM.
Provision for Joint secretary	Provision includes take over as Secretary after two years	–
Method of forming ECs, size of committee.	Under the approval of the Gram Sabha, from 10 to 21 members	The EC will have at least two women members and a representative of the concerned Panchayat, one representative of NGO (where a NGO is facilitating), one representative of funding agency (if any).
Tenure of EC	Five years	Five years
Involvement of women in ECs	Minimum 33% in EC and 33% of chairpersons or vice chairpersons of committees must be women	
SCs and STs	Involvement in committee of STs as per their proportion of population	
Role of village institutions in forest management	Provisions for their inclusion in committee duly recognized and	Involvement of NGO's (wherever associated) for MHRD support and for organizing VLOs. The GFD extends such support in the absence of NGO's.
Landless and poor in executive	At least two in executive	–

(contd...)

(contd...)

Particulars	MP	Gujarat
Micro-planning	For forest improvement as well as economic well-being	Action Plan is prepared for approval by DCFs. Working scheme to be approved before harvesting. No working in forest allowed without sanctioned working scheme.
Role of Panchayat	The executive members of the Panchayat and the Sarpanch are on JFMC executive as ex-officio members. Rights to non-nationalized MFPs as per Panchayat (Extension to Scheduled Areas) Act 1996	Gram Panchayat may also act as a VLO.
Rights to members	Usufructs, MFPs income	Non-wood products, Usufructs
Responsibilities	Forest protection; preparation and implementation of micro-plan	Conservation and management of degraded forests
Benefits sharing	Equal (50%) to the members in cash, 30% in village resource development and 20% forest improvements from the amount obtained from final felling.	100% usufruct benefits of (non- wood) intermediate products. 50% sharing of wood products between FD and VLO. 50% sharing of net at final harvest. No monetary benefit to NGOs.

Source: Field data, (2010).
Notes: DFO: Divisional Forest Officer, EDC: Eco-development Committee, FPC: Forest Protection Committee, GFD: Gujarat Forest Department, MHRD: Ministry of Human Resources Development, MFP: minor forest products, NGO: Non-governmental Organization, VFC: Village Forest Committee, VLO: (Village Level Organization).

9. Land Use Pattern and Status of Forest Capital in MP and Gujarat

The complexity of institutional mechanisms to control forest resources depends on the extent and nature of CPRs. The following section provides the status of land use and forest stock in the two states.

9.1. Land Use Pattern in Madhya Pradesh

As per the data gathered from the office of the Commissioner of Land Records 2008, MP is the second largest state of the country with an area of 308,000 sq. km, constituting 9.38 per cent of the geographical area of the country. The recorded forest area of the state is 8,699,000 ha. Land not available for cultivation is more than 3,398,000 ha (11.05%) as compared to cultivable wasteland (1,177 ha). However the NSA in MP state is 14,735,000 ha (47.91%).

9.2. Forests in Madhya Pradesh

The forest cover in the state, based on interpretation of satellite data for October–December, 2006, was 308,274 ha, which was the second highest in the country. As Table 6.3 shows, in terms of forest canopy density classes, the state had 6,647 ha of Very Dense Forests (VDF),[6] 35,007 ha of Moderately Dense Forests (MDF)[7] and 36,014 ha of open forest (OF).[8]

Table 6.3

Forest Cover Under Different Categories in MP (ha)

	Forest Area				Non-forest	Total
Category	VDF	MDF	OF	Scrub		
Very dense forest	6,647	0	0	0	1	6,648
Moderately dense forest	0	35,007	16	1	11	35,035
Open Forest	0	0	36,014	0	42	36,056
Scrub	0	0	1	6,389	1	6,391
Non-forest	0	0	15	11	224,089	224,144
TOTAL	6,647	35,007	36,046	6,400	224,144	308,274

Source: State of Forest Report, Forest Survey of India, (2009: 111).

---

[6] All land with tree cover (including mangrove cover) of canopy density of 70 per cent and above.

[7] All land with tree cover (including mangrove cover) of canopy density between 40 per cent and 70 per cent above.

[8] All land with tree cover (including mangrove cover) of canopy density between 10 per cent and 40 per cent.

Table 6.4

Forest Cover in Selected Districts in MP (ha) in 2010

Geographical Area of District	VDF	MDF	OF	Scrub	Total	Forest as % of Geographical Area
Harda 3,330	19	546	463	8	1,028	30.87
Seoni 8,758	241	1,812	1,031	61	3,084	35.21
Balaghat 9,229	1,339	2,711	946	56	4,996	54.13
Sehore 6,578	25	654	703	124	1,382	21.01

Source: State of Forest Report, Forest Survey of India, (2009: 112).

Four districts of MP, that is, Harda, Seoni, Balaghat and Sehore were selected for this study, out of which Balaghat was the largest, having an area of 9,229 ha (Table 6.4). Harda district was the smallest (3,330 ha). Very dense forest were more in Balaghat (1,339 ha) covering only 25 ha in Sehore district. Maximum moderately dense forests were also found in Balaghat district (2,711 ha) as compared to much less in Sehore district (654 ha). Scrub area was found more in Sehore district (124 ha), and less in Harda district (8 ha).

9.3. Land Use Pattern in Gujarat

As per the data provided by the Directorate of Economics and Statistics (Government of Gujarat 2009–10), Gujarat is situated on the western coast of the country and has the longest coastline amongst all the states. The geographical area of the state is 196,000 sq. km, which constitutes 5.96 per cent of the country's geographical area. The recorded forest area in the state is 1,854 ha, which is 9.66 per cent of the geographic area. Land not available for cultivation is more, that is, 3,744 ha (19.90%) as compared to culturable wasteland (1,982 ha). However, the NSA in Gujarat state is 9,443 ha (50.20%).

9.4. Forests in Gujarat

The recorded forest area in the state of Gujarat is 195,337 ha, out of which VDF is only 376 ha, and 5,319 ha is moderately dense forest

Table 6.5

Forest Cover Under Different Categories in Gujarat (ha) in 2010

Category	Forest Area				Non-forest	Total
	VDF	MDF	OF	Scrub		
Very dense forest	376	0	0	0	0	376
Moderately dense forest	0	5,064	122	9	124	5,319
Open Forest	0	75	8,397	41	396	8,909
Scrub	0	0	44	1270	105	1,419
Non-forest	0	110	432	143	179,314	179,999
Total	376	5,249	8,995	1463	179,939	196,022

Source: *State of Forest Report,* Forest Survey of India, (2009: 83).

Table 6.6

Forest Cover in the Selected Districts of Gujarat (ha)

District	Geographical Area	VDF	MDF	OF	Scrub	Total	% of GA
Panchmahal	4,461	0	176	394	35	570	12.78
Sabarkantha	7,390	29	305	468	90	802	10.85
Surat	7,657	84	778	445	26	1,307	17.07
Junagadh	8,281	15	952	633	24	1600	19.32

Source: *State of Forest Report,* Forest Survey of India, (2009: 83).

(Table 6.5). The maximum forest area comes under open forest, that is, 8,909 ha, while scrub constitutes only 1,419 ha. The remaining 179,314 ha comes under non-forest area (Directorate of Economics and Statistics, Government of Gujarat, 2009–10).

Four districts from Gujarat state, that is, Panchmahal, Sabarkantha, Surat and Junagadh were selected for this study, of which Junagadh was the largest, having an area of 8,281 ha (Table 6.6). Panchmahals district was the smallest (4,461 ha). Very dense forest was found in Surat (84 ha) while there was none in Panchmahals district. The maximum forest cover was found in the moderately dense forest in Junagadh district (952 ha) which was much lesser in Panchmahals district (176 ha). Scrub area was found more in Sabarkantha district (90 ha), while lesser in Junagadh district (24 ha).

There were 1,734 JFMCs in Gujarat managing 0.24 ha of forest area since the JFM programme began in the state in 1991. The number of JFMC members was 0.81 million, of these 0.14 million families belonged to STs. The forest area allotted to the JFMCs was approximately 238,242 ha (Present Status of JFM, 2011).

10. Methodology for the Village Level Survey

To conduct a detailed survey of selected villages in order to understand the linkages between participatory forest management and its impact or otherwise on poverty, the tools of FGD, Participatory Rural Appraisal (PRA) and a HHS were employed for data collection. The Sustainable Livelihoods Framework (SLF) was used to analyze the efficacy of JFM and its impact on poverty levels at the study sites.

The policy response and implementation at the village level in the two states was captured through data collected on socio-economic status and household level participation in JFM, current status of JFM and interventions taken by the JFM committees in the villages along with a pebble distribution method (PDM) exercise.

10.1. Focus Group Discussions

A common checklist for all the resource institutions was prepared for preliminary discussion in villages at the purposively selected sites. For the JFM component, clusters were selected based on the existing literature and information on institutional activities done at the division level of forests. A preliminary discussion was conducted in three–five villages in all the clusters and then one village in each cluster was selected for detailed study. The final site selection also tried to choose a mix of JFM institutions (the three types of JFMCs, namely VFC, FPC and EDC that have been discussed earlier) and villages by official status (revenue vs forest villages), to include a wide range of institutional settings and backgrounds under which JFM had been introduced and made operational.

A total of eight villages were selected as per the filters mentioned above, four in each state, for a detailed study of JFM and poverty. The FGD and survey tools along with other PRA techniques such as forest resource ranking, the PDM, activity mapping exercise and village transects aimed at developing a basic understanding of forest-livelihood linkages. The concerns of various stakeholders including farmers, women, tenants and the landless and resource management aspects were also covered in the detailed discussions. In addition, semi-structured interviews were carried out with JFMC presidents and secretaries. Separate meetings were held with FD officials and field staff to get their opinion and feedback on JFM activities and community participation under JFM.

10.2. Household Survey

An HHS of sample JFM members in each of the eight selected villages was conducted in order to represent the diversity of each village's demography and socio-economic structure. The survey questionnaire covered issues of socio-economic importance to land holders and landless villagers as well as participation of different groups in JFM activities, including women, tribals and other marginalized communities, higher and lower caste households, etc. The central aim was to discover (a) the processes of implementing the new management systems under JFM, (b) community processes related to managing natural resources, (c) the impact on the community including benefits and problems perceived by members under the new system and (d) the ultimate effect on poverty levels.

In each of the villages, 50 households were selected purposively to represent three land-related categories: landed, tenants and the landless. The head of the household was interviewed on factual data regarding size of holdings, assets, cultivation and JFM activities including income from forests. Various questions related to governance such as accountability, transparency and household participation were also asked to substantiate the FGDs and PRA findings. An entire village census was carried out in villages with less than 50 households; however, some families had temporarily out-migrated during the survey and thus their information has not been not included in the study.

10.3. The Pebble Distribution Method

The PDM has been developed by the Center for International Forestry Research (CIFOR) and presented in one of the NET working Forest Plantations (NETFOP) draft reports (van der Meer, Bairaktari, de Groot, van Heist and Schmerbeck, 2007). The important characteristic of the method is its quantitative capturing of 'importance' that includes local priorities and provides a qualitative justification behind the importance that people assign to each alternative (Table 6.7). However, in the context of PDM, 'importance' as described in the NETFOP report is a relative judgment which can be subjective depending on personal experiences and knowledge and can be related or not related to tangible costs and benefits.

Table 6.7

Two Mutually Exclusive Sets Used in the Pebble Distribution Method

First Set	Second Set
Increase in Forest Cover	Decrease in Forest Cover
Self-awareness	Negligence of government officials
FD Guidance	Encroachment for agriculture
FPC Establishment	Dormant FPC
Plantation Activity	Illicit Felling
Poverty Reduction	Poverty in the village

Source: Focus group discussion, (2010).

Two sets of factors were prepared for the pebble distribution exercise, one to quantify the importance of each factor leading to a perceived increase in forest cover by villagers and the other to quantify the importance of each factor that had led to a perceived decrease in forest cover. Both sets were exclusive of each other, that is, in villages where a majority believed that the forest cover had increased, the exercise was conducted only for the factors that could have led to this increase. Similarly, in villages where the forest cover was believed to have decreased, the pebble distribution exercise was conducted for the factors leading to the decrease.

The pebbles were distributed by informants according to the total importance of each factor. All the images were placed on a single chart paper which contained their meanings in the local language. The meanings were also explained and a demonstration was given with five pebbles by the facilitator before beginning the task. The informant group was then invited to distribute the pebbles onto the images and were left alone during their discussions. The informants in all the selected villages undertook the exercise enthusiastically and discussed all the factors present in front of them while assigning pebbles. They were given the option of rearranging the pebbles as the discussion progressed and were nowhere in-between disturbed by the facilitator until the distribution was over. At this stage the facilitator counted the pebbles placed on each factor and asked the group members whether they wished to change their choices. The members carefully looked at the chart containing pebbles placed on the different factors and approved the outcome of the exercise. They also explained to the facilitator why they had attached high weight to any particular factor.

11. The Study of JFM Villages in Madhya Pradesh

11.1. Village Khumi, Harda District

Khumi is a forest village located in the Rehatgaon range in the Timarni block of Harda district (also forest division) in MP. It is 20 km away from the FD Rehatgaon range office and was

Image 6.1

Damawas JFM Committee with Forest Department Official

Image 6.2

Beat Guard at Mandoranan

Source: John R. Wood.

Source: John R. Wood.

Image 6.3

Future Forests Begin in a Seedling Nursery

Source: John R. Wood.

Image 6.4

Korku Adivasis of Khatpura Village

Source: Peter Wood.

Image 6.5

Building a Check dam in Khumi's Forest

Source: John R. Wood.

Image 6.6

Ghurshivera: Oustees from Kanha National Park

Source: John R. Wood.

inhabited by the Gowal, Yadav and Gond communities with a total population of 196 divided amongst 35 households. The major sources of livelihood for the villagers were labour and agriculture. Most of the villagers had their own land allocated by the FD; however, inconsistent income from agriculture has made the village vulnerable to poverty and deprivation. The village was surrounded by teak-dominated dense forests with a total area of 1,100 ha, approximately (Field Observations, 2010). The FPC was created in 1992 with the objective of benefitting both the forest and the community, and had 96 members at the time of the survey. The FPC had protected the forest in the surrounding region by preventing illicit felling. According to the villagers, the forest cover had improved and this could easily be observed by looking at the dense forest around the village settlement.

According to the JFM guidelines, 25 per cent of the revenue generated from harvesting of timber done under the FD working plan is to be credited to the FPC account. Besides aggregating funds in the community account, several development activities have been initiated under the JFM programme, including construction of a cement road and bridges in the region, digging trenches, building check dams, a stop dam to conserve water in the village, contour bunding for increasing moisture content in the soil, uprooting the *lantana camara* weed and planting, thinning and pruning in the forest. All these activities have helped generate employment for Khumi villagers. However, Khumi's FPC was inactive at the time of the survey, and the villagers lacked any motivation to conduct regular meetings. Earlier the villagers were interested and attended meetings because of FD incentives, but because of the lack of such incentives they have been rarely attending the same.

Table 6.8 shows the range of income earned by participating households in forest activity. A total of 15 households worked in the forest in 2008 and earned a total income of ₹27,380 (an average income of ₹1,825 per household).

Khumi's FPC at the time of the survey had ₹349,000 in its account that was lying unutilized. Several FPC proposals such as the construction of houses and the installation of a high powered electric transformer were pending with the FD. The funds were earlier used to provide credit to villagers at an interest rate of

Table 6.8

Non-timber Forest Product (NTFP) Income per Household in Khumi

NTFPs	Income-wise No. of HH Participated		Average HH Income
	<1,000	b/w 1,000 & 3,000	
Tendu Leaves	6	3	
Mahua Fruits	0	7	
Other NTFPs	5	3	

NTFPs	Income-wise No. of HHs that Participated			Average HH Income		
	<1,000	b/w 1,000 & 3,000	>3,000	< 1,000	b/w 1,000 & 3,000	>3,000
Tendu Leaves	6	3	8	₹533	₹2,333	₹3,862
Mahua Fruits	0	7	2	0	₹2,072	₹3,750
Other NTFPs	5	3	0	₹430	₹1,333	0

Source: Field survey, (2010).

4 per cent p.a. However, non-repayment of loans forced the FD to stop the sanctioning of loans from this fund. Villagers agreed that many of them had not repaid their loans, and they had to repay loans taken from the local money lenders at a much higher interest rate of 3 per cent, payable monthly. However, the villagers believed that the outstanding debtors of the FPC were not in any condition to repay their loans, hence the Khumi village community was not emphasizing repayment. However, they expected further utilization of FPC funds for the development of the village.

11.2. Village Khatpura, Sehore District

Khatpura is a forest village located in Budhni taluka of Sehore district in MP. The village had a population of 778, divided amongst 175 families. Five families had migrated away. The villagers said that previously a lot more people migrated for work, but since 2002 there were plenty of labour opportunity locally because of the construction of the Narmada Water Pipeline. Most of the villagers belonged to the STs. Approximately 60–70 per cent of them were

Korku adivasis, and there were additionally four Dharoi and four Bhil families. Among the non-STs, there were 55 Jatav (SC) families and three Harijan (SC) families, a Muslim and a Sikh family, as well as one Yadav, five Banjara and three Meena families. The village's main sources of livelihood included farming, local labour and gathering NTFPs. About 25 per cent of the adults worked in a stone quarry and 50 per cent worked in the Narmada Pipeline project. About 10 per cent got regular income from *kullu* gum extraction.

The Khatpura FPC was established in 1996 through the efforts of the Forest Department. The entry point activity was clearing and pruning work in the forest, for which participating villagers were paid. Villagers were also engaged in fire protection activities. Under the JFM programme, they agreed to undertake the protection of the forest in return for usufruct rights over various forest products. The households were also allowed to collect dried wood stock and sell it in the neighbouring villages.

The villagers told us at the time of the survey that the FPC was not functioning as it should have. They were very forthcoming about the irregularities that plagued the FPC Committee; for example, one FPC member had left the village but was still on the committee. Secondly, the election for the FPC president was not conducted fairly and was to a large extent influenced by FD officials. In another instance in 2004, the FD officials had asked 20 households to manage the bamboo grove in the forest and promised monetary incentives for harvesting and thinning the bamboo culms, apart from their wage labour. These households claimed to have worked for almost two years at a wage rate of ₹1200 per month but were not paid the promised bonus from the sale of the bamboo culms. FD officials explained that the reason for this was the low productivity of the villagers and losses incurred by the FD. This offended the villagers and they withdrew their support for the JFM programme, including their voluntary help in extinguishing forest fires and reporting illicit fellings inside the forest.

The beat guard of the village said that the FPC had had problems in keeping to the rules and understanding what role they were to play. For example, there was the problem of a migrant Bhil community encroaching on the forest land, but the locals did nothing to stop them. According to the beat guard, the villagers were only interested in activities from which they could get immediate money. The FPC had extended loans to villagers but the borrowers, including the president of the FPC himself, had defaulted in paying back their loans, leading to a halt in this activity. The money lenders in the region provided credit at a monthly interest rate of 10 per cent. This credit was only available to landholders and thus the landless in the village now had no credit facility.

Under the FPC's development activities, four stop dams and more than 10 check dams had been constructed in the village. In addition, more than 1,000 trenches had been dug to conserve water and improve agricultural productivity. Several training exercises for livelihood generation had been carried out in the village periodically, including candle and incense stick making, cultivation, apiculture, the processing of lemon grass and bamboo boat making. All these activities were initiated by the FD with the help of NGOs or in consultation with the Indian Institute of Forest Management based in Bhopal. The villagers believed that the lack of a market in which they could sell their produce and costs exceeding revenues were the major reasons for the failure of all of the livelihood interventions.

Training for the sustainable harvesting of *kullu* gum, which is a nationalized forest product exported internationally, was also provided, but continued only for short periods ranging from six months to two years. At the time of the survey, the beat guard complained about the over-harvesting of *kullu* gum. Around 20 households had been granted a permit to extract *kullu* gum, along with the correct tools for doing the same and given several training sessions on the importance of sustainable practices for collection. Despite being told several times to extract the gum in a sustainable way by making only a small cut in the bark of the tree, the collectors had been causing damage to the trees and as a result several trees in the forest were in a degraded state.

In the forest beside Khatpura, the villagers were allowed to collect NTFP for local consumption as well as for selling purposes. Altogether, 41 families were involved in NTFP collection. The range of income earned by participating households in NTFP collection is presented in Table 6.9. The beat guard complained about the unsustainable practices used in harvesting NTFPs, including not only *kullu* tree damage, but also setting fires for *mahuva* flower

Table 6.9

NTFP Income per Household in Khatpura

NTFPs	Income-wise No. of HH Participated			Average HH Income		
	<1,000	b/w 1,000 & 3,000	>3,000	<1,000	b/w 1,000 & 3,000	>3,000
Tendu Leaves	10	2	0	₹480	₹1,500	0
Mahuva Fruits	4	31	6	₹325	₹1,780	₹4,000
Other NTFPs	6	30	0	₹517	₹1,510	0

Source: Field survey, (2010).

collection and the cutting of tree branches to gather fruits. Out of 50 households surveyed, 10 had members who worked in the forest in 2009. They earned a total income of ₹18,600, or an average income of ₹1,860 per household.

11.3. Village Gurshivehra, Balaghat District

Gurshivehra is a forest village in Garhi taluka of Balaghat district populated by families displaced from the Kanha National Park in the 1970s. They lived in the buffer zone outside the Park. There were about 250 people, divided into 55 families. They were very open to discussion about their current economic status, the role of the forest in their life and the current Eco-development forest management regime under JFM. Apart from the families (five households) that had temporarily migrated out of the village and one family that had been outcast by the entire village community, everyone else was willing to talk and share their experiences with respect to EDC activities, the FD and their own socio-economic life in the village.

There were 30 Baiga families, 15 Gond families and three OBC families (including one blacksmith) in the village; 75 per cent of them made a living from farming and 25 per cent got agricultural labour jobs. Fuel wood was the only major benefit that they got from the forest. NTFPs had ceased to exist in the nearby forest due to unsustainable harvesting techniques employed in the past;

however, several fruit bearing trees had been planted inside the village settlement within the boundary of various households and the fruits were consumed by the villagers. The village community had given up their practice of fishing and eating fish and mutton. The reasons cited were the ban imposed on fishing inside the Kanha National Park and the high cost of purchasing mutton that made it unaffordable for a majority of the village households.

The Gurshivehra villagers liked their new farms and new environment, but they complained about the lack of electricity in the village. They also desired more wells and gave high priority to the construction of new wells in the vicinity of households so that no one had to go more than 500 m to get drinking water. Meanwhile, more development work was required on the agricultural fields including fencing and the completion of land levelling. Electricity generation for pumps was also needed. Clearly, there was a need for the villagers to understand the importance of village level planning and of making efforts to use government and community funds for the overall development of the village, rather than demanding wells near every household when there were enough wells to meet their drinking water requirements.

The Gurshivehra EDC Committee was formed in 2002 and had 12 members in its EC, including five women members and a president who was selected by consensus among the EDC general body members and was serving his second term. There had been three General Body meetings (GBMs) conducted up until the survey. Information about the meetings was spread by a *kotwar* (messenger). Everybody participated, including the women. Minutes were taken and those who were at the meeting took it upon themselves to convey what happened to anyone who did not get there. The EDC had appointed one villager as a forest watcher in the three months of summer at a salary of ₹1,000/month on a rotational basis. Apart from FD support, no other source of funding was available for the EDC. Extinguishing forest fires was considered to be the village community's duty and was carried out through voluntary labour.

When the EDC was formed, Gurshivehra's villagers were asked to protect the forest and avoid the felling of trees, and in return, they were promised that they would receive bamboo at subsidized rates and other employment activities under the EDC. So far the activities have included agricultural land levelling, for which the villagers have received wages, as well as building a school, digging three wells, installing one hand pump and constructing a road. A majority of the activities have been conducted in the last two years (2007–08), thereby lowering the out-migration rate in these two years. Nothing significant was found to be happening during the time of our research study in 2009, with the villagers predicting that migration would be on the rise again. The villagers believed that the most beneficial EDC work had been land levelling in the crop fields, of which 50 per cent remained to be completed. They did not think the programme could be considered a success until this work was completed. Their demands included more wells, bio-gas plants and electricity. In 2008, pedal pumps for irrigating crops were offered to the villagers at a subsidized price of ₹1,200 per pump. They were bought by 12 households, while others could not afford to pay for the same. In addition, two bio-gas stoves had been installed and a proposal for more such stoves was in the pipeline.

These findings again raise concerns about village level development planning and allocation of resources, because nobody in Gurshivehra was being trained for the maintenance of bio-gas plants and the manure required for their operation was scarce as the villagers did not have enough livestock. A canal and a pond had also been constructed under EDC activities, but stop dams were needed to conserve water in the canal which otherwise became dry in the non-monsoon season. The moisture content in the fields adjoining the pond and canal was significantly higher than in other fields, thus demonstrating improved crop yields under EDC activities.

Previously, Gurshivehra villagers used to collect NTFP for local consumption but at the time of the survey, due to over-harvesting of produce, NTFPs like *aonla* (*embilica officianalis*) and white *musli* had ceased to exist inside the forest. Villagers were involved in the collection of *sal* seeds which were available once in every two years. The seeds were purchased by the FD from all the villages situated in the buffer region of the national park. The average income earned per person through *sal* seed collection was ₹250. All the villagers worked in the land levelling project initiated by the FD in 2008 as well as the construction of a road. Some villagers migrated to cities like Surat and Mumbai for a full three–four month period once or twice a year.

11.4. Village Jhilmili, Seoni District

Jhilmili village is situated in Chappara taluka on the highway connecting Seoni to Jabalpur and had a VFC that was established in 1995–96. The village had a degraded forest until the early 1990s, but even before the VFC was established the community members decided to stop the felling trees. Their efforts resulted in strong regeneration of the forest area within two–three years and led the FD to establish a formal JFM institution in the village. The VFC was established in 1995–96 and the EC comprised of 21 members and a president from the village community.

Jhilmili villagers were very proud of their achievement of successfully conserving their forest, which in two decades had been converted into a dense forest. There was a sense of ownership and belonging to the forest amongst the community because no external agencies were involved in the conservation. This distinguished Jhilmili's VFC from other VFCs during our preliminary discussions. Throughout our FGD, the villagers kept narrating instances where they had captured timber thieves and charged a fine as per VFC norms and then handed over the case to the FD. This included an instance where a renowned politician's men were caught harvesting timber in the night. The villagers seized their tractor and trolley for three days and ignoring threats, charged a fine before releasing the seized vehicle. After this instance, nobody had ever tried to illicitly cut trees in Jhilmili's forest.

Jhilmili was inhabited by 80 households comprising a mix of Gowal, Bagri (Patel), Deharia (Marar), Gond and Ahirwar communities. While there were a few big farmers primarily from the Patel community, a majority of the households were dependent on agricultural labour and stone crushing work for their livelihoods. During the time of the survey there were three SHGs in the village, one of them operational for 12 years. They lent money to members at a monthly interest rate of 3 per cent. The village however had its own issues related to the domination of the Patel community and lack of sufficient resources for some households.

The village had a stock of regenerating teak forest covering a total area of approximately 1,000 acres (data obtained from field notes, 2010). According to the agreement signed with the Forest Department, 40 per cent of revenue generated from the sale of forest products, including timber, was credited to the VFC account. These funds were utilized to implement various development proposals in the village. Some of the proposals included: construction of a cemented road, digging trenches, building check dams to conserve water in the village and planting, thinning and pruning trees in the forest. Another proposal implemented by the VFC was the provision of common and private connections for drinking water by constructing water outlets near small clusters of households and installing pipes to make water available at each doorstep.

The documentation work done in the VFC was one of the main reasons for including the village in our research. Various documented records included: Fodder distribution register, Forest product distribution register, Membership record register, Plant distribution register, Watcher Payment records file, VFC Loan register, Micro plan, Attendance register, Proposal Book, Case Book (Income), Ledger and Receipt book for the sale of timber.

At the time of the survey, the Jhilmili VFC had only ₹746 in its account. Its MJSI included proceeds from the sale of forest products including intermediate yields and funds granted by the FD. The members also stated that previously the VFC had around ₹1 lakh in its account but it was spent on arranging the logistics for a politician's visit to the taluka. The two forest watch guards appointed through the VFC were paid monthly incomes by the FD. The large farmers were seeking a warehouse to be constructed for storing their agricultural produce. They wanted to sell their produce directly in the market and eliminate middlemen, thus increasing their profits. The poorer villagers wanted a pond to be constructed on the western side of the village settlement. This pond could serve the twin purposes of providing employment and water for the villagers and their livestock.

The need for a pond had been included in the village micro plan but the work had not started as the final proposal had not been passed by the VFC. While development activities were expected to be pro-poor, the decision-making power lay in the hands of the Patels who needed labour on their crop fields. They would not allow the Jhilmili VFC to make decisions that would divert village labour to other infrastructural development activities.

The Patel community was the dominant sub-group in the village. Two persons had served as VFC president and both belonged to the Patel community. Both were educated and had large farms. The president of the VFC was well aware of the objectives of JFM as well as current issues including climate change and farmer suicides. He played an important role in mobilizing the community for forest protection and passing resolutions under the VFC.

Jhilmili's villagers were only allowed to collect NTFP for local consumption, except for *tendu patta* which is a nationalized product. The regenerating forest also contained NTFP fruits like *chironji*, *achar* and *sitaphal* (custard apple) that could be collected for domestic consumption. The VFC gave the *sitaphal* contract to a bidding group of villagers who would then harvest all the fruit and sell it in the taluka of Chappara. Out of 50 households surveyed, six had members who worked in the forest in 2009 and earned a total income of ₹11,500, or an average income of ₹1,916 per household; additionally, 22 families were involved in NTFP collection. The range of income earned by participating households in NTFP collection is given in Table 6.10 below:

Table 6.10

NTFP Income per Household in Jhilmili

NTFPs	Income-wise No. of HH Participated			Average HH Income		
	<1000	b/w 1000 & 3000	>3000	<1000	b/w 1000 & 3000	>3000
Tendu Leaves	7	7	7	₹428	₹2,357	₹3,857
Mahuva Fruits	0	7	2	0	₹2,543	₹3,450
Other NTFPs	0	7	5	0	₹2,215	₹3,800

Source: Field survey, (2010).

12. The JFM Study Villages in Gujarat

12.1. Village Khatardevi, Surat District

Khatardevi is a forest village in the middle of the Mandavi taluka forest in Surat district. It is 20 km away from the Mandavi range office of the Gujarat FD. This forest village was inhabited entirely by Vasawa adivasis, with the total population estimated to be 250, divided into 55 households. There is a section of landless households whose ancestors migrated from a nearby region and settled in the village. The major sources of livelihood for the villagers were milk selling and agriculture. Most of the farmers had small landholdings as a result of the growing population and partition of land among separating households. Several interventions had been made under the JFM programme to improve agricultural productivity and the income from agriculture.

The village is surrounded by a reserve forest with a total area of 733 ha (approximate). The Khatardevi JFMC was created in 2000 with the objective of benefitting both the forest and the community. The FD staff said that dense forest area was left only in the patch containing Khatardevi and its neighbouring villages. The rest of the area in the Mandavi forest range was heavily degraded. The forest in this patch was also targeted for timber and the villagers were not able to control illicit felling despite witnessing it on several occasions. Owing to a lack of feeling of ownership of the forest, little was done. Khatardevi villagers and the FD staff believed that overall the forest cover had decreased under JFM and although the villagers had refrained from cutting trees and had also participated in protecting the forest from fire, illicit felling by outsiders was one of the major reasons for the decrease in forest cover.

About 50 per cent of the villagers turned up for JFMC meetings, including 10–15 per cent of the women. All the financial records were held by the FD. At the time of the survey there were ₹500 in the account. Whenever there was a conflict in Khatardevi, it was resolved by voting. Though the villagers did not mention any conflict details during the FGDs, we learned during the HHS that the first President of the JFMC was charged with misusing JFMC funds and therefore he quit the post and the villagers selected a new President.

Water scarcity was a major issue for the villagers; several efforts had been initiated, including the construction of a water tank by the JFMC which was abandoned midway. Incomplete projects and the inequitable distribution of benefits were two striking features of Khatardevi's JFM programme that otherwise had been effective in livelihood generation for the village. An additional problem area was that the villagers had not received their MGNREGA job cards which were lying with the *sarpanch* of the village.

Several proposals had been implemented by the Khatardevi JFMC such as construction of three *pukka* (brick) houses, providing bore well connections and pipes for irrigation on a daily payment basis, renting a tractor for land levelling in a few crop fields and distribution of milch cattle to 25 households. However, there had been little effort to distribute JFM benefits equitably and little had been done for the landless households. The villagers did not know about the distribution of milch cattle and none of the landless members were given cattle for their livelihood. Similarly, agriculture-related developments had also not contributed to poverty reductions for the landless members of the community. Milk selling had become an important year-long livelihood activity for a majority of villagers because credit for buying livestock was easily available to them.

Khatardevi's villagers were allowed to collect NTFP for local consumption. They sold *tendu patta* and *bili* fruit which were available in large quantities despite a decline in the past due to monsoon failures. The villagers received ₹50 per hundred packs of *tendu* leaves last year where each pack consisted of 50 leaves. *Bili* was sold at ₹20 per kg. Out of 50 households surveyed, 21 had members who had worked in the forest in 2009. They had earned a total income of ₹41,800, or an average income of ₹1,990.47 per household per annum.

12.2. Village Kotra, Panchmahal District

Kotra is a revenue village located in Santrampura taluka of Panchmahal district in Gujarat, 65 km away from the district capital, Godhra. All the villagers were Bhils, but of different groups—Bamaniya (40%), Taviad (35%), Chandana (10–15%), Tadavi (5%) and Katara (5%). The main sources of livelihood in the village included farming (50%) and agricultural labour (50%). The villagers got many products from the forest, including fuel wood and fodder, *mahuva* flowers, *tendu patta* and *sitaphal* (custard apple). The growing population and increasing number of households had reduced the land ownership status per household. A majority of households were in the small and marginal farmer category. This had increased the dependence on alternative sources of livelihood in the village.

The JFM programme was initiated in Kotra by the Foundation for Ecological Security (FES), an NGO that had prepared a micro plan for the village on behalf of the FD. The plan's major emphasis was on the protection of the existing forest area (which was largely degraded), using a habitation strategy such that the households situated near particular patches of the forest were made responsible for protecting their particular patch from illicit felling. The Kotra JFMC EC met every month and the General Body two–three times a year. These meetings regularly had a 60–70 per cent turnout. All the villagers were informed of the meetings two days in advance. Minutes were kept by the secretary and were available to all. The JFMC records maintained in the village included: (a) the payment voucher book for forest labour, (b) the JFMC meeting attendance register, (c) cash book, (d) proposal book, (e) general register and (f) accounts book.

Overall, Kotra's villagers perceived that the FES had all the power to implement proposals and though everybody had benefited from JFM, poverty was still a problem. The BPL card distribution system was an important issue discussed during the FGDs. Earlier, 180 BPL cards had been issued, but after the government's survey of 2004, there were only 20 BPL households. In the eyes of one FGD group this did not reflect a true picture of the village. They estimated that around 25 per cent of the village was still very poor. Everybody agreed, however, that the poverty problem was worse before the JFM programme started. Post-JFM, agricultural productivity had improved; the forest was more productive, and fodder was available for the livestock. In 2008, an MGNREGA project was effectively implemented in the village and several wells and a forest boundary wall were constructed. Apart from minor cases of proxy beneficiaries, the MGNREGA generated livelihood support for the entire village and thus the out-migration rate was lower in 2008 compared to previous years.

The Bamaniya sub-group is the largest sub-group and holds important positions decided through elections, such as the village *sarpanch*, the JFMC president and secretary positions. The Taviad candidates had contested in all the elections with support from other sub-group households situated near their settlement. The JFM EC had 15 members (five Bamaniya, four Taviad, one Solanki and one Chandana) out of which four were women (three Bamania and one Taviad). Intra-group marriages were not allowed, but inter-group marriages did happen between all the sub-groups of Bhils living in the village.

The JFM programme in Kotra was introduced by the FES and started officially on 7 February 1998. The main activities were designed to protect what little degraded forest remained. Plantation work and seeding of grass were also initiated. In 1999, the village registered for an *adhikar patra* covering 200 ha. The FES also sent a team of five members to Netrang, well-known in Gujarat for its AKRSP training in operational aspects of JFM. After starting a nursery for seedlings, the Kotra JFMC began replanting the degraded forest. Around 80–85 gully plugs were built to increase soil moisture. JFM's main benefits, according to the villagers, have been the stoppage of erosion and the beginnings of a more organic form of agriculture with worm composting and an increased flow of leaf litter from upstream forest land to crop fields. The groundwater level had also increased, but the wells still became dry in summer and thus there was a need to construct more water harvesting structures, including check dams. The availability of *kalra* leaves (whose seeds can be sold) and fruits like custard apple had also increased in the regenerating forest. One major intervention that the villagers felt was required was land levelling, as many crop fields were situated on sloping grounds and produced low agricultural yields.

Table 6.11

NTFP Income per Household in Kotra

NTFPs	Income-wise No. of HH Participated			Average HH Income		
	<1,000	b/w 1,000 & 3,000	>3,000	<1,000	b/w 1,000 & 3,000	>3,000
Tendu Leaves	13	20	0	₹423	₹1,585	0
Bili Fruit	7	11	2	₹442	₹1,790.90	₹3,500

Source: Field survey, (2010).

The villagers were allowed to collect NTFP for local consumption including *mahuva* and custard apple. *Bili* trees were also present in the forest but in small quantities.

The villagers were unaware of their utility and hence did not collect the fruits or leaves. *Tendu patta* was used as livestock fodder and also sold to a contractor. Out of the 50 households surveyed, 44 had members who worked in the forest in 2009; they earned a total income of ₹62,500, or an average income of ₹1,420 per household in 2009. Additionally, 32 families were involved in *tendu* leaves collection, which earned them a total sum of ₹9,250, or an average income of ₹289 per household (Table 6.11).

12.3. Village Damawas, Sabarkantha District

Damawas is a village comprising approximately 3,000 people and is situated near the Gujarat–Rajasthan border in Khedbrahma taluka of Gujarat's northern Sabarkantha district. There were about 450 households, 70 per cent of which were Dungri Bhils and 30 per cent Baxi Panch (the Gujarati designation for OBCs). One-third of the Damawas villagers earned their livelihood from farming, another one-third from forest work and the remaining one-third from other pursuits, primarily agricultural labour. The village was surrounded by a reserve forest with a total area of 257 ha.

The Damawas JFMC was created in 2003 with the objective of benefiting both the forest and the village community. The JFM had contributed to increased forest cover which was a great source of pride for the village. The villagers refrained from cutting trees and participated in activities to protect the forest. During the time of the survey, the forest area was being fenced with barbed wire in order to prevent encroachment. Inside the forest area there were several check dams, and the planting of new trees and shrubs had resulted in the growth of several NTFPs, including google gum, *tendu* leaves and *mahuva* flowers. There were 90 members in the general body of the JFMC. The EC included 11 members (eight Dungri Bhils and three OBCs), of which two were women (both OBC).

The villagers said there had never been a conflict in the Damawas JFMC and that there had been no problems. Periodically, there had been forest fires, mostly caused by the burning of dry leaves by people collecting honey. The village had about 35 motorcycles owned by agricultural labourers who used them to get to work. Apparently, it was common to have four riders on one motorcycle, who shared the cost of the petrol. Some villagers migrated for three–four months once or twice a year.

Several interventions had been made by the FD under the JFM programme, including organizing a veterinary camp for the entire village, constructing check dams and a bore well to provide water to the planting sites as well as drinking water for the households. Three sewing machines had also been distributed under the JFM and the beneficiaries were undergoing training from the village tailor to use those machines. Platforms had been constructed under trees for celebrating festivals and dancing. As mentioned above, fencing of the forest boundary was underway to prevent encroachment by outsiders, allegedly from Rajasthan. Villagers recounted how in 2007 some 250 outsiders made an unsuccessful attempt to encroach the reserved forest land but were driven away by the Damawas villagers and the FD.

No development proposal as such had been put forward by the Damawas villagers, who were totally unaware of any such privilege. Thus the Damawas JFMC had been working at the sole discretion of the FD. The villagers were mostly not interested in JFMC meetings as most of them spent their days in the fields earning their daily living. Since its inception, the JFM programme had not included the Patel families of Damawas, who neither come to JFM meetings nor got involved in JFM activities. All the Dungri Bhil and OBC members attended JFM GBMs, but none ever raised any issue, thus indicating that JFM activities were tightly controlled by the FD.

The Damavas villagers were allowed to collect NTFP for local consumption. They sold the *tendu patta* and *mahuva* flowers which were found in large quantities. The villagers received ₹50 per hundred packs of *tendu* leaves in 2008 with each pack consisting of 50 leaves. *Mahuva* flowers were consumed in the manufacturing of local liquor within the village. Several households extracted gum from the forest and earned ₹60 per kg. Out of the 50 households surveyed, 15 had members who worked in the forest in 2009 on various construction and plantation jobs and earned a total income of ₹20,060, or an average annual income of ₹1,337 per household. Additionally, 30 families were involved in NTFP collection. The range of income earned by participating households in the NTFP collection is presented in Table 6.12 below.

Table 6.12

NTFP Income per Household in Damawas

NTFPs	Income-wise No. of HH Participating			Average HH Income from NTFP		
	<1,000	b/w 1,000 & 3,000	>3,000	<1000	b/w 1,000 & 3,000	>3,000
Tendu Leaves	23	6	0	₹391	₹1,283	0
Mahuva Flowers	24	6	0	₹525	₹1,267	0
Other NTFPs	2	0	0	₹230	0	0

Source: Field survey, (2010).

12.4. Village Mandoranan, Junagadh District

Mandoranan is a forest village located in Talala taluka, Junagadh district, in the buffer zone surrounding the Gir National Forest. It was dominated by the Patel community, while other communities that lived there included the Kolis, Ahirs, Rabaris, Harijans, Lohars, Mochis, etc. It was a big village with a population of approximately 4,000. The major sources of livelihood included agriculture and horticulture, including mango cultivation. Wage labour was another economic activity but the men and women earned different wages, ₹100 per day for men and ₹60 per day for women. The argument given was that men did more physically demanding activities compared to women. Women were represented on the EC of the EDC but as in all the other villages studied, the women did not speak in front of the men of the village.

The major reason for the prosperity of Mandoranan was the income from the annual mango crop. While some farmers sold their entire crop to contractors, others sold mangoes by themselves in cities like Surat, Rajkot and Junagadh. During the mango harvesting period, the wage rate was more than for any other activity and hence all the labour was diverted to this single activity during the months of April and May.

The villagers perceived that the EDC programme had been beneficial for both the Gir forest and the village community. Not only had infrastructure been developed but forest health had also improved and good mutual understanding had developed between the village community and the FD. The villagers were confident about the success of the EDC in their village and believe that its achievements deserved more attention. They did not shy away from site visits by visitors.

In Mandoranan, EDC funds had been used to construct concrete roads in the village, a boundary wall for the primary school and the village cremation ground, street lights, two check dams and two ponds. Most recently, a computer had been purchased for Mandoranan's primary school. In addition, the EDC undertook the fencing of crop lands (with 25% of the cost of fencing borne by the beneficiaries), and the distribution of gas cylinders. Because the collection of fuel wood was prohibited in the forest, 240 gas cylinders were distributed by the FD to reduce dependence on fuel wood.

The LPG and building stones were to be provided by the FD and villagers recalled how at the beginning of the EDC programme, they were told that these would be financed by the FD. In reality, the villagers had been charged 25 per cent of the cost and an additional amount was levied by the EDC. The villagers continued to face fuel problems, including irregularity in the refilling of LPG cylinders and the non-availability of kerosene following LPG distribution to the beneficiaries in the village.

Mandoranan's EDC programme was aimed to benefit the entire village community, but the dominant Patel community appeared to have benefited the most. Several OBC households were not represented in the EDC. Many EDC members had not used the LPG and other benefits as they could not afford to pay the 25 per cent of the total cost as was required of them. LPG cylinders were not easily available or refillable despite frequent EDC complaints. Well-off members got their LPG cylinders refilled by paying a higher price in the black market. Kerosene was not distributed to households eligible for LPG, thus the poorer households were forced to switch to fuel wood taken from cropfields and barren land in the village. Other interventions like the fencing of crop fields and construction of check dams and ponds also benefitted the landholding class in the village. The marginalized sub-groups, however, got indirect benefits through increased labour opportunities.

Mandoranan's villagers were strictly prohibited from collecting any NTFP from the neighbouring protected Gir National Forest, thus there was no contribution of the NTFP to the village economy. Out of the 50 households surveyed, however, seven had members who worked for the FD in the forest in 2009 and earned a total income of ₹16,400, or an average income of ₹2,342.85 per household. The villagers were also not allowed to collect any fodder from the forest since the time of the formation of the EDC. Crop residues and cultivated *jowar* (sorghum) served as fodder for the village livestock.

13. Comparing the Study Villages in MP and Gujarat

A brief comparative profile of all the JFM villages studied is given in Table 6.13; the villages vary in terms of total households ranging from 35 to 500 and forest areas ranging from 200 to over 3,500 ha.

Table 6.13
Profile of the Study Villages

Village Name	State	Year of JFM Initiation	Forest Area (in ha)	No. of Households	Population	Major Groups/Castes
Khumi	MP	1992	1,100	35	196	Gowal, Yadav, Gond
Khatpura	MP	1996	3,568.49	175	778	Korku, Dharoi, Bhil, Jatav (SC), Harijan, Muslim Ahirwar, Thakur
Gurshivehra	MP	2002	622.66	55	250	Gond, Baiga
Jhilmili	MP	1995	404.68	80	350	Patel, Ahirwar, Gond, Rajak (OBC), Deharia
Khatardevi	Gujarat	1998	200	184	1,187	Vasava
Kotra	Gujarat	2000	733	55	250	Bhil (Bamania, Taviad, Tadavi)
Damawas	Gujarat	2003	257	450	3,000	Adivasi (Bhil, Thakker, Banjara), Rabari, Patel
Mandoranan	Gujarat	1999	500	500	4,000	Patel, Maldhari, Harijan, Korhie

Source: Field survey, (2010).

In every village, JFMC has been established for more than a decade. Except for Khatardevi, all the villages were inhabited by a variety of different castes and tribes.

The comparative facts related to key decision makers, overall perceived changes in forest cover by the villagers, and women's participation are given in Table 6.14. While women were represented in all the JFM ECs, they hardly spoke in any of the meetings. Only in Jhilmili did women actively participate in the meetings but they did not have any say in the final decision-making, which was mostly in the hands of the FD staff. The women in Jhilmili were also successfully operating three SHGs in the village that lent money to individual members.

In Khatpura only 66 per cent of the households surveyed were able to tell the mode of appointment of their JFMC president, though according to many of the respondents the election was influenced by the FD. In Khumi, Gurshivehra, Jhilmili, Khatardevi, Kotra and, Damawas, all (100%) the households surveyed were able to tell the mode of appointment of their JFMC President. Almost invariably, all were selected by consensus and without any election. In Mandoranan, only 30 per cent of the households surveyed were able to tell whether their JFMC president had been selected by consensus and without any election.

In the case of Jhilmili, the DFO and the FD ranger said that their degraded forest had been converted to a dense forest primarily because of the efforts of the village community. However, during the FGD, when the villagers were asked about any shortcomings of the JFM programme they became silent and later told us that in the last two years nothing significant had been done by the VFC. No proposal had been implemented nor had any employment been generated except for two forest watch guards paid through the VFC account.

13.1. JFM and Poverty in the Study Villages

The BPL and APL (above poverty line) card distribution in the sample households is presented in Table 6.15. Khumi villagers had around ₹340,000 locked up in community funds but not a single

Table 6.14

Comparing Governance and Economic Contexts in the Study Villages

Issues	Villages in MP					Villages in Gujarat		
	Khumi	Khatpura	Ghursivehra	Jhilmili	Khatardevi	Kotra	Damawas	Mandoranan
JFM governance (decision making for interventions)	Forest department	Forest department	Forest department	Dominant caste (Patel community) and FD	FD and Landholders	NGO (FES)	FD	FD & dominant caste (Patels)
Forest Cover (Assessed using PDM and FGD)	Increase	Decrease	Increase	Increase	Decrease	Increase	crease	Increase
Women's Participation	Low	Low	Low	Moderate	Low	Low	ow	Low
Funds available with JFMC	₹340,000	₹7,500	₹114,000	₹746	₹500	₹15,000	N/A	₹6.60 lakhs
Economic Activity								
Agriculture	Subsistence	Subsistence	Subsistence	Agriculture: Commercial (Patel) / Subsistence (Poor)	Commercial	Subsistence	Commercial (Patel farmers) / Subsistence (Poor)	Commercial (Patel farmers) / Subsistence (Poor)
NTFPs	Tendu, Mahuva, Achar, Aonla, Achar	Tendu, Mahuva, Achar, Gum, Aonla	Sal seeds	Tendu, Mahuva, Achar Bili	Tendu and Bili	Tendu	Tendu, Mahuva, Gum	NA

Forest Employment	Plantation, harvesting	Plantation, pruning	Infrastructure (wells, land levelling, road, pond, canal)	Plantation, pruning	Infrastructure (check dam, roads, well)	Plantation	Plantation and infrastructure (check dam, bore well, fencing of forest land)	Plantation and infrastructure (check dam, road, bridges)
Alternative Livelihood	Migration	Construction; Misc. labour in the region	MGNREGA (2008)/ Migration	Wage labour at crop fields and stone mine	Livestock management	MGNREGA (2008) Migration	Wage labour at crop fields; Misc. labour in the region	Wage labour at crop fields; Migration
Voluntary Labour	Yes (road construction)	Yes (forest fire control)	No	Yes (Forest Protection before JFM)	No	No	No	No

Source: Field survey, (2010).

Table 6.15

Below Poverty Line (BPL) Statistics of Sample Households in the Study Villages (%)

	After JFM Introduced			Before JFM Introduced		
	Below Poverty Line	*Above Poverty Line*	*NA*	*BPL*	*APL*	*NA*
Khumi	88.89%	0%	11.11%	96.29%	0%	3.70%
Khatpura	80%	2%	18%	36%	4%	58%
Gurshivehra	70.45%	13.63%	15.90%	63.63%	15.90%	20.45%
Jhilmili	58%	22%	20%	52%	4%	44%
Khatardevi	66%	10%	24%	76%	0%	24%
Kotra	36%	48%	16%	84%	0%	16%
Damawas	76%	14%	10%	76%	14%	10%
Mandoranan	42%	50%	8%	44%	50%	6%

Source: Field survey, (2010).

Khumi household was above the BPL with the villagers continuing to live a poor and stressed life. The villagers in Kotra were not satisfied with the BPL allocation system of 2004 and believed that the sudden reduction in the number of BPL card holders was not due to any development success or increased income but solely to the new system of BPL card allocations. In both the EDC villages (Gurshivehra and Mandoranan) a segment of the population was poor. Gurshivehra was a forest village deprived of basic facilities including electricity and other alternative livelihood opportunities other than rain-fed agriculture. The village was dependent solely on the FD for its development.

The numbers of landless and landholders and their economic activities covered in the HH survey are given in Tables 6.16 and 6.17. The number of farming households possessing BPL cards and one or more members migrating for some part of the year is also presented. The high percentage of BPL cardholders in the landholders sub-group in most of the villages reflects subsistence agriculture practised in these villages. The very fact that the major economic activity for most of the surveyed households in all the villages was either agriculture or agricultural labour suggests

Table 6.16

Agricultural Households Possessing BPL Cards and Dependent on Involuntary Migration

Village	Landless	Agriculture-related HHs				No. of BPL HHs	No. of HHs practising Migration	HHs Raising Issues in JFMC Meeting
		Land <= 5 Acres	Land <= 10 Acres	Land => 10 Acres	Total			
Khumi	7	16	4	0	20	18	17	9
Khatpura	21	26	3	0	29	19	13	8
Ghursivehra	1	37	6		3	31	17	13
Jhilmili	24	23	1	2	6	1	8	9
Khatardevi	20	27	3	0	30	22	8	7
Kotra	0	50	0	0	50	8	31	3
Damawas	4	41	0	5	46	35	12	0
Mandoranan	45	5	0	0	5	1	2	4

Source: Field survey, (2010).

Notes: A distinction is drawn between involuntary and voluntary migration. When migration is a consequence of economic or social stress, it is involuntary. When migration happens for improving economic opportunities, it is considered voluntary.

Table 6.17

Number of Households Involved in Various Economic Activities in the Study Villages

Economic Activity	Khumi		Khatpura		Ghursivehra		Jhilmili		Khatardevi		Kotra		Damawas		Mandoranan	
	M	S	M	S	M	S	M	S	M	S	M	S	M	S	M	S
Agriculture	17	3	15	16	35	8	11	10	22	7	36	13	12	32	3	1
Agri and Wage labour	7	16	7	18	9	29	31	18	13	10	12	34	36	6	34	3
Migration	2	7	0	0	0	0	0	7	7	4	1	3	0	0	4	6
Milk Selling	0	0	0	0	0	0	0	0	4	23	0	0	0	0	0	0
Construction labour	0	0	25	0	0	0	0	0	0	0	0	0	0	0	0	0
Other*	1	0	3	10	0	5	8	3	4	3	1	0	2	2	9	4

Source: Field survey, (2010).

Note: * The other economic activities reported were forest watcher/watchmen, cattle grazing, anganwadi worker, NTFP collection, shopkeeper, vendor, old age pension and service outside village e.g, in army, private firms, etc.

Table 6.18

Average Income from the Sale of Milk in JFM Villages

Village	Livestock	Total Milk Produced Per Day for Sale (litres)	Price Per Litre (₹)	Total Direct Income	No. of HH Selling Milk	Average Income Per Household Per Day	Average Monthly Income
Khatardevi	Cow	45	15	675	14	₹48.2	₹1,446.43
	Buffalo	101	22	2,222	27	₹82.3	₹2,468.89
Damawas	Cow	52	15	780	15	₹52	₹1,560
	Buffalo	28	22	616	10	₹61.6	₹1,848
Mandoranan	Cow	7	17	119	3	₹39.67	₹1,190
	Buffalo	9	22	198	3	₹66	₹1,980

Source: Field survey, (2010).

that the communities were highly vulnerable to risks related to agriculture and lacked any alternative for consistent income in the village.

As Table 6.18 shows, income from selling milk only happened in the Gujarat villages. Khatardevi was the only village where this dairy activity played an important role in the overall village economy and where almost all households were involved. In the other villages, a majority of the livestock was unproductive and although bullocks were employed in the crop fields, the milk was consumed within the households and no household sold its milk in the market. In Damawas, where there was little dairy activity, the landless members of the village community generally did not take the livestock loan and were dependent on wage labour for their livelihood.

13.2. Governance and the Decision-Making Systems

By design, a JFM committee is a two-tiered institution. The leadership consists of the President, the Secretary and the EC. The second tier is the general body comprising all members of the village community. This generally includes members from all the families residing in the village at the time of initiation of the JFM committee in the village. JFMC members are intended to meet to develop a village micro-plan, to discuss development issues specific to their village and to draft proposals with the help of the village beat guard who submits the proposals to the FD for its execution.

The de jure objective was first, to decentralize decision making to the JFMC as an institution that would ensure the local community was being listened to and there was an equitable distribution of benefits. Second, community members would become responsible for protecting their forests from fires and illicit felling. Developing a feeling of forest ownership was intended to motivate communities to participate in the protection and management activities as equal partners with the FD. During the FGDs and at the household level, villagers in Khumi, Jhilmili and Kotra demonstrated a strong spirit of ownership of the forest under JFM, largely due to an exceptional JFM implementation experience. This could be attributed to the presence of a dedicated DFO (Khumi), an NGO (FES in Kotra), strong leadership and a dedicated beat guard (Jhilmili) during the implementation of JFM in these villages. Other villages also mentioned the ownership they felt at the time of the initiation of JFM, but in practice they had seen that their JFMC and forests were controlled by the FD.

Village-specific proposals had been identified in the micro plan documents and certain proposals had been implemented under JFM. They included proposals such as construction of irrigation facilities, land leveling, provision of credit at low interest rates and the distribution of productive cattle. However, the FD had the final authority to approve and implement any proposal in the village. The pace of implementation of proposals was regarded as slow everywhere, retarding the pace of overall village development. In villages like Khumi, the proposals had been pending for so long that it had broken the spirit of community participation. Several instances of inequitable distribution of benefits had raised questions over who was maximizing the benefits of the existing JFM institutions in village development.

In all eight JFMCs included in this study, the power to frame proposals remained in the hands of the FD-appointed beat guard who was the ex-officio member secretary. If the beat guard was not present in a JFMC meeting, the members could not frame proposals.

In effect, despite the participatory management regime, the village community was dependent on the FD staff for all interventions.

The general body membership was open to all adult members in the village. The EC comprised of representatives of all the castes or tribes, and women were also represented in the committee. The president of the JFMC was elected for five years. For an ordinary member, the scope for direct action was limited to the GBM that occurred twice or thrice in a year. The monthly EC meeting was the key event that addressed issues related to decision making and administrative action at the community level. However, in all the JFMCs studied, it was found that the GBM as well as the EC meetings were not conducted at specified intervals. According to the HHS results, attendance varied greatly. In some cases, we were told that except for a few elites of the village community and a few other individuals, nobody came to the meetings. Table 6.19 shows the variations in villager responses to questions about their attendance and participation in meetings.

Deficiencies also appeared when social sub group and gender representation was considered. Although there usually were women members in the ECs, they either did not attend or remained silent

Table 6.19

Household Participation in JFMC Meetings and Activities (%)

Village	Regularly Attending Meetings	Ever Involved in JFM Activities	Present in First Ever Meeting of JFMC	Ever Raised Any Issues in the JFM Meetings
Madhya Pradesh				
Khumi (FPC)	92.60%	74%	55.50%	33.33%
Khatpura (FPC)	24%	70%	34%	26%
Gurshivehra (EDC)	50%	95.50%	70.50%	29.55%
Jhilmili (VFC)	78%	84%	72%	18%
Gujarat				
Khatardevi (JFMC)	34%	68%	60%	14%
Kotra (JFMC)	50%	96%	84%	6%
Damawas (JFMC)	20%	58%	44%	0%
Mandoranan EDC	10%	10%	26%	8%

Source: Field survey, (2010).
Note: Percentage indicates 'Yes' answers.

throughout the meetings. Every JFMC as per its constitutional requirements had formal provisions for members from all the sub groups in the village to be represented on the EC. In Jhilmili and Mandoranan some sub groups complained about the dominance of the Patel community, which controlled JFMC decision making. On the other hand, in Damawas, the Patel community absented itself from JFMC activities altogether.

When contacted at the individual household level, only a few individuals claimed to have raised a proposal or issue in the meetings. Awareness regarding the minutes of the JFMC meetings and the JFM accounts was also found to range from very good to very poor amongst the study villages, as Tables 6.20 and 6.21 make clear.

13.3. Enhancement Strategies

To meet the demand for funds, innovative strategies could include: linking JFM with the Payment for Ecosystem Services tool and other market instruments for biodiversity conservation, payment for carbon sequestration, ecotourism and watershed protection as well as other ecosystem goods and services provided by the forests at global, national and regional levels thereby creating new

Table 6.20

Awareness of the JFM Programme in the Sample JFMCs of MP

Village	Khumi	Khatpura	Gurshivehra	Jhilmili
JFM Programme	FPC	FPC	EDC	VFC
Know that JFM accounts were handled by the beat guard	88.89%	20%	54.54%	78%
Know that JFM meetings minutes were written by the beat guard	100%	38%	56.81%	82%
Know whether minutes and accounts were available for members to review	96%	38%	25%	84%
Ever sought information regarding JFM funds	29.62%	2%	11.36%	0%

Source: Field survey, (2010).

Table 6.21

Awareness of the JFM Programme in the Sample JFMCs of Gujarat

	Khatardevi	Kotra	Damawas	Mandoranan
	(JFMC)	(JFMC)	(JFMC)	(EDC)
Know that JFM accounts were handled by the beat guard	66%	74%	42%	32%
Know that JFM meetings minutes were written by the beat guard	66%	74%	42%	32%
Know whether minutes and accounts are available for members to review	52%	54%	42%	30%
Ever sought information regarding JFM funds	0%	0%	4%	4%

Source: Field survey, (2010).

opportunities for JFMC incomes.[9] These along with long term development planning could contribute to livelihood improvements and socio-economic welfare of participating community members, who otherwise are not adequately compensated for protecting the forests that are supposedly providing global services.

Some possible interventions that could be facilitated by conservation funds might include: (a) constitution of a village level credit society to lend low interest loans to JFMC members; (b) part transfer of funding from international and national conservation projects to individual households as direct incomes or virtual cash crop traded under the ecosystem goods and services markets and (c) creation of village infrastructure like cemented roads and bridges, community centres or water pipelines.

The presence of an NGO or an active DFO in specific villages has led to improved communication and overall better coordination between forest protection and implementing proposals for village development. Increased interaction between FD officials (DFO and higher ranks) and communities also provides additional incentives for members to attend meetings and participate in JFM activities. Further, involvement of higher officials could also speed up the

[9] For further information on enhancement strategies see Kumar and Thiaw 2013.

pace of proposals being implemented and improved awareness of issues related to forest management.

The effective implementation of JFM under the proposed enhancement strategy would be an effective incentive for communities to become involved in conservation. Thus far, the focus had been on overall village development, and the JFM institution had not effectively included all of the households. Decision making remained with the FD staff and in some cases the elite members of the village. Most members did not perceive any direct benefits and many of them were either not aware or did not enquire about the status of various JFMC decisions. Increasing their incentives in the form of direct incomes, a credit facility and more attention and meeting with higher officials would certainly provide a catalytic effect in increasing community participation in JFMC decision making. A combination of incentives and monitoring along with proper communication of a forest conservation agenda could also mobilize communities to work towards improving forest health and productivity through assisted natural regeneration and forest protection activities.

Enhanced JFM outcomes can be measured on the parameters of equity, efficiency, community satisfaction and sustainability of the resource. Table 6.22 provides a list of performance indicators for measuring such improved outcomes.

Table 6.22

Indicators for Measuring Enhanced JFM Performance

Value	Performance Indicators
Equity	• Role of community in forest management • Usufruct rights and distribution of benefits • Membership criteria in JFM committee
Efficiency	• Collective decision making and household representation in JFM • Compliance with Rules • Status of Proposals drafted by JFMC
Satisfaction	• Contribution of JFM to village development • Employment opportunities in the village
Sustainable Forest Conservation	• Forest Protection from clear felling and grazing • Regeneration of degraded forest area • Plantation activity

Source: Author's own.

14. Answers to Comparative Questions

1. At the village level, how was the CNRM project and institution introduced?

After the promulgation of the JFM Mandate in MP, 14,428 VFCs, including 9,137 VFCs, 4,470 FPCs and 821 EDCs were constituted (JFM, 2011). This was largely a 'top-down' procedure carried out by FD officials, although during study we discovered in Jhilmili a case where the villagers had earlier taken forest protection into their own hands and had later applied to the FD to become part of the JFM programme. At the start of the MP programme, there were some forest officers who were dedicated to the JFM idea, such as the one in Harda District who made Khumi a model of community forest management. Unfortunately, he was soon transferred from the division and real community participatory management came to a halt.

In Gujarat, efforts by the FD to protect forests resulted in conflicts with local communities and damage to forest resources. This data is based on an interview with NGO informants in 2010. Thus, efforts to involve local people in the protection and regeneration of forests based on the principle of care and usufruct benefits were initiated in south Gujarat in 1986–87, especially in the Vyara and Rajpipla forest divisions. In Gujarat, the introduction of JFM was more bottom-up, with NGOs like the AKRSP playing a prominent role in village implementation (Iyengar and Hirway, 2001: 330–38). In general, in the early days of JFM, the results were encouraging not only in the protection and regeneration of forest resources but also in reducing the conflicts between the locals and FD personnel.

2. How did the project and institution perform, both de jure and de facto, in terms of the CNRM goals?

JFM seems to have taken the shape of an incentive-driven mechanism rather than a programme creating self-reliant institution with a feeling of ownership and responsibility for resource management among village communities. Villagers responded to direct benefits such as jobs in the forest or for permission to collect NTFPs. Most incentives such as support for the conversion to agriculture or animal husbandry or training in new skills were accepted, but not because the villagers had any choice. The entire initiative and control belonged to the FD.

When asked about possible steps to improve the working of JFM, most of our respondents were not able to give us any response. A majority of those who did respond (which was a small number) emphasized the development of infrastructure to suit their own needs and some demanded access to individual benefits such as the digging of wells near their homes. There was more community spirit in Khumi but that was because their community members were aware of funds lying unspent in the JFMC account. The Khumi villagers proposed use of funds for construction of houses and securing electricity connections for irrigation. The longer that their proposals lay pending at the divisional forest office, the more they lost interest in JFM activities. The villagers in Khatpura lost all interest in JFM activities due to the availability of regular wage labour at the Narmada pipeline construction site near the village. The FD at the time of the survey was finding it difficult to gather the villagers for extinguishing forest fires or for other work inside the forest. In Damawas, Khatardevi and Mandoranan, very few community members regularly attended meetings. With ample agricultural labour work available nearby on large crop fields, attending these meetings came at a high opportunity cost in terms of foregone wages for the day. This tendency suggested that JFM communities may not have been interested in forest resource management without any direct financial incentives provided to them. Moreover, these incentives would also have to be high enough to compensate their existing socio-economic activities.

3. What was the extent of productivity and income increase?

The objective of the JFM programme was less to increase productivity and incomes and more to increase forest cover, and according to PDM results, the latter was achieved in six out of the eight villages studied. Villagers cited new awareness of the importance of their forest as the most important reason, followed by FD and JFMC efforts. In the two villages (Khatpura, MP and Khatardevi, Gujarat) where respondents indicated a decrease in forest cover, FD negligence and illicit felling were cited as the main causes of the same.

Where the JFM programme was found to be protecting the forest resources well, the FD was blunt about its determination to strictly regulate (in the case of NTFP harvesting) or bar (in the EDC cases) villager access to the forest. From the villagers point of view, FD efforts at providing alternate means for producing energy (e.g., bio-gas plants) or earning a livelihood (farming or animal husbandry) or training for a new skill (e.g., tailoring) had been less than successful. The ultimate reason was the villagers' lack of decision-making control. Meanwhile, the lack of a cordial relationship between the community and the FD resulted in poor sense of stewardship amongst the community which in turn led to deterioration of the forest itself.

4. How decentralized and inclusive was the governance of the CNRM institution?

In both states, the FDs have been reluctant to decentralize any control over forest management to JFMCs and the latter, under the 'guidance' of the beat guards, have neither administrative, fiscal nor political autonomy. In several cases, it was found that even JFMC meetings could not be called without the beat guard's approval. The centralizing trend is a reversal of what started as local initiative-taking. In Jhilmili, the villagers were so enthusiastic about forest protection that the initiative for joining the JFM programme was theirs. They were proud of their accomplishment of regenerating a previously degraded forest, but privately many had confided that there had been no JFM activity for two years. In Kotra awareness regarding benefits of forest conservation began with the help of an NGO but even then only half of the respondents interviewed claimed to be regular in attending JFMC meetings and only 6 per cent had raised any issues in such meetings. The small proportion of respondents who engaged in raising issues in all the study villages indicates that forest governance has not changed much and communities have been only involved in employment generation activities under JFM.

5. What has been the impact on the poor members of the village?

On the issue of equitable distribution of benefits under JFM, the Khatardevi villagers complained that a majority of JFM interventions had benefitted the landholding group, thereby increasing the economic gap between the landless and landholders in the village. All the JFM interventions in the village such as the provision of a borewell, pipes for irrigation, the distribution of livestock to select households and provision of *pucca* houses to three families had benefited the landholders. Similarly, several respondents in Jhilmili took pride in the regeneration of their forest due to the community's collective efforts but resented JFMC decisions which they considered biased. For example, proposals before the JFMC such as the construction of a pond were rejected by the dominant landowning group, who feared the diversion of labour from their crop fields. Significantly, the JFMC was instead considering the construction of a warehouse for storing agricultural produce.

Similarly, in Mandoranan interventions such as the distribution of LPG cylinders were intended to benefit more than 250 out of the 350 households but they were used by very few households as the majority could not afford the initial 25 per cent payment for availing the LPG, nor pay for LPG operational expenses. In contrast to Jhilmili and Mandoranan, however, in the larger village of Damawas, the elite group absented themselves from JFMC activities because there were few economic benefits to be gained and labour availability was not a problem.

6. How integrated was the project intervention and what was the extent of the outreach?

JFM project interventions were invariably FD-controlled and focussed primarily on protecting and extending forest cover, not only by fencing and patrolling existing stock but by regenerating degraded land, planting new trees or constructing check dams. But since the overall FD objective was to reduce the dependency of villagers on forests and to limit or bar their access to forest products, numerous other interventions were undertaken. In EDC villages such as Gurshivehra (MP) where former forest dwellers were being transformed into farmers, the FD undertook land levelling and well digging. A bio-gas unit was installed and solar cookers were distributed. The project was integrated and the outreach extensive, but the villagers, still impoverished following their eviction from their homes in the Kanha National Park, had many unfulfilled needs. Totally dependent on FD handouts, perhaps their greatest need was to regain control over their own livelihoods.

7. How had the project and institution contributed to effective, equitable and sustainable resource management?

The literature on JFM and discussions with many JFM stakeholders suggest that the institutional mechanism that is., the JFMC, had been an influential factor in achieving its deliverables. In reality, however, the impact of JFM has been both positive and negative, depending on the project and the stakeholder interviewed. Positive evidence which varied by stakeholder, includes: (a) an increase in forest cover and the availability of fuel wood, (b) motivation to raise issues and resolve conflicts by members, (c) equitable distribution of benefits among members of the JFMC, (d) capacity to carry out proper harvesting, value addition and marketing of forest produce, (e) maintenance of financial transparency in financial matters, (f) regular meeting and management decision-making through consensus of all members, (g) support by the FD to the JFMC in the management of the forest, resolving conflicts and the extraction, transportation and sale of forest produce, (h) preparation of micro plans and their implementation by the community, (i) capacity to conduct meetings, writing of minutes, maintaining records by the JFMC and (j) generation of adequate employment in the village to reduce rural to urban migration.

As against the above perceived gains, there was also evidence that varied by stakeholders, that the desired outcome of JFM could not be attained due to constraints such as: (a) inadequate consultation of the FD with stakeholders, (b) government-driven projects and target-oriented projects instead of people-oriented projects, (c) lack of transparency in decision-making, (d) lack of regular GBMs and follow-up action, (e) lack of awareness among the majority of JFM members about future yields, income and their share, (f) inadequate involvement of women, (g) lack of training and skill building to manage the forest, (h) unresolved conflicts with neighbouring villagers dependent on the same patch of forest, (i) improper boundary demarcations leading to inter-village and intra-village conflicts, (j) lack of alternative sources of livelihood for forest-dependent communities, (k) poor marketing of forest produce, (l) inadequate funding and investment in projects and (m) lack of effective communication, publicity and incentives.

15. Conclusion: The Way Forward

When asked about the possible steps to improve the working of JFM, most of the respondents said they wanted JFM to continue, but were not able to give any suggestions for change. A majority of those who did respond called for the development of village infrastructure to suit only their own needs. The case of Khumi was unique because the community members were aware of unspent JFMC funds and were demanding constructed houses and an electricity connection, but Khumi's community spirit was seen to be dwindling and many members had lost interest in JFM activities. The villagers in Khatpura had also lost all interest in JFM activities due to wage labour opportunities available at the construction site near the village. The FD found it difficult to gather Khatpura villagers for extinguishing forest fires in the region and other work inside the forest requiring human labour.

While it was clear that proper awareness had not been developed regarding the JFM objectives of decentralized management and ownership of forest resources, another school of thought suggested that villagers were indifferent to JFM simply because they have not yet received their fair share of benefits under the JFM intervention. Thus future policymakers need to ensure that sustainable livelihood interventions need to be accompanied by communication on the local project's benefits and the importance of forest conservation.

This study aims to provide feedback to policymakers, analysts and practitioners on issues related to community involvement in the administrative, fiscal and decision making aspects of JFM institutions. The decentralized management anticipated for JFM in the National Forest Policy of 1988 has not materialized and the key institution, the JFMC, has been marked by low participation of forest community members, especially those from marginalized sub-groups such as women, backward castes/groups and the landless. In most project villages their participation in meetings has been weak and they have shown poor awareness regarding the minutes and funds managed by the JFMC president and secretary.

In some villages the forest has actually been further degraded despite the constitution of a JFMC. At the time of this study, JFM seemed to be losing focus with many committees becoming inactive. There was a need to reorganize them, release funds for JFM activities, implement existing proposals and organize regular meetings between FD officials and community members. Allocating a fixed percentage of JFMC funds to implement proposals for marginalized sub-groups could have possibly countered the dominance of powerful sub-groups and increased the stake of the marginalized in the functioning of JFMC in their village.

In the case of Khumi village, the funds derived from timber harvesting were shared between the FD and the JFMC, but the inaccessibility of these funds to reduce poverty through the creation of alternative livelihood opportunities violated JFM principles and led to a decline in the interest of community members to participate in conservation efforts. Direct monitoring and active involvement of FD higher officials, that is, the Chief Conservator of Forests (CCF) and the Additional Principal Chief Conservator of Forests (APCCF), is likely to motivate lower level staff of FD to put to use the community funds, currently locked up for activities proposed by Khumi JFMC.

The presence of an NGO as seen in the case of Kotra village had led to improved communication and overall better coordination between forest protection and implementing proposals for village development. This suggests that greater involvement of NGOs specializing in CNRM projects could produce better results. The increased communication that NGOs could facilitate between FD officials and communities may very well provide additional incentive for JFMC members to attend meetings and participate in JFM activities.

Finally, JFM villages and especially the EDCs in protected areas could be considered as platforms for compensating local communities involved in the protection and conservation of areas of high ecological importance. Also, taking a cue from the Mexican example (which shows that community forest enterprises could be economically profitable and yet maintain forest cover in the area at rates similar to protected areas),[10] provisioning of skill up-grading and capacity building for forest-based micro-enterprises in the villages (e.g., Khumi, Kotra, Damawas, Jhilmili) where dense forests managed under JFM could lead to sustainable income opportunities through forest management.

In all the villages, subsistence agriculture and agricultural labour were the major economic activities, thus several proposals were centered on improving agricultural productivity. In this regard, interventions such as renting irrigation equipment (diesel pumps, pipes, etc.) at subsidized rates and carrying out land leveling and fencing work in the crop fields could become standardized tasks taken up by JFMCs. These interventions could provide increased benefits to a majority of community members through increased agricultural productivity and protection of crops from wildlife. They also could be earned by the beneficiaries as payment for

---

[10] See Bray and Perez (2002).

their active involvement in forest protection. Money channelized through global conservation markets as well as through the national conservation regime can provide regular incentives to EDCs. These funds can be directly provided as cash rewards or in the form of development initiatives such as better provisioning of schools, strengthening of health centres, providing drinking water or constructing roads and community centres. If the poor members of India's forest communities can become involved in these kinds of work and receive its benefits through a more decentralized JFM, they will be more likely to associate strongly with forest management through the JFM regime in perpetuity.

7

Conclusion: Comparing CNRM Institutions and Their Impact on Poverty in Gujarat and Madhya Pradesh

John R. Wood

The previous four chapters have investigated in considerable detail, four of India's most important programmes in community natural resource programmes as they operated in Gujarat and MP during our research in 2008–10. Despite the change in government in 2012, their operation continues more or less the same way. The studies on PIM, IFCs, Watershed Development and JFM amply demonstrate the challenges involved in intervening in the socio-economic complexity of rural India with new programmes and new institutions. They further demonstrate the difficulties—conceptual, programmatic and analytical—faced in dealing with poverty in India. The studies bring forth a variety of cases where the CNRM shows positive results, both in terms of productivity increases, energetic self-governance and benefits for the poor. They also reveal how programme design flaws, implementation failures, resistance to change and lack of capacity building have defeated many of the CNRM's objectives. What remains is to comparatively assess the performance of the four programmes in Gujarat and MP in terms of the effectiveness of their resource management and impact on rural poverty, and to analyze the ingredients of both their success and their failure.

In reviewing the results of the research presented here, it is well to remember that there were several special features in our approach to this study. First, although each specialist studied and wrote about a particular programme, each also studied the central problems of institutional performance and the impact on poverty as a team with a common agenda of theoretical interests and analytical questions. Second, rather than study a scattering of cases across India, we focused on two states, Gujarat and MP, so that we could investigate patterns of CNRM programme implementation and performance in a comparative perspective, both resource-wise and state-wise. And third, while we learned about the programmes from all possible sources of information—governmental, NGO, donor, academic—we gave priority to our own field investigation. We wanted to study CNRM projects inductively, on the ground in real villages, and to learn from the real end-users whom we considered the most important stakeholders in CNRM.

At the outset of Chapter 1, while we listed the similarities shared by the four CNRM programmes, increasing familiarity with their implementation and performance has further revealed a number of significant differences between them as well. It is important to understand these, as they will qualify any generalizations we can make about CNRM institutions and their impact on poverty. Some may find it inappropriate or unfair to dwell on the differences, for the resources vary in their nature and potential and the four programmes in their goals and strategies. Yet that is what is valuable about such comparisons: it forces us to think about why similarities and differences exist, and to ask why and how the success of strategy 'A' might or might not be copied and the failure of strategy 'B' might or might not be avoided.

In order to carry out a comparison of the four CNRM programmes and institutions, on the one hand, and their impact on poverty, on the other, we refer back to the initial seven questions each author was asked to answer regarding the villages he/she studied:

1. At the village level, how was the CNRM project and institution introduced?
2. How did the project and institution perform, both de jure and de facto, in terms of CNRM goals?
3. What was the extent of productivity and income increase?

4. How decentralized and inclusive was the governance of the CNRM institution?
5. What had been the impact on the poor members of the village?
6. How integrated was the project intervention and what had been the extent of the outreach?
7. How had the project and institution contributed to effective, equitable and sustainable resource management?

In this first of two concluding chapters, we will review comparatively the answers to these questions for each of the four resource management programmes presented in Chapters 3–6. Then in Chapter 8, we will engage in a critique that suggests needed policy changes and a way forward for CNRM in Gujarat and MP.

1. At the village level, how were the CNRM projects and institutions introduced?

This question focuses on how the CNRM process of decentralizing control over resource management to a community of end-users began and how the institution that would govern it was established. It breaks down into several other questions. First, who were regarded as members of 'the community'? Did the CNRM institutional membership extend to all villagers, or were there de jure or de facto exclusions? Second, was the decentralization to be carried out by legislation, or simply by an administrative directive? The de jure provisions in the rules and regulations of a new CNRM project needed to reveal the decentralizing intentions of the government, define rights and procedures and tell members how much decision-making autonomy they could expect.

Third, was the control that was decentralized simply administrative, or did it include more significant fiscal and political responsibilities? Across the four kinds of resource management studied here, we have seen repeatedly that the more significant the responsibilities that were devolved, the greater the interest and participation was aroused in the community. Fourth, what was the CNRM PIA and to whom in the village did the PIA's agents introduce the project? This involved the pivotal questions of whether, and how the government or an NGO took charge of introducing the project. Which villagers were informed about the rights and responsibilities that accompanied decentralization? Were motivation and capacity-building provided?

Fifth, what kind of institution was created to receive the decentralized resource management control? What offices were created, and were they filled using democratic procedures? Were there institutional rules that ensured transparency and accountability? How autonomous would the institution be from elite capture or outside pressures?

Each of our authors has shown how the answers to these questions on the CNRM project's introduction are keys to determining the CNRM institution's performance in the longer run and who would receive how much of the CNRM project's benefits. More often than not, where the CNRM has failed, the problem can be traced back to an institutional design defect or a flawed beginning.

First, with regard to membership of and participation in the CNRM institution, WDP and JFM projects are designed de jure as CPR projects involving all community members—in WDP projects defined by the geography of a watershed, while in JFM projects defined by the nature of a forest and the relationship a community has with it. However, in the case of WDP projects, despite the CPR rhetoric, the landless are de facto often excluded from the benefits of the project and have little incentive to participate. In the case of JFM projects, since the whole community is restricted or altogether excluded in its access to the common resource, the forest, membership in the JFMC results in few, strictly regulated benefits. In both WDP and JFM projects, however, limited labour opportunities (e.g., construction of check dam policing of forests) may occur.

PIM is not a CPR project, as WUA membership is restricted to those who use irrigation water, that is, landowners who pay joining fees and water rates. In the case of FCs, only FC members are legally eligible to fish in the reservoirs. In addition, Ukai FC membership is restricted to ST oustees, that is, those displaced by the reservoir construction. These exclusions result in extensive illegal fishing in the Ukai reservoir, where policing is inadequate.

In the case of PIM, MP's rapid legislative approach to introducing PIM led to the top-down control of decision-making that stultified participation by end-users. Not only fiscal and political but even administrative initiative was kept beyond the reach of MP WUAs by placing an ID sub-engineer in the WUA's most powerful executive position. Meanwhile, in Gujarat, the bottom-up approach carried out prior to the enactment of PIM legislation, created better opportunities for WUAs to take up administrative, operational and maintenance functions and in some cases fiscal initiatives. Significantly, the best productivity and redistribution successes in both states occurred where NGOs led the PIM introduction process, a subject to which we will return.

In the case of FCs, the MP government placed control of local fishing management in the hands of a contractor, leaving only minimal administrative functions for the FC EC. The FCs of Gandhi Sagar reservoir not only lack control over marketing and the price received for their catch, but are forced to sell their fish only to the contractor. In Gujarat, the FCs of the Ukai reservoir are also forced to sell their fish to a contractor, albeit because the government sets a fishing lease's price so high that they have to give up control to a contractor who will pay for it in return for exclusive control over all fish caught. Institutional decision-making autonomy is impossible for the FCs under such circumstances, in both states.

With reference to the question of the role of PIA, there were some marked contrasts across both the states and resource management programmes. In the FC programme, the Department played a dominant role in introducing the projects at the village level. In neither Gujarat nor MP, were NGOs invited to cooperate with the government in implementing FCs. That left the introduction of FCs in the hands of the Department officials whose sole concern was the fishery's revenue potential. A pathetic lack of interest and initiative among FC members ensued in both states—in Gujarat because of governmental negligence in curbing illegal fishing practices, and in MP because the decision-making control remained in the hands of self-interested contractors working for the government.

In the case of JFM in Gujarat, NGOs, especially the AKRSP, originally played a significant role in introducing JFM and persuading villagers to participate in forest protection and the regeneration of degraded forests. In MP (and eventually in Gujarat, although the NGO FES in Kotra village was an impressive exception), NGO involvement weakened due to FD indifference and delay tactics. The only hope for village participation lay in projects initiated by the few forest officers who took a sincere interest in JFM. The FDs in both states looked upon JFM principally as a means to limit villagers' access to the forest and to extend forest cover. This conflicted with villagers' expectations of NTFP, fuel wood or grazing access for cattle. With forest beat guards as the controllers of records and financial matters on JFM committees in both states, JFM was structured to fail as a CNRM institution.

2. How did the project and institution perform, both de jure and de facto, in terms of CNRM goals?

It has already been demonstrated that the performance of CNRM institutions was strongly determined by the nature of their design and introduction. Once the CNRM project was underway, however, further factors emerged that affected their performance. First, how the new CNRM institution performed in relation to CNRM goals could be gauged by the quality of its governance. Ideally this would have meant that the CNRM institution operated democratically, that is: (a) its officials and executive body were elected through periodic elections; (b) they were responsible and accountable to the membership; (c) all of their transactions and accounts were transparent, so that both executives and members could make and implement informed, collective decisions and (d) adherence by officials and members to collectively agreed rules was ensured by appropriate sanctions devised by the membership.

Only a few of the CNRM institutions described in the snapshots of each study village came close to such a standard. Out of the 30 CNRM institutions studied only five had democratically elected executives while most were 'selected' with little or no competition. Our research discovered a variety of factors that affected the democratic/non-democratic governance in CNRM institutions: the nature of the village leadership that steered the project; how the social composition of the membership affected participation in CNRM activities; attitudes regarding inclusiveness of marginalized groups, especially women, and the nature of the PIA's commitment to good governance and capacity-building support. On the latter point, it is worth noting that where the government was the PIA, the officials involved usually preferred selection of executive members, perhaps because doing so gave them greater control.

Some examples drawn from the case studies should suffice to illustrate these factors. In the PIM village of Kiyadar in Gujarat, two men, Haribhai and Jesing Choudhary had managed to implement the PIM programme so well that its institutionalization could be regarded as irreversible. In the JFM village of Jhilmili in MP, a more collective kind of leadership by the larger Patel landowners was instrumental in undertaking numerous forest-protection initiatives even before the JFM programme commenced—in fact, it was the Jhilmili leaders who approached the FD asking to take part in the programme. The key in both cases lies in the ability of the leaders to take initiatives, to inspire trust and produce results. In the case of Kiyadar, they were also able to institutionalize robust democratic decision-making practices.

In all CNRM villages, one might have expected that social homogeneity would have made for an easier task of uniting members behind common goals, while social heterogeneity might have led to friction among both members and executives. In fact, some of the most successful CNRM cases occurred where social heterogeneity was the most extensive—for example, Valuna in the case of the WDP, or Kiyadar in the case of PIM. Meanwhile, social homogeneity was no guarantee of success in the WDP case of Kalakhunt or the JFM case of Khatardevi. What seemed to matter more was a history of cooperation amongst the village social groups on which the new programme could be built. There were several examples in Gujarat where dairy or credit cooperatives provided such training. In the FCs of both states, meanwhile, fishermen joined primarily because of the benefits offered and neither social homogeneity nor heterogeneity had had any effect on the unity or otherwise of the FCs.

3. What was the extent of productivity or income increase?

Measuring, with confidence, any increase or decrease in productivity and/or income resulting from CNRM turned out to be the most difficult of the MDG Project's challenges. With no reliable benchmark data available for the pre-CNRM years in a given village, we had to ask villagers to remember whatever they could of the amounts grown or cut or caught and the prices paid or received for production and harvest. It soon became obvious that this was leading to considerable guessing at, and fabrication of numbers. We even found our own field investigators trying to help villagers with the invention of numbers so as not to return from the field with empty blanks in the survey questionnaires.

Whatever the numbers given, we had no objective way to verify them. In the case of JFM, fearing that illiteracy was a problem, researchers resorted to a method of pebble distribution. In the case of PIM it seemed that FGDs, where a number of villagers could compare estimates and recall prices collectively, would produce more reliable data. In the end, with each of the four partners given the latitude to collect data as he/she saw fit, there was inevitably a varying margin of error.

Another major problem arose as we began to analyze the impact of CNRM institutions on productivity and income: the problem of attribution. How could it be proved that the CNRM programme and institution at the village level was the cause of an increase in productivity or income when many other influencing factors were also present? Such factors could range from the extent of rainfall to the amount of fertilizer used, or the vagaries of the market for the crop or fish catch or forest produce. For some household members, alternative employment opportunities were available, for example, through anti-poverty programmes such as MNEGRA. In some villages situated near cities or towns (e.g., in the cases of the PIM village Kanipur or the WDP village Jamsar), or rural construction sites (in the case of the JFM in village Khatpura), household income increases were attributable to external employment opportunities. In several FC and JFM villages, household income from forest or fishing work was less important than that from agricultural labour.

Still, the introduction of CNRM can be shown to be the decisive change that improved productivity and income in several locations and in several ways. First, in PIM villages where the WUA took the decision to distribute irrigation water to the tail section (in the best cases, distributing it there *first*), the expansion of irrigated area clearly was the direct cause of productivity and income increases. In WDP villages, where groundwater recharge and soil moisture retention dramatically improved after project interventions, it created a powerful argument that the productivity increases were due primarily to the WDP interventions. Amita Shah's finding that 92 per cent of her respondents, in eight different villages spread across two states, reported that their incomes increased after their village's WDP intervention, suggests strongly that however many other factors contributed to the increases, WDP interventions deserved major credit. Similarly, Madhu Verma's statistics on the expansion of forest cover after the implementation of JFM strongly suggests that JFM protection and rehabilitation strategies were having an effect.

Then there were the indirect effects, where, for example, increases in irrigation due to PIM or WDP projects caused productivity increases that required more labour for crop harvesting, and consequently a rise in wages for agricultural labourers. These indirectly benefitted the poor, as Shashidharan Enarth has argued. He also cites a further indirect benefit in some PIM villages (e.g., Chopadvav and Dagarkot), where migration reduced when CNRM-induced productivity increases created a demand for more household labour. Other indirect effects included the spinoffs from WDP or JFM SHGs' microfinance efforts, and in general the increase in purchasing power resulting from enhanced incomes.

4. How decentralized and inclusive was the governance of the CNRM institution?

A great deal of the analysis of the four CNRM programmes studied here reveals a resistance to decentralization on the part of NRM government departments and officials. In the case of the JFM and FC programmes, the Forestry and Fishery Departments respectively wanted to not only manage but also maximize revenue gains from the sale of the resource. Thus, the autonomy of the community institution was de jure blocked by the departmental control exercised through the beat guard or contractor respectively. The same was true for the PIM programme in MP, where there was no expectation of revenue earning but an ID SE controlled irrigation decision-making as well as records and account books.

The usual stated reasons given for the unwillingness to really decentralize control to the CNRM institution included a lack of confidence in the capacity of the end-users' to manage the resource effectively and the fear that money would be misspent or stolen. Unstated reasons often included bureaucratic officiousness and condescending attitudes towards villagers. But the main reason was that NRM officials were unwilling to dilute their control over decision-making about resources and public money. Moreover, according to numerous end-user complaints, for many officials the bribes and kickbacks extracted from villagers or contractors, respectively, were the overriding concern.

Among the CNRM institutions reviewed here, only two Gujarat and one MP WUA created under the PIM programme seemed to have acquired truly decentralized self-governing capabilities. All three had NGOs as the PIA and had achieved the most in terms of productivity and equity. NGOs had been highly active in both states in the WDP programme, but their roles were circumscribed in several significant ways. First, WDP projects were of short duration, leaving NGOs inadequate time to build WDCs as institutions based on end-user participatory governance. Second, in both states the most critical authority over all WDP projects lay with the DRDA, the government channel through which money passed on to the villages and the barriers where technical approval was to be obtained. The technical protocol set by the DRDA engineers was intimidating for most villagers, especially the landless ones, reinforcing the need for technically-adept NGOs as intermediaries. The problem remained, however, for either NGO or government PIAs to transfer project initiatives to the WDC. The NGOs could be as top-down and controlling as government in this regard.

As Jharna Pathak reports from discussions with FC members, the latter suspected that collusion among government and contractors robbed them of their fair share of CNRM benefits. She describes the MP approach as 'cooperative coercion,' whereby poor fishermen because of their poverty had no alternative to working in a highly exploitative industry in which they had no control over the resource or the terms of their employment. Several of the JFM cases revealed the same 'sham' decentralization: the villagers of Khumi, MP received a share of income from coupe felling, but had not been allowed to spend the money even though it was in their own JFMC account. In Ghurshivehra MP, the villagers who had been evicted from Kanha National Park had no alternative but to receive government help in land levelling and other agricultural improvements through JFM. CNRM meant little if the prescribed measure of decision-making autonomy was not devolved by the government.

Almost inevitably, the result of end-user powerlessness was apathy that could lead to indifference when the resource management rules designed to protect the resource and for sharing the benefits equitably were ignored or flouted. The FCs of the Ukai reservoir provided ample illustration of how FC members behaved when policing was lacking in the reservoir. Illegal fishing by both members and non-members destroyed the credibility of the FC and endangered the resource itself. Similarly in JFM villages, if the end-users saw others violating forest management rules and getting away with it, their morale and self-restraint declined. Thus the ultimate test for governance was, did the new CNRM institution have enough credibility and the community enough sense of ownership of resource management responsibility that members would adopt the new norms regarding their individual and collective behaviour?

5. What has been the impact on the poor members of the village?

It is too easy to conclude that CNRM did not impact poverty, although it was clear that it was not a poverty-reduction programme. While none of the four programmes had the explicitly stated objective of poverty reduction, there was an implicit assumption of equity in the de jure provisions for the formation and operation of the CNRM institutions at the village level. Several of the better NGOs involved in CNRM institution building have fought doggedly for equity as a principle to be incorporated in each project they implemented. Generally, however, equity consciousness, arguably the most important institutional condition for fighting poverty, had not been instilled during the decentralization process.

In both the PIM and WDP programmes, the major beneficiaries were landowners. Where PIM was most successful, it achieved an equitable delivery of water to the more marginal landowners in the tail section of the irrigation projects, thereby substantially improving their productivity and livelihoods. To that extent, the relative poverty of the worse-off landowners of the village community was reduced. But the key issue was, what happens to the really deprived, namely the landless and the poor, tenants, sharecroppers and the 'weaker elements' such as SC, ST and other marginalized village members, especially women? Shashidharan Enarth's analysis of PIM villages indicates that although PIM primarily benefitted those owning land, the latter were forced to pay higher wages for agricultural labour. For most of his landless respondents, this had resulted in increased incomes. As for women, although most of the CNRM institutions we studied had reserved a seat for one or more female member(s), their participation in decision-making in all but one case (the PIM village of Dagarkot in MP) was negligible. Except in CNRM projects that featured the introduction of Self-help Projects operated by and for women, they received only minimal benefits.

6. How integrated was the project intervention and what was the extent of the outreach?

Some of the individual projects we studied involved much more than resource management per se. They were mainly what we referred to earlier as CPR projects and usually (but not only) the ones where an NGO was the PIA. The latter were also those with the most effective, sustained outreach, that is, they reached out to all segments of the community with support that built capacity and self-reliance.

The WDP programme was ostensibly the most integrated intervention, because de jure it involved multiple development activities geared towards improving the livelihoods of all the inhabitants of a micro watershed. The main WDP focus may have been on the recharge of groundwater and the retention of soil moisture, but it also included animal husbandry, new crop technology, the greening of the commons, orchard development and interventions such as microfinance and skill development for earning a livelihood (tailoring, jewellry-making, etc.). The outreach in the form of agricultural extension work with farmers or the development of SHGs was usually more extensive if effective NGOs were selected as the PIA.

However, as Amita Shah makes clear, the de facto WDP focus was often more narrowly on building check dams. Ridge-to-valley procedures and greening of the commons were often ignored. Project duration was so short that institution building was weak. While 'the community' was led to expect improvements in their livelihoods, in reality it was those who owned land close to the new structures built during the project who benefitted more.

The JFM programme, and within it the Eco-development Programme had an impressively broad programme of benefits which were delivered to the forest dwellers who had been evicted or completely excluded from protected areas. EDC activities were clearly aimed at weaning them away from the forest for their daily needs such as fuel wood and fodder and providing them with alternative livelihood options. In that sense the EDC was not a programme that decentralized resource management, because the resource was taken away from the community. Thus in the EDC villages that we studied, a wide range of benefits were provided to lure forest dwellers away from their forest dependency with land and farming assistance (Gurshivehra), animal husbandry and veterinarian services (Khatardevi) and even sewing machines and tailoring lessons (Kotra).

7. How have the project and institution contributed to effective, equitable and sustainable resource management?

In many of the CNRM projects studied in our research, there was a great deal of concentration on the first of this question's adjectives and not enough on the other two. The reasons were clear. At the outset of CNRM projects, effectiveness was usually perceived as the paramount objective because of the mismanagement of resources that had prevailed. Equity would have to wait until the results of the mismanagement that had accumulated under government control had been corrected. That way too, skeptical villagers would be more likely to sign up for membership. But the more serious reason was that to give priority to the equity objective would be to risk continual confrontation with the social, economic and political hierarchy of each village, and potentially face failure. Only the most determined NGO PIAs were resolute and strong enough to give equity the same emphasis as effectiveness.

As for the sustainability objective, in the study villages, except in the JFM programme (where it was of greatest concern) and only latterly in the FCs, not much attention was given to the same. Two kinds of sustainability eventually became concerns in all CNRM projects. While environmental sustainability was a major issue from the 1980s onwards in India, in the CNRM projects (apart from JFM) it was largely ignored until the lack of it threatened productivity. Thus, in CNRM projects involving water, the threat of salinization forced a new awareness about the danger of waterlogging for soil health in PIM projects. The exhaustion (or salinization, in coastal areas) of groundwater in WDP projects revealed limits beyond which CNRM could not go. The sustainability of CNRM institutions was another vital issue to which we will return in Chapter 8.

The priority given to effectiveness could be most clearly seen in the PIM programme, where from the outset canal rehabilitation was the crucial need after years of neglect and breakdown. Farmers were reluctant to 'buy in' to the community management proposal until the ID invested in and constructed a rehabilitated system of effective water delivery. In particular, tail end farmers were reluctant to join a WUA unless they could be shown that renovated field channels were bringing water to their fields. In the cases of Kiyadar, Chopadvav and Dagarkot the WUA was able to decide on and implement a policy of delivering water to the tail end first. In these villages the goals of effectiveness and equity became mutually supportive.

Similarly, skeptical farmers in drought-ridden villages had to be won over to the WDP by investments in any useful entry point activity. Given their urgent need for water, the same emphasis on effectiveness explained the priority given to constructing check dams. The WDP did offer other significant opportunities that would enhance resource use efficiency and equity. However, funds for activities such as soil and water conservation for dry land farmers, or upland forestry to arrest erosion, though available under the WDP were frequently underutilized due to low participation by the poor. This not only impacted resource use efficiency but also project equity performance.

In the case of the JFM programme, mismanagement and encroachment had degraded some forests so badly that the first priority was protection of whatever forest was left, followed by planting new trees or facilitating the regrowth of rootstock. One could argue that effectiveness here meant sustainability. But in several places in both states we were shown degraded forests which had been rehabilitated under JFM, but which had subsequently become degraded again through illicit felling. Thus sustainability depended on more than just enforcement by protection committees.

Lack of effectiveness had become a major stumbling block for FCs in the Ukai reservoir, because of their failure to develop a system for policing the reservoir to prevent illegal fishing. In the case of the Gandhi Sagar FCs, policing of the reservoir by the contractors was effective. However, with the fishermen not responsible for the resource's sustainability, the result was overfishing, especially of the more valuable species.

Conclusion

Effectiveness, equity and sustainability, all basic values in CNRM rhetoric, are demonstrably interconnected and mutually supportive. However, our research findings strongly indicate that as objectives, they could only be fully met if the CNRM institutions were given, and exercised, greater responsibility in managing their resources. Some NGO activists and authors have insisted that equity and sustainability will only get the attention they deserve if they are given the same priority as effectiveness at the beginning of each CNRM project. They maintain that equity and sustainability cannot be treated as 'add-ons' that are to be dealt with in CNRM projects at a later date and they do have a point. As suggested earlier, what happens during the introduction of the CNRM programme sets in motion patterns of behaviour, relationships between stakeholders and a process of institutionalization which might be very difficult to change later on in the project. Thus it is essential that PIAs, whether they be government officials or NGO activists, set the terms early on as to how equity and sustainability are to be achieved, and follow through on both.

Such a suggestion indicates a shift in our discussion to critique and proposals for change. Thus, our concluding observations turn now to the way forward for CNRM in Gujarat and MP.

8

CNRM and Poverty in India: The Way Forward

John R. Wood

CNRM is not only a new strategy for improving local resource management in India, but also a strategic policy change that will empower India's village communities to achieve new productivity, greater social equity and democratic control over their livelihoods.

Alas, from 1947 onwards such optimistic statements have greeted many new rural development initiatives in India, at first raising hopes, but later breeding frustration and cynicism, not only in the villagers who have 'heard it all before', but also in policy-makers, NGO activists and academic analysts. Have initiatives like PIM, IFCs, Watershed Development and JFM become like so many other Indian rural development initiatives which have been a mixed bag of some successes and some failures and much in-between, thereby largely making only a scattered and marginal impact on the status quo? Our findings certainly seem to support this view. Moreover the point of our study of CNRM programmes in Gujarat and MP, has CNRM made a significant impact on rural poverty? The answer is similar, albeit more uncertain because of the controversy over the measurement of poverty and questions about data reliability.

In brief, our findings indicate a mixed bag. If we take 'success' to mean competent management of the resource, an increase in productivity and governance that shows indications of participation, accountability and inclusiveness, then based on our studies, three PIM projects have been successful, two have been failures and the remaining three have been in-between. All of the WDP projects have been successful, but only in terms of increased productivity and incomes; they have, on the other hand, been mostly failures with regard to equity and governance indicators. In the JFM projects and FCs there have been some gains in income, but also losses and we are reluctant to say whether either of them has been due to CNRM because community control of resource management decision-making has been either weak or non-existent. In the case of JFM, governmental (i.e., FD) control has been so overwhelming that forest dwellers could hardly be called 'joint managers' of the JFM projects in their villages. In the case of the FCs, government proxies, namely the government-appointed contractors, had the control. This is not to say that participating FC or JFMC members had not received any benefits. They had, but only as a result of 'coercive cooperation' (Jharna Pathak's phrase) or 'incentive driven mechanisms' (Madhu Verma's phrase), not community management.

In the villages covered by the 30 CNRM institutions we have studied, we can roughly conclude that only some of the poor households were better off than before CNRM was introduced. When we break it down by resource, the poor in eight PIM villages improved their situation markedly in three villages (Dagarkot, Kiyadar and Chopadvav), only marginally in two villages (Akala and Bamandi) and not at all in three villages (Kanipur, Banji and Neemkheda). In the WDP villages, the poor in all the eight villages were only marginally better off than before the commencement of the programme. In the villages covered by the six FCs, the status of the poor improved marginally in four villages and worsened in two villages. In the eight JFM villages there was only a marginal improvement for the poor in three villages and no improvement in five of the villages. And again the caveat prevailed that any gains or losses for the poor in the FC or JFM villages occurred for reasons other than community management, of which there was little or none.

Given this mixed but generally unimpressive assessment, our first question should perhaps be whether CNRM strategies ought to be abandoned in favour of some other NRM strategy, or whether they have enough merit to warrant an overhaul of several of their most deficient aspects? Would a reformed CNRM work any better than the current programmes?

Elinor Ostrom won the Nobel Prize in Economics (2009) by demonstrating how and why CNRM was better than the only other alternatives, namely, management by government or private management.[1] Resource management by government has been universally criticized for its inefficiencies, rigidity and corruption, and these have been amply illustrated in our case studies. We have also seen how government officials were reluctant to lose their control over the resource and quick to reassert it when CNRM faltered or failed. Hopefully, with improved and tighter legislation and a revised approach to selecting and training new recruits to NRM ministries, changes in departmental attitudes may gradually evolve. It has to be recognized, however, that no matter how excellent the CNRM projects and institutions may become, the NRM government departments will always be major stakeholders in resource management and will undoubtedly assert their claim to control NRM decision-making. This is because in India the state owns the resources and/or the means to access and develop them. It owns the reservoirs, dams and canals, forests and forest land, the administrative apparatus and the physical infrastructure that enables NRM and it also employs thousands of people who, for better or for worse, work in and for NRM departments.

Private management of natural resources such as water has been discussed in India, but given little credence because of public aversion to the profit motive in the management of resources so fundamental to the survival of millions of poor people. In the new economic climate favouring privatization and deregulation however, private management of natural resources may not be ruled out. Private management of water distribution is already being considered in cities like New Delhi although running into stiff opposition.

The main evidence our research offers to the private versus public debate comes from the IFCs studied by Jharna Pathak. She shows

---

[1] Ostrom, 1990; and see Jayanta Bandyopadhyay et al., 2009.

how in Gujarat's Ukai fishery, where the government had allowed private contractors to control the price and marketing of the FCs' fish catch, the result was the exploitation of fishermen and what she calls a 'crony capitalist' relationship between government officials, contractors and the FF leaders. The same exploitation was visible in MP, although the role of the contractor there was less private and more as a government proxy. The overriding concern in both cases, however, was that the profit motive had led not only to exploitation of fishermen, but also to an overexploitation of the fish resource which may have proven unsustainable.

There are many unanswered questions regarding private NRM suggested by the FC case. If private management were to be extended to water and forests, how would the much larger end-user populations react? Given their stakes in both these resources, what role would different levels of government insist on retaining? Would there be any regulation of profit-taking, working conditions or exploitation of the resource? If so, by whom? Would community institutions play any role, and if not, would end-users have any inputs at all in private NRM policy-making? Would NGOs or foreign donor agencies still have roles to play? And most pertinent to our research concern: would the 'weaker elements' fare any better, or worse, under private management?

It bears repetition that what we have learnt from our study of the 30 CNRM institutions in Gujarat and MP barely scratches the surface of CNRM performance in these states, let alone in the ever more vast and complex arena of India as a whole. Nonetheless, the evidence uncovered in the research reported in Chapters 3–6 and the comparative analysis presented in Chapter 7 points to recurring patterns of institutional, group and individual behaviour that largely explains why CNRM, while producing some impressive results, has fallen short of the expectations of planners, NGO activists and especially the people so dependent on what this 'new paradigm' in resource management promised. In this final chapter we therefore felt that it was incumbent on us to suggest a way forward for the improved implementation of CNRM.

In each section below we first state our general findings regarding the shortcomings both in the current concept and in the implementation of central CNRM principles and then turn to recommendations for reform.

1. The commitments made by government departments regarding decentralization of control over resource management and the decision-making autonomy of CNRM institutions run by end-users have not been adequately fulfilled.

In one way or another, this criticism applies to all four programmes. The de jure provisions of the bureaucratic regulations setting up JFM and FCs in both states gave a false appearance of decentralization, while the Ministries of Environment, Forests and Fishing respectively had not really devolved the control and autonomy necessary to build effective CNRM institutions to the end-users. The same can be said about PIM in MP where no real devolution of control had occurred and in one village in Gujarat (Kanipur) ID officials had actually taken back control of irrigation management. In the case of WDP, the initial community decision-making control became negligible first, because government engineers made the crucial technical decisions about the construction of water-harvesting and distribution structures. Second, the WDP projects thus far had not lasted long enough to institutionalize end-user control, and ended up under *panchayat* control. Fortunately, the time allotted to WDP projects was to be increased, but it was yet to been demonstrated to the community that their control would also increase.

Our research clearly shows that the inadequacy of decentralization had several corrosive effects at the village level and these included: (a) lack of participation in meaningful decision-making had resulted in a loss of interest and enthusiasm for the programme among the membership, particularly among the marginalized groups; (b) loss of interest often resulted in institutional control getting exercised by a small leadership group who lacked the incentive to act responsibly, transparently and accountably; (c) thus weakened, the leadership group was more easily manipulated by government officials and lost its decision-making autonomy; (d) this loss of control resulted in more frequent breaking of rules and the spread of an 'anything goes' attitude which ultimately undermined the institution and its management and protection of the resource.

Thus the policy changes required is a new or amended legislation and regulations that commit NRM ministries to ensure the full and meaningful transfer of democratic control of the relevant resource to village community institutions for each programme. Where such legislation already exists or new legislations are required, incentives for decentralization and strict penalties for non-decentralization will need to be established, along with reasonable but definite implementation timelines.

A comparison of Gujarat versus MP CNRM implementation experience clearly indicates that legislation alone does not ensure that decentralization takes place, and hence the other recommendations listed here are of vital importance. Enacting a law which overnight 'creates' CNRM institutions on paper—often called the 'top-down' or 'big bang' approach to CNRM—does little to change realities at the village level.[2] It was supposed to shock NRM officials into accepting a new dispensation and changed roles, but in Gujarat and MP, the officials quickly moved to protect their prerogatives and control.

Nonetheless, the legislative route does have some advantages. Theoretically, at least, it formalizes the decentralization of authority, endorses it with legality and political commitment, and makes it harder to undo. Officials feel more pressure to make decentralization work. At the village level the existence of a law that lays out governance expectations and spells out sanctions that deter cheating and protect the resource helps prevent arbitrariness and solidifies the authority of CNRM institutions. Notwithstanding the addition to India's litigation overload, new laws and regulations need to provide end-users a means by which to redress their grievances.

---

[2] Significant lessons can be gleaned from the experience of Andhra Pradesh in legislating and implementing The Andhra Pradesh Farmers Management of Irrigation Act of 1997.

2. Inadequate attention has been paid to the initial introduction of CNRM projects at the village level.

As can be seen from the village snapshots, in most of the cases that we have studied, not enough effort was made at the outset to promote and explain the project to the end-user community, especially to its poorer sections. In a majority of cases, villagers learned only indirectly about the objectives and benefits of the project, the institutional changes that were forthcoming and the role they were expected to play. The evidence on this point is somewhat surprising. In fact, awareness of FC members regarding their cooperative and its functioning, the responsibilities of executive members or rules that protected fish stock were fairly high in both reservoirs. In JFM villages, there were more disparities in the levels of awareness from village to village. But in both FC and JFM villagers, the incidence of participation in meetings—even if merely by asking a question—was uniformly and abysmally low. One plausible explanation could have been that the involvement in an FC or JFMC occurred principally because of the benefits offered by government officials; in other words, member participation was a response to incentives, not an indication of a community coming together to discuss and resolve common problems. Meanwhile, in the WDP villages, where one might have expected greater awareness and participation, only in villages where an NGO had been the PIA was there actually much awareness or participation.

Wherever government officials had introduced the CNRM project at the village level, our research indicates that their efforts at disseminating information and mobilizing all segments of the community were usually inadequate. Too often, there were brief visits by well-attired officials in a motorcade of jeeps, who visited the home of the *sarpanch*, met members of the village elite and, after an obligatory cup of *chai*, were soon on their way to the next village. The communication was top-down and hurried, mostly one-way, and the information itself inadequately dispersed. If information was power, the prevalent procedures for its dissemination in CNRM project villages left too many villagers powerless.

We will argue below that NGOs should carry out both the introduction and implementation of CNRM projects, but if government officials must be the PIA, their training for this part of their job requires an overhaul that includes learning techniques for teaching, social mobilization, democratic decision-making, transparent and accountable administration and conflict resolution.

3. CNRM projects that are introduced and implemented by NGOs stand a better chance of success, but NGOs also may fail as PIAs.

Our research suggests that the best PIAs were experienced, effective NGOs with expertise in both engineering (or forest or fish management) and social mobilization. Using PRA methods, they first carry out extensive research to study the project village's geography, topography, resource usage and needs, social structure and economic record. At the project's outset itself they lay out clearly to every household in the village all the aspects of the project, including O&M procedures, governance expectations and the new emphasis on inclusiveness. Their major task is capacity building aimed at self-reliant and self-governing management by end-users. It might also be called sustainable institution building, because it is essential that by the time the project is completed, the WUAs or WDCs or JFMCs or FCs that the NGOs leave behind are equipped for effective, equitable and sustainable resource management.

At the outset of a PIM project, the NGO's immediate challenge is to work with government officials to complete management transfers and prepare the end-users to take up what was previously a government responsibility. They also have the challenge of winning the confidence of the villagers. The NGO thus finds itself thrust into an intermediary role between the government and the end-users. NGO activists are invariably more confident, technically knowledgeable and also more assertive than villagers when dealing with officials. This can easily lead to problems of village dependency on the NGO, whereas it is crucial that the end-users become self-reliant. Some NGOs have turned this dependency into a controlling relationship where they make the decisions and the villagers carry them out. The better NGOs learn to 'lead from behind,' rather than make all the decisions and anticipate everything that could go wrong. They let the villagers make the decisions and learn from their mistakes.

We did not find any NGO playing a role in a JFM project in MP, but the presence of a beat guard in the JFMC infrequently did provide an intermediary who could communicate, however inadequately, the community's needs or demands to government. The same could be said about the SEs in the MP PIM projects. We met a few who were energetic and responsive enough to take some initiative, even though structurally their role was severely limited.

The next two sections will emphasize that the most crucial contribution an NGO could make is to teach good governance by promoting meaningful participation, robust democratic behaviour, transparent and accountable administration, as well as inclusive and equitable sharing of resource management control and benefits.

4. In the formation of CNRM institutions at the village level there was inadequate insistence on democratic governance and inclusion of representatives of the marginalized groups.

It is ironic that while India has been developing a robust democracy at the national level and in many of the states too, at the village level one often finds residual feudal practices and attitudes that are anything but democratic. Traditional hierarchies based on caste, land tenure, work relations, gender relations or indebtedness still persist and may assert themselves when an intervention such as a CNRM initiative begins to threaten the status quo. The problem usually arises with the issue of electing the President, Secretary and EC that are to guide the CNRM project. Despite clear de jure provisions for election of executives in all four programmes, real elections featuring public contests between candidates, campaigns where issues and positions are identified and debated and the election results determined by secret voting and ballot boxes, rarely take place. In fact, there is often a deliberate avoidance of democratic procedure for fear that it will create or exacerbate conflicts between contending groups in the village. Even a strong NGO would find it difficult, in the face of what looks like a village consensus for choosing particular candidates, to insist that democratic procedures be followed. With hardly any deliberation, the new office holders are selected, not elected. As Amita Shah notes, 'in most cases it reproduces the existing power structure obtaining in the village.' During our research, we often identified this as 'elite capture' of the new institution. In the PIM and WDP villages, this would most frequently mean capture by members of the dominant land-owning caste; less frequently, where the dominance was less concentrated, a more pluralistic leadership might emerge.

Let it quickly be said that 'elite capture' is not necessarily a wholly bad outcome. In many villages if the new CNRM institution's leaders, and the PIA, ignored the de facto control of the elite group, they would soon find themselves powerless to carry out decisions. In fact, the chances of the new institution surviving at all would be in jeopardy. The optimal solution would then be to insist on strictly following the procedures for a democratic election, even if the result was the same as that obtained through 'selection.' This way, the elite that would inevitably win control of the new CNRM institution might come to understand that they had a responsibility towards those who elected them. The electors know their leadership is legitimate and may discern that they have the votes with which to change it in the future. Fair elections, which in the beginning might only be achieved through NGO insistence and support, are also the optimal route to learning about accountability, the rule of law and the larger goal of community empowerment. Initially, democratic elections might only confirm the status quo, but eventually, they will be the only route to changing it. Democracy involves a learning process, but it is essential to get the procedure right from the beginning.

There may have to be penalties for non-compliance with democratic procedures by individuals, or indeed the whole community. If these are laid out in legislation or regulations, they should be clearly announced at the outset. Usually the most effective penalties are withdrawal of access to the resource and other benefits that are gained by membership. What matters most is that the extent of the penalty for each infraction be set and imposed by the community through its representatives on the EC. When penalties are imposed, the entire membership of the CNRM institution should be informed.

Representatives of marginalized groups are often not given a seat on the EC, and if they are, their participation in decision-making is weak and their stake in resource management ignored. Existing rules that govern the formation of CNRM ECs vary, but in keeping with general reservation policy in India, they usually provide a place(s) for 'the weaker elements,' or socially marginalized groups. The latter consists of people who have a right to the resource and a stake in its management, even if they lack the power to exercise the same. They are pushed to the margins, literally, by the weight of traditions that enforce exclusion or dependence. Even if their stake in the CNRM project is recognized and they were to be included in the EC, their representative would be usually selected by the village elite, who would tend to pick a representative(s) who will not be troublesome.

We saw frequently that women's participation in CNRM institutions was weak. Often their non-participation occurred as a result of meetings being held at night, because daytime for both men and women is meant for work in the fields, forests or fishing boats. At night, women's family duties would inevitably take priority, and in several conservative villages we were told that no self-respecting woman would walk through the dark to the place of the meeting. Clearly, the only answer to this problem can be a determined stand by an NGO that employs female activists who are experienced in mobilizing the village women. They can make arrangements for other women to temporarily take the female representative's place at home, and ensure her safe passage to and from meetings.

The reason why special arrangements should be made to accommodate the participation of the marginalized villagers is not because, initially at least, their presence in meetings is going to make a difference in decision-making outcomes. What matters is first, that the marginalized, perhaps for the first time in their village's history, are recognized as stakeholders in resource management and as participants in, or at least witnesses to decision-making that affects them, and from which they have previously been excluded. Second, like others in the CNRM institution, they too are at the beginning of a learning process and will need special encouragement from supportive NGO mentors.

Of course, the foregoing discussion applies differently in the case of the STs in both JFM and FC villages because they often are the majority group and face no participation barriers, even if they are not given significant decision-making power in these programmes. Our research included several JFM cases where there was a minority group of *adivasis* from tribes different from the dominant one or even of non-*adivasis*. However, the usual marginalization was not a factor in the operation of the CNRM project or institution. The mentoring of NGOs was of vital importance, especially if real decentralization was to be achieved.

One proposal requiring further discussion is that representatives of significant marginalized groups should be elected by their marginalized group meeting separately, and that such representatives need to not only be voting members of the EC, but would also report back to their respective groups.

5. CNRM projects are often too unifocal; they could be more successful and have a greater impact on poverty if they involve more than resource management.

Only in WDP and in some JFM projects was the approach to resource management holistic, that is, the management of the resource was supplemented by additional activities which addressed larger developmental issues at the village level. We have already noted this in relation to the WDP and JFM projects. The WDP's mandate embraced the developmental needs of an entire watershed at the same time that it focused on drought relief. It was designed to benefit all parts and inhabitants of the watershed. Unfortunately, because of the limited time allotted to WDP projects, the usual concentration was on quick-fix efforts, such as building check dams, which primarily benefitted the landed. In the case of JFM projects, especially the EDC projects designed to benefit forest dwellers evicted from protected areas, the FD was confronted with the need to supply multiple benefits, such as bio-gas plants, solar cookers or drinking water supply, along with alternative livelihood supports in agriculture and animal husbandry. The problem was that the hand-out of such benefits only reinforced the dependence of EDC communities on the Forest Department, and defeated any hope of self-reliance and long-range sustainability. The same could be said about the FD's provision of benefits (loans for housing and boats, subsidized nets, etc.) to FC members.

Meanwhile, the PIM's focus on irrigation served the interests of landed households but provided only indirect benefits for the non-landed, thus driving an ever larger wedge between the haves and the have-nots. In the case of FCs, the sole concentration of the programme on fish productivity seemed to miss the point that many fishermen, particularly those that were studied in Gujarat's Ukai reservoir, earned a larger part of their income through agriculture or wage labour. In both PIM projects and the FCs, more emphasis is on creating income sources for poorer households, for example, with MNEGRA project that enables better resource management performance.

Conclusion

CNRM as practised in the four programmes studied here is unlikely to be abandoned by either the Gujarat or the MP governments, but the absence or erosion of crucial components of CNRM in these programmes has dangerously undermined its value as a rural development strategy. If the control and responsibility for resource management are not fully decentralized—at least to the extent prescribed in existing legislations and regulations—a fiction is created which allows government officials to retain or take back decision-making authority that has been promised to end-user communities. It is important to remember that it is the latter who take the greatest risk in signing up for CNRM. And it is not only they who have much to lose in a reversion to government control. For India as a whole it requires little imagination to calculate the impact on the economy of a return to pre-CNRM performance in agriculture, forestry or fishing.

Despite official rhetoric, CNRM is at a crossroads where most projects are still in an experimental phase. One can find model villages—the PIM projects in Kiyadar, Chopadvav and Dagarkot come to mind—where the CNRM experiment has made a very positive change in the livelihoods of participating households. In most of the other PIM projects and many of the WDP projects studied, the evidence is mixed and the jury still out: in some the CNRM institution is functioning reasonably well and households have registered some increase in income, while in others governance has been indifferent or weak, and productivity has remained hardly greater than before the project. Where NGOs have been the PIA it is often not completely certain whether progress would become self-sustaining after the NGO winds up its implementation role. Then there are the outright failures, such as the PIM village of Kanipur or the WDP village of Kalakhunt where, the CNRM project had been abandoned or ground to a halt by insurmountable challenges respectively.

The JFM and FC experiments, meanwhile, show potential, but strictly speaking, they are not truly CNRM experiments for all the reasons given earlier. In most cases, villagers have found that they have entered a commitment under false pretences and have lost faith and interest in their local project. In the JFM cases the irony has been that in the beginning, the experiments, such as those undertaken in the late 1980s and early 1990s in Harda District in MP or Bharuch District in Gujarat, were genuine CNRM experiments and gave excellent results. In the FC cases there were cooperatives where productivity and incomes had increased, but if so, it was not because of community management of the resource.

We have witnessed enough evidence of success or partial success, however, to remain optimistic that the CNRM experiment in India, if improved in the ways outlined above, is worth pursuing as a vehicle for reaching the goal of 'inclusive growth.' In villages where CNRM institutions, aided by NGO support, have been able to grow, they have fostered a learning process and a demonstration effect which despite setbacks would be very difficult if not impossible to stop. The growth is already horizontal. Villages without CNRM are continually seeking to join PIM, FC, WDP or JFM programmes after witnessing what they have achieved in neighbouring villages. The initial motive may just be to gain the benefits available under the various programmes, be they canal rehabilitation or check dams or solar cookers or fishing nets. Beyond these benefits, however, lies the prospect of a new and better way to manage water, the forests and fish. There are indications that the growth will also be vertical, in the form of federations of CNRM institutions at higher levels. These are already in existence in the FC federations, and under discussion in the PIM programme, although yet to be formed.

At the policy-making level, the perspective and motivation regarding CNRM are quite different. There is still a lot of skepticism and political uncertainty that hesitates to look beyond the next election. However, the pressures of several long-range trends that support CNRM in India, well-understood by policy-makers, seem likely to prevail. First, due to population increase, the need to raise productivity levels continues to grow and where CNRM projects can contribute to greater productivity they will be supported by all stakeholders, including planners and politicians as well as end-users. (In the case of JFM, the targets will be different: both increased forest cover as well as better livelihoods for forest dwellers.)

Second, where CNRM can be institutionalized and made inclusive both in its design and implementation, it will help to mobilize and make more productive villagers who have hitherto barely subsisted. Third, decentralization, like economic liberalization, is valued by political and economic elites because it offloads some of the costs of development (in this case costs of NRM), from the government to the end-users. And, in view of the current movement in India to end corruption, one might add here that wherever CNRM results in real decentralization of resource management to democratic end-user control, there will be a greater chance of curbing the corruption of government officials. Will their corruption be replaced by the corruption of CNRM officials at the village level? Our evidence indicates that this could happen, but when it does, the corrupt CNRM official would usually be removed by fellow end-users. If they have the authority to act, they are unlikely to tolerate corrupt behaviour by a fellow end-user since it means that the resource they depend on is getting depleted or degraded, thereby diminishing their own share of benefits.

Finally, despite its frequent manipulation and abuse, democratization appears to be an irreversible process in India. However, in most of the CNRM institutions studied here democratization faces many difficulties, the greatest of which is the unwillingness of government departments to decentralize control over resource management. CNRM can benefit from democratization as well as contribute to it. However, the two most important research findings presented in these pages are that first, CNRM institutions cannot function democratically unless the decision-making authority and autonomy due to them are truly decentralized, and that second, only if they function democratically can there be hope that their management of resources will be equitable.

Glossary

achar: (*Buchanian lanza*) NTFP fruit used for making sweets
adhikar patra: agreement on rights between Forest Department and
    village-level organization
adivasi: aboriginal; in India often referred to as 'tribal'
amin: water distributor
anganwadi: village day care facility for young children
aonla: (*Embilica officialis*) NTFP, used in ayurvedic medicines
aquifer: subterranean water source

bajri: millet
bamboo: (*Dendrocalamus strictus*) NTFP used in house construction
beat guard: Forest Department official at village level
bili: (*Aegle marmelos*) NTFP fruit
Borewell: a well constructed by rotary drilling
bori bandh: rainwater harvesting structure made of sand bags
bottom-up approach: refers to development initiatives that
    encourage grassroots participation by local people, empowering
    them to make and implement their own self-reliant decisions.

canal outlet: structure in canal allowing water release
check dam: earth, rock or cement barrier built across dry river bed
    to trap monsoon rain and recharge groundwater
Chief Engineer: the senior-most irrigation department official
Chipko Movement: Uttarakhand people's forest protection
    movement
Chironji: (*Buchanania lanzan*) NTFP; same as *achar*, used in
    ayurvedic medicines
Congress: Indian National Congress, a major political party
contour bund: trenching to impede monsoon run-off, retain
    moisture and prevent soil erosion on sloping land

contractor: fishing manager hired privately or by government
coupe felling: select felling of timber to enhance FD revenues
crore: ten million (10,000,000)

decentralization: transfer of control from a higher to a lower
    body
de facto: actual, real
de jure: by right, legal, official
distributory: major link in canal network
drawdown crop: crop grown on land exposed when reservoir
    empties

end-users: those most closely working with and depending on a
    resource for their livelihood
Executive Engineer: a mid-ranking ID official

field channel: irrigation link between canal outlet and fields
fingerling: junior fish fry deposited in reservoir by FD
forest village: village on land under Forest Department jurisdiction

google gum: NTFP gum from google (*Commiphora wightii*) tree,
    used in medicine
gram vatika: village garden managed by Gram Panchayat
groundwater: subterranean water
gully plug: earth, rock or concrete structure built across narrow
    natural drainage lines to trap monsoon rain

Haryali: a set of MoRD guidelines for micro-watershed development
head count ratio: poverty estimate reflecting the proportion of
    people living below the poverty line
heading: piling-up of debris in field channel to raise water level
head-end or (-reach): irrigation zone closest to canal outlet;
    reservoir fishing zone closest to dam
hectare (ha): 2.47 acres

inclusive growth: development that involves and benefits everyone,
    regardless of social or economic status

jowar: sorghum

kachcha: (lit. 'unbaked') structure made with mud, straw
kalra leaves: curry leaves from the curry tree (*Murraya koenigii*), used in many dishes
kharif crop: crop watered by monsoon rain
kullu gum: (*Sterculia urens*) major NTFP used in ice-cream and sweets manufacture

lakh: one hundred thousand (100,000)
lantana camara: obnoxious weed, uprooted because it is damaging to grass and seedlings
lift irrigation: irrigation that requires raising water to a higher level

mahua flower: major NTFP; flower of *madhuca latifolia* tree used in making liquor
middle reach: irrigation zone midway between canal and tail-end or fishing zone in the middle of a reservoir
minor: irrigation canal system link below a distributory
monsoon: rainy season
musli: (*Chlorophytum borivilianum*) NTFP herb, used in ayurvedic medicine; aphrodisiac

nullah plug: earth, rock or concrete structure used to trap monsoon rain in natural drainage formation
nistar: permission given by Forest Department to collect minor forest produce on forest land
non-timber forest: any forest product except wood (includes leaves, flowers, herbs, gum etc.) product

oustees: people displaced by development projects (e.g., reservoir construction) or by government order (e.g., people evicted from protected forests)
panchayat: village government council
pucca: (lit. 'baked') solid, made of permanent materials
rabi crop: crop watered by winter rains
RCC road: reinforced cement concrete road

revenue village: village on land under Revenue Department
  jurisdiction
ridge-to-valley procedure: high to low or periphery to core
  progression of interventions in watershed development

sal: (*Shorea robusta*) a large tree; NTFPs include its leaves, fruit,
  gum and seeds
salinization: environmentally harmful build-up of salts in soil
sarpanch: village head; leader of the panchayat
siphon: U-shaped chamber used for carrying water across a stream
sitaphal: (NTFP fruit) custard apple
stopdam: generic term for watershed run-off barriers
Sub-engineer: minor Irrigation Department official

tail-end or -reach, -section: irrigation zone furthest from canal
  outlet, often deprived of water; reservoir zone furthest from
  dam which dries first as reservoir empties
tail-ender: farmer or fisherman working in the tail-end
talati: village record keeper
tamarind: (*Tamarindus indica, imli*) NTFP used as a flavouring
  agent
tank: large pond or monsoon water storage area
tendu patta: major NTFP; leaf of tendu (*Diospyros meanoxylon*) tree
  used in *bidi* (indigenous cigarette) rolling
top-down approach: refers to development initiatives, now largely
  discredited as unsustainable, that depend on government
  initiative and maintenance
tubewell: borewell that penetrates to a very deep level

usufruct rights: entitlement to NTFP

Van Kalyan Samiti: Forest Welfare Committee
van talavdi: pond constructed in forest

water course: layout of field channels down to the field level
waterlogging: process by which soil becomes saturated with water
water rates: irrigation charges

watershed: area in which water drains to a single point

watershed plus: a set of activities that follow a watershed project providing agricultural extension and credit

water table: level of sub-surface water

weaker elements: refers to poor, vulnerable groups such as women, Scheduled Castes, Scheduled Tribes, the landless

References and Select Bibliography

Agarwal, Anil and Sunita Narain. 1989. *Towards Green Village: A Strategy for Environmentally Sound and Participatory Rural Development*. New Delhi: Centre for Science and Environment.

———(eds.). 1997. *Dying Wisdom: Rise, Fall and Potential of India's Traditional Water Harvesting Systems*. State of India's Environment: A Citizens' Report, No. 4. New Delhi: Centre for Science and Environment.

———. 2000. 'Water harvesting: Community-led Natural Resource Management'. *ILEIA Newsletter* (March):.

Ahmed, Meera. 2013. 'The Curious Case of Purshottam Solanki'. Available at www.truthofgujarat.com/the-curious-case-of-purshottam-solanki/#.UgaloJKkpET (Accessed on 11 June 2013).

Angelsen, A. and S. Wunder. 2003. 'Exploring the Forest-poverty Link: Key Concepts, Issues and Research Implications'. CIFOR Occasional Paper No. 40. Bogor: CIFOR.

Bahl, R. W. 1999. 'Implementation Rule for Fiscal Decentralization'. *Development, Poverty and Fiscal Policy*. Washington, DC: Economic Development Institute, The World Bank.

Bandhyopadhyay, Jayant, Kanchan Chopra, Purnamita Dasgupta and Nilanjan Ghosh. 2009. 'A Nobel for the Commons: A Tribute to Elinor Ostrom'. *Economic and Political Weekly* 44(45), 7 November: 16–18.

Baumann, P. 2006. *Forest-poverty Linkages in West and Central Asia: The Outlook from a Sustainable Livelihoods Perspective*. Rome: FAO.

Beck, Tony. 1994. *The Experience of Poverty: Fighting for Respect and Resources in Village India*. London: Intermediate Technology Publications.

Beck, T. and C. Nesmith. 2001. 'Building on Poor People's Capacities: The Case of Common Property Resources in India and West Africa'. *World Development* 29(1): 119–33.

Bene, C., K. Mindjimba, E. Belal and T. Jolley. 2000. 'Evaluating Livelihood Strategies and the Rol'. Available at http://www.worldbank.org/html/extpb/wdr2000_2001.htm (Accessed on 15 October 2011).

———. 2001. 'Attacking Poverty: Opportunity, Empowerment and Security'. Available at http://www.worldbank.org/html/extpb/wdr2000_2001.htm (Accessed on 15 October 2011).

Bhattacharya, Ajoy Kumar, ed. 2007. *Forestry for the Next Decade: Managing Thrust Areas*, Two volumes. New Delhi: Concept Publishing Co.

Bhattacharya, P., L. Pradhan and G. Yadav. 2009. 'Joint Forest Management in India: Experiences of Two decades'. *Resources, Conservation and Recycling* 54(8): 469–80.

Bhide, Shashanka and Aasha Kapur Mehta. 2005. 'Tracking Poverty through Panel Data: Rural Poverty in India 1970–1998'. Working Paper No. 28, Chronic Poverty Research Centre, Indian Institute of Public Administration, New Delhi.

Bhide, Shashanka and Aasha Kapur Mehta. 2008. 'Economic Growth and Poverty Dynamics'. Working Paper No. 36, Chronic Poverty Research Centre, Indian Institute of Public Administration, New Delhi.

Bland, S. and S. Donda. 1995. 'Common Property and Poverty: Fisheries Co-management in Malawi', (abstract). 5th Annual Conference of the International Association for the Study of Common Property, Malawi, May 24–28.

Bray, D. B. and L. M. Perez. 2002. *Community Forests of Mexico: Achievements and Challenges*. Mexico City, Sierra Madre:

Brewer, J., S. Kolavalli, A.H. Kalro, G. Naik, S. Ramnarayan, K.V. Raju and R. Sakthivadivel. 1999. *Irrigation Management Transfer in India: Policies, Processes and Performance*. New Delhi: Oxford and IBH Publishing.

Brewer, J. S. 2000. *Irrigation Management Transfer in Indian Canal Systems*. New Delhi: Rawat Publications.

Carney, D. 1995. 'Management and Supply in Agriculture and Natural Resources: Is Decentralization the Answer?' *Natural Resource Perspectives* 4(June): 1–4.

Chambers, R. 1988. *Managing Canal Irrigation: Practical Analysis from South Asia*. New Delhi: Oxford and IBH Publishing Co. Pvt. Ltd.

Chambers, Robert, N. C. Saxena and Tushaar Shah. 1989. *To the Hands of the Poor: Water and Trees*. New Delhi: Oxford and IBH Publishing Co. Pvt. Ltd.

Chambers, R., M. Leach and C. Conroy. 1993. 'Trees as Savings and Security for the Rural Poor'. *Gatekeeper Series*, No. 3. London: International Institute for Environment and Development. Available at http://www.iied.org/pubs/pdfs/6025IIED.pdf (Accessed on 10 September 2011).

Coudouel, Aline, Jesko S. Hentschel and Quentin T. Wodon. 2002. 'Poverty Measurement and Analysis'. In J. Klugman (ed.), *A Sourcebook for Poverty Reduction Strategies*. Washington, DC: The World Bank. Available at http//www.worldbank.org/INTPRS1/resources/383606- (Accessed on 23 May 2010).

Crase, Lin and Vasant P. Gandhi (eds.). 2009. *Reforming Institutions in Water Resource Management: Policy Performance for Sustainable Development*. London: Earthscan.

Datye, K. R. and R. K. Patil. 1987. *Farmer Managed Irrigation Systems: Indian Experiences*. Pune: CASAD.

Davidson, Ogunlade R. and J. W. Martens, eds. 2001. *Methodological and Technological Issues in Technology Transfer*. Cambridge, UK and New York: Cambridge University Press.

Davies, Jonathan and Michael Richards. 1999. *The Use of Economics to Assess Stakeholder Incentives in Participatory Forest Management: A Review*. London and Brussels: Overseas Development Institute and European Commission.

Deaton, A. and J. Dreze. 2000. 'Indian Food Puzzles: Growth, Poverty and (Mal)nutrition'. Unpublished manuscript, Princeton University, London.

de Groot, R. S., M. Wilson and R. Boumans. 2002. 'A Typology for the Description, Classification and Valuation of Ecosystem Functions'. *Ecological Economics* 41: 393–408.

Dev, S. Mahendra. 2007. *Inclusive Growth in India: Agriculture, Poverty and Human Development*. New Delhi: Oxford University Press.

Dev, S. Mahendra and C. Ravi. 2007. 'Poverty and Inequality: All-India and States, 1983–2005'. *Economic and Political Weekly* 42(6), 10 February: 519–20.

Dhamija, Nidhi and Shashanka Bhide. 2010. 'Dynamics of Poverty in India: A Panel Data Analysis'. *Economic and Political Weekly* 45(13), 27 March: 91–96.

Dhawan, B. D. 1997. 'Production Benefits from Large-Scale-Canal Irrigation.' *Economic and Political Weekly* 32(52) 27 Dec, Mumbai. Available at http://www.epw.in/

journal/1997/52/review-agriculture-review-issues-specials/production-benefits-large-scale-canal#sthash.UgLo2Ku3.dpuf

———. 1999. *Studies in Indian Irrigation.* New Delhi: Commonwealth Publishers.

Directorate of Economics and Statistics. 2004. *Agriculture Statistics at a Glance.* New Delhi: IFFCO.

Droogers, P. 2002. *Global Irrigated Area Mapping.* Colombo: International Water Management Institute.

DSC (Development Support Centre). 2010. 'Post-project Management and Use of Watershed Development Fund in Four States of India'. *Policy Brief.* Ahmedabad: DSC.

Eswaran, Mukesh and Ashok Kotwal. 1994. *Why Poverty Persists in India: An Analytical Framework for Understanding the Indian Economy.* Delhi: Oxford University Press.

FAO (Food and Agricultural Organization). 1993. *Marine Fisheries and the Law of the Sea: A Decade of Change,* FAO Fisheries Circular, No. 853. Rome: FAO.

———. 2005. *The State of Food Insecurity in the World, Eradicating World Hunger—Key to Achieving the Millennium Development Goals.* Rome: FAO.

Farrington, J., C. Turton and A. J. James. 1999. *Participatory Watershed Development: Challenges for the Twenty-first Century.* New Delhi: Oxford University Press.

Ghate, Rucha. 2004. *Uncommons in the Commons: Community Initiated Forest Resource Management.* New Delhi: Concept Publishing Co.

Gordon, S. 1954. 'The Economic Theory of a Common-Property Resource: The Fishery'. *Journal of Political Economy* 62 (2):124–42.

Government of Andhra Pradesh (GoAP). 1997. *Andhra Pradesh Farmers Management of Irrigation Systems Act (Act 11 of 1997). Act and Rules,* Department of Irrigation and Command Area Development. Hyderabad: The Co-operative Press Ltd.

Government of Gujarat (GoG). 2005. *Report of the Committee to Study the Backwardness of the Talukas of Gujarat,* Volumes I, II and III, Cowlagi Committee. Gandhinagar: Government of Gujarat Press.

Government of India (GoI). 1994. *Guidelines for Watershed Development.* New Delhi: Ministry of Rural Areas and Employment, Department of Wastelands Development.

———. 1994. *Handbook on Fisheries Statistics, 1993.* New Delhi: Ministry of Agriculture, Department of Agriculture and Cooperation (Fisheries Division).

———. 2005. *The Gazetteer of India.* New Delhi: Department of Animal Husbandry, Dairying and Fisheries.

———. 2007. *Report of the Working Group on Natural Resource Management (NRM) for the Eleventh Plan.* New Delhi: Planning Commission.

———. 2008. *Common Guidelines for Watershed Development.* New Delhi: National Rainfed Area Authority, Ministry of Agriculture.

———. 2009. *Report of the Expert Group to Review the Methodology for Estimation of Poverty.* Chairman: Suresh D. Tendulkar. New Delhi: Planning Commission.

———. 2011. *Common Guidelines for Watershed Projects, 2008.* Revised Edition, New Delhi: National Rainfed Area Authority, Planning Commission.

———. 2012. *Poverty Estimates in India.* New Delhi: Planning Commission. Available at http://planningcommission.nic.in/ (Accessed on 24 July 2012).

———. 2012. *Press Note on Poverty Estimates 2009–10.* New Delhi: Planning Commission. Available at http://planningcommission.nic.in/news/press_pov1903.pdf (Accessed on 2 June 2012).

Government of Madhya Pradesh (GoMP). 2010. Progress Report on Water Users Association (WUA). PIM Monitoring Cell, Water Resource Department: Bhopal.

Gupta, M. V. and M. M. Dey. 1999. 'A Framework for Assessing the Impact of Small-scale Rural Aquaculture Projects on Poverty Alleviation and Food Security'. *FAO Aquaculture Newsletter* 23: 22–25. Rome: Food and Agricultural Organization.

Hickey, Samuel and Giles Mohan (eds.). 2004. *Participation: From Tyranny to Transformation?* New York: Zed Books Ltd.

Hill, I. and D. Shields. 1998. *Incentives for Joint Forest Management in India: Analytical Methods and Case Studies.* Washington, DC: The World Bank.

Himanshu. 2007. 'Recent Trends in Poverty and Inequality Some Preliminary Results'. *Economic and Political Weekly* 42(6), 10 February: 497–508.

———. 2010. 'Towards New Poverty Lines for India'. *Economic and Political Weekly* 45(1), 2 January: 38–48.

Hirway, Indira ,Kashyap, S. P. and Shah, Amita. 2002. Dynamics of Development in Gujarat. New Delhi: Concept Publishing Company.

Huntington, Samuel. 1968. *Political Change in Developing Societies.* New London: Yale University Press.

Iyengar, Sudarshan and Indira Hirway, (eds.) 2001. *In the Hands of the People: Selected Papers of Anil C. Shah.* Ahmedabad: Gujarat Institute of Development Research, Centre for Development Alternatives and Development Support Centre.

Jain, Sachin Kumar. 2009. 'Poverty hidden in numbers'. *Hard News.* Available at http://www.hardnewsmedia.com/2009/04/2850 (Accessed on 10 November 2010).

Jodha, N. S. 1986. 'Common property resources and rural poor in a dry region of India'. *Economic and Political Weekly* 21(27), 5 July: 1169–81.

———. 1995. 'Common Property Resources and the Environmental Context: Role of Biophysical versus Social Stresses.' *Economic and Political Weekly* 30 (51), 23 December: 3278–83.

Joint Forest Management (JFM). 2011. Forest Department, Government of Madhya Pradesh. Available at http://mpforest.org/jointforestmanagement.html. Accessed on 4 February 2016.

Joshi, L. K. (ed.) 1997. *Management of Irrigation, A New Paradigm: Participatory Irrigation.* New Delhi: Ministry of Water Resources.

———.1999. 'Irrigation and its Management in India'. In T. Beck, P. Bose and B. Morrison (eds.), *The Cooperative Management of Water Resources in South Asia.* Vancouver: Centre for India and South Asia Research, Institute of Asian Research, University of British Columbia.

Joshi, L. K. and Rakesh Hooja (eds.). 2000. *Participatory Irrigation Management: Paradigm for the 21st Century,* Volumes 1 and 2. Jaipur and New Delhi: Rawat Publications.

Joy, K. J. and S. Paranjape. 2004. *Watershed Development Review: Issues and Prospects.* Technical Report, Centre for Interdisciplinary Studies in Environment and Development (CISED), Bangalore.

Joy, K. J., Amita Shah, Suhas Paranjape, Srinivas Badiger and Sharachchandra Lele. 2006. 'Reorienting the Watershed Development Programme in India'. Occasional Paper, Forum for Watershed Research and Policy Dialogue (A consortium of SOPPECOM, GIDR and CISED). Available at http://www.cised.org/wp-content/uploads/occasional-paper-2006-r-66.pdf (Accessed on 8 March 2016).

Jyotishi, Amalendu and R. Parthasarathy. 2007. 'Reservoir Fisheries Management: Experience of Tawa in Madhya Pradesh'. *Economic and Political Weekly* 42(5), 3 February: 409–15. Available at http://www.jstor.org/stable/4419212 (Accessed on 13 April 2011).

Kapila, Raj and Kapila, Uma. 2006. India's Economy: A Journey in Time and Space. New Delhi: Academic Foundation.

Kartha, K. N. and K. S. Rao. 1993. 'A Study on the Piscifauna of Gandhisagar Reservoir with Particular Reference to the Abundance of Commercial Varieties of Fish'. *Fishery Technology*, 30: 11–14.

Kerr, J., Pangare, G., Lokur-Pangare, V., George, P.J. and Kolavalli, S. 1998. The role of watershed projects in developing rainfed agriculture in India. Study for the Indian Council for Agricultural Research. World Bank: Washington DC.

Khare, A., M. Sarin, N. Saxena, S. Palit, S. Bathla, F. Vania and M. Satyanarayana. 2000. *Joint Forest Management: Policy, Practice and Prospects—Policy that Works for Forests and People*, Series no. 3. United Kingdom & World Wide Fund for Nature—India. London: International Institute for Environment and Development (IIED).

Kishore, A. 2002. 'Social Impact of Canal Irrigation: A Review of 30 years of Research'. Paper presented at First Annual Partners' Meeting of IWMI-TATA Water Policy Programme, Anand.

Kone, A. 1985. 'Traditional Fishing Rights in the Central Delta of the Niger and the Lake Region: Conflicts and Recommendations with a View to Equitable and Rational Management of Fishery Resources'. FAO Fisheries Report No. 360, Food and Agricultural Organization pp. 95–103. Rome.

Kumar, M. Dinesh, Ankit Patel, R. Ravindranath and O. P. Singh. 2008. 'Chasing a Mirage: Water Harvesting and Artificial Recharge in Naturally Water-Scarce Regions'. *Economic and Political Weekly* 43(35), 5 September: 61–71.

Kumar, M. Dinesh, Shantanu Ghosh, Ankit Patel, O. P. Singh and R. Ravindranath. 2006. 'Rainwater Harvesting in India: Some Critical Issues for Basin Planning and Research'. *Land Use and Water Resources Research*', 6(1): 1–17.

Kumar, Pushpam and Ibrahim Thiaw, eds (with Tom Barker). 2013. *Values, Payments and Institutions for Ecosystem Management: A Developing Country Perspective*. United Nations Environment Programme. Cheltenham and Northampton: Edward Elgar Publishing Ltd.

Kumar, Suresh D. 2007. 'Can Participatory Watershed Management be Sustained? Evidence From Southern India'. Working Paper No. 22–07, South Asian Network for Development and Environmental Economics (SANDEE), Kathmandu.

Lal, R. 2003. *Food Security and Environmental Quality in the Developing World*. Boca Raton and London: Lewis Publishers.

Lal, R., D. Hansen and Norman Uphoff. 2002. *Food Security and Environmental Quality in the Developing World*. New York: Lewis Publishers.

LEAD India. 2008. 'India's National Action Plan on Climate Change'. Available at http://www.climate-leaders.org/climate-change-resources/india-and-climate-change/indias-national-action-plan-on-climate-change (Accessed on 10 February 2010).

Lele, S., G. Madhavai, S. Badigar and A. Vadivelu. 2009. 'Watershed Development in Karnataka: A Large Scale Assessment of Processes, Sustainability and Impact'. Draft report, Centre for Interdisciplinary Studies in Environment and Development (CISED), Bangalore.

Lele. S. K. and R. K. Patil. 1994. *Farmer Participation in Irrigation Management—A Case Study of Maharashtra*. SOPPECOM. Delhi: Horizon India Books.

Lobo, L. and S. Kumar. 2009. *Land Acquisition, Displacement and Resettlement in Gujarat, 1947–2004*. New Delhi: SAGE Publications.

Manna, G. C. 2007. 'On Calibrating the Poverty Line for Poverty Estimation in India'. *Economic and Political Weekly* 42(30), 28 July: 3108–15.

Manor, James. 1999. *The Political Economy of Democratic Decentralization*. Washington, DC: The World Bank.

Marothia, Dinesh. 1997. 'Agricultural Technology and Environmental Quality: An Institutional Perspective'. Keynote Paper, *Indian Journal of Agricultural Economics* 52(3): 473–87.

———. 2012. 'Performance of Culture Fisheries under Alternative Property Rights Regimes in Chhattisgarh'. *International Journal of Ecology and Environmental Sciences* 38(4): 163–207.

Mathew, George, ed. 2000. *Status of Panchayati Raj in the States and Union Territories of India*. New Delhi: Concept Publishing Co.

Mathur, P. C. 1999. 'Political Dynamics of the Institutional Pendulum of Democratic Decentralization: An Overview'. In S. N. Jha and P. C. Mathur (eds.), *Decentralization and Local Politics: Readings in Indian Government and Politics—2*. New Delhi: SAGE Publications.

Mehta, Aasha Kapur. 2010. 'Poverty Persistence, Entry and Escape.' Chapter in Michele Kelley and Deepika D'Souza (eds.), *The World Bank in India: Undermining Sovereignty, Distorting Development–Independent People's Tribunal on the World Bank in India*. New Delhi: Orient Blackswan Pvt. Ltd.

Menon, A., P. Singh, A. Shah, S. Lele, S. Paranjape and K. J. Joy. 2007. *Community-based Natural Resource Management: Issue and Cases from South Asia*. New Delhi: SAGE Publications.

Mishra, Sib Ranjan. 1987. *Fisheries in India*. New Delhi: Ashish Publishing House.

Mitra, Subrata K. 2006. *The Puzzle of India's Governance: Culture, Context and Comparative Theory*. New Delhi: Routledge.

MoEF (Ministry of Environment and Forests). 1990. Joint Forest Management Resolution, Order No. 6.21/89-FP, 1 June 1990. New Delhi: Wildlife Division, MoEF.

Mollinga, P. P. (ed.). 2000. *Water for Food and Rural Development: Approaches and Initiatives in South Asia*. Thousand Oaks, New Delhi and London: SAGE Publications.

Mukherji, B. 1961. *Community Development in India*. Calcutta: Orient Longmans.

Myers, Norman. 1996. 'The World's Forests: Problems and Potentials'. *Environmental Conservation* 23(02; June): 156–68.

Naoroji, Dadabhai. 1901. 'Poverty and Un-British Rule in India—1901'. Available at http://www.vifindia.org

Narayana, D. 2005. 'Local Governance Without Capacity-building: Ten Years of Panchayati Raj'. *Economic and Political Weekly* 40(26), 25 June: 2822–32.

Narmada and Water Resource Department (NWRD). 2009. *Irrigation Utilization Report*. Government of Gujarat, Gandhinagar.

Oblitas, K. and R. Peter. 1999. *Transferring Irrigation Management to Farmers in Andhra Pradesh, India*. Washington, DC: The World Bank.

Olomola, A. 1998. 'Sources and Resolution of Conflicts in Nigerian Artisanal Fisheries'. *Society and Natural Resources* 11:121–35.

Pai, R. and S. Datta. 2006. *Measuring Milestones: Proceedings of the National Workshop on Joint Forest Management*. National Workshop on JFM. New Delhi: MoEF and Winrock International India.

Parker, A. 1995. *Decentralization: The Way Forward for Rural Development?* Washington, DC: The World Bank.

Parthasarathy, R. 1998. Reforms in Irrigation Management: Bottoms-up versus Top-down Models. Working paper No. 104. Gota, Ahmedabad: Gujarat Institute of Development Research.

Patnaik, Utsa. 2007. 'Neoliberalism and Rural Poverty in India'. *Economic and Political Weekly* 42(30), 28 July: 3132–50.

Paustian, P. W. 1968. *Canal Irrigation in the Punjab*. New York: AMS Press.

Platteau, J. P., J. Murickan and E. Delbar. 1985. *Technology, Credit and Indebtedness in Marine Fishing: A Case Study of Three Villages in South Kerala*. Delhi: Hindustan Publishing Corporation.

Postel, S. L. 1993. *The Last Oasis: Facing Water Scarcity*. New York: Worldwatch Institute.

Present Status of JFM. 2011. Department of Forest and Environment, Government of Gujarat. Available at http://gujenvfor.gswan.gov.in/e-citizen/joint-forest-management/e-citizen-Jointforest-manage-presentstatus.htm. Accessed on 4 February 2016.

Project Office. 2010. Satak Irrigation Scheme, Department of Water Resources, Government of Madhya Pradesh.

Rahim, K. B. M. and Katar Singh. 1992. 'The Marine Fishermen's Co-operative Societies in West Bengal: An Exploratory Study'. Paper presented at the Workshop on Cooperatives in Natural Resources Management, 7–11 December 1992, Institute of Rural Management, Anand.

Ramchandradu, M. V. 2007. 'Integrating Equity Concerns in Watershed Development Projects—Policy Provisions, Processes Followed and Lessons Learned'. In A. Shah, S. P. Wani and T. K. Sreedevi (eds.), *Impact of Watershed Management on Women and Vulnerable Groups—Proceedings of the Workshop on Comprehensive Assessment of Watershed Programs in India*. Patancheru: ICRISAT.

Ravallion, M. 2008. 'A Global Perspective on Poverty in India'. *Economic and Political Weekly* 43(43), 25 October: 31–37.

Ravindranath, N. H. and P. Sudha. 2000. 'Carbon Sequestration Benefits of Reduced Impact of Logging'. In *Methodological and Technological Issues in Technology Transfer*. Intergovernmental Governmental Panel on Climate Change. Cambridge University Press.

Reddy, V. Ratna. 1999. '"Wealth Ranking" in Socio-economic Research: Substitute or Complement?' *Indian Journal of Agricultural Economics* 54(1), January–March): 93.

———. 2001. 'Watershed Development and Livelihood Security: An Assessment of Linkage and Impact'. Project Report, Centre for Economic and Social Studies, Hyderabad.

Reddy, R.V. and Soussan, J. 2004. 'Assessing the Impacts of Watershed Development Programmes: A Sustainable Rural Livelihoods Framework.' in Bekele Shiferaw and H. Ade Freeman (eds.), *Methods for Assessing the Impacts of Natural Resource Management Research*. International Crops Research Institute for the Semi-Arid Tropics: Hyderabad.

Rondinelli, D. 1981. 'Government Decentralization in Comparative Perspective: Developing Countries'. *International Review of Administrative Science* 47(2): 133–45.

Sachs, Jeffrey. 2005. *The End of Poverty: How We Can Make it Happen in our Lifetime*. London: Penguin Books.

Saith, Ashwani. 2005. 'Poverty Lines versus the Poor: Methodology versus Meaning'. *Economic and Political Weekly* 40(43), 22 October: 4601–10.

Samal, Kishor and Shibalal Meher. 2003. 'Fishing Communities on Chilika Lake: Comparative Socio-economic Study'. *Economic and Political Weekly* 38(31), 2 August: 3319–25.

Sarch, M. T. and E. A. Allison. 2000. 'Fluctuating Fisheries in Africa's Inland Waters: Well Adapted Livelihoods, Maladapted Management'. Available at http://oregonstate.edu/dept/IIFET/2000/papers/sarch.pdf. (Accessed on 13 March 2010).

Scott, J. C. 1985. *Weapons of the Weak: Everyday Forms of Resistance*. New Haven and London: Yale University Press.

Sen, P. 2005. 'Of Calories and Things: Reflections on Nutritional Norms, Poverty Lines and Consumption Behaviour in India'. *Economic and Political Weekly* 40(43), 22 October: 4611–18.

Sen, S., Amita Shah and Animesh Kumar. 2007. 'Watershed Development Programmes in Madhya Pradesh: Present Scenario and Issues for Convergence'. Technical Report, Forum for Watershed Research and Policy Dialogue (A consortium of SOPPECOM, GIDR and CISED).

Sethna, Armin. 2000. 'Emergence of Joint Forest Management in India (Post Script by Anil C. Shah) (Journalistic Documentation)'. Unpublished paper, Aga Khan Rural Support Programme, India (AKRSP-I).

Shah, Amita. 1998. 'Watershed Development Programmes: Emerging Environment Perspectives'. *Economic and Political Weekly* 33(26), 27 June: A66–80.

———. 2001. 'Who Benefits from Participatory Watershed Development? Lessons from Gujarat, India'. *GateKeeper Series*, No. 97. London: International Institute for Environment and Development.

———. 2004. 'Benchmark Survey for Impact Assessment of Participatory Watershed Development Projects in India'. Report submitted to Planning Commission (with Technical Support from SOPPECOM, Pune), New Delhi.

———. 2007. 'Impact of Watershed Development in Central Western Region: Evidence and Way Forward'. A Synthesis Report Prepared for Community Watershed as a Growth Engine for Development of Dryland Areas, Global Theme on Agroecosystems, Report No. 47. Patancheru: ICRISAT (International Crop Research Institute for the Semi-Arid Tropics).

Shah, Amita., A. Samuel and K. J. Joy. 2011a. 'Equity in Watershed Development: Imperatives for Property Rights, Resource Allocation and Institutions'. In Suhas P. Wani, Johan Rockstrom and K. L. Sahrawat (eds.), *Integrated Watershed Management in Rainfed Agriculture*. London: CRC Press.

Shah, Amita, Hasmukh Joshi and Jayaram Desai. 2009. 'Revisiting Watershed Development in Madhya Pradesh: Evidence from a Large Survey'. Technical Report, Forum for Watershed Research and Policy Dialogue (A consortium of SOPPECOM, GIDR and CISED),

Shah, Amita, Hasmukh Joshi and Vinit Raskar (supported by Jayaram Desai). 2011b. 'Assessing the Impact of Watershed Projects in Ratlam, Madhya Pradesh: A Post-facto Analysis'. Technical Report, Forum for Watershed Research and Policy Dialogue (A consortium of SOPPECOM, GIDR and CISED),

Shah, Amita, Hasmukh Joshi and Dipak Nandani. 2012. 'Impact of Investment in Watershed Projects in Gujarat: A Comprehensive Study'. Draft Report submitted to the National Institute of Rural Development, Hyderabad. Ahmedabad: Gujarat Institute of Development Research.

Shah, Anil C. 2002. *Joint Forest Management*. Ahmedabad and New Delhi: DSC and SPWD.

———. 2003. *The Deprived—Study of Problems in Irrigation Programs in India*. Ahmedabad: Development Support Centre.

Shah, Anwar. 1998. 'Balance, Accountability and Responsiveness: Lessons about Decentralisation'. Policy Research Working Paper 2021, The World Bank, Washington, DC.

Sheil, D., R. K. Puri, I. Basuki, M. van Heist, Syaefuddin Rukmiyati, M.A. Agung Sardjono, I. Samsoedin, K. Sidiyasa, E. Permana Chrisandini, E. Mangopo Angi, F. Gatzweiler, B. Johnson and A. Wijaya. 2002. *Exploring Biological Diversity, Environment and Local People's Perspectives in Forest Landscapes: Methods for a Multidisciplinary Landscape Assessment*. Bogor: CIFOR.

Singh, K. 1994. *Managing Common Pool Resources: Principles and Case Studies*. Delhi: Oxford University Press.

Singh, S., A. J. James, R. Reddy, A. Shah and K. N. Joshi. 2011.'Water User Groups as a Building Block for IWRM'. A Joint Review Mission Special Study submitted to the European Commission Sector Policy Support Programme, Institute of Development Studies, Jaipur.

Sinha, M. and B. C. Jha. 1997. 'Ecology and Fisheries of Ox-Bow Lakes (Maun) of North Bihar', Central Inland Fisheries Research Institute, Barrackpore, Bulletin No. 74: 65.

Sinha, M. and Pradeep K. Katiha. 2002. 'Management of Inland Fisheries Resources under Different Property Regimes'. In Dinesh Marothia (ed.), *Institutionalising Common Pool Resources*. New Delhi: Concept Publishing Company.

Smith, J. and S. Scherr. 2002. 'Forest Carbon and Local Livelihood: Assessment of Opportunities and Policy Recommendations'. Occasional Paper 37, CIFOR, Bogor.

SPWD (Society for the Promotion of Wasteland Development). 1992. *Joint Forest Management: Concept and Opportunities*. Proceedings of a National Workshop held at Surajkund, August, SPWD, New Delhi.

Srinivasan, T. N. 2007. 'Poverty Lines in India: Reflections after the Patna Conference.' *Economic and Political Weekly* 42(41), 13 October: 4155–65.

Srivastava, U. K., M. Dharma Reddy and V. K. Gupta. 1983. 'Reservoir Fisheries in India: Some Issues and Problems'. In U. K. Srivastava and M. Dharma Reddy (eds.), *Fisheries Development in India: Some Aspects of Policy Management*. New Delhi: Concept Publishing Co.

Stackhouse, John. 2000. *Out of Poverty and into Something More Comfortable*. Toronto: Vintage Canada (Random House).

State Planning Commission (GoMP). 2009. District-wise Poverty Estimates for Madhya Pradesh, Bhopal. Available at https://www.google.co.in/#q=State+Planning+Commission%2C+Madhya+Pradesh.+2009.+District-wise+Poverty+Estimates+for+Madhya+Pradesh%2C+Bhopal (Accessed on 1 April 2016).

Sudha, P. and N. H. Ravindranath. 2001. 'Carbon Sequestration Benefits of Reduced Impact Logging'. In B. L. Metzger, L. McGrory, S. Van Rooijen, O. R. Davidson and J.W. Martens (eds.), *Methodological and Technological Issues in Technology Transfer*. Cambridge, UK and New York: Cambridge University Press.

Sugunan, V. V. 1995. 'Reservoir Fishing in India'. Central Inland Capture Fisheries Research Institute, Barrackpore, India. Rome: FAO. Available at http://www.fao.org/DOCREP/003/V5930E/V5930E01.htm#ch1.3 (Accessed on 10 December 2010).

Sultana, Parvin and M. Paul Thompson. 2007. 'Community Based Fisheries Management and Fisher Livelihoods: Bangladesh Case Studies'. *Human Ecology* 35(5), Marine Resources: 527–46.

Suryanarayana, M. H. 2008. 'Inclusive Growth: What Is so Exclusive About it?' Working Papers 2008–09, Indira Gandhi Institute of Development Research (IGIDR), Mumbai.

Taylor, Carl C. 1956. *A Critical Analysis of India's Community Development Programme*. Delhi: CPA Publications.

The Acorn. (n.d.). 'A Universally Accepted Poverty Line'. Available at http://acorn.nationalinterest.in/2007/11/07/a-universally-accepted-poverty-line (Accessed on 14 August 2009).

Tiwari, D. and A. Dinar (eds.). 2002. *Role and Use of Economic Incentives in Irrigated Agriculture*. Washington, DC: The World Bank.

Townsend, R. E. and Pooley, S. G. 1995. 'Distributed Governance in Fisheries'. In Susan Hanna and Munasinghe (eds.), *Property Rights and the Environment, Social and*

Ecological Issues. Washington, DC: The Beijer International Institute of Ecological Economics and the World Bank.

Turton, Cathryn. 2000. 'Enhancing Livelihoods through Participatory Watershed Development in India'. Working Paper 131 (April), Overseas Development Institute London.

United Nations Development Programme. 1997. Governance for Sustainable Human Development. New York: UNDP.

———. 2005. *Decentralized Governance Monograph: A Global Sampling of Experiences.* New York: Management Development and Governance Division.

UN Millennium Project. 2005. *Investing in Development: A Practical Plan to Achieve the Millennium Development Goals.* London and Sterling: Earthscan.

Uphoff, N. 1986. *Improving International Irrigation Management with Farmer Participation— Getting the Process Right.* Boulder: Westview Press.

Vaidyanathan, A. 1999. *Water Resource Management: Institutions and Irrigation Development in India.* New Delhi: Oxford University Press.

———. 2006. *India's Water Resources: Contemporary Issues on Irrigation.* New Delhi: Oxford University Press.

van der Meer, P. J., C. Bairaktari, R. S. de Groot, M. van Heist and J. Schmerbeck. 2007. *Methodology for Assessing Benefits of Afforested Community and Forest Land.* Wageningen, Netherlands: Wageningen University.

Vermillion, D. L. 1997. *Impacts of Irrigation Management Transfer: A Review of the Evidence.* Colombo: IIMI.

———. 1997. 'Management Devolution and the Sustainability of Irrigation: Results of Comprehensive versus Partial Strategies'. Rome: FAO/World Bank Technical Consultation on Decentralization and Rural Development.

Vira, B. 2005. 'Deconstructing the Harda Experience: Limits of Bureaucratic Participation.' *Economic and Political Weekly* 40(48), 26 November: 5068–75.

Wood, John R. 2002. 'Decentralization, Democratization and Development: The Case of India's Water Users Associations'. Workshop on Democratization in Latin America and South Asia: 'Creating and Revitalizing Democratic Institutions: Context and Challenge in Latin America and South Asia'. Vancouver: University of British Columbia.

———. 2007. *The Politics of Water Resource Development in India: The Narmada Dams Controversy.* New Delhi: SAGE Publications.

World Bank. 1982. *Fisheries Sector Policy Paper.* Washington, DC: The World Bank.

———. 1998. *INDIA—Water Resources Management Sector Review: Report on the Irrigation Sector.* New Delhi and Washington, DC: The World Bank.

———. 2007. *India at a Glance.* Washington, DC: The World Bank.

World Development Report. 2001. 'Attacking Poverty: Opportunity, Empowerment and Security'. Available at http://www.worldbank.org/html/extpb/wdr2000_2001.htm (Accessed on 15 October 2011).

Index

About the Authors

Shashidharan Enarth is Senior Advisor at the Institute of Livelihood Research and Training, Hyderabad. With over two decades of professional experience in development sector spread across three Indian NGOs—LOCOST, AKRSP and DSC—he has promoted programmes ranging from holistic health to natural resources development and good governance. He has also worked as a consultant to the World Bank on NRM programmes in Nigeria, Tanzania and India. After a PhD from University of British Columbia, he pursued research interests on decentralization, democratization and role of civil society in creating system changes. He was also closely involved in watershed and irrigation policy reforms and the introduction of Participatory Irrigation Management (PIM) in various states of India.

Jharna Pathak is Assistant Professor, Gujarat Institute of Development Research, Ahmedabad. Her research interests include dryland farming and institutions in managing natural resources. Dr Pathak is also a visiting professor at Gujarat University and various management institutes in Ahmedabad. Her research mainly concerns issues in policy and institutional development in the areas of managing natural resources, dryland agriculture, innovations in farms and agriculture and sustainable development. She has edited a volume of essays (jointly with Amita Shah) titled *Tribal Development in Western India*, (2014).

Amita Shah is Professor of Economics and former Director of Gujarat Institute of Development Research, Ahmedabad. Her major areas of research are dryland agriculture and forestry, environmental impact assessment, gender and environment, agriculture-industry interface, employment and livelihood issues and chronic poverty. She has published several books and over 75 research papers in reputed journals. She has worked closely with a number of government, non-government and international organizations. She has also been a consultant to various donor agencies within and outside India.

Madhu Verma is Professor, Indian Institute of Forest Management (IIFM), Bhopal. She has 27 years of work experience with postdoctoral research work at University of California (Berkeley) and University of Massachusetts (Amherst), USA. She has more than 40 publications in international and national journals/books to her credit and has conducted projects on valuation, green accounting and payment for ecosystem services with the support of the World Bank, United Nations Environment Programme (UNEP), European Union (EU), Department for International Development (DFID), Asian Development Bank (ADB), International Institute for Environment and Development (IIED), Winrock International and various ministries of the Government of India, the National Forestry Commission and the 13th Finance Commission of India. She has also contributed to the world acclaimed projects on Millennium Ecosystem Assessment and on The Economics of Ecosystems and Biodiversity.

John R. Wood is Professor Emeritus of the Department of Political Science, University of British Columbia (UBC), Vancouver. He taught Comparative Politics with a special focus on India at UBC for 36 years and was Founder/Director of its Centre for India and South Asia Research. Throughout his career, he was involved with the Shastri Indo-Canadian Institute (SICI) which promotes academic exchange and research collaboration between India and Canada. He served as the Resident Director at SICI's India Office (New Delhi) between 1973–75, 1989–90 and 2004–06. He was the author of *The Politics of Water Resources Development in India—The Narmada Dam Controversy* (SAGE, 2007) and co-translator/editor of *The Autobiography of Indulal Yagnik* (2012).

nal